Sackcloth and Ashes

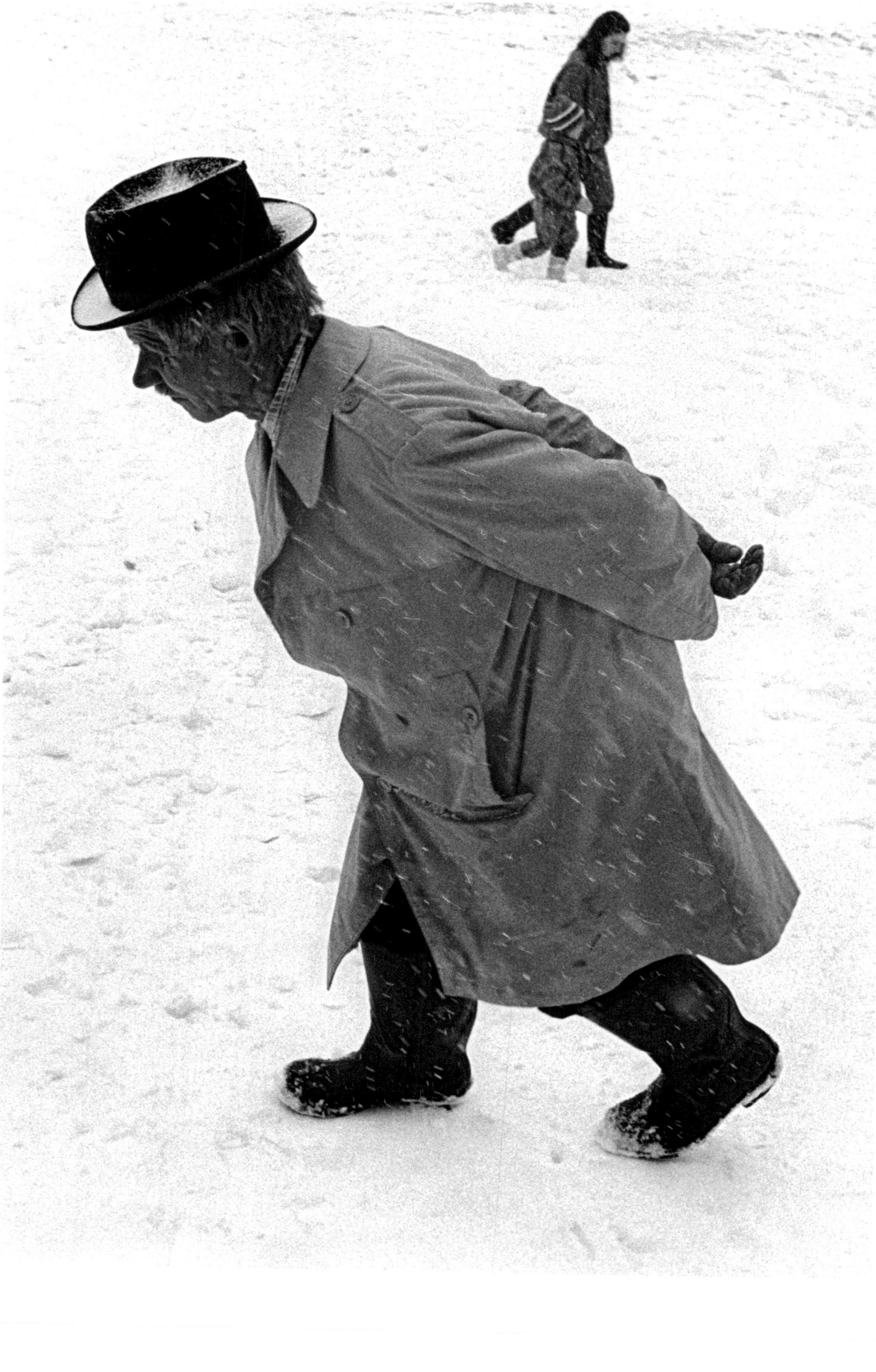

Witold Krassowski

Sackcloth and Ashes

GOST

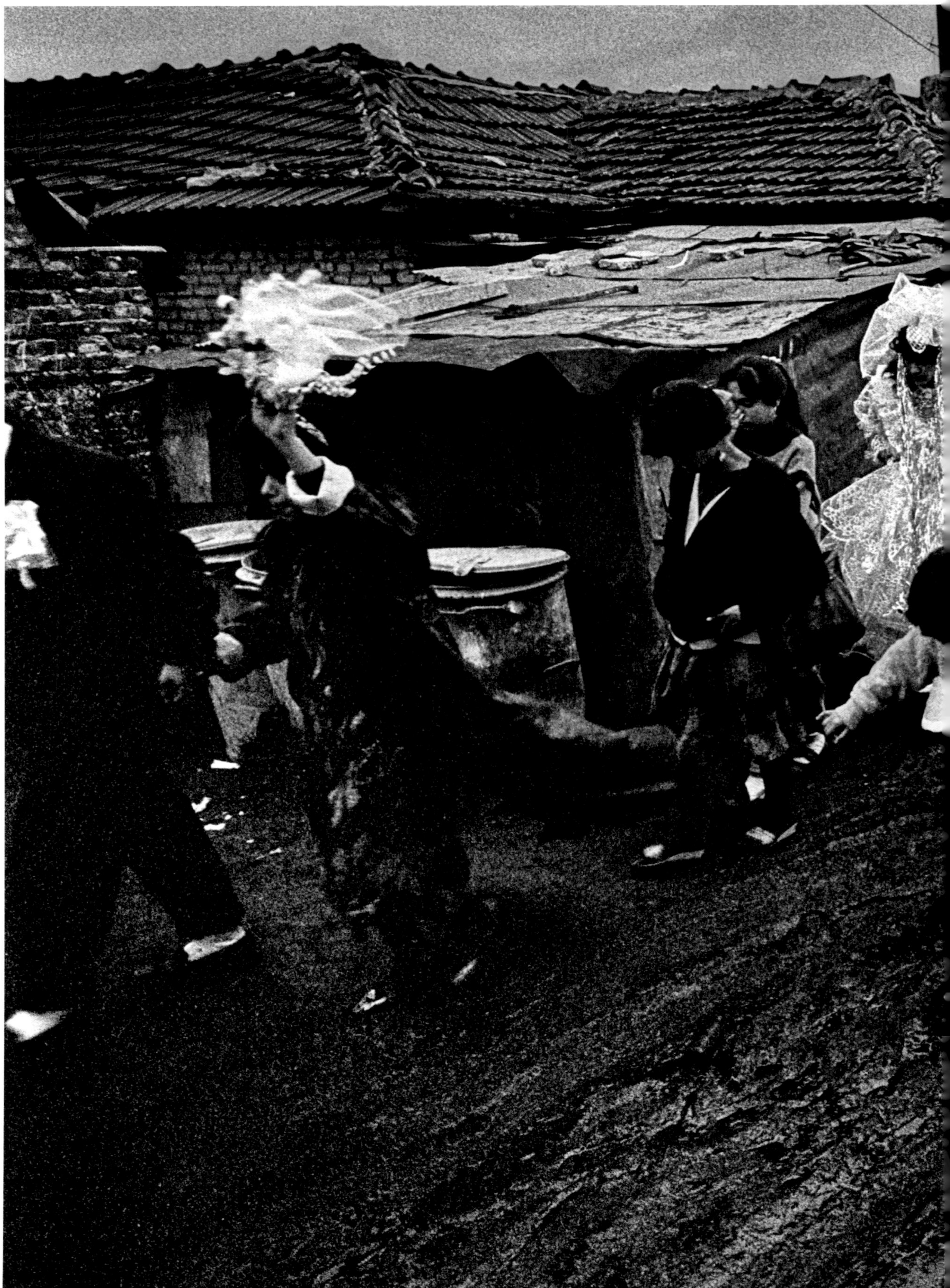

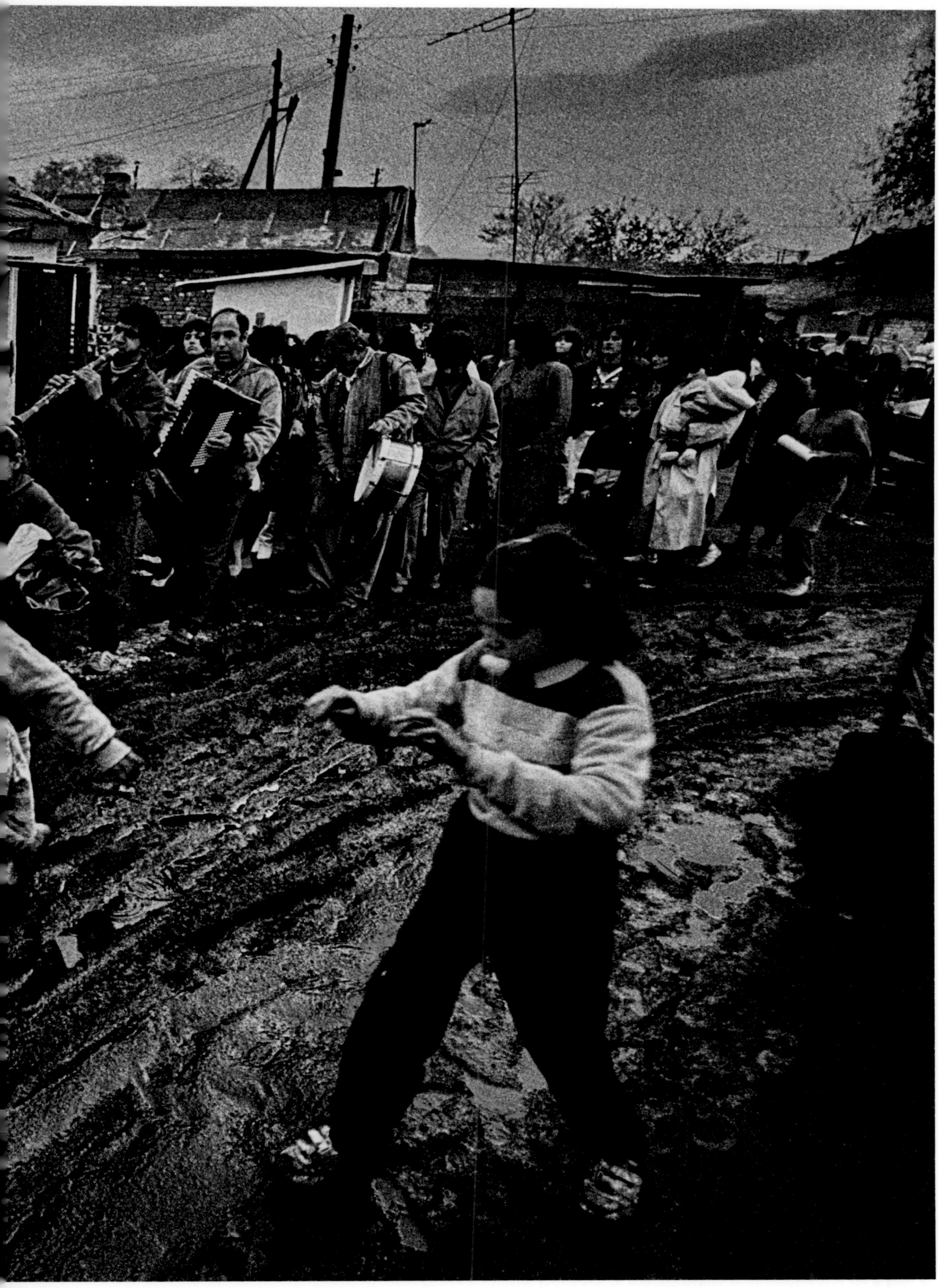

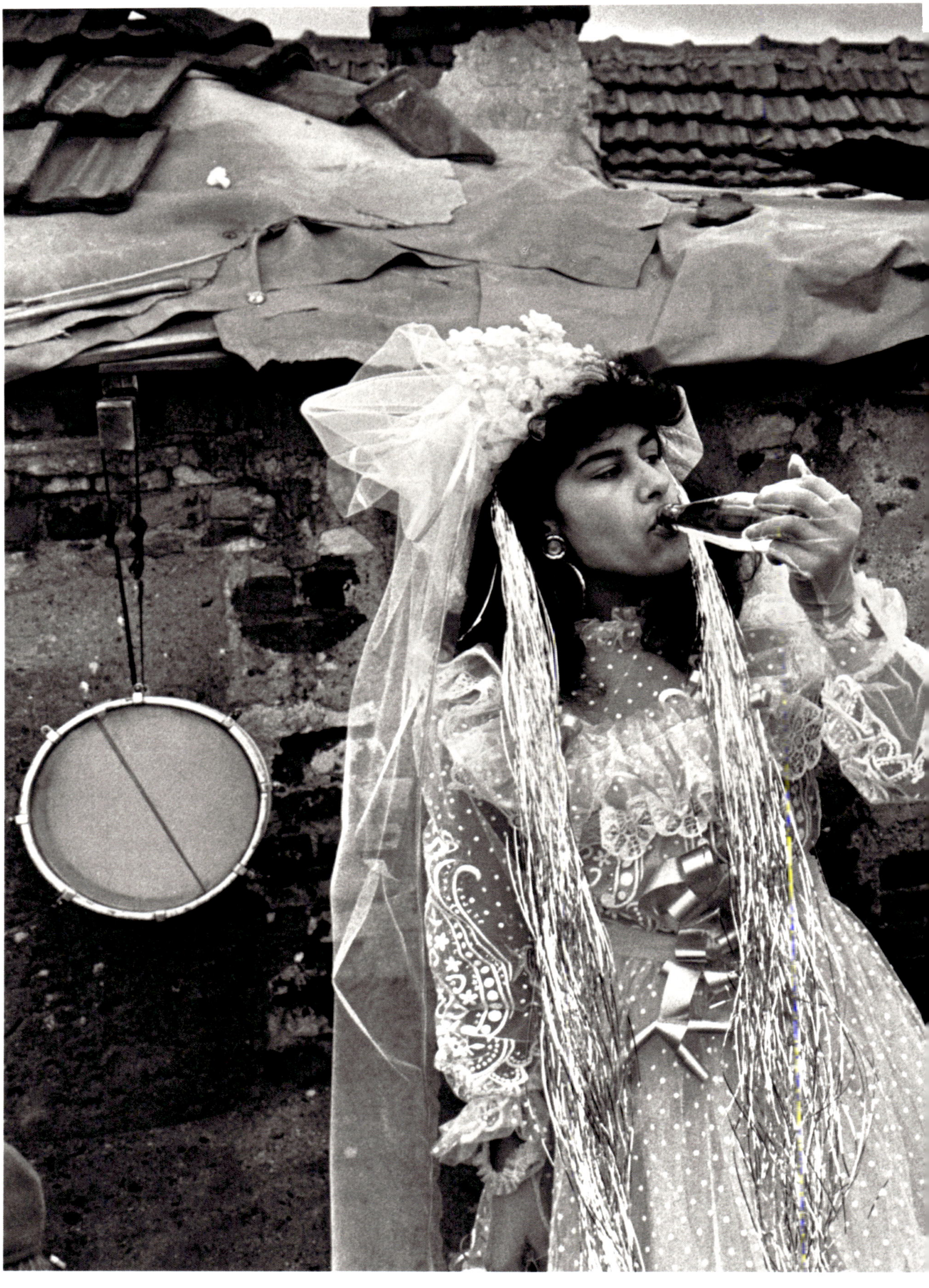

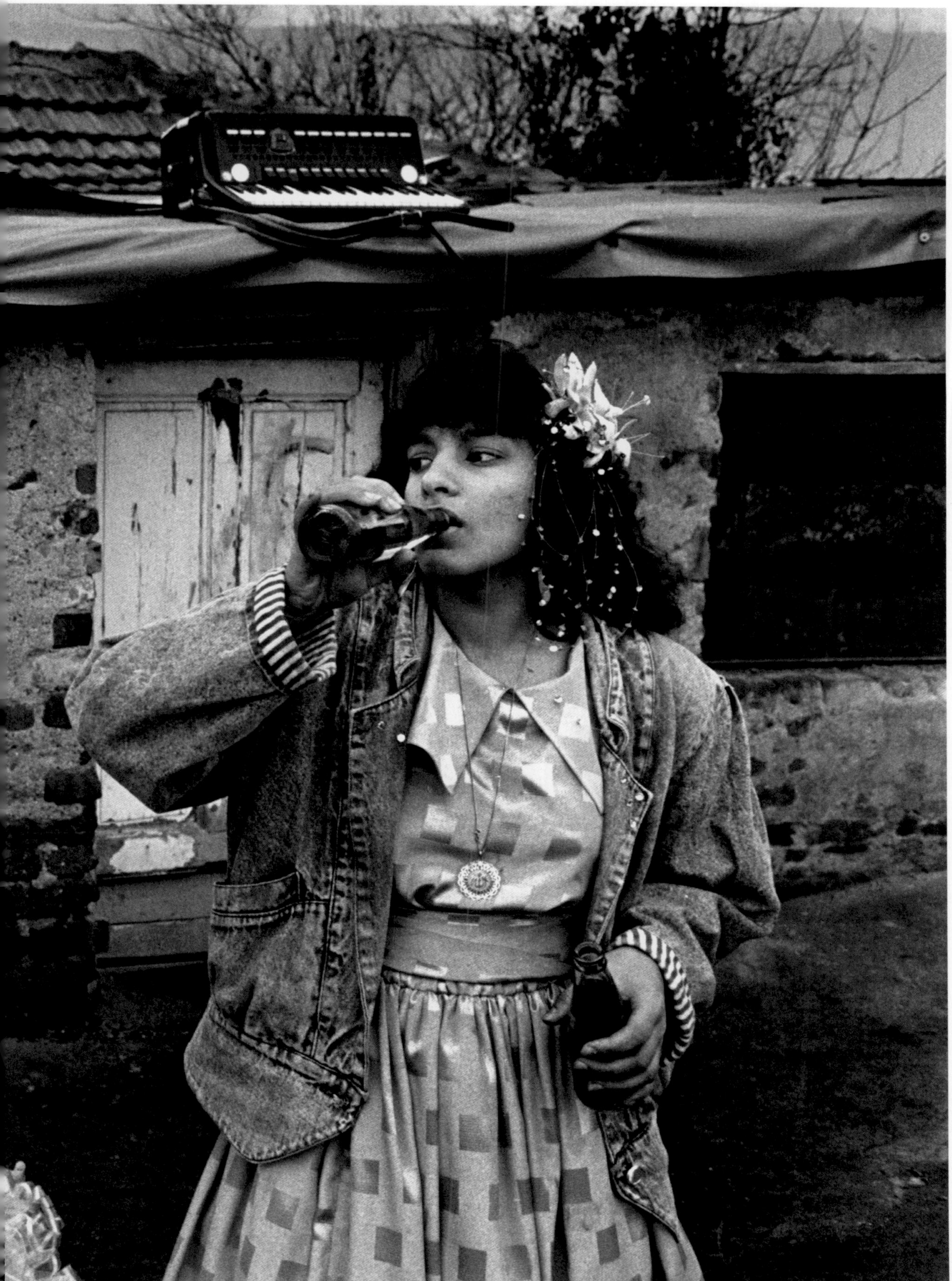

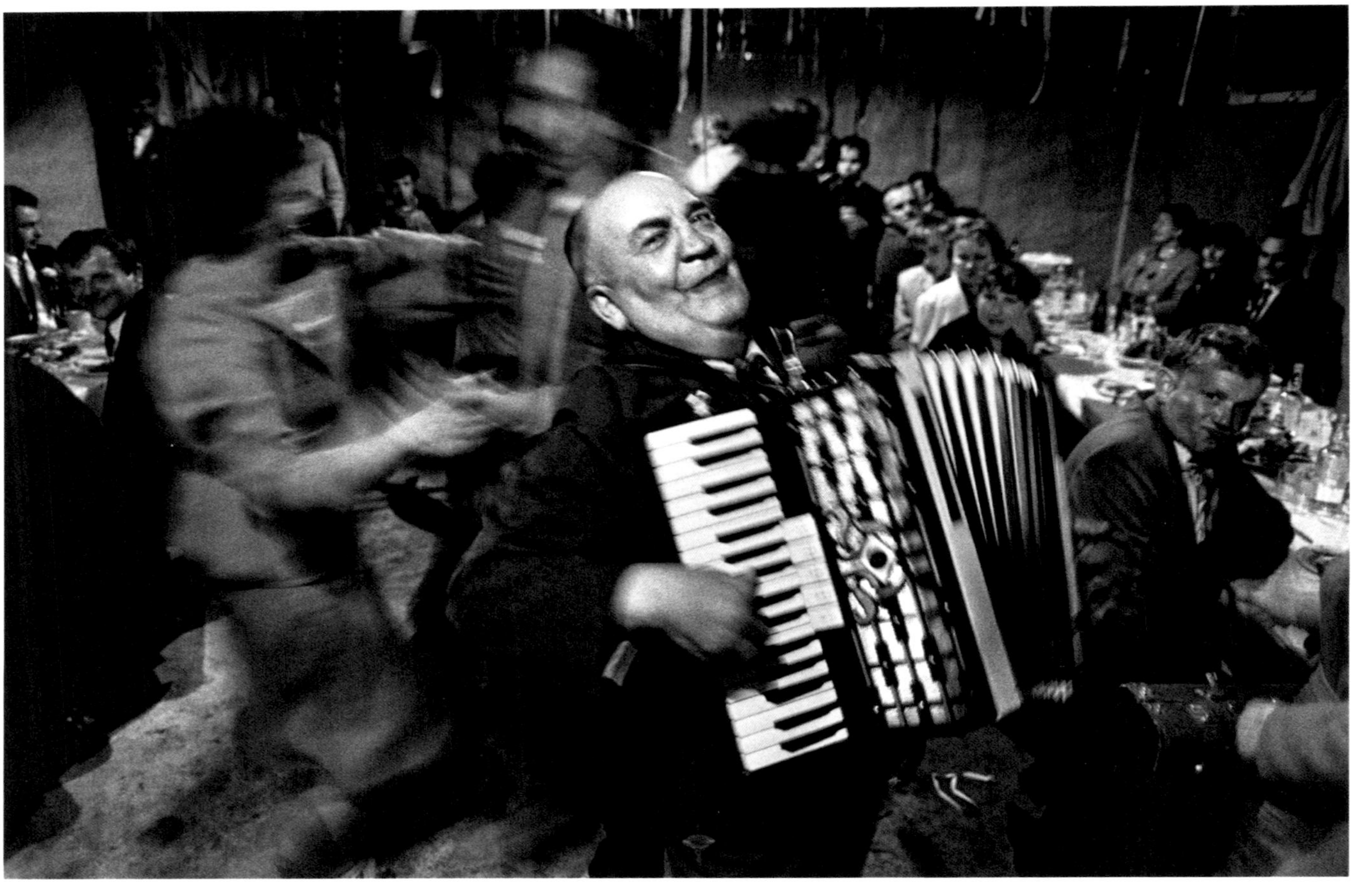

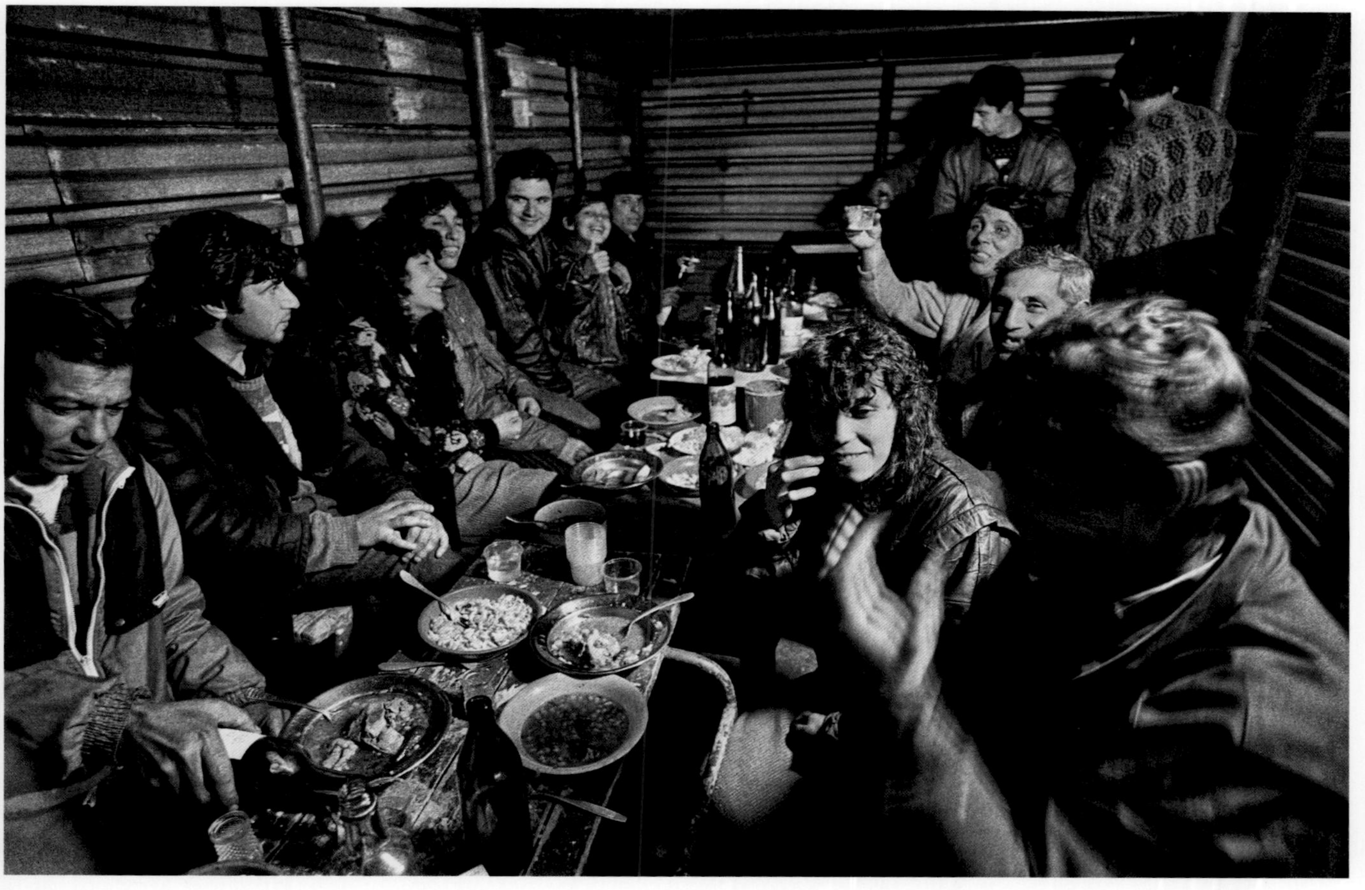

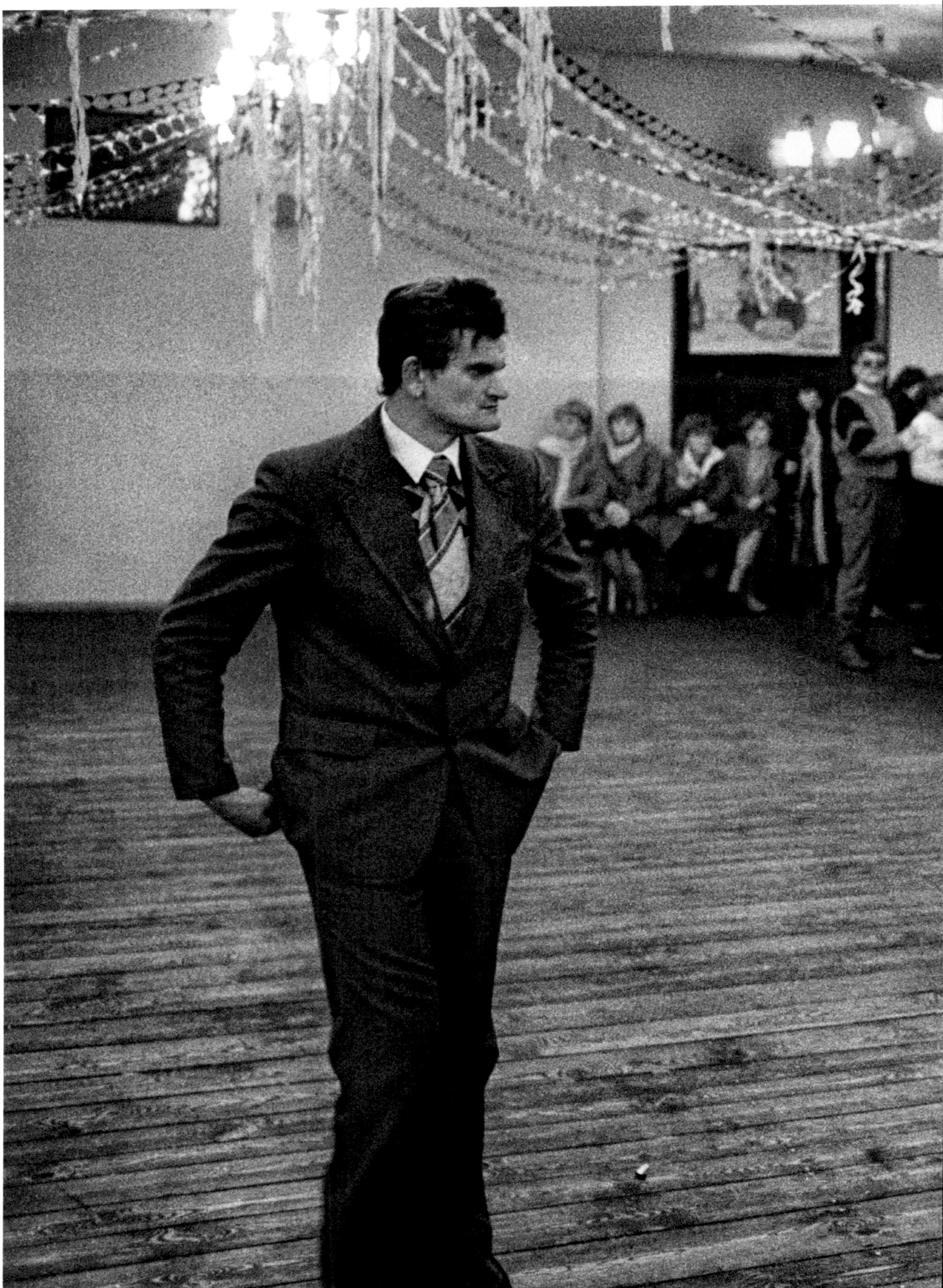

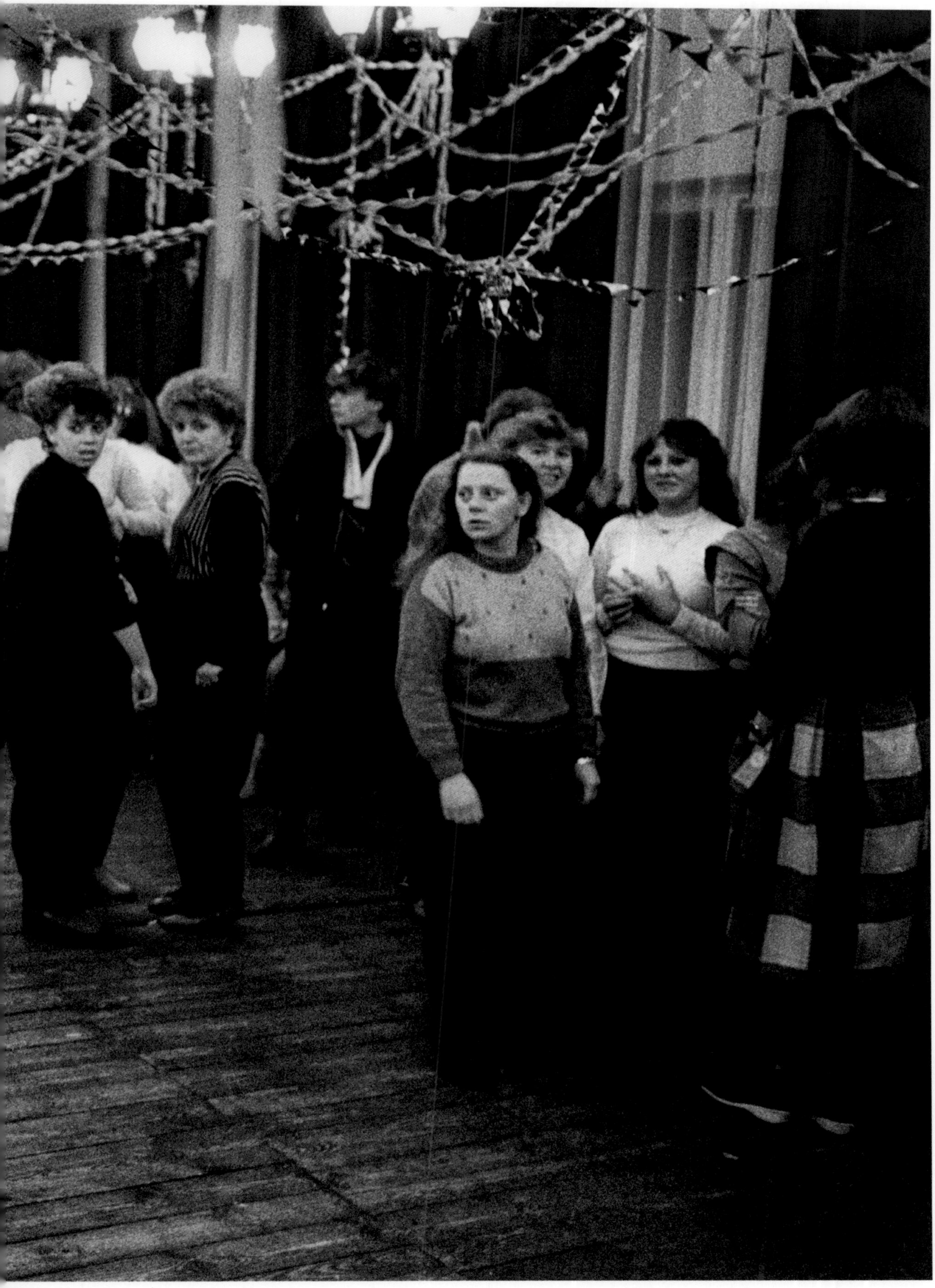

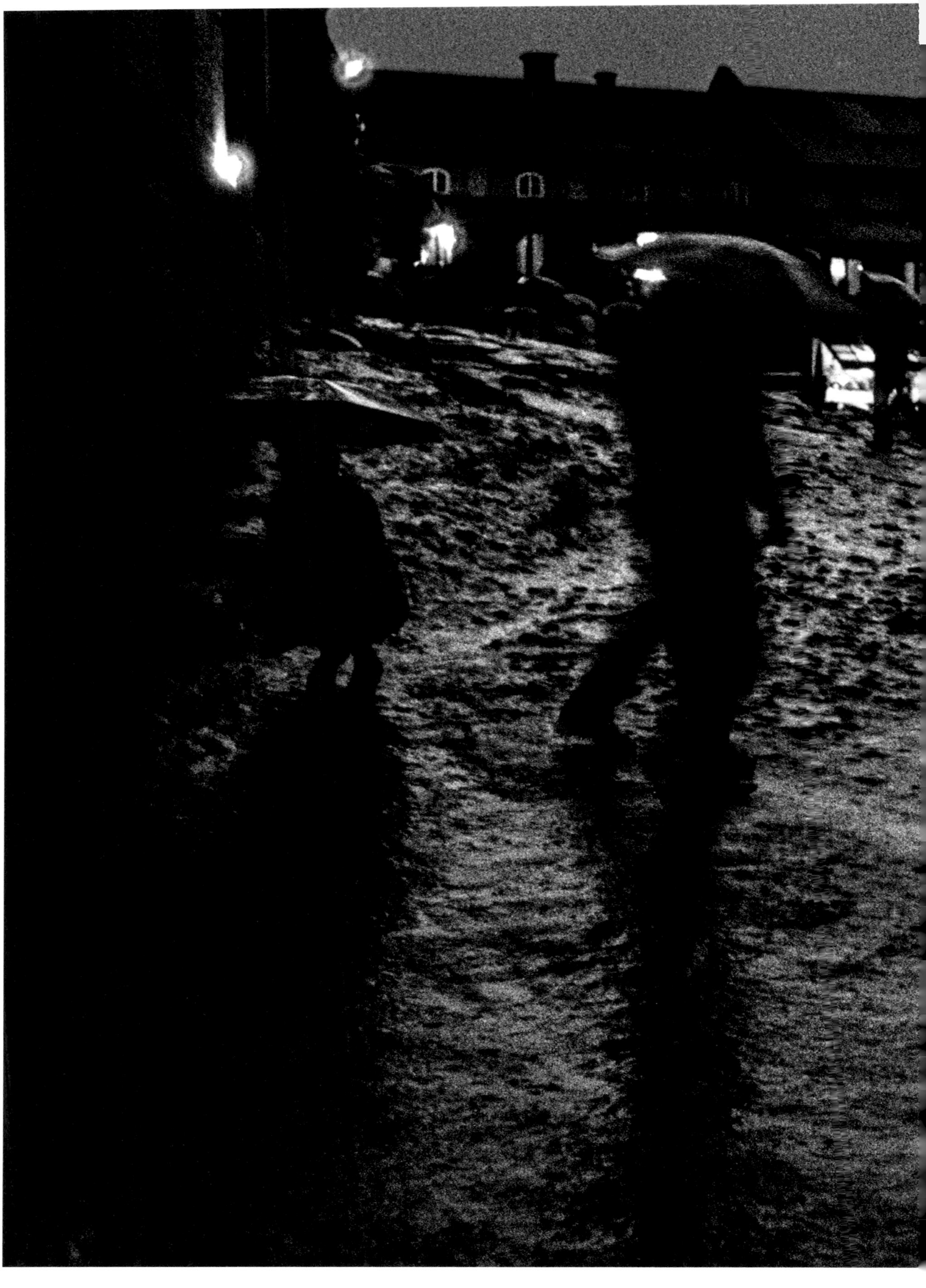

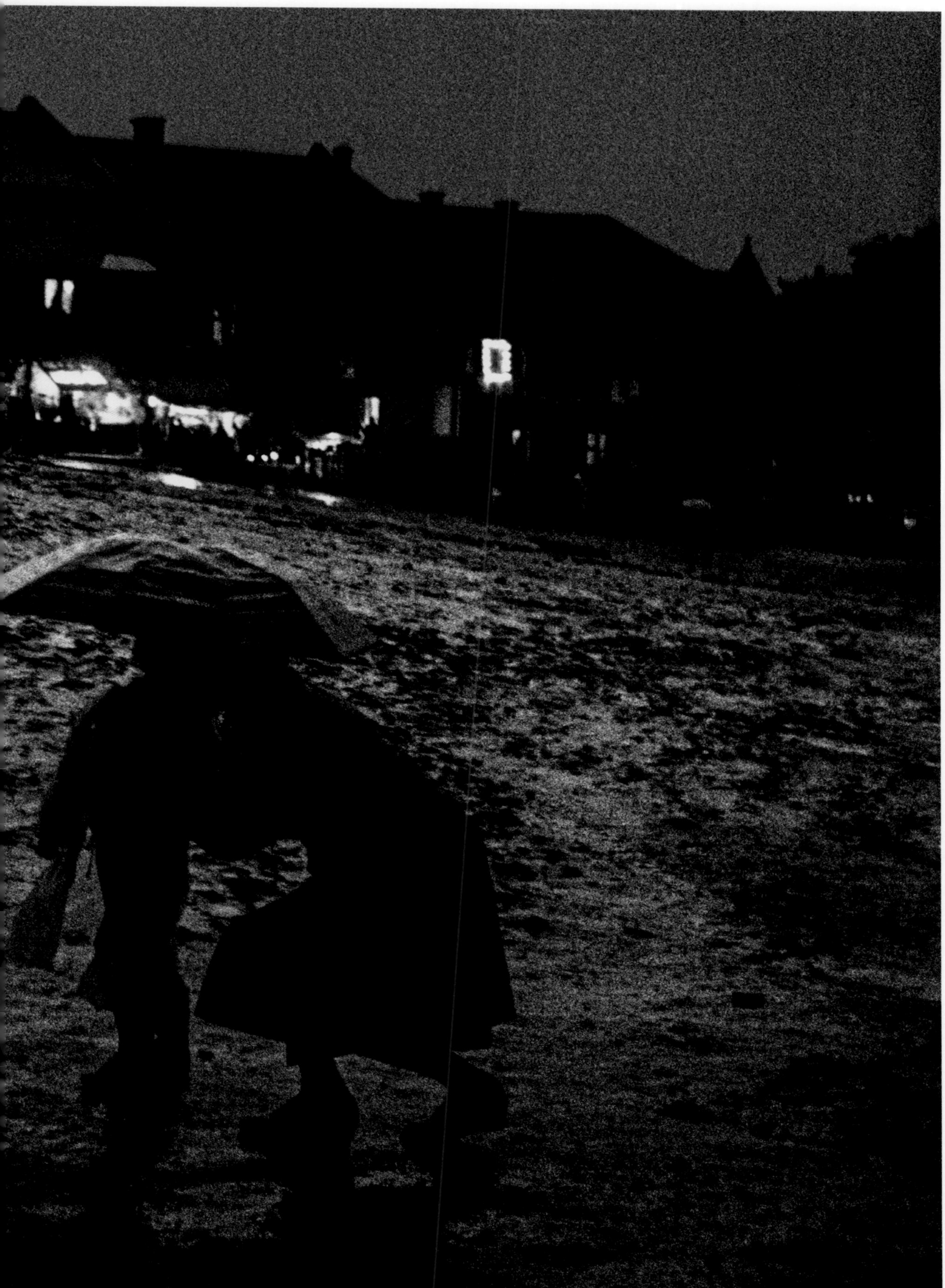

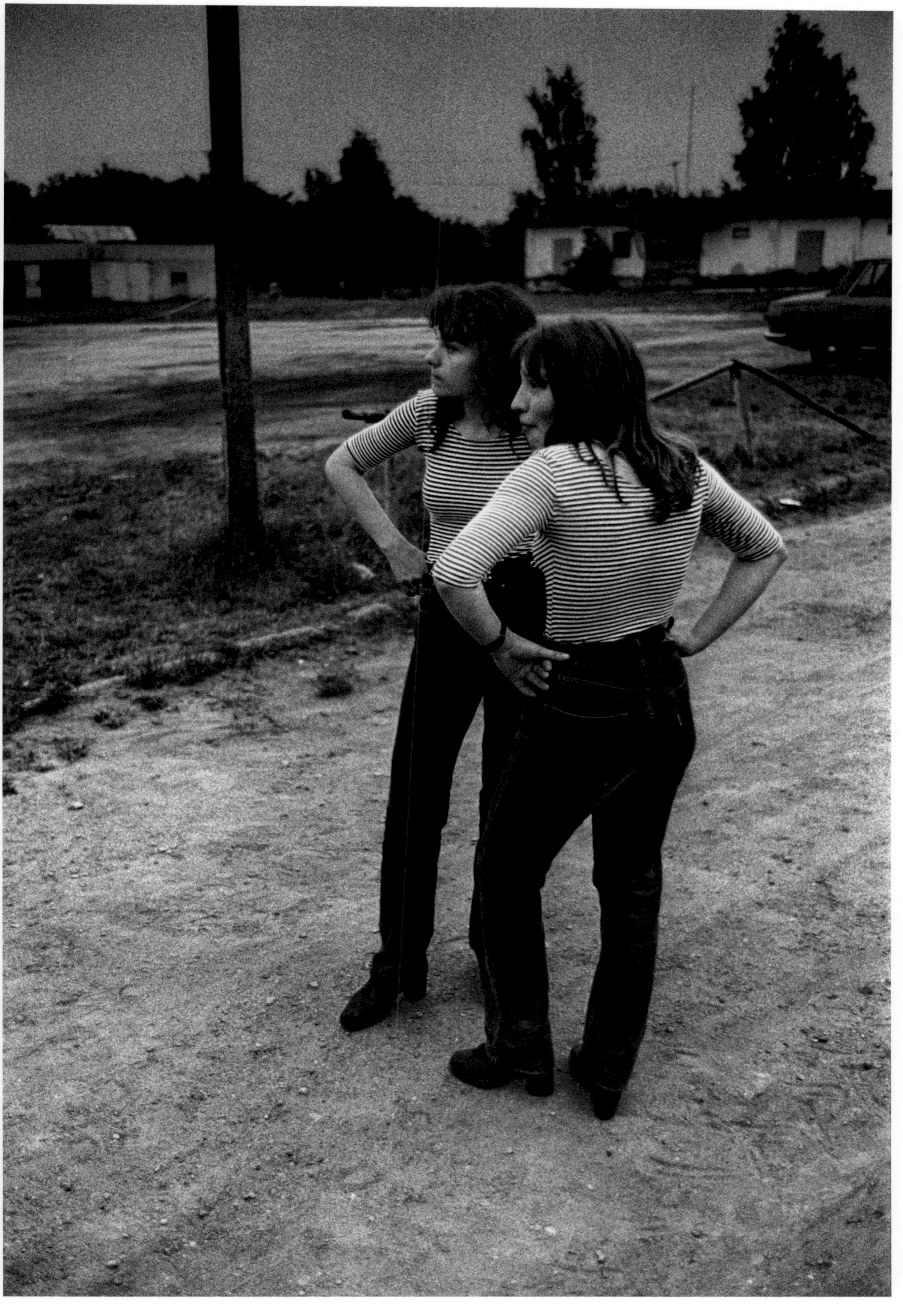

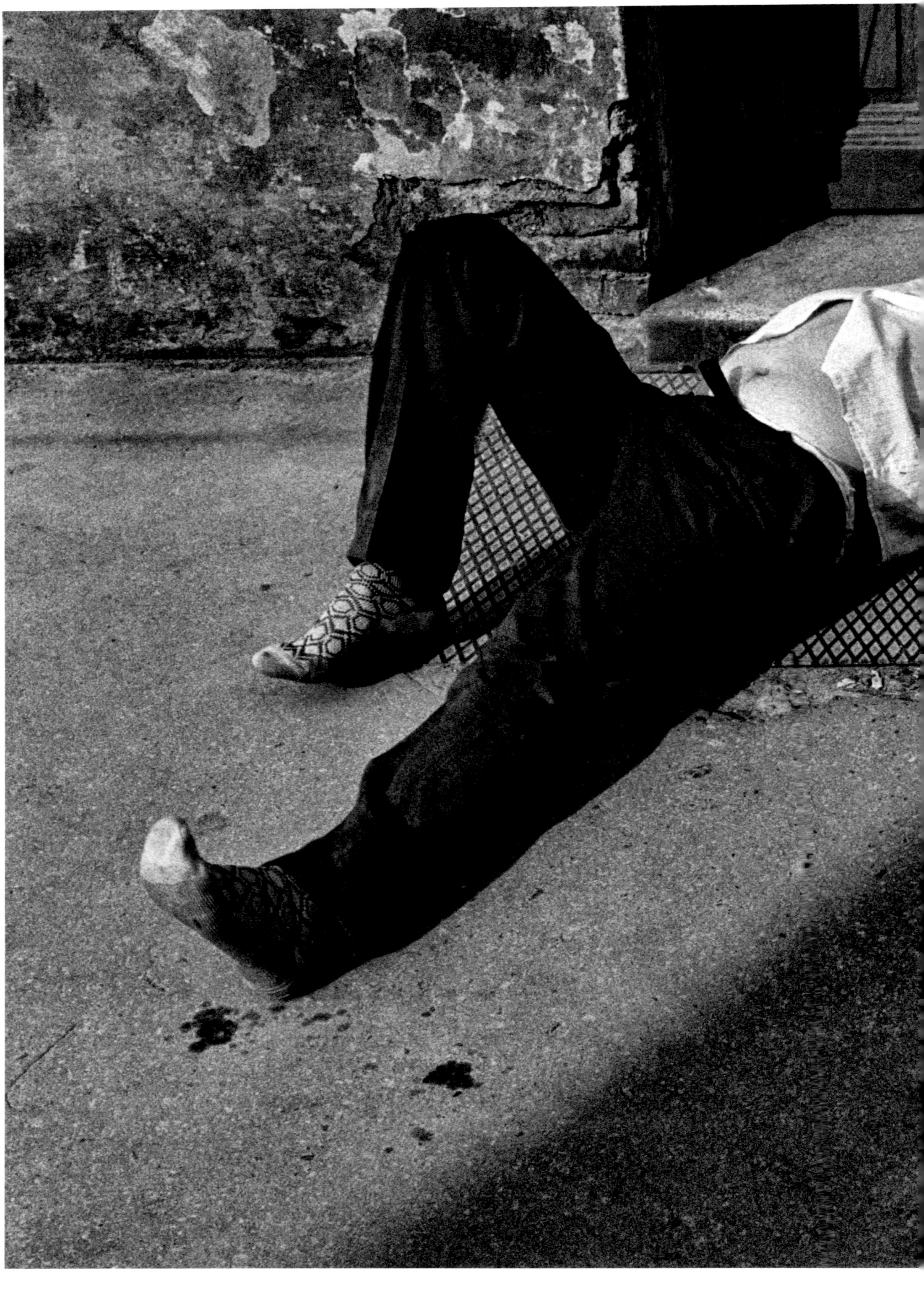

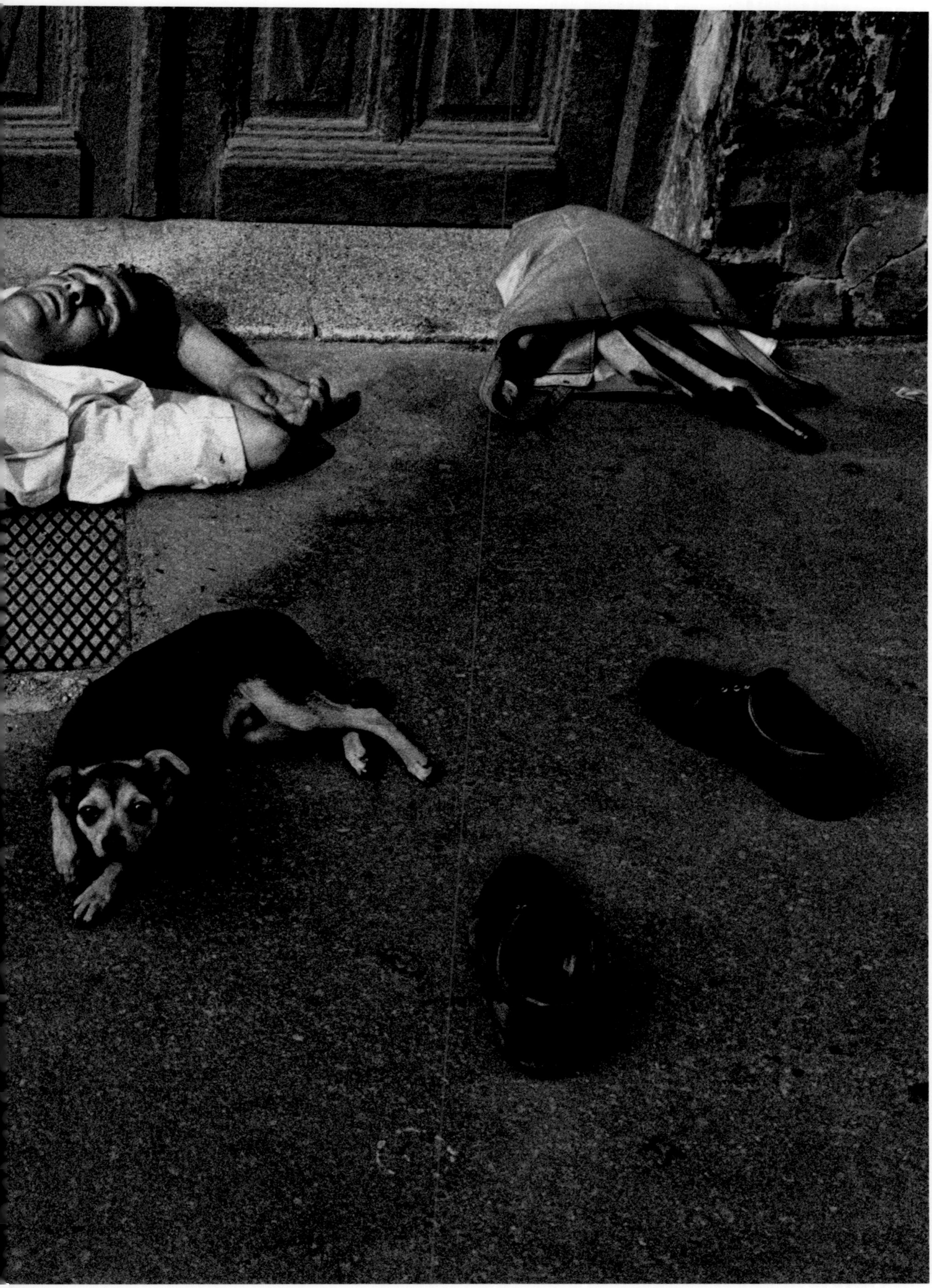

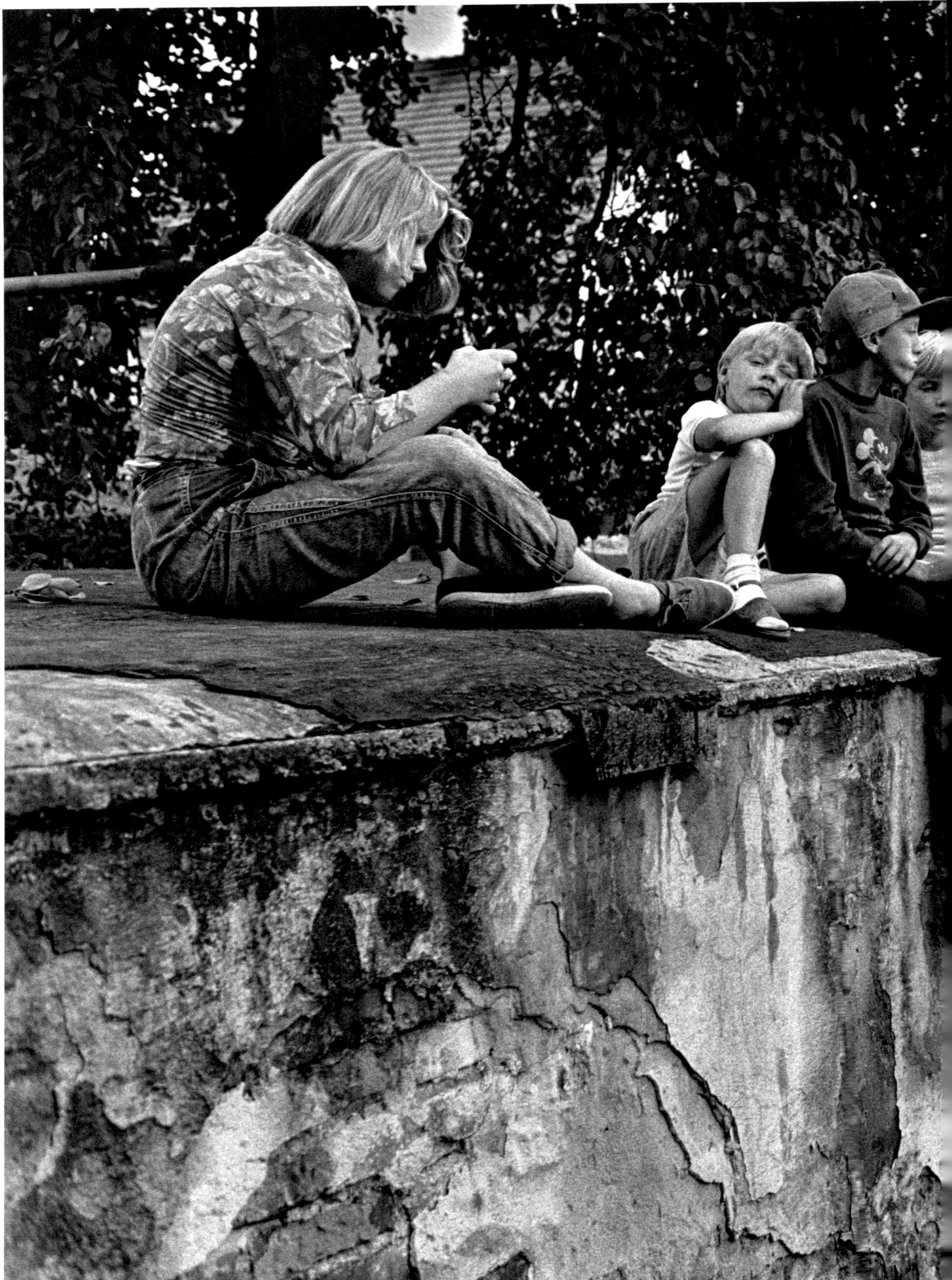

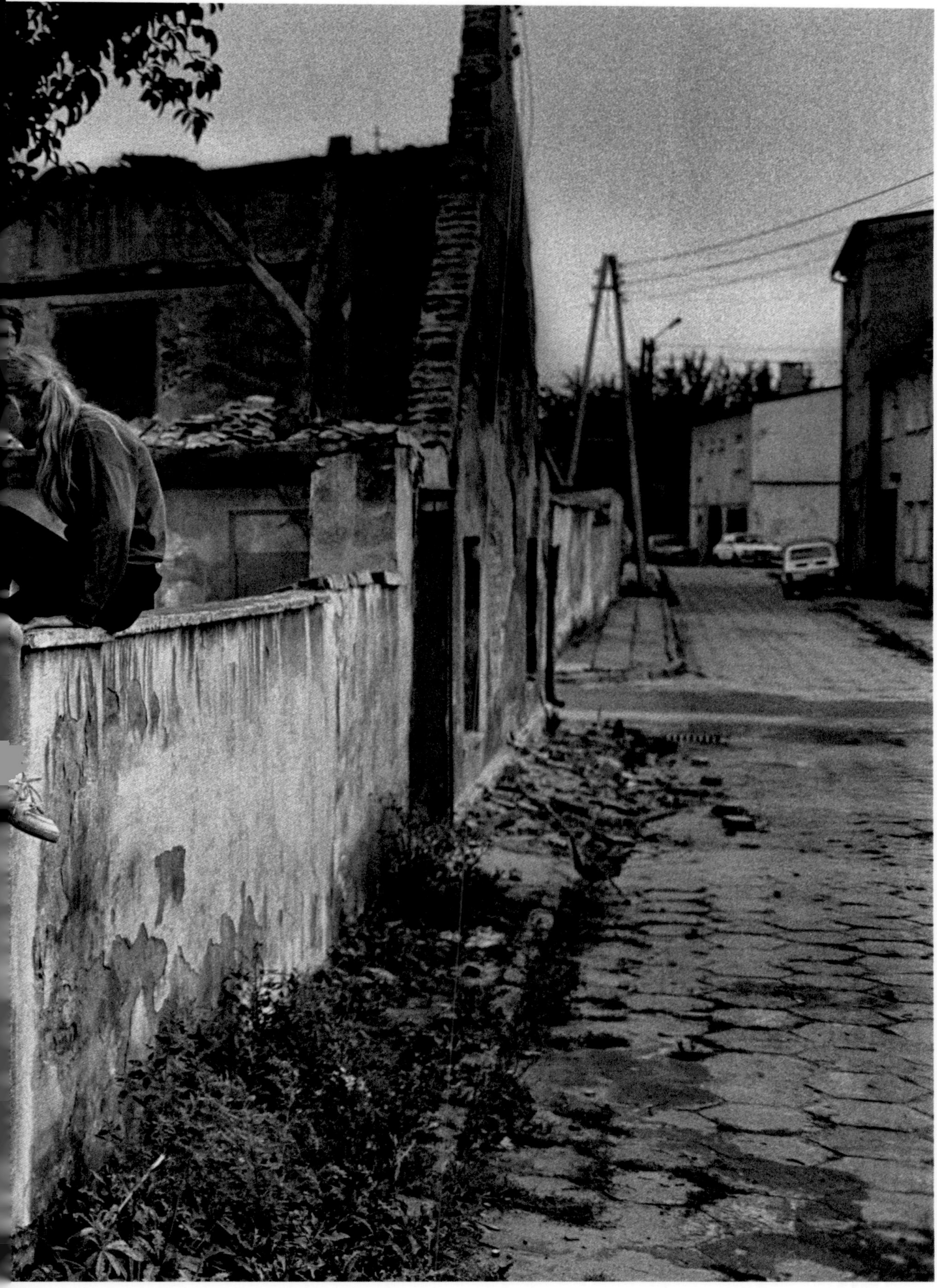

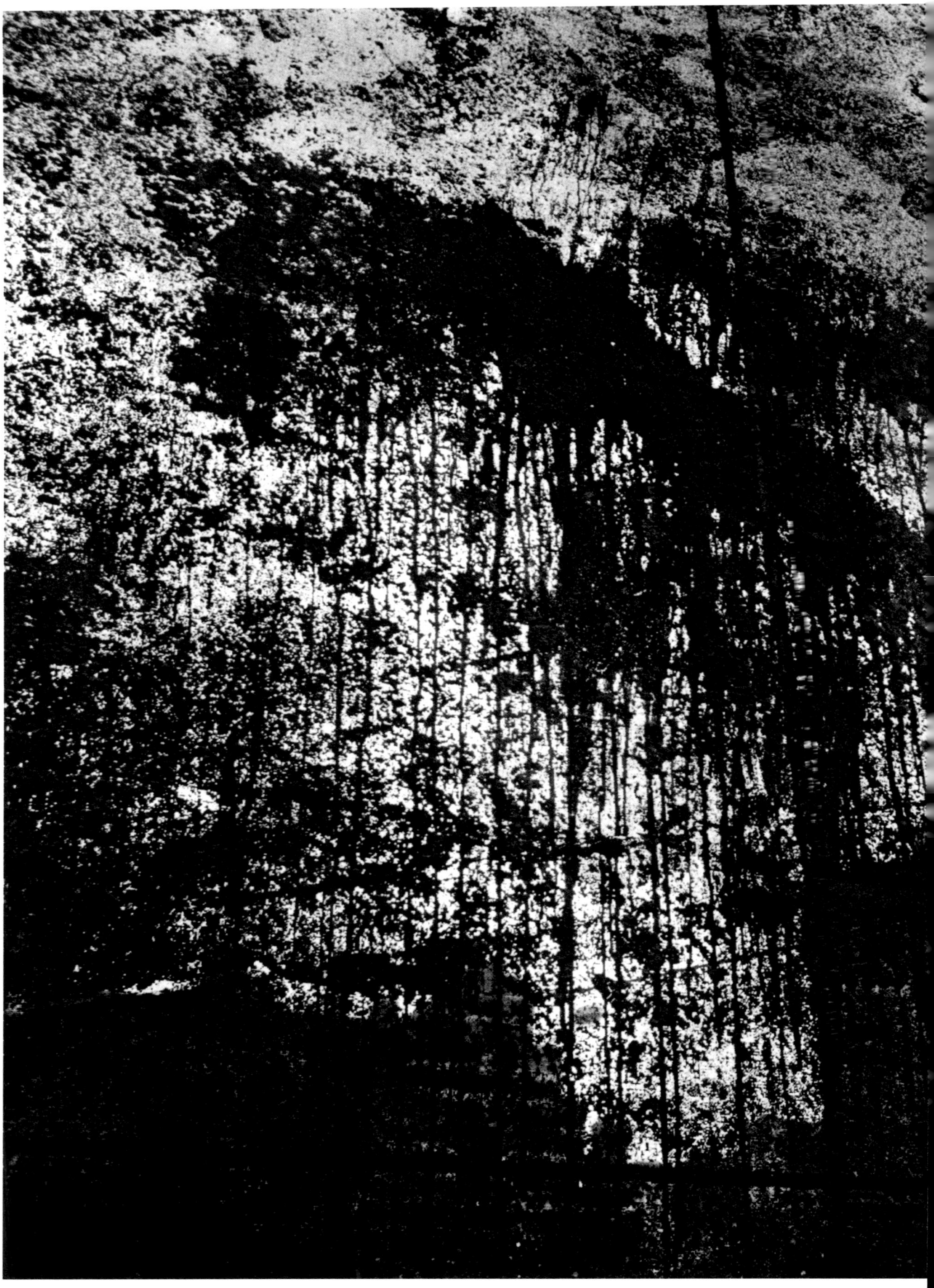

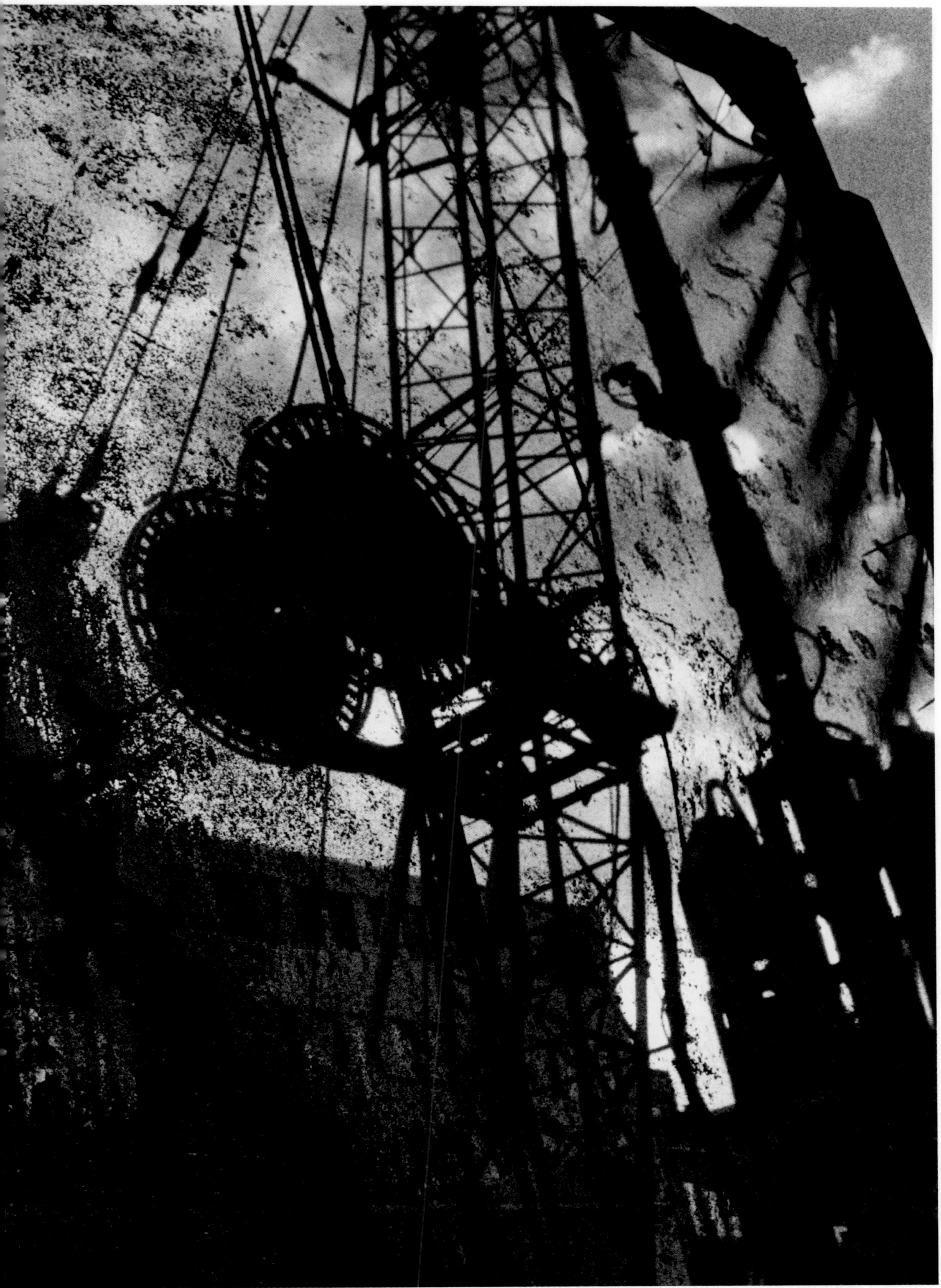

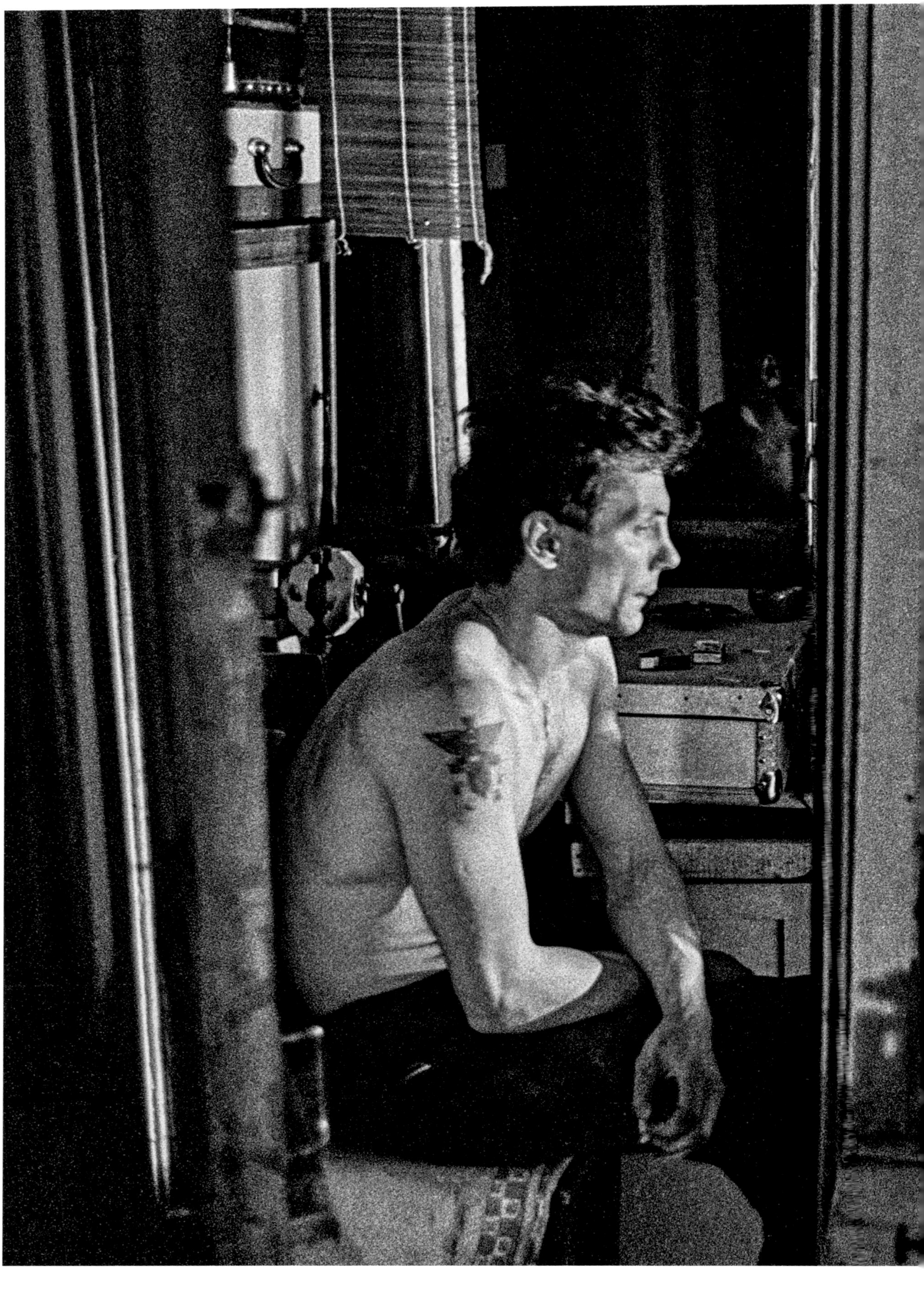

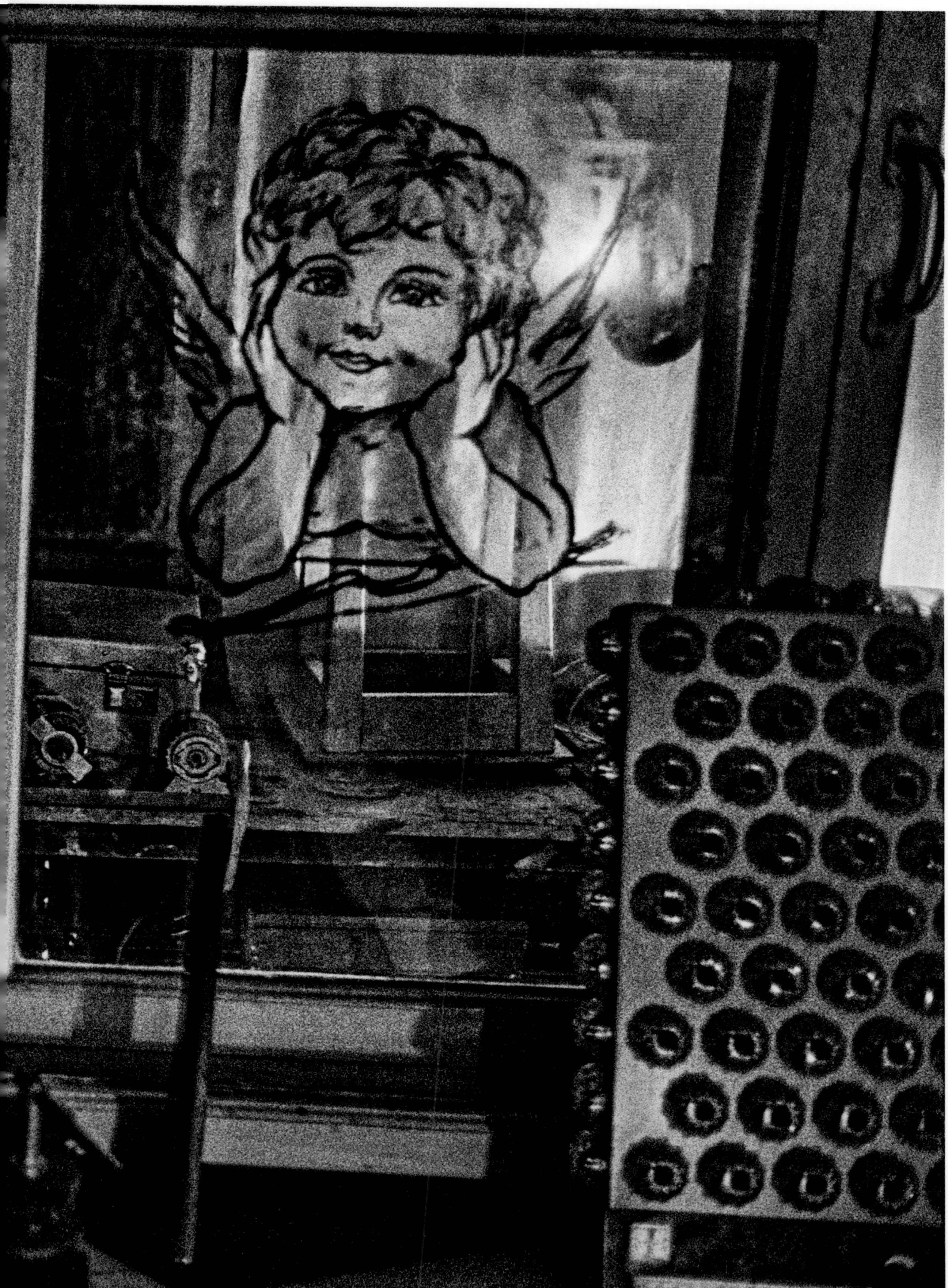

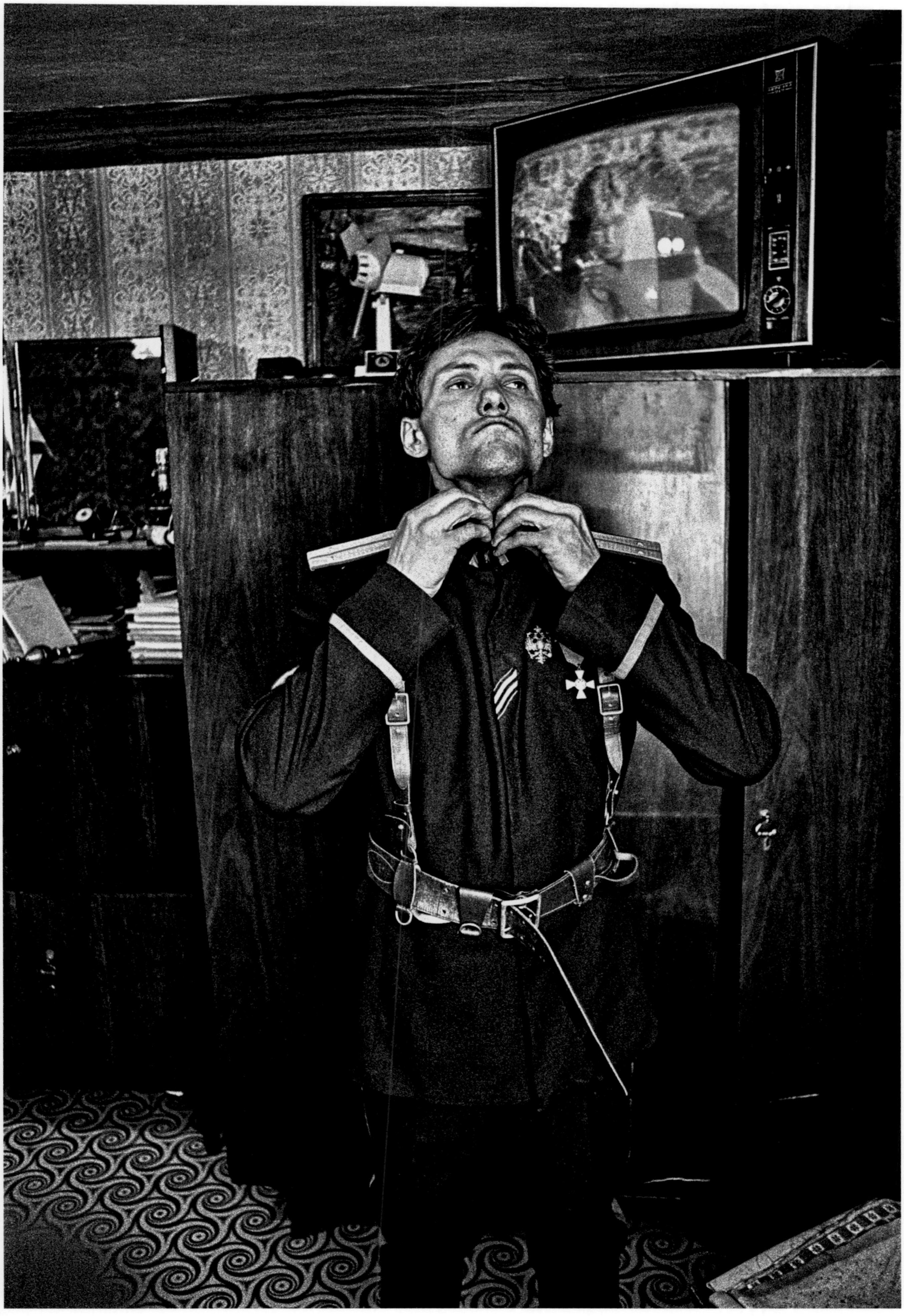

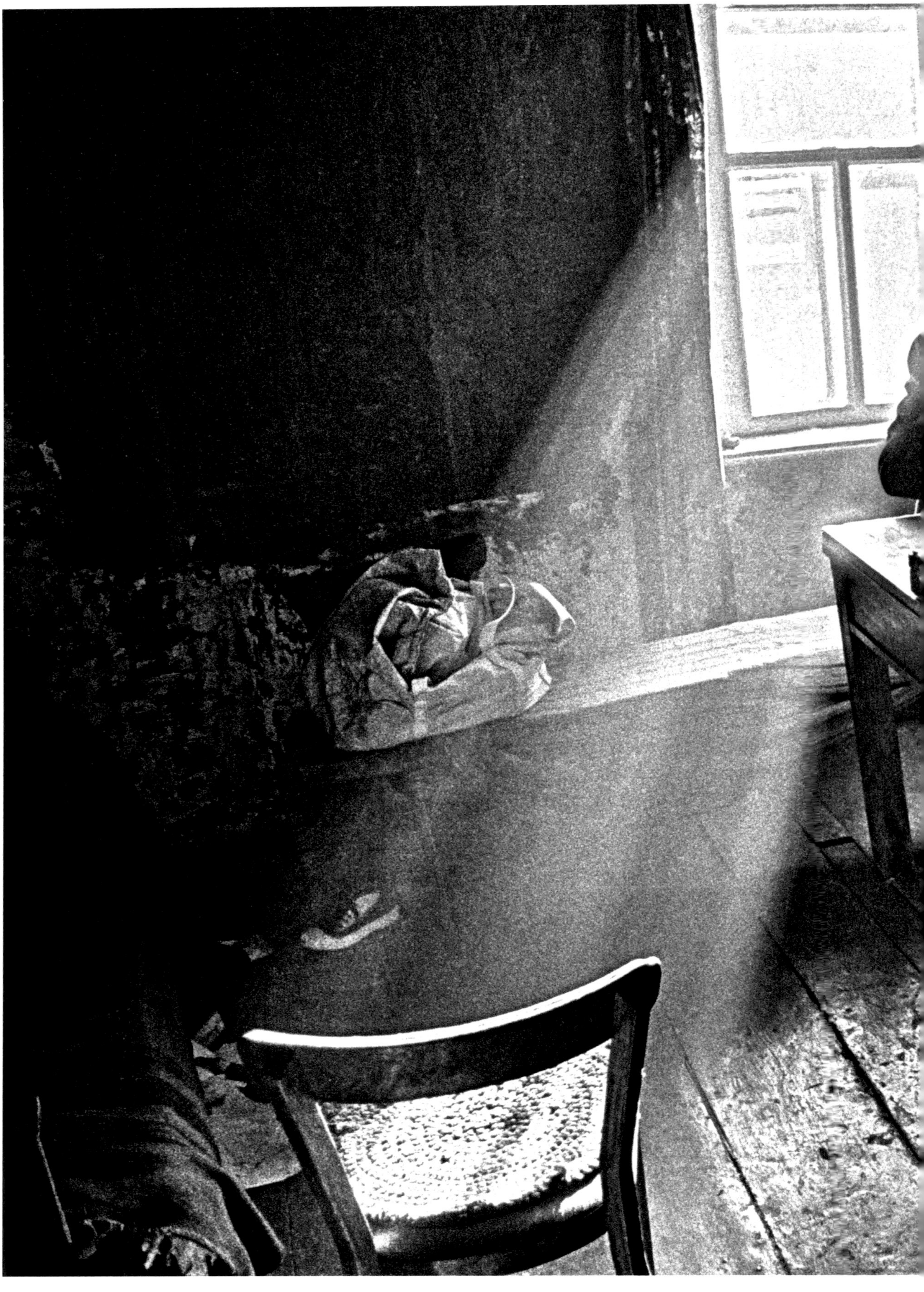

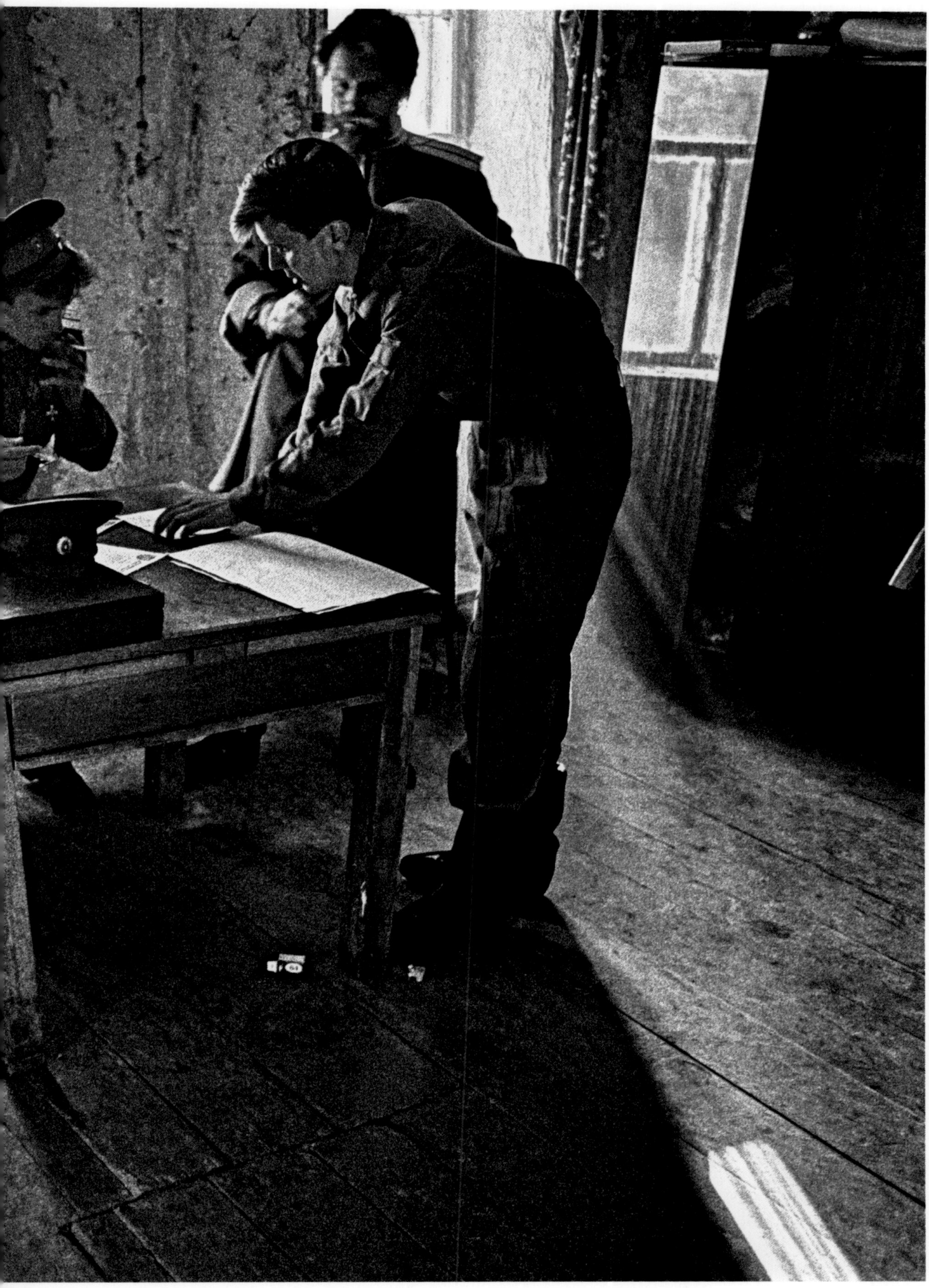

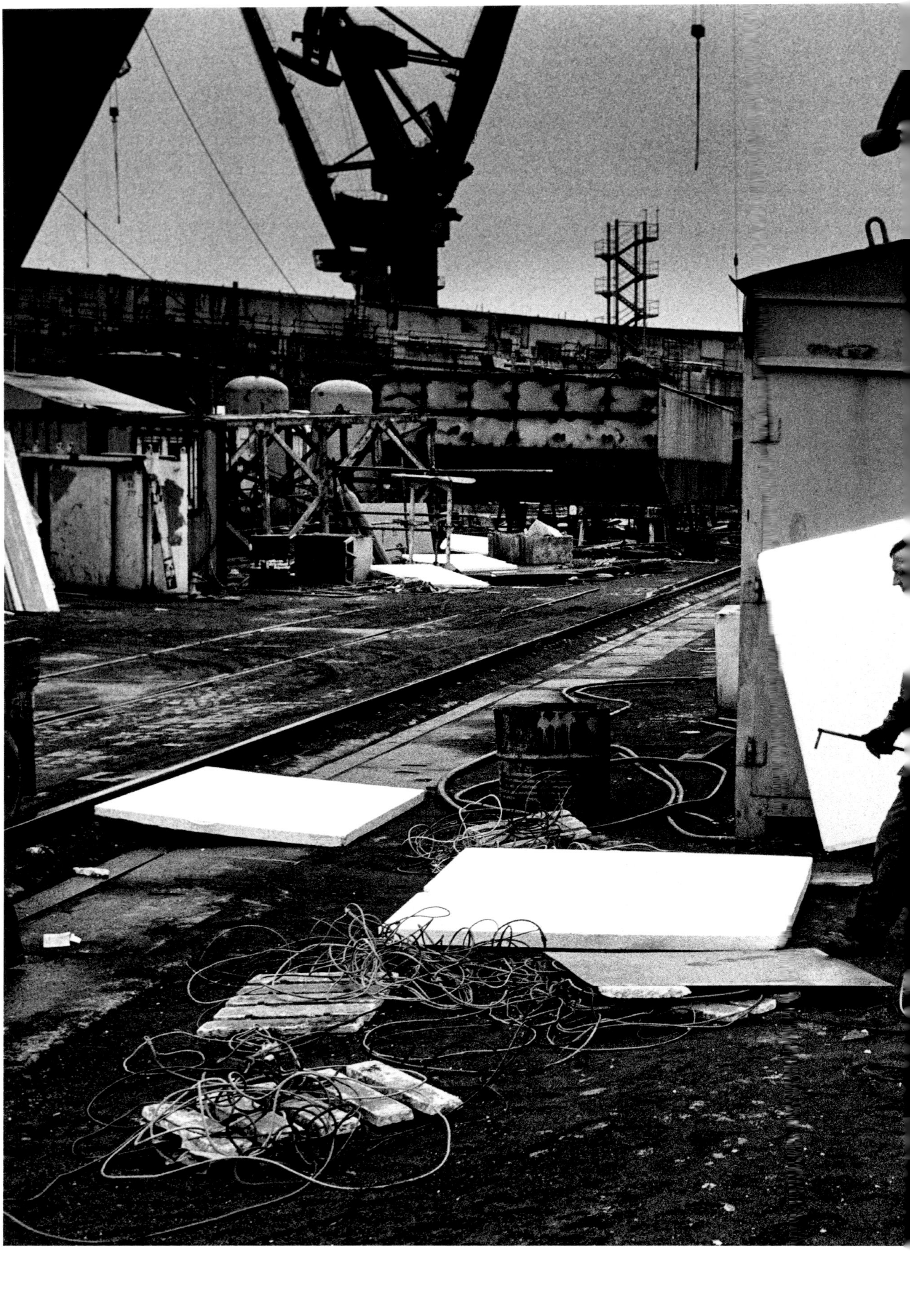

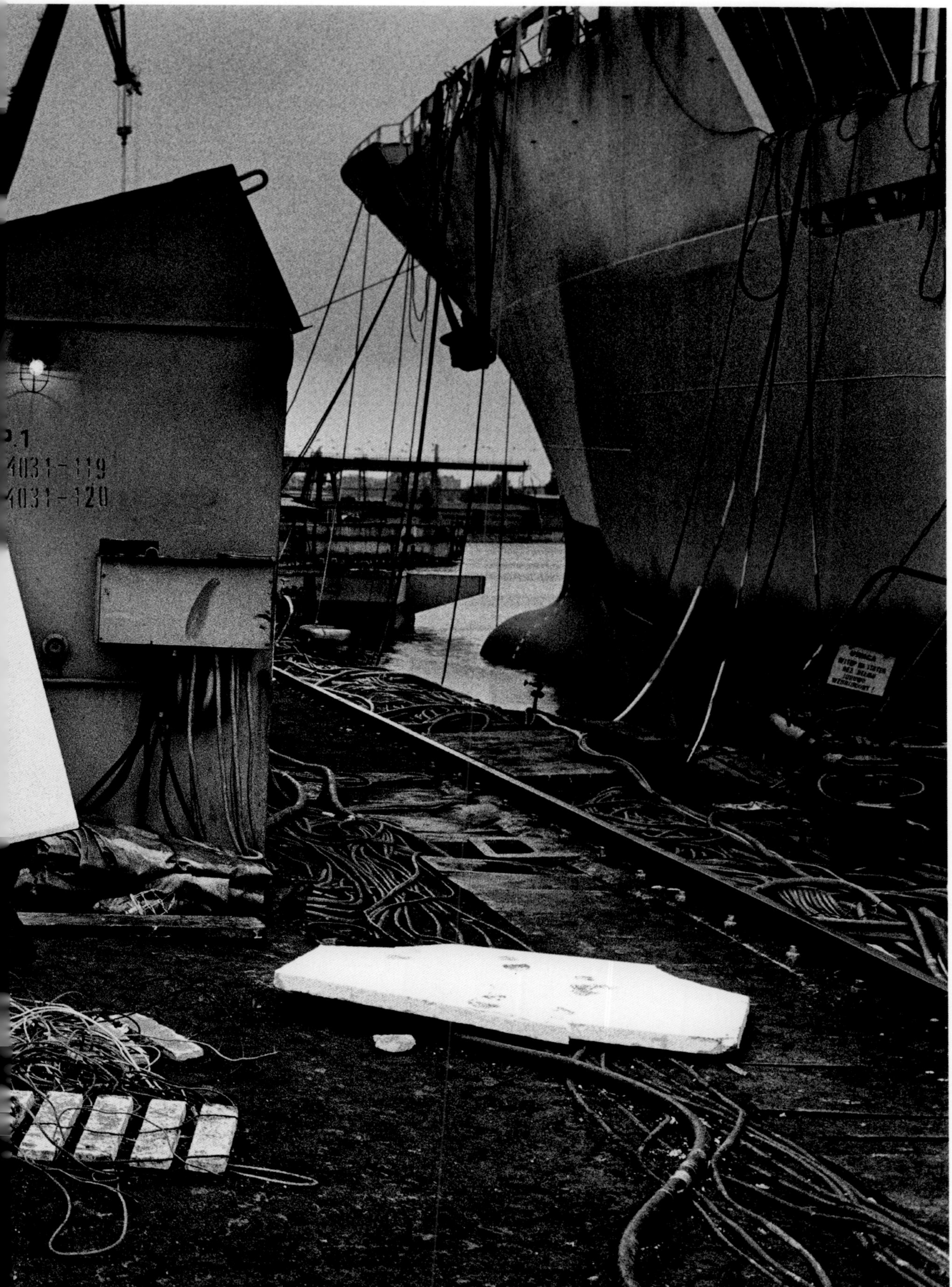
4031-119
4031-120

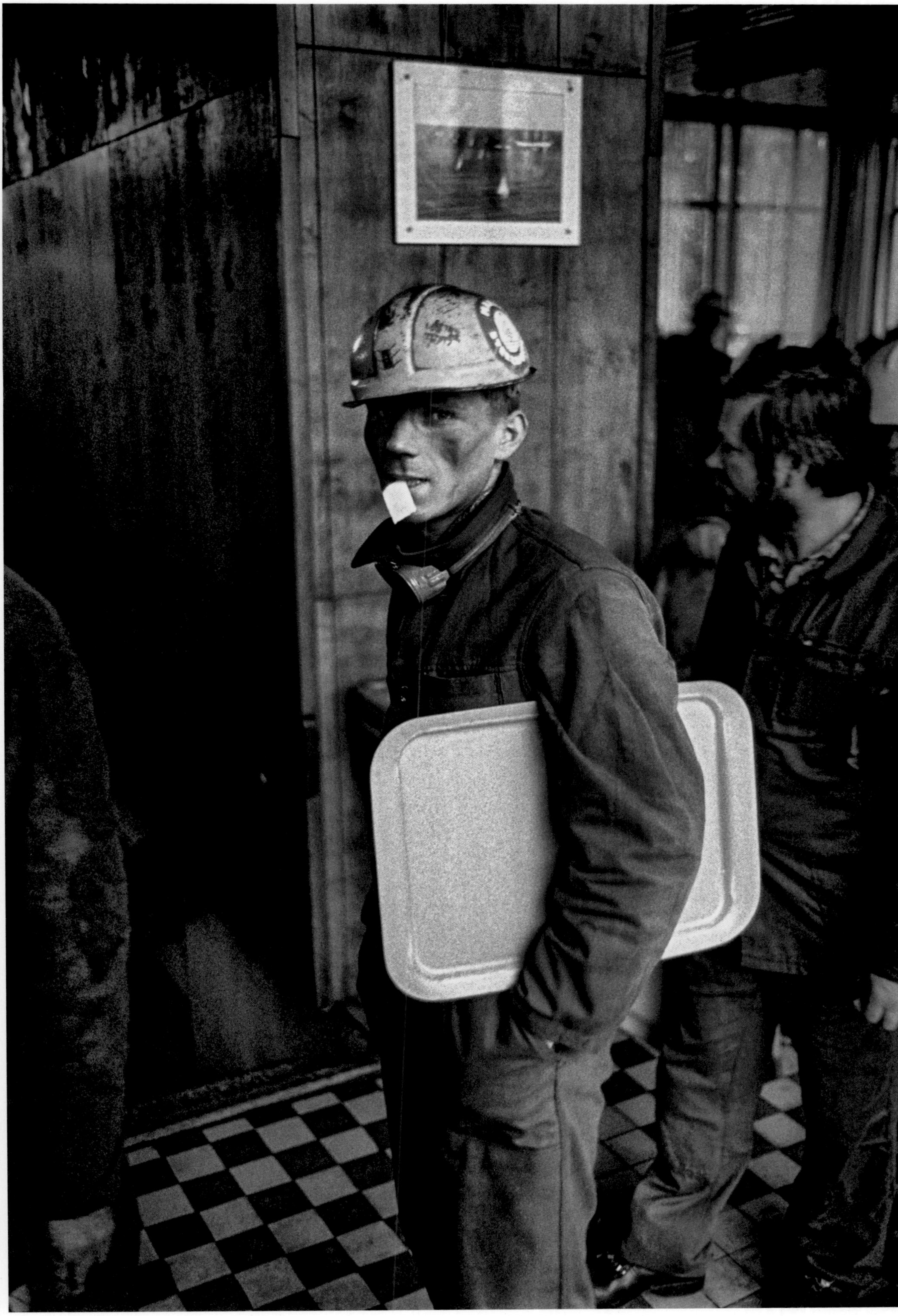

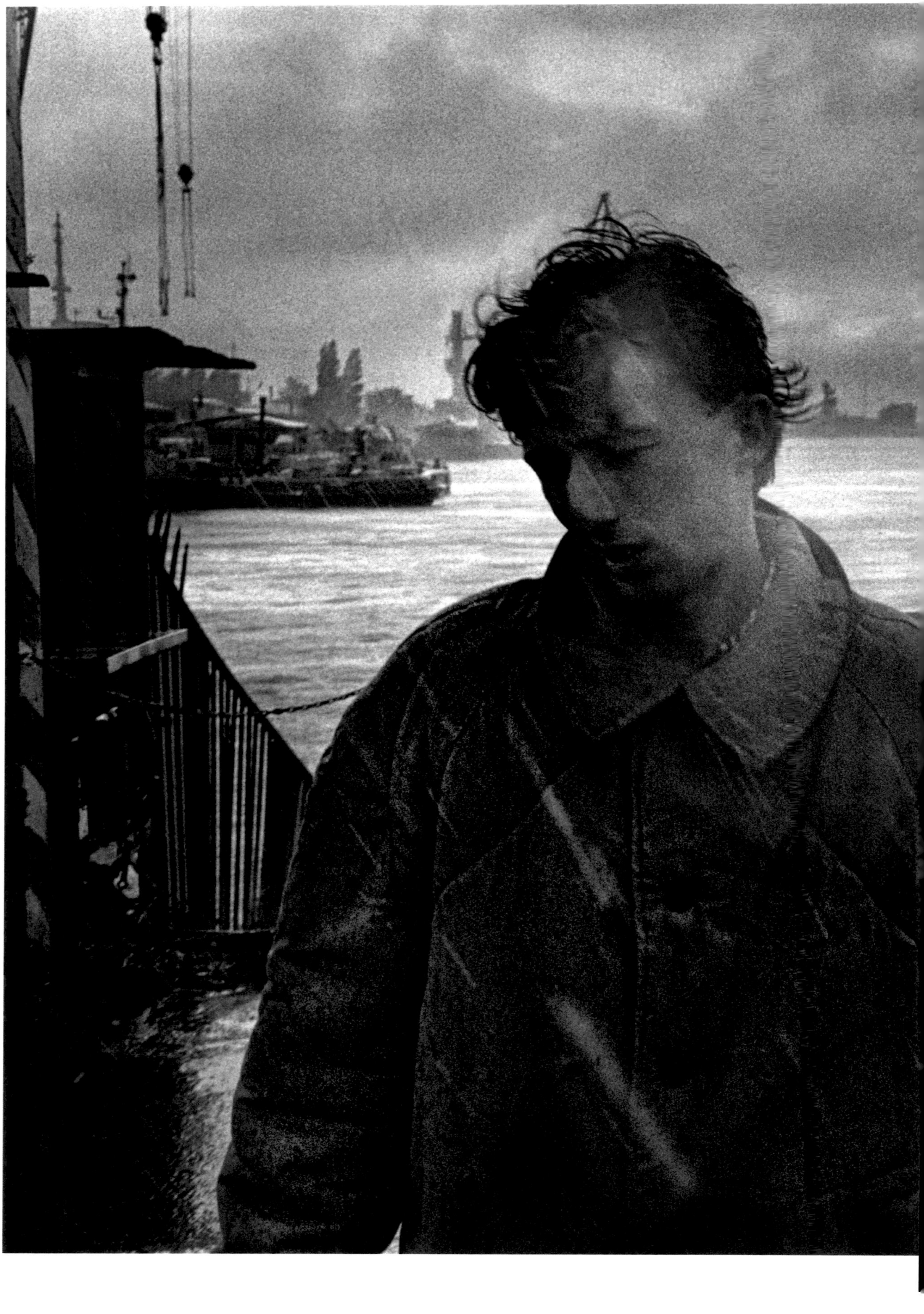

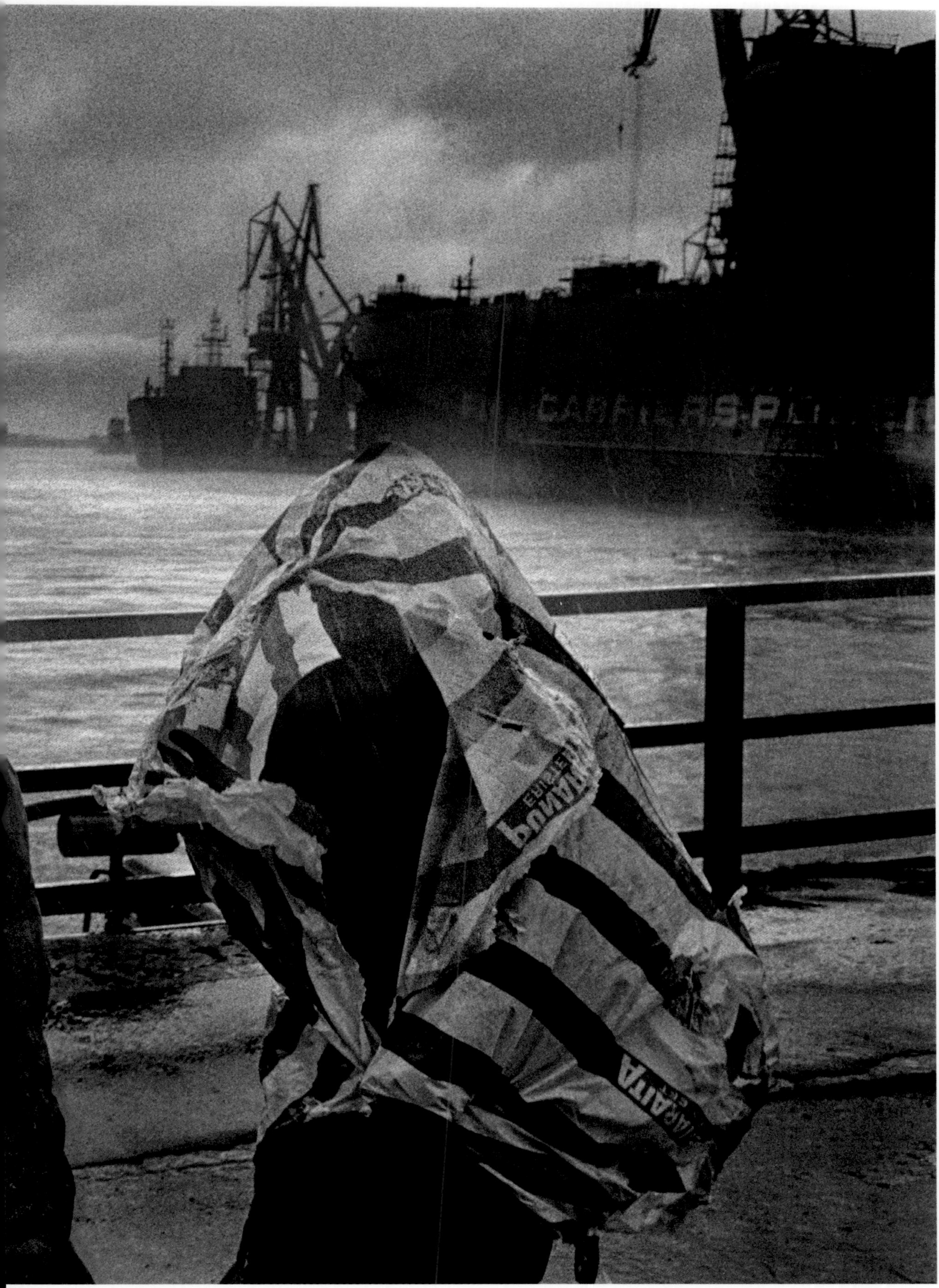

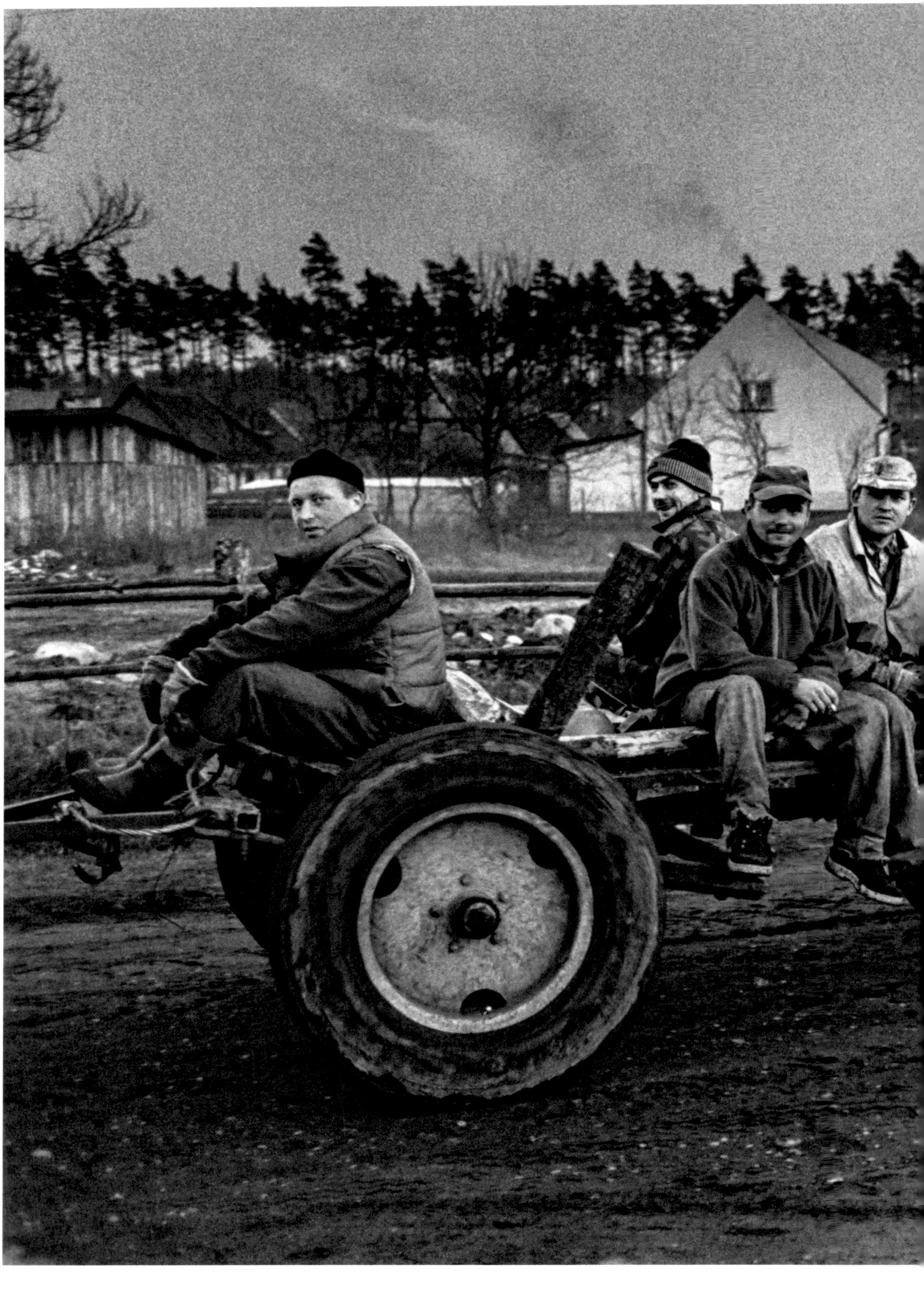

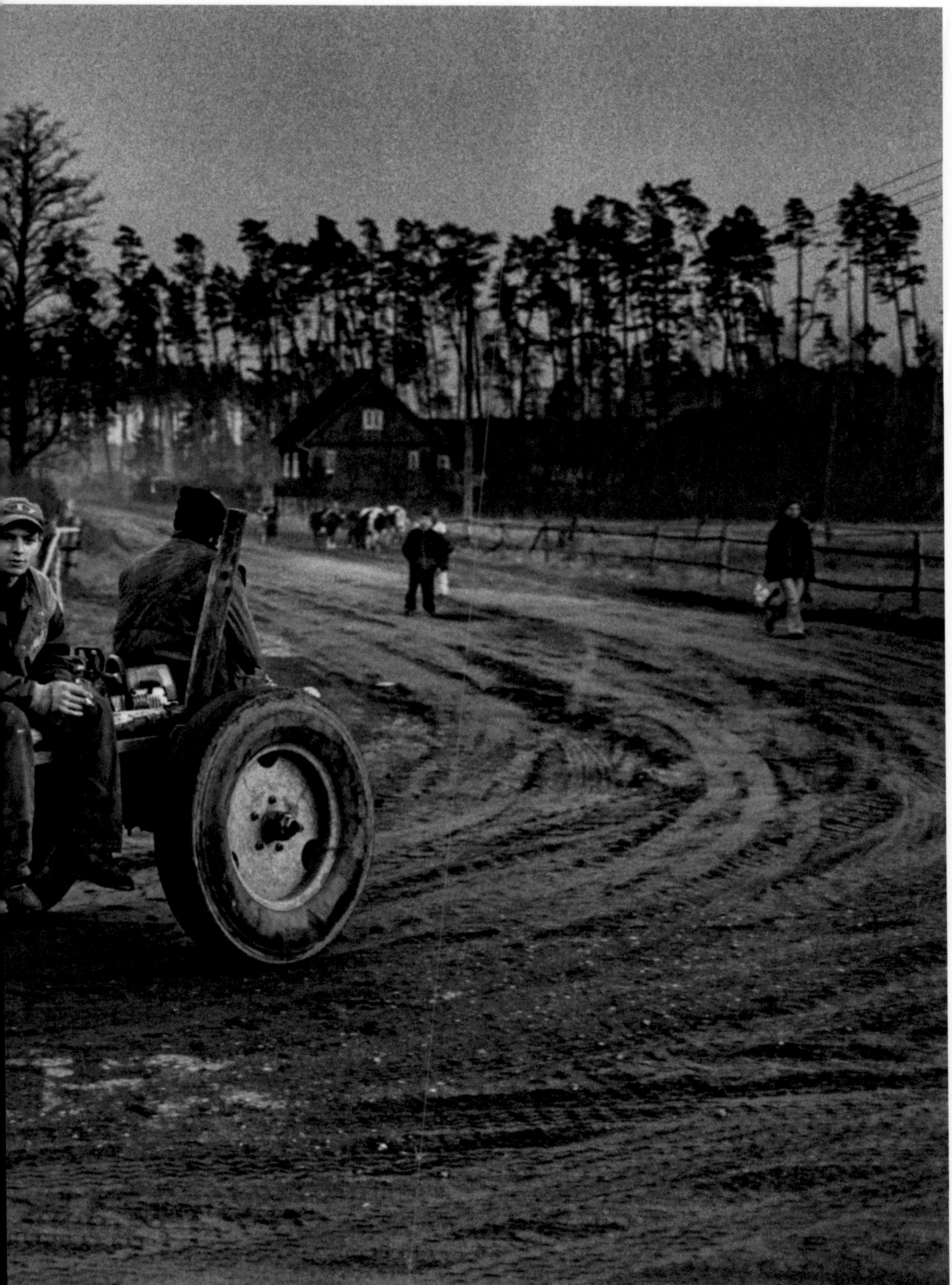

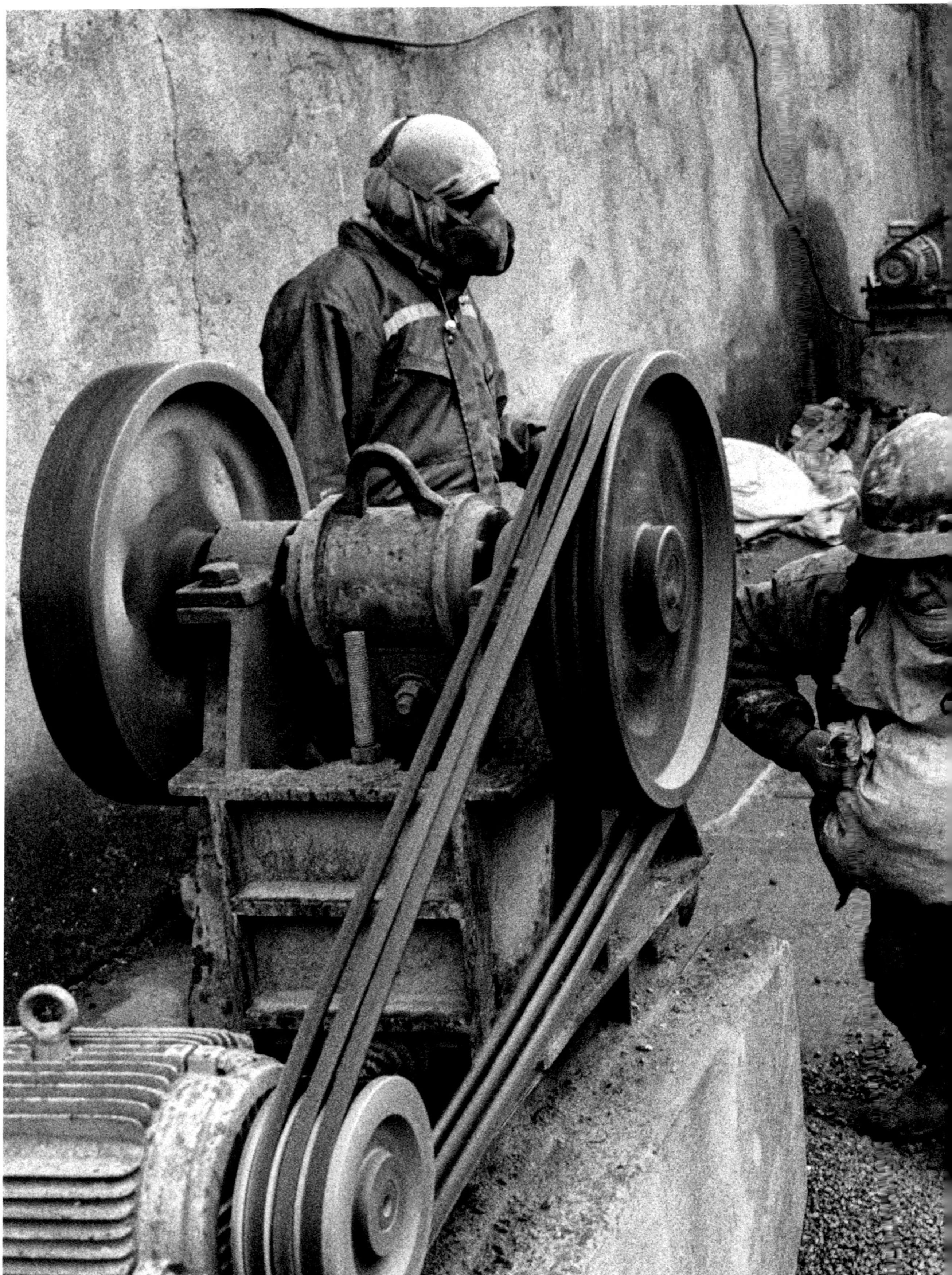

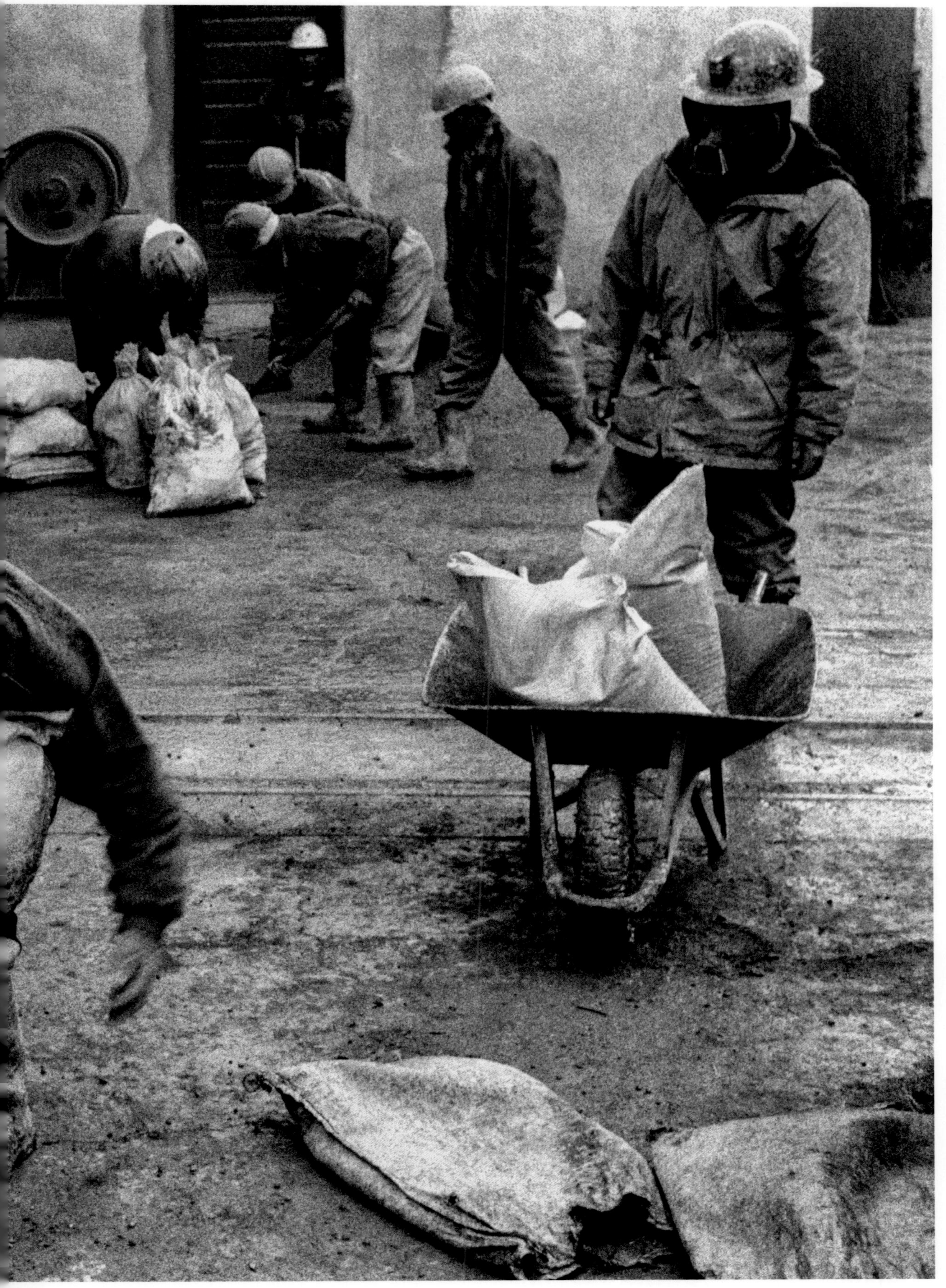

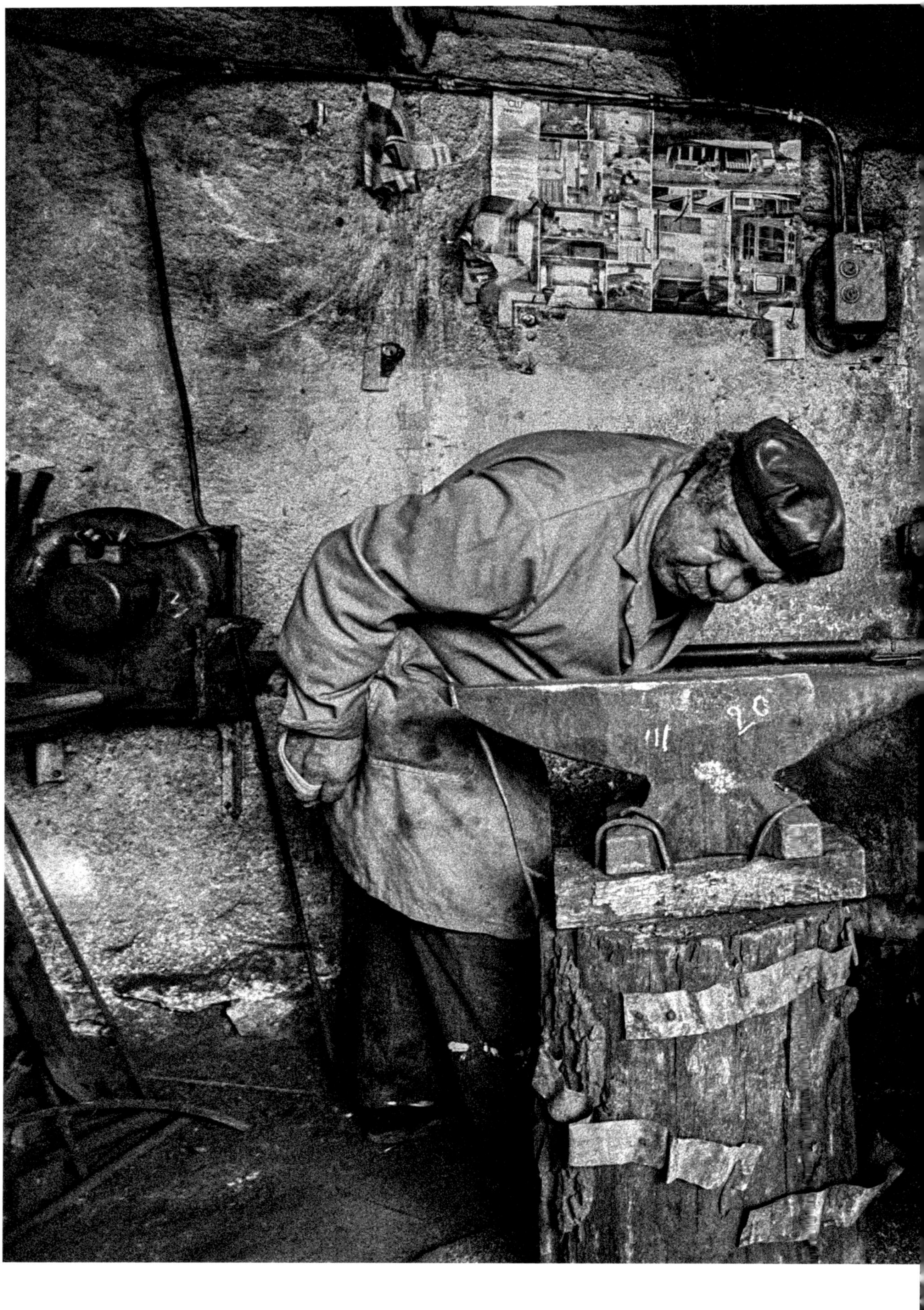

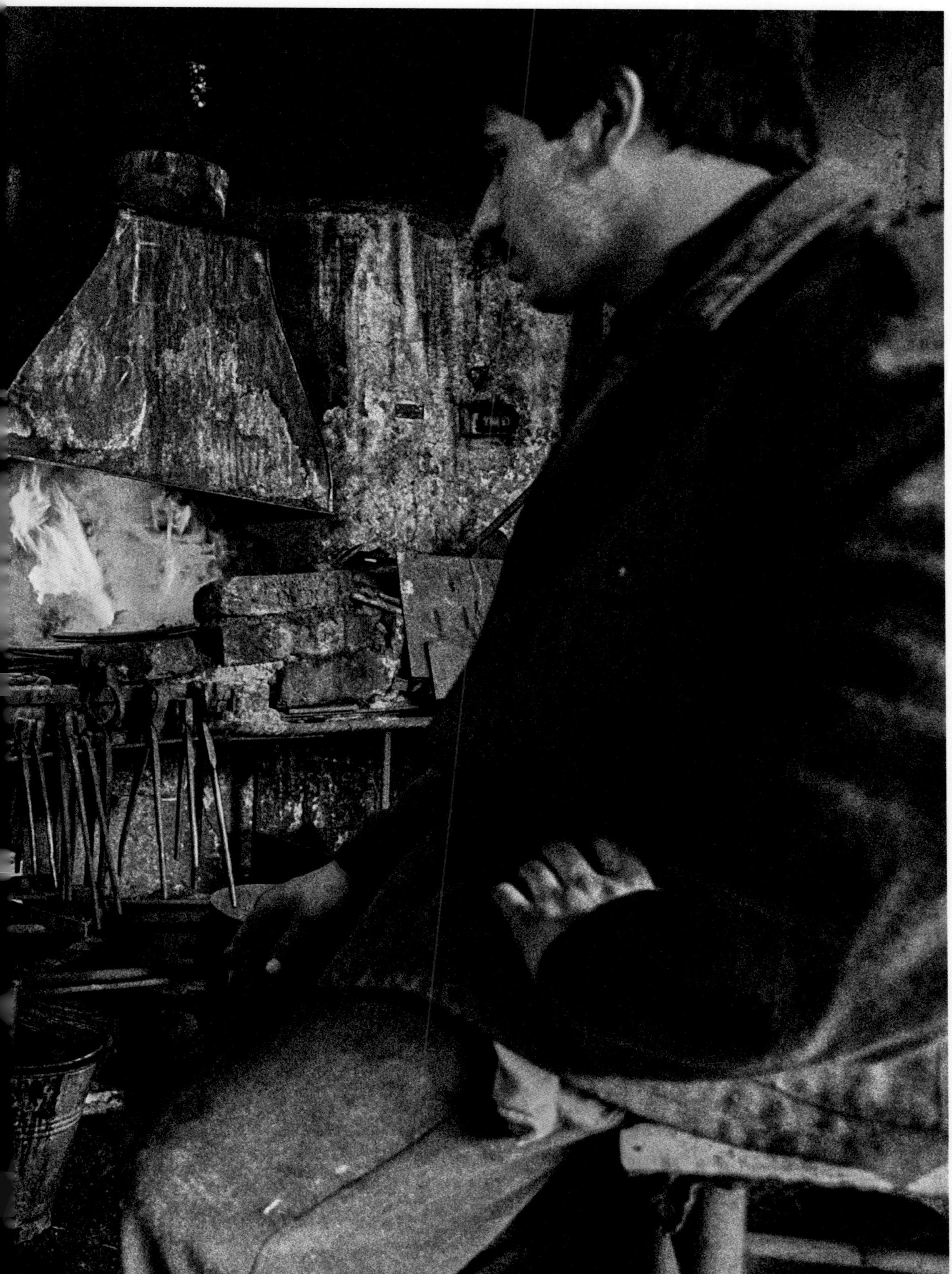

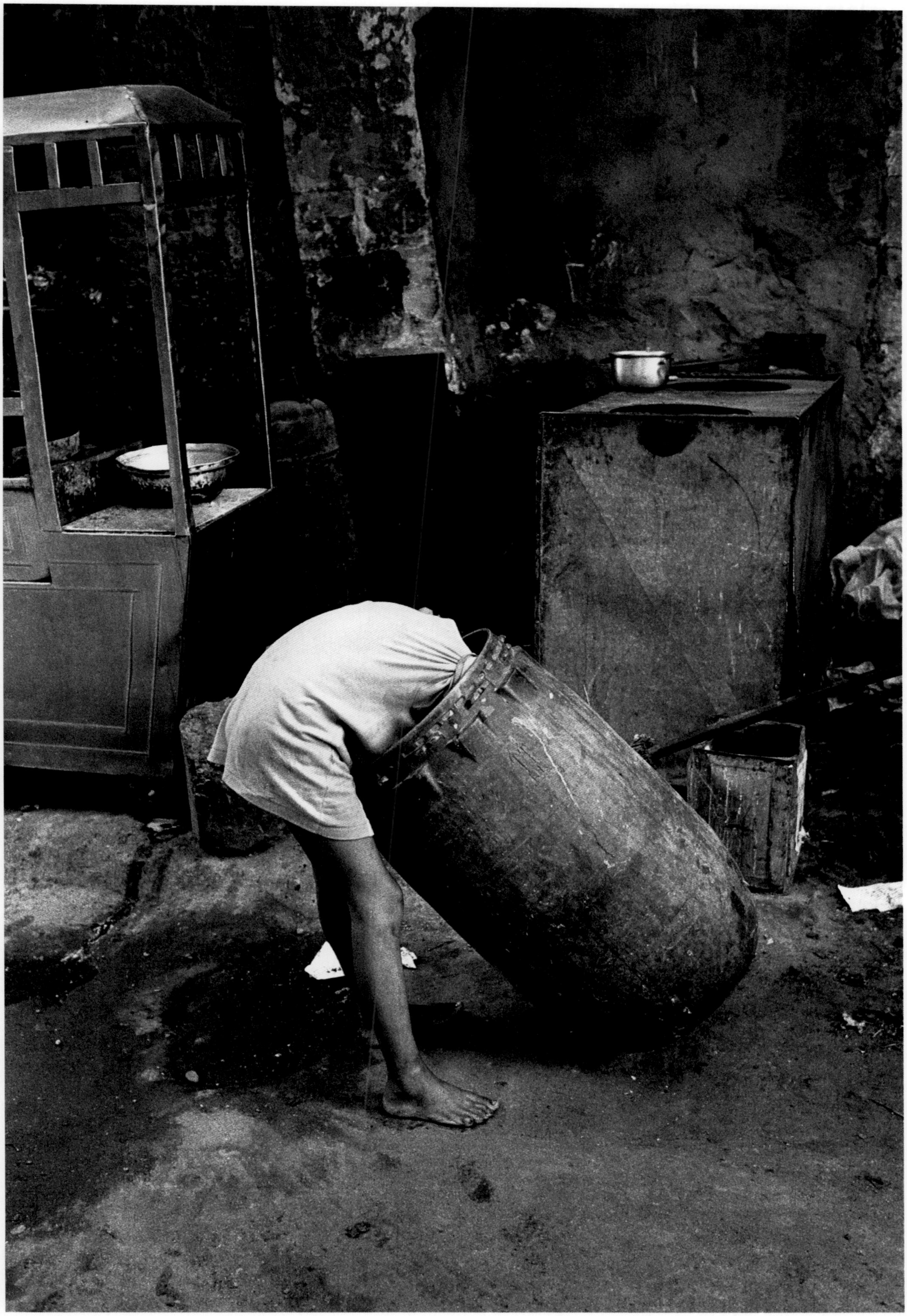

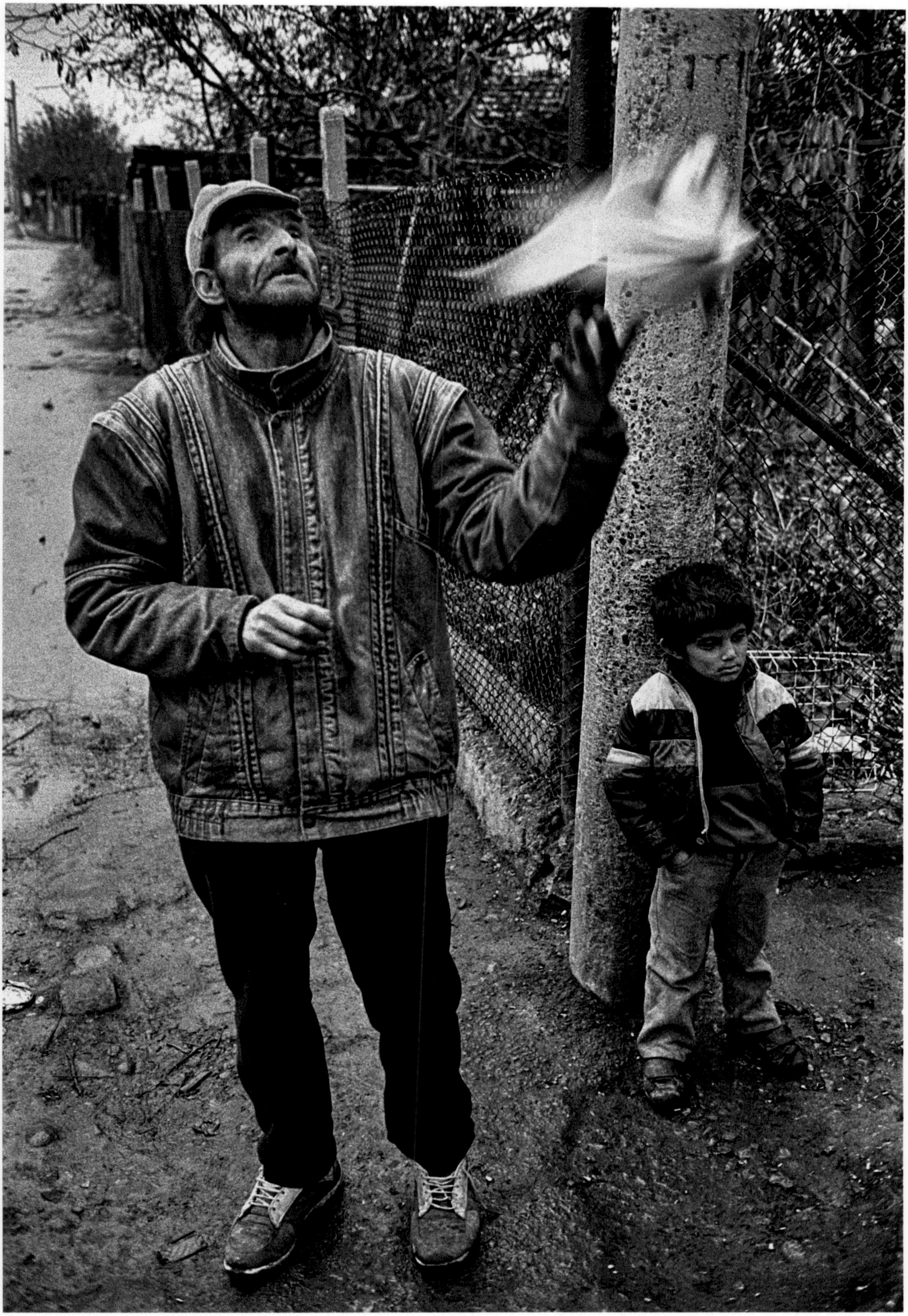

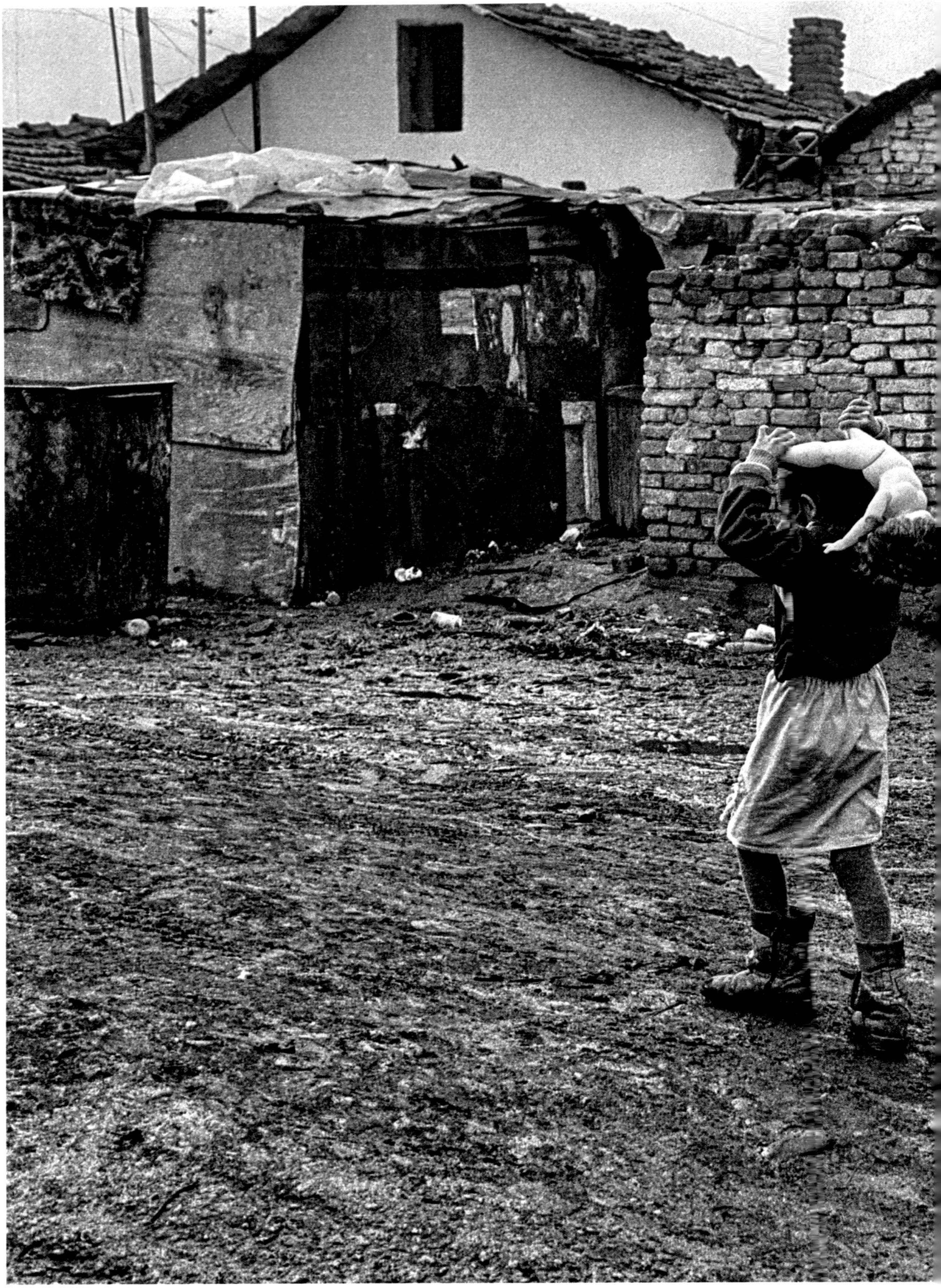

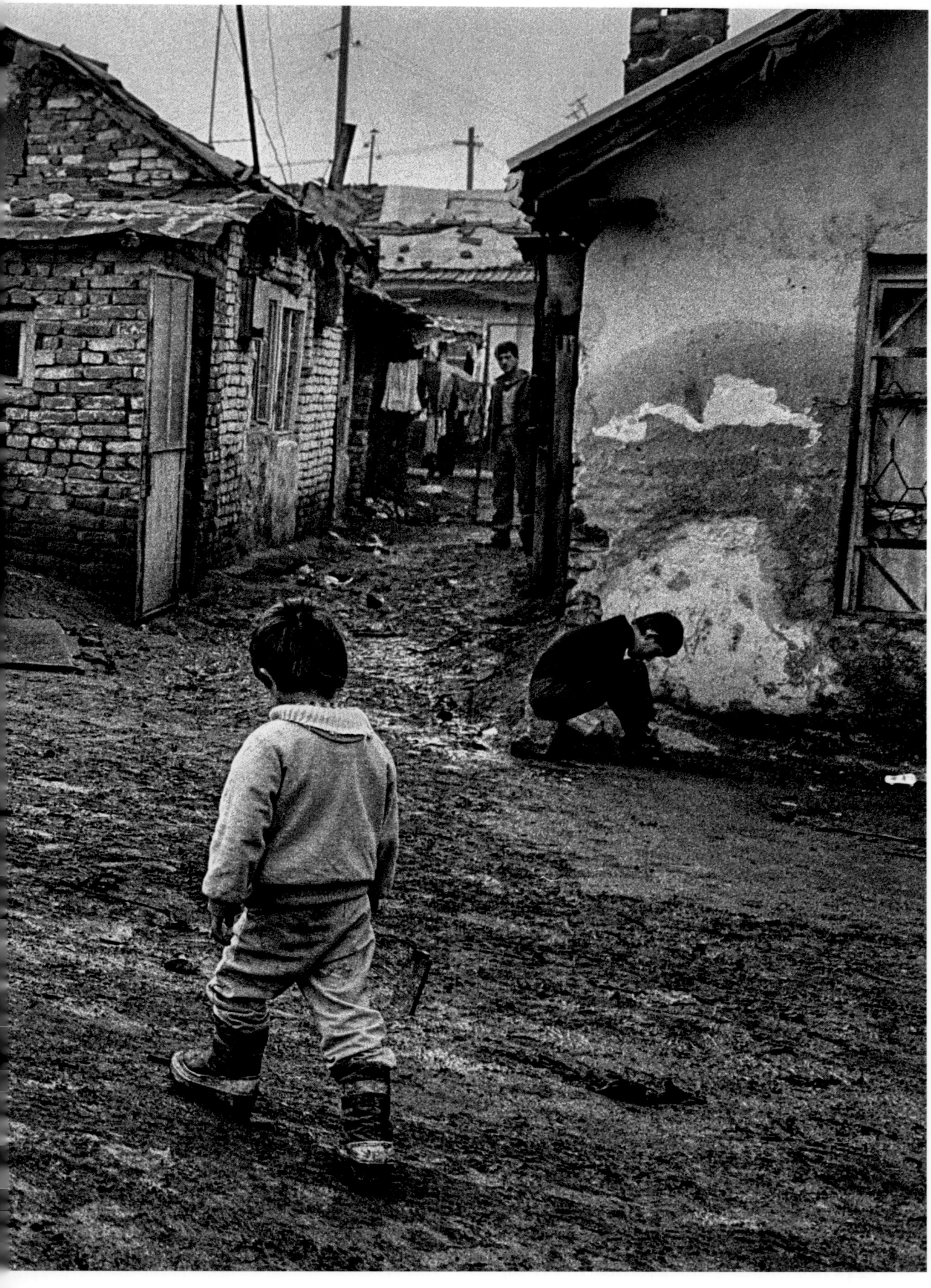

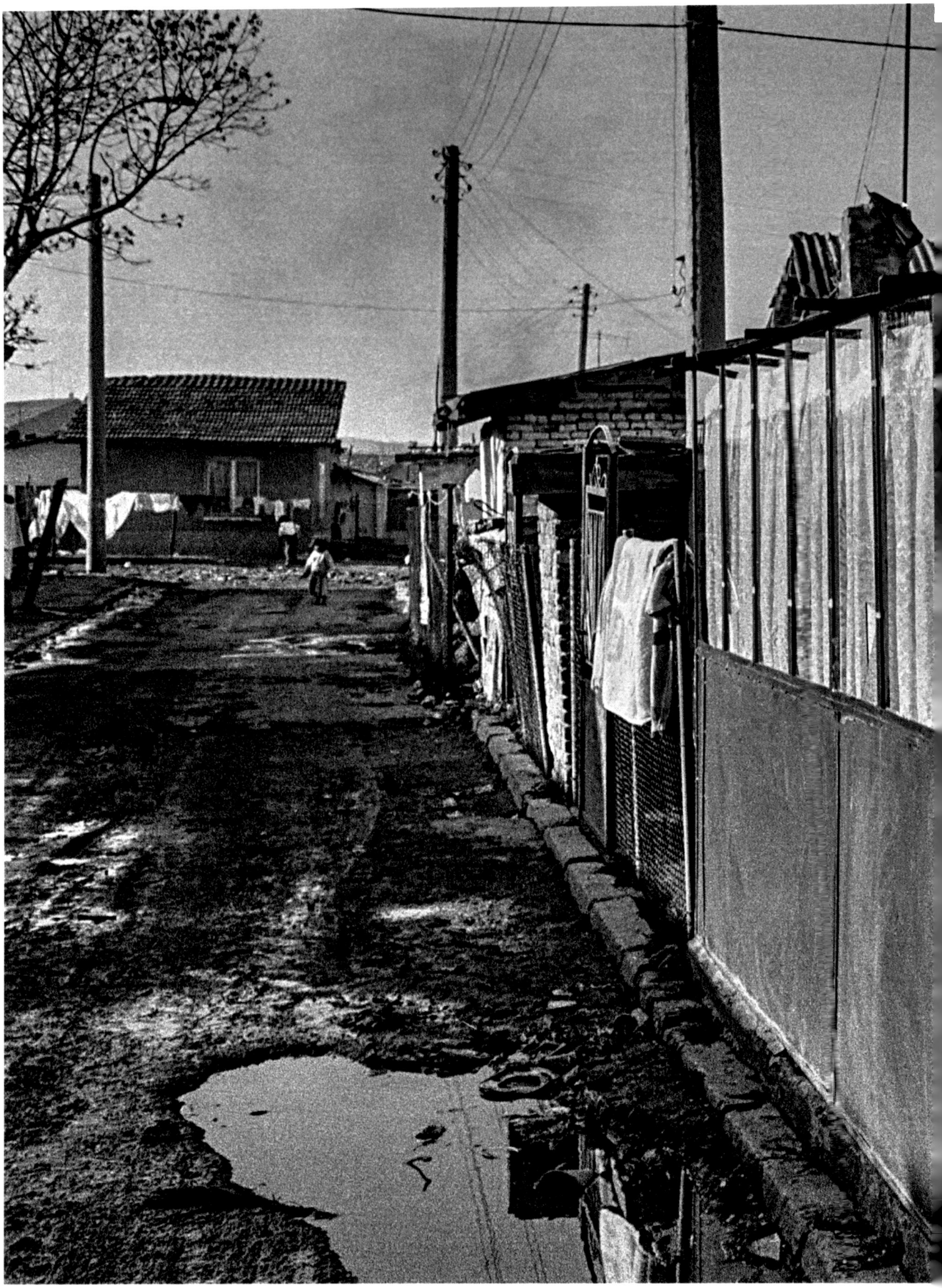

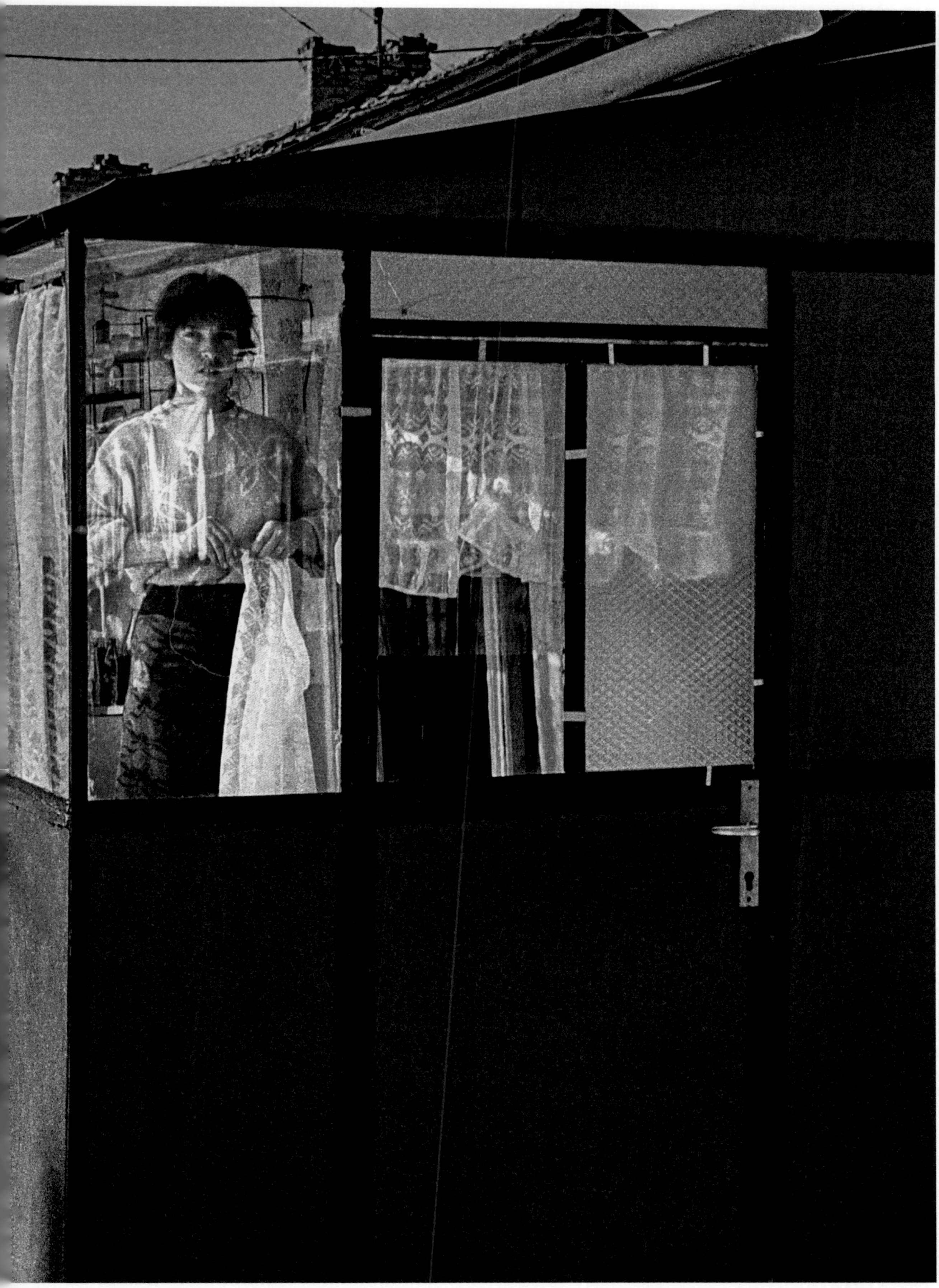

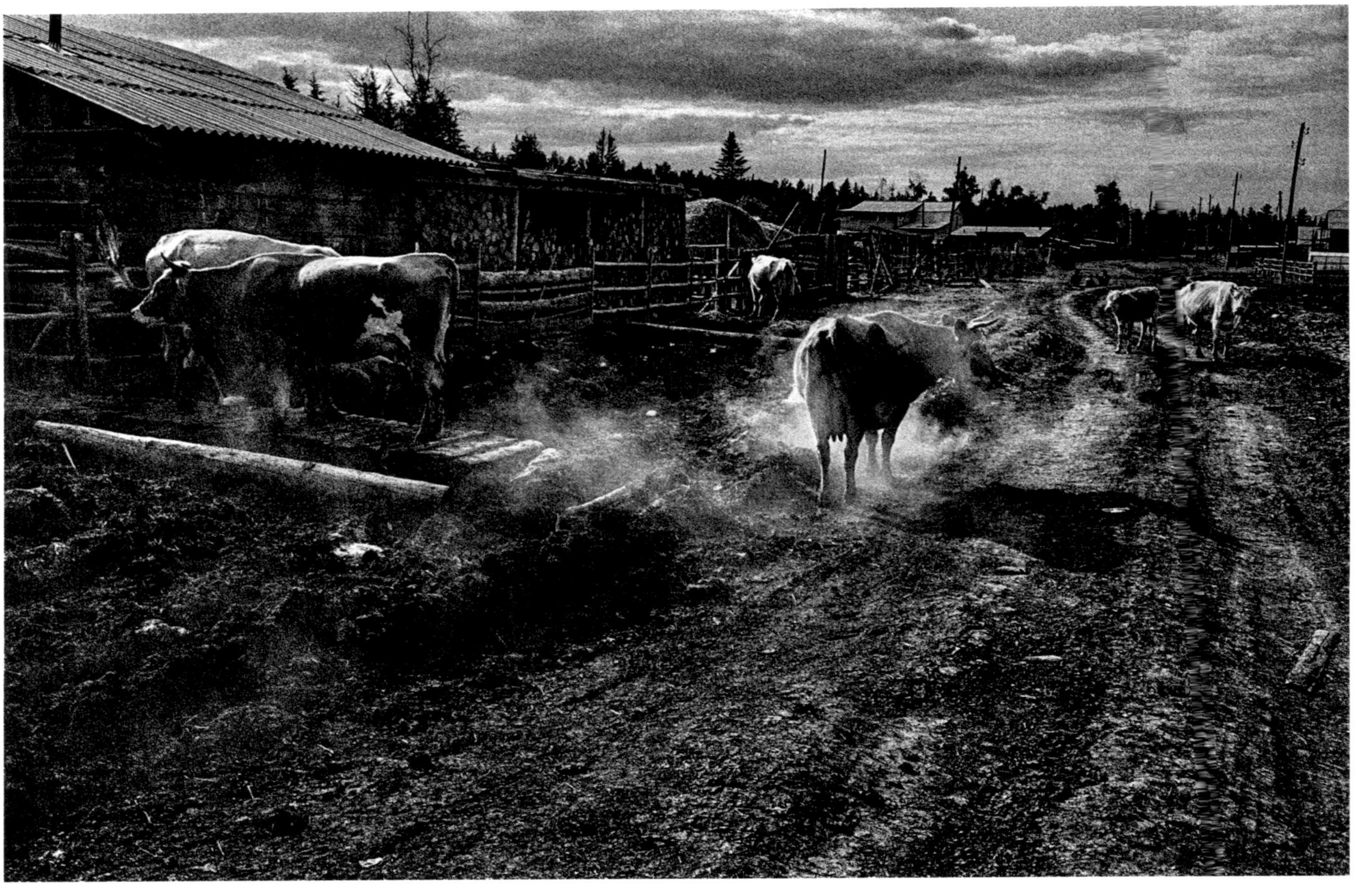

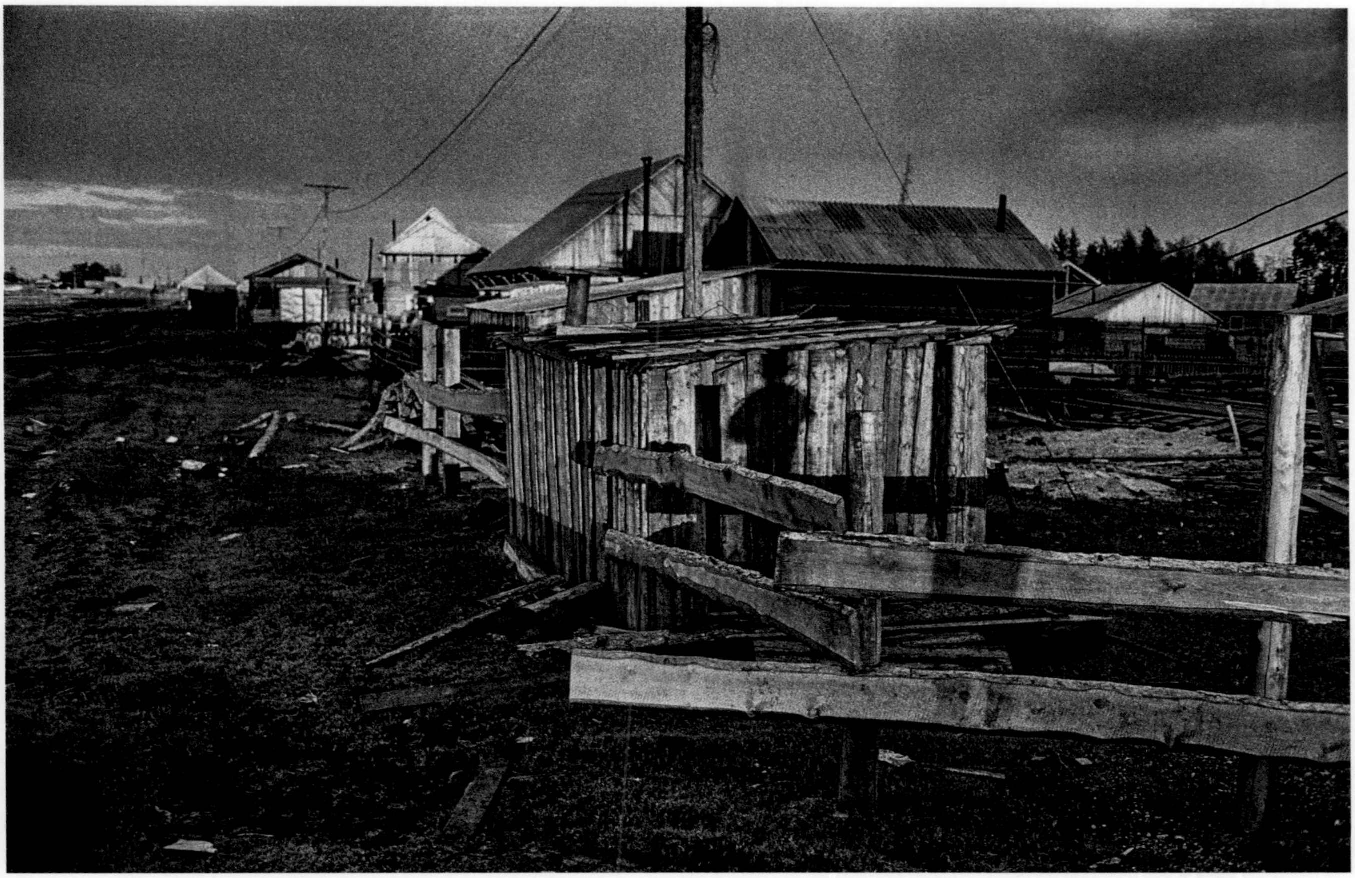

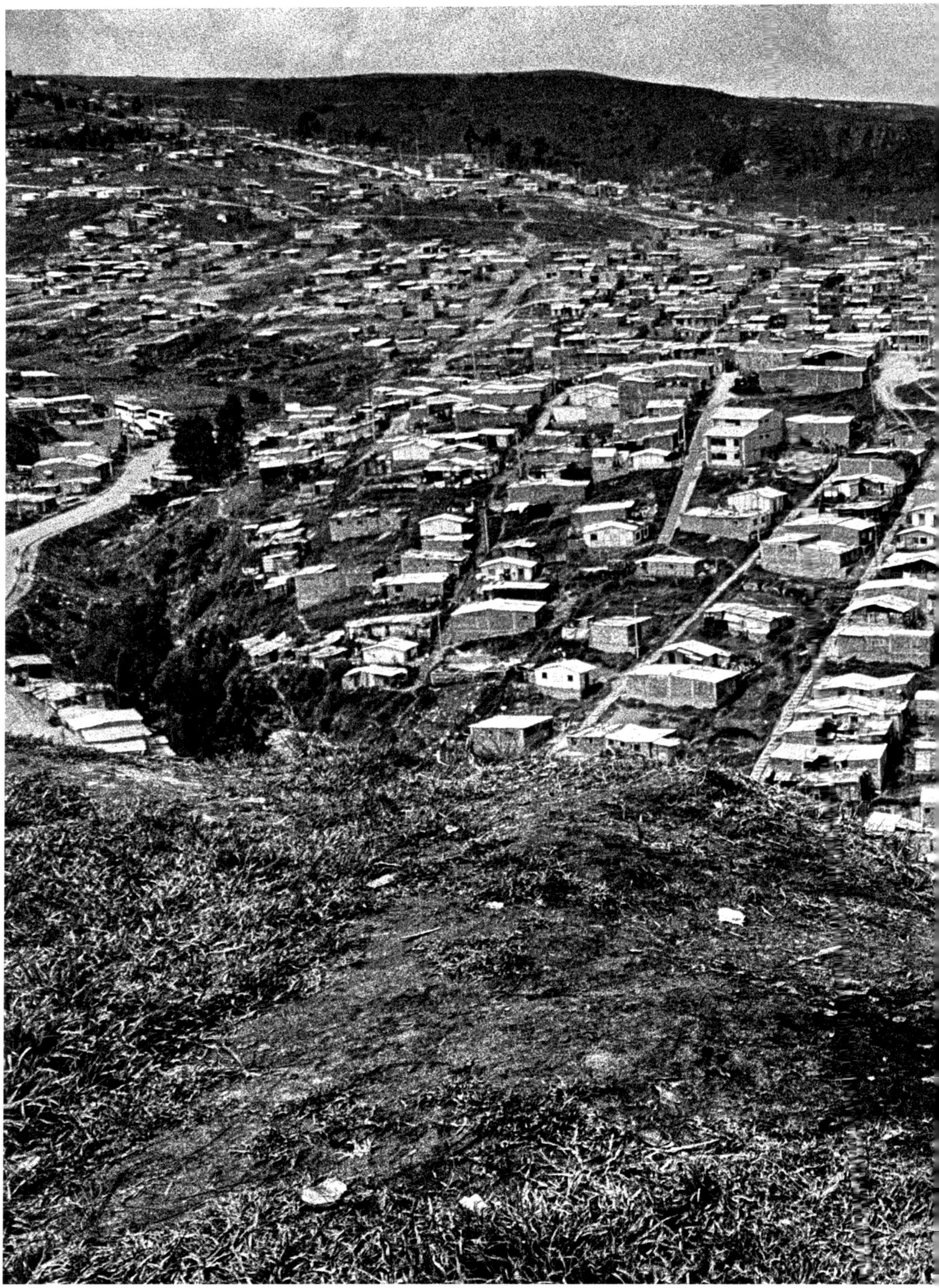

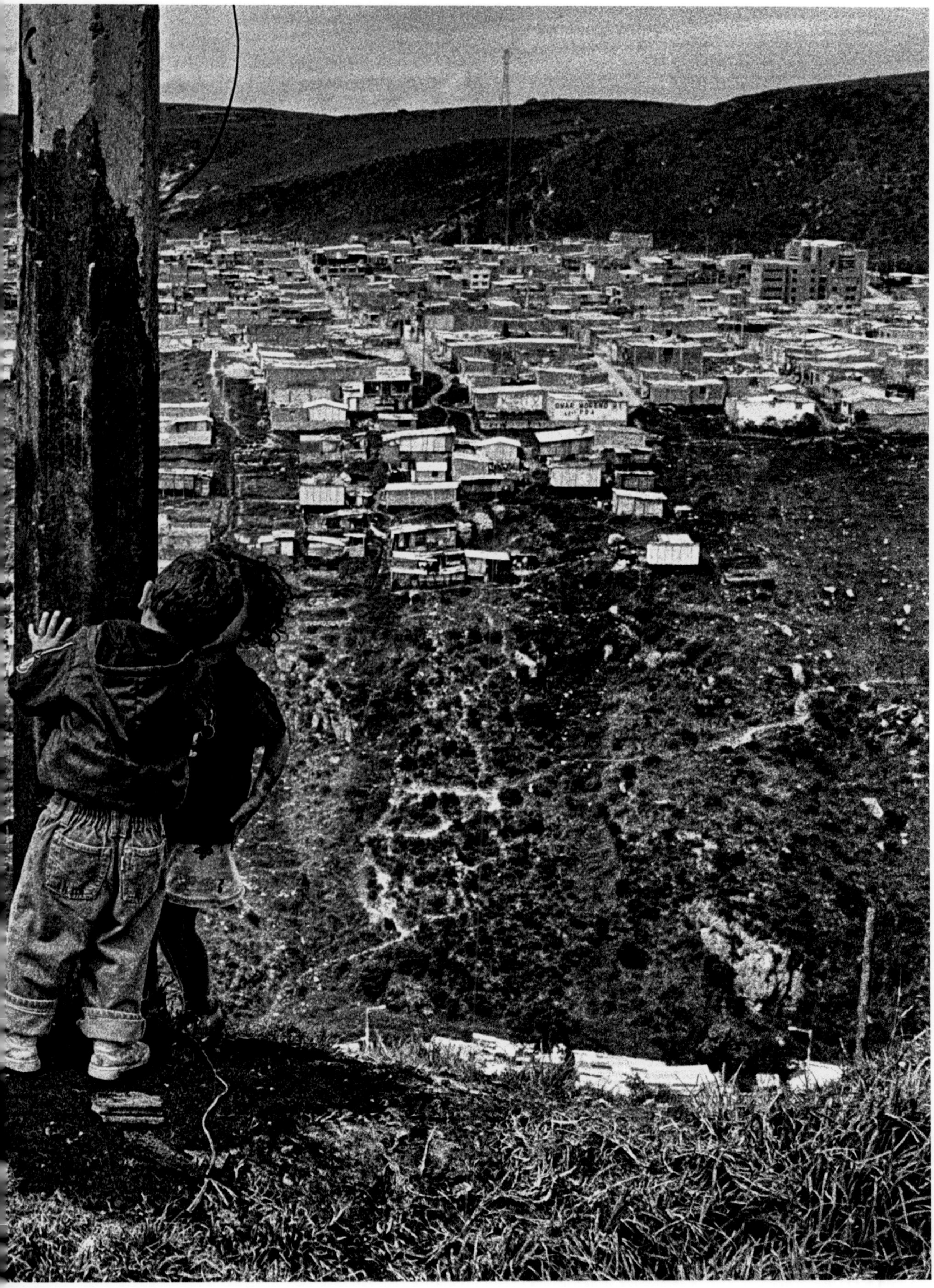

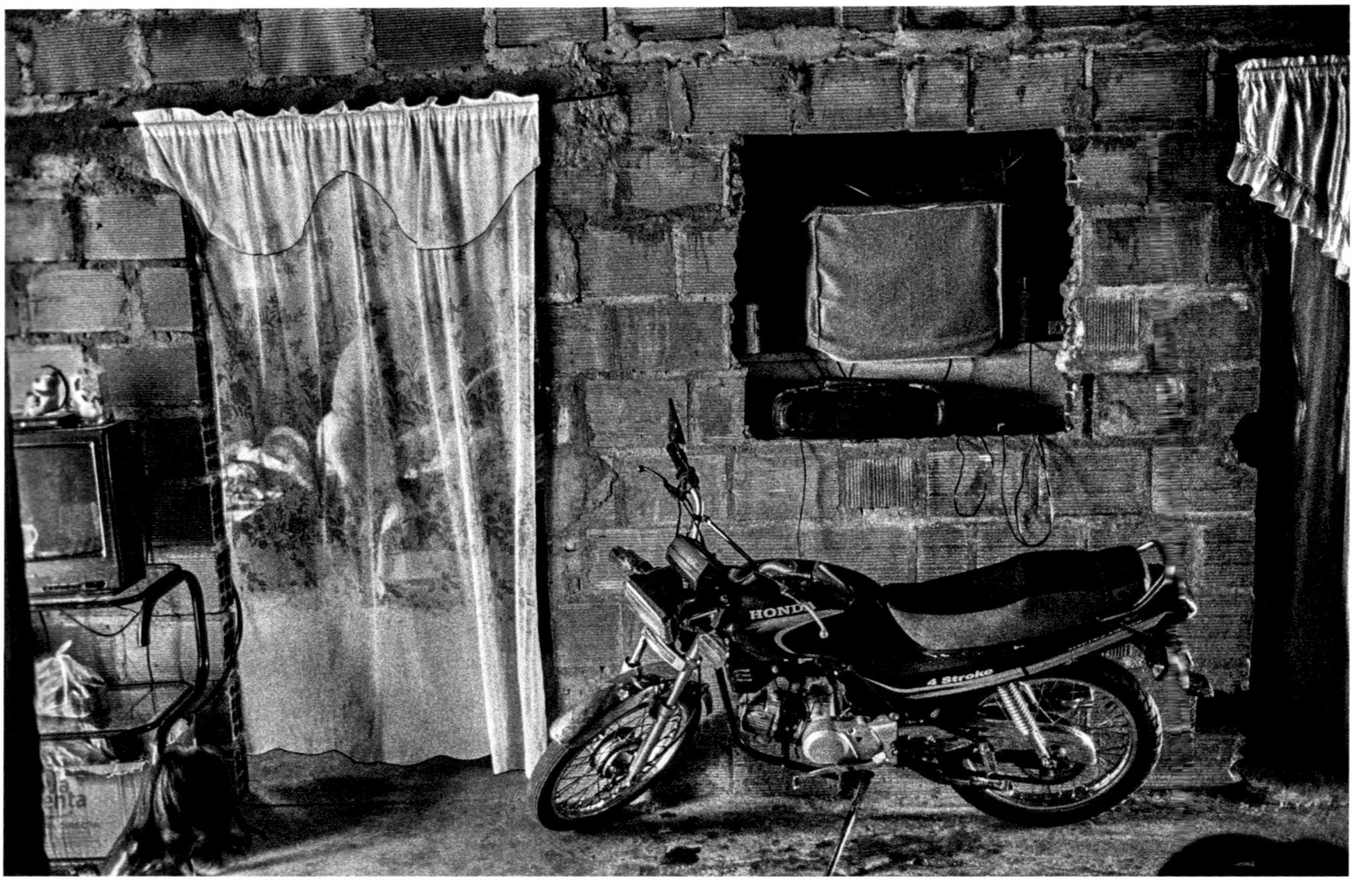
HOND
4 Stroke

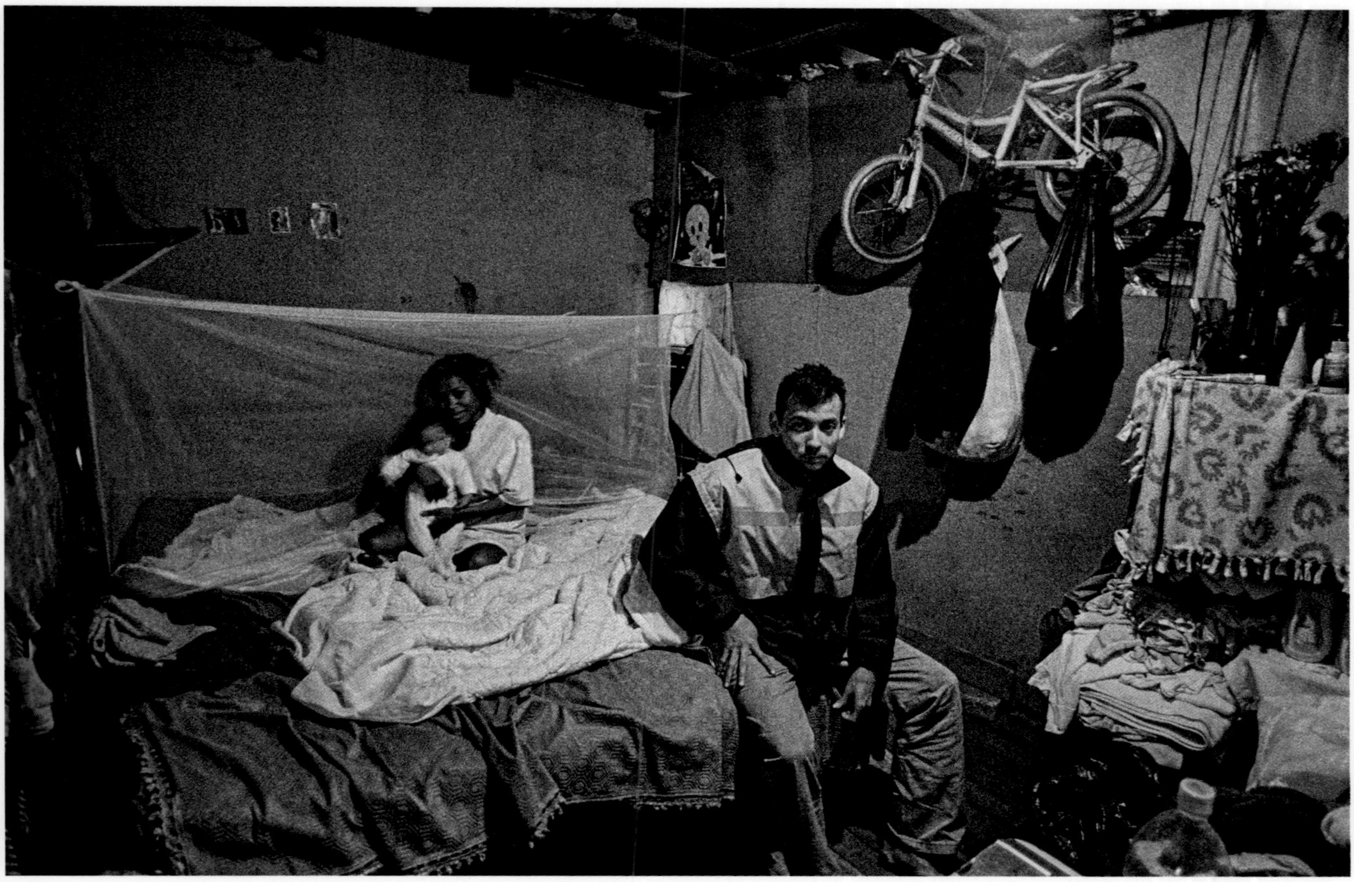

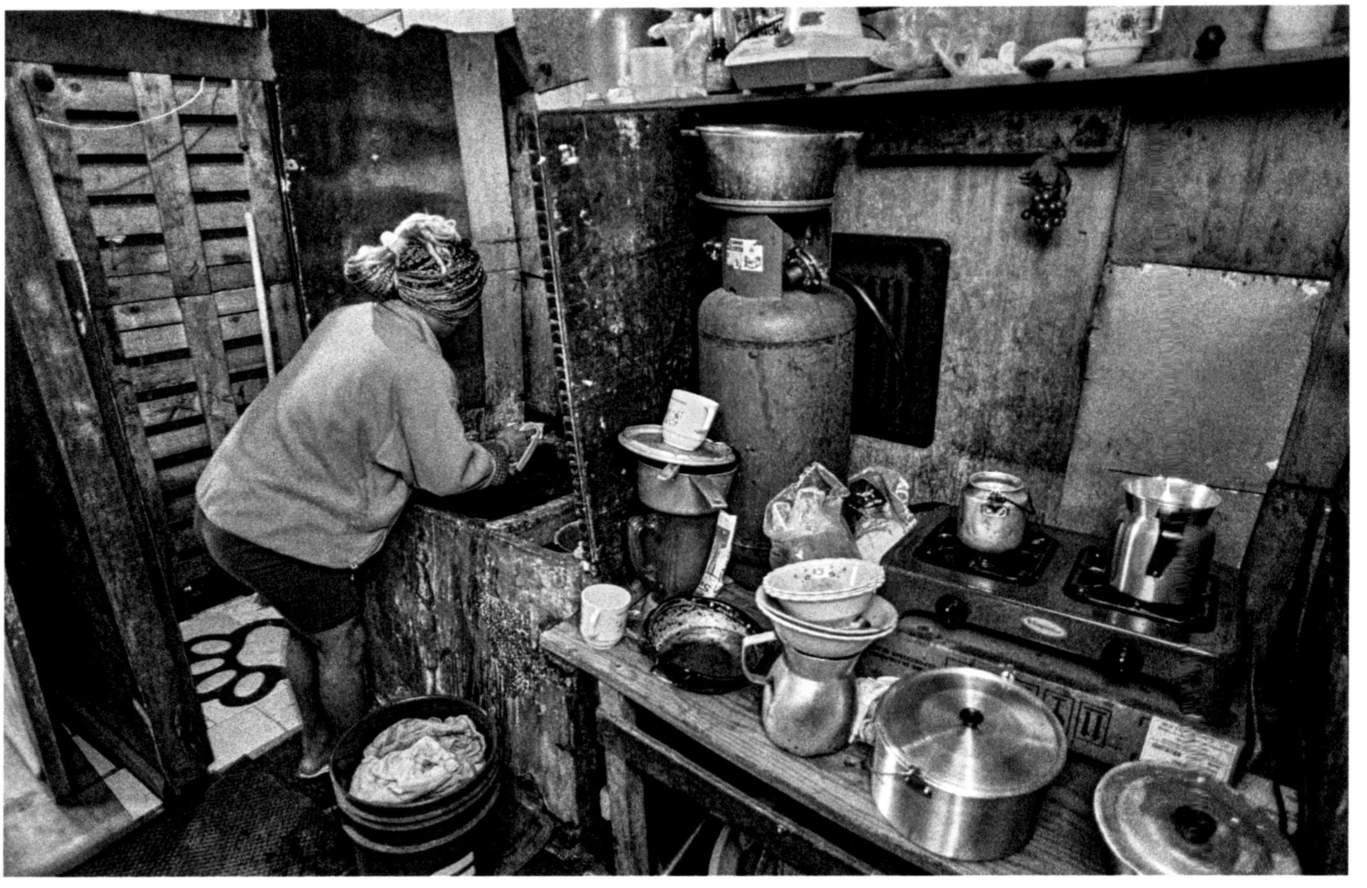

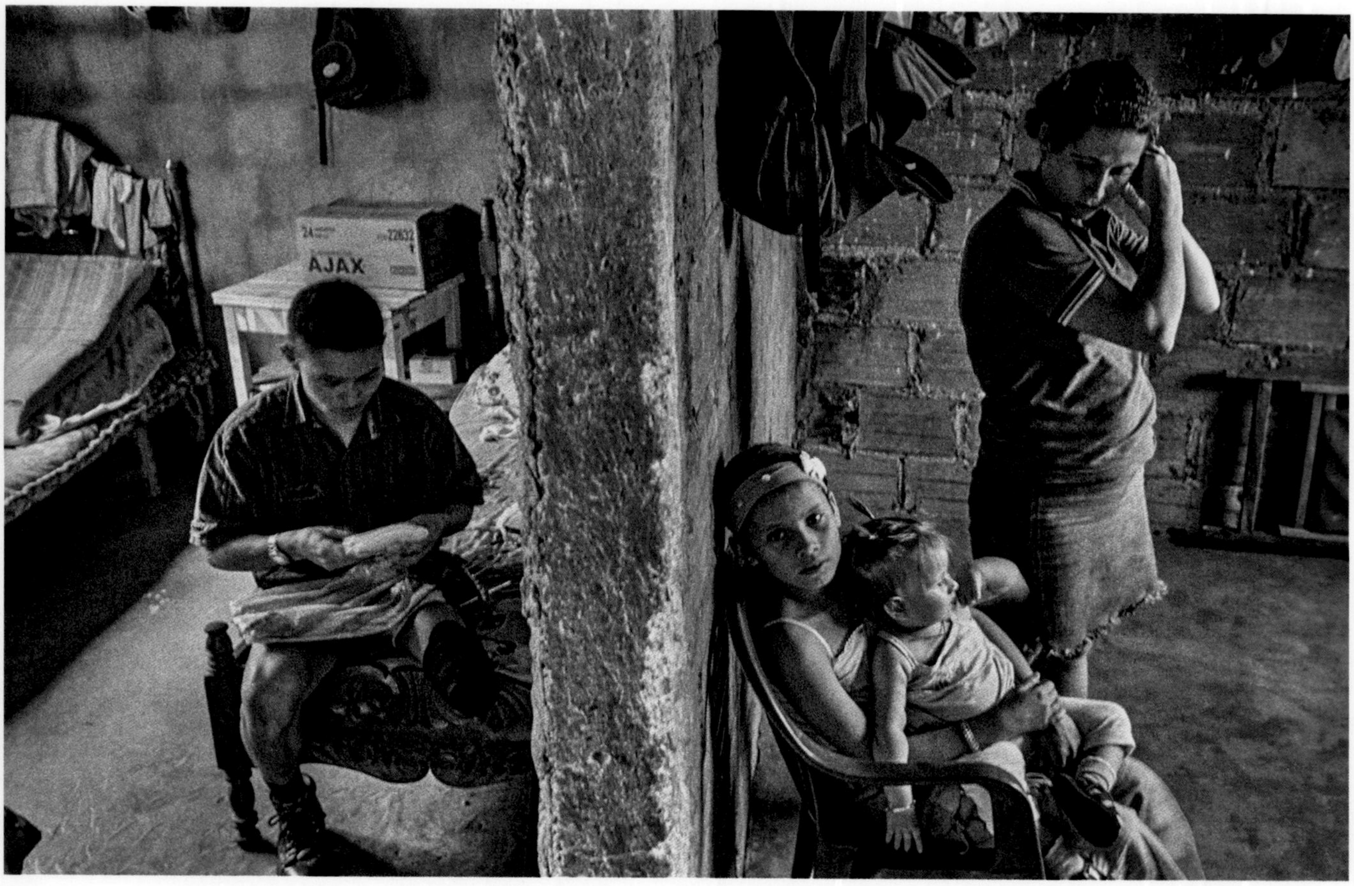
AJAX

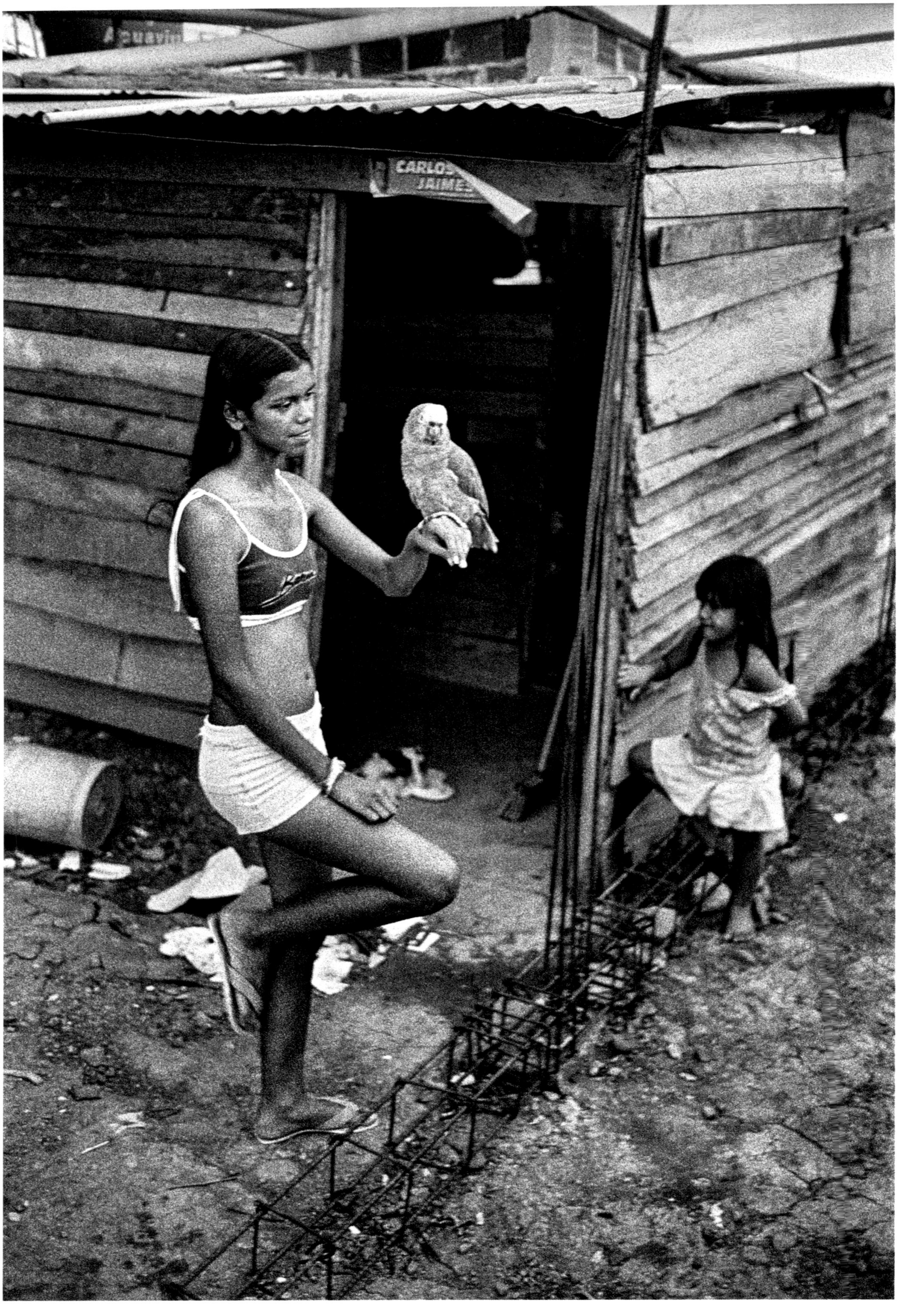
CARLOS
JAIME

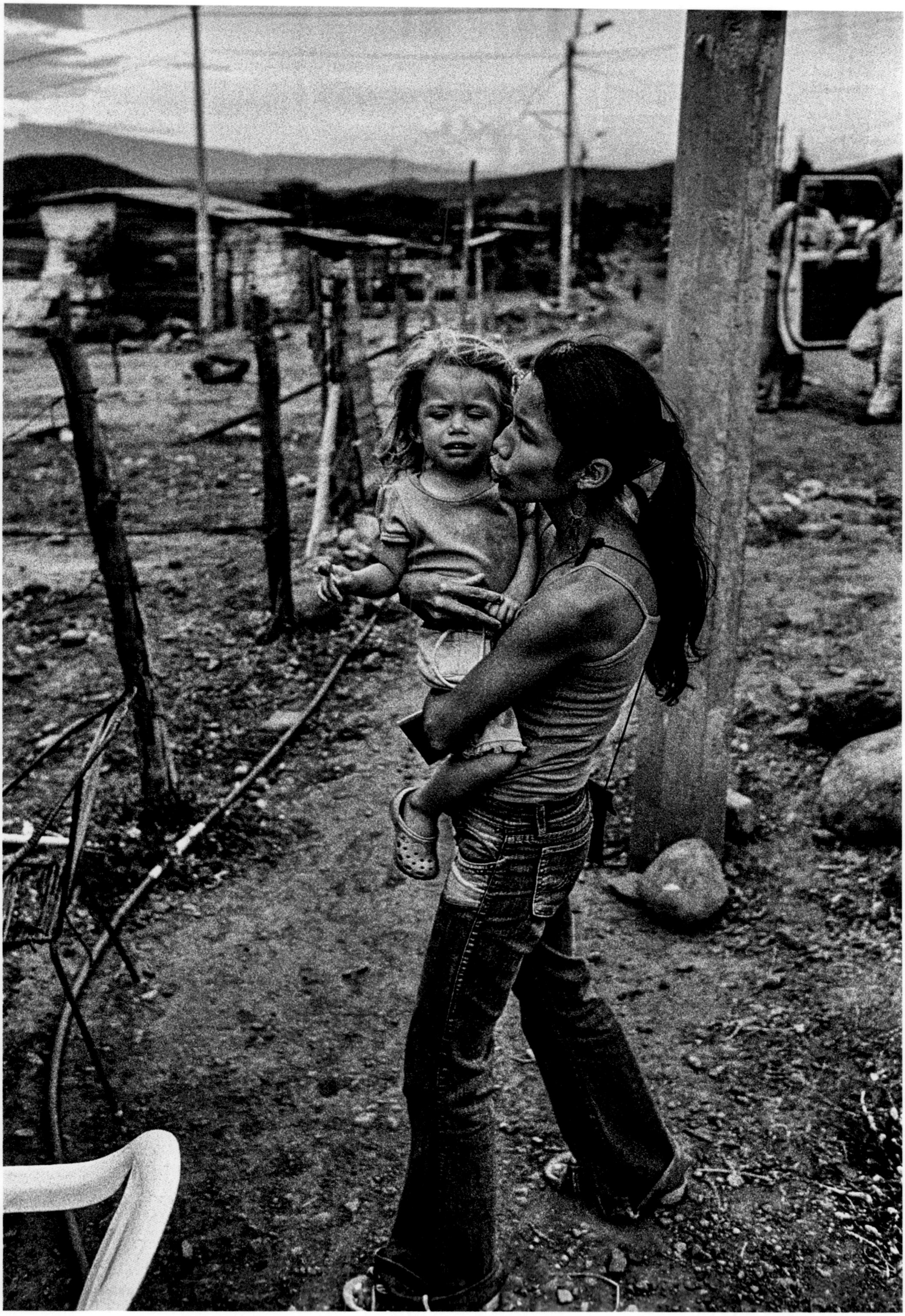

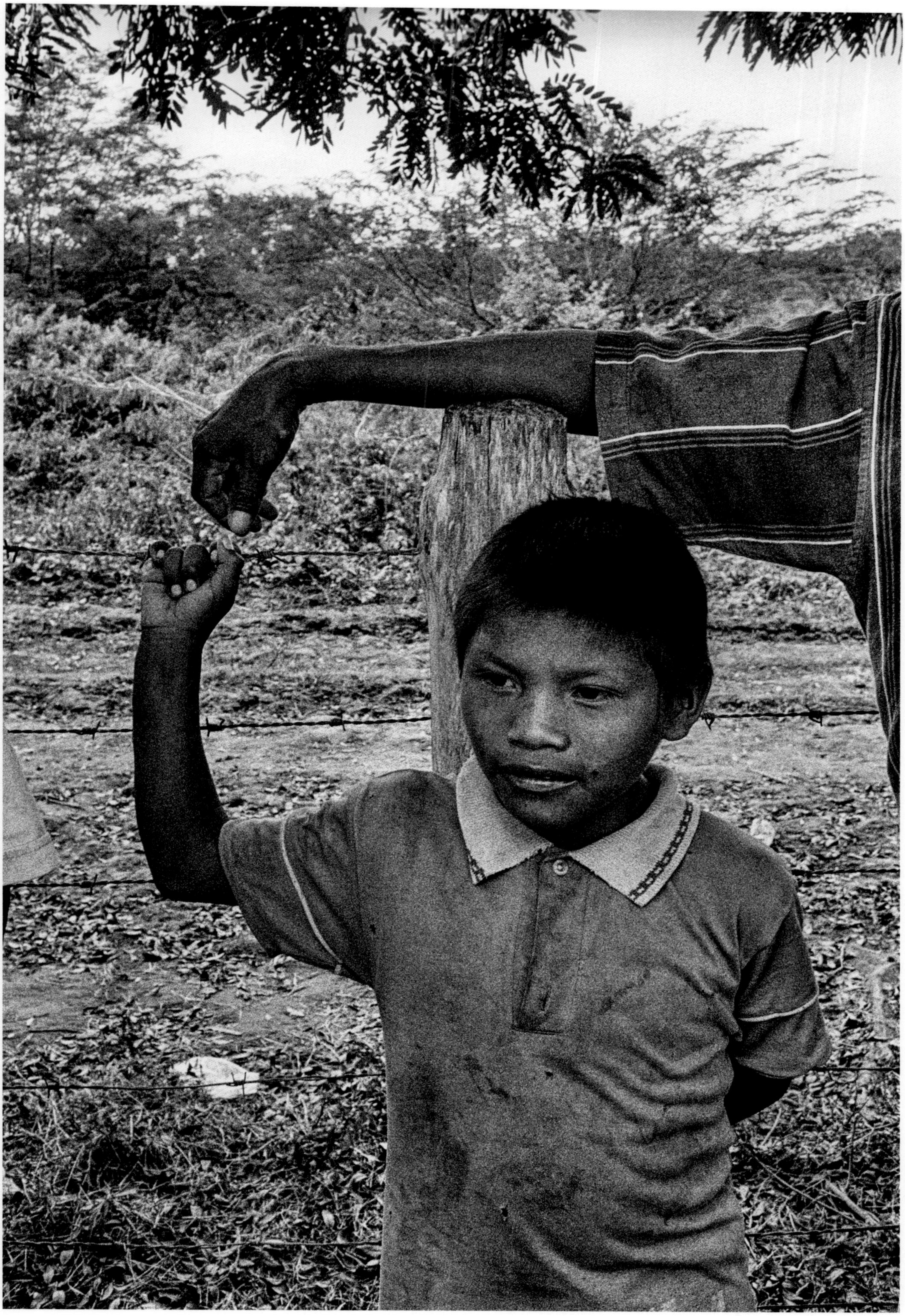

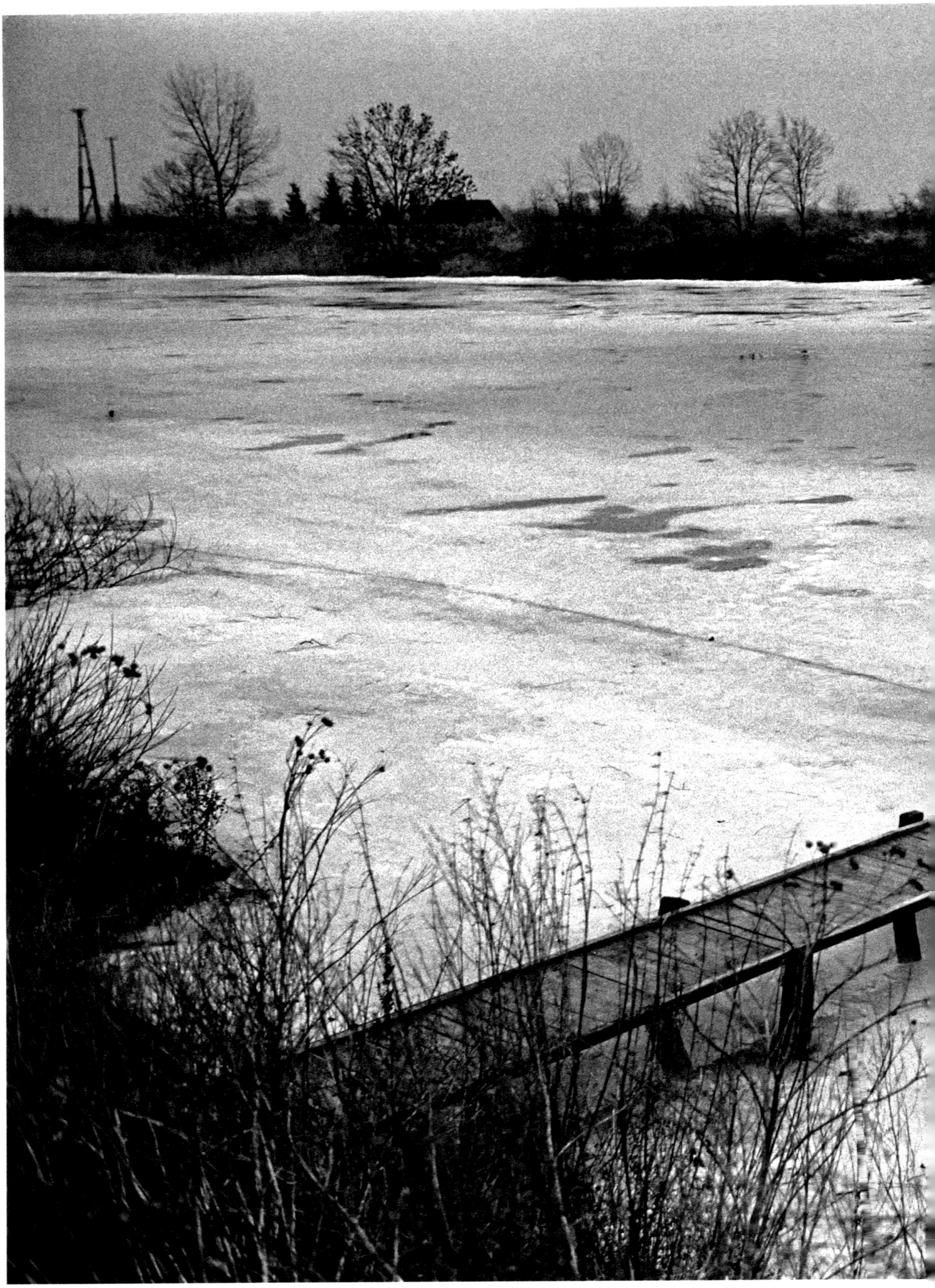

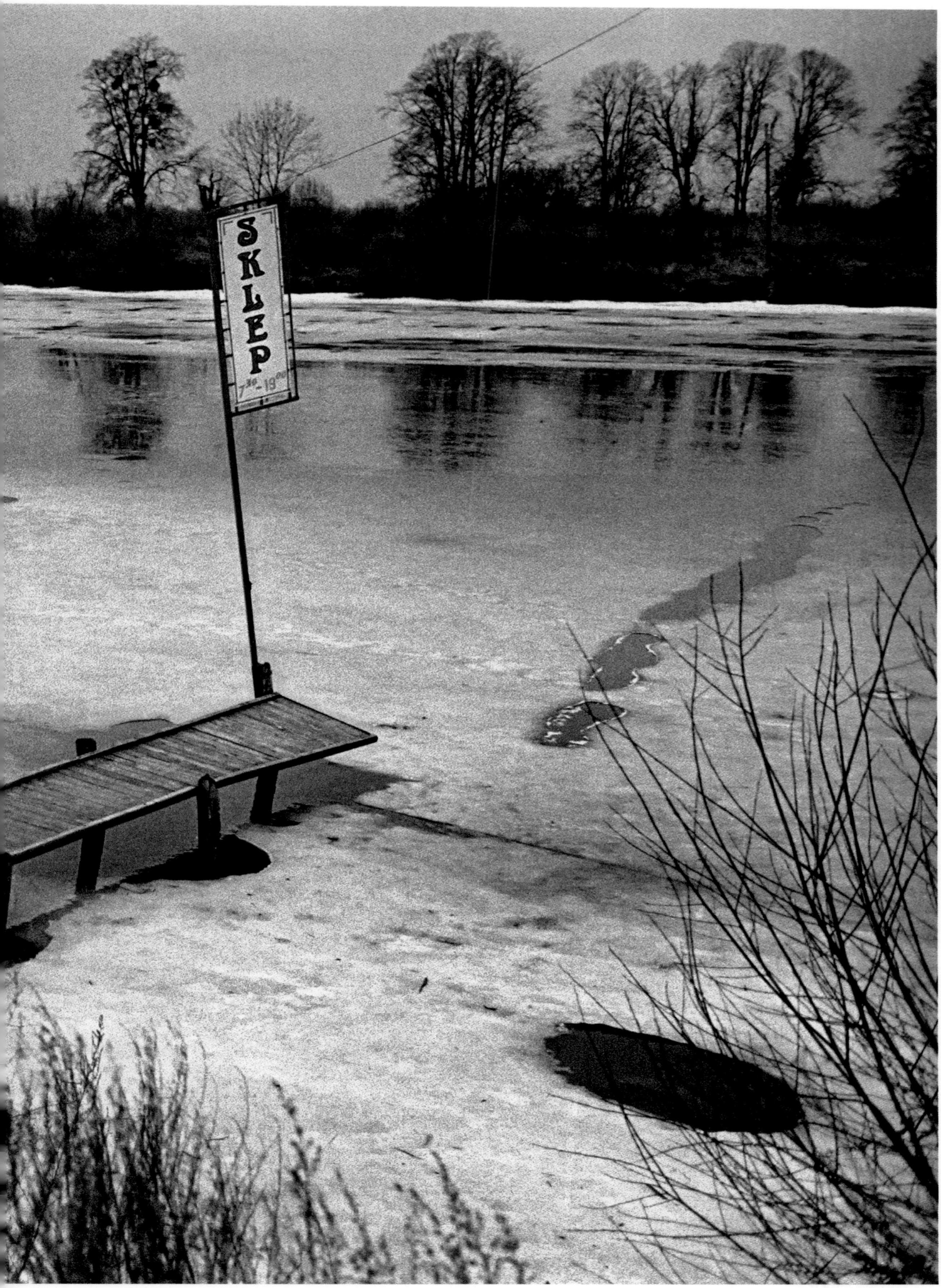
SKLEP

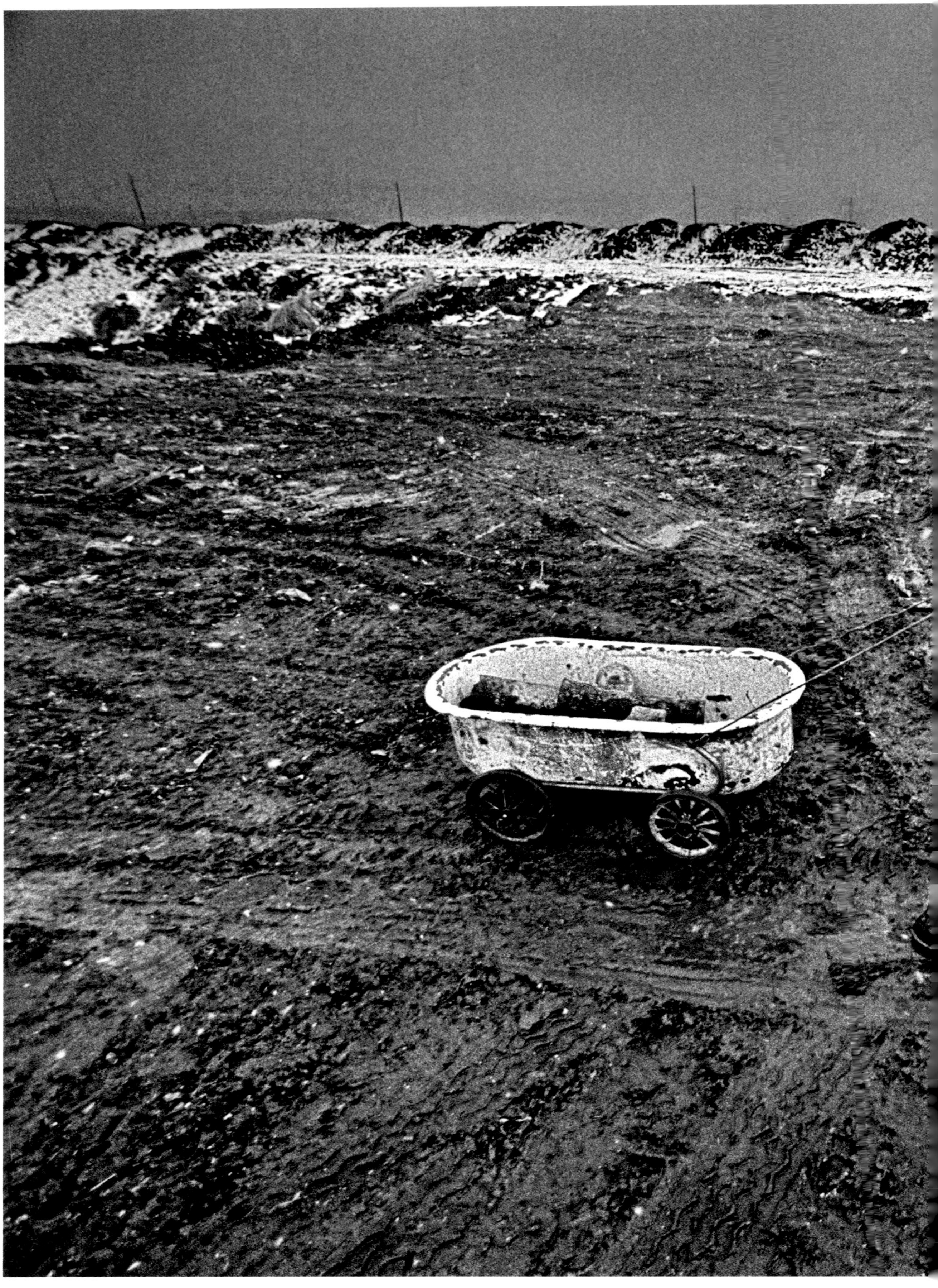

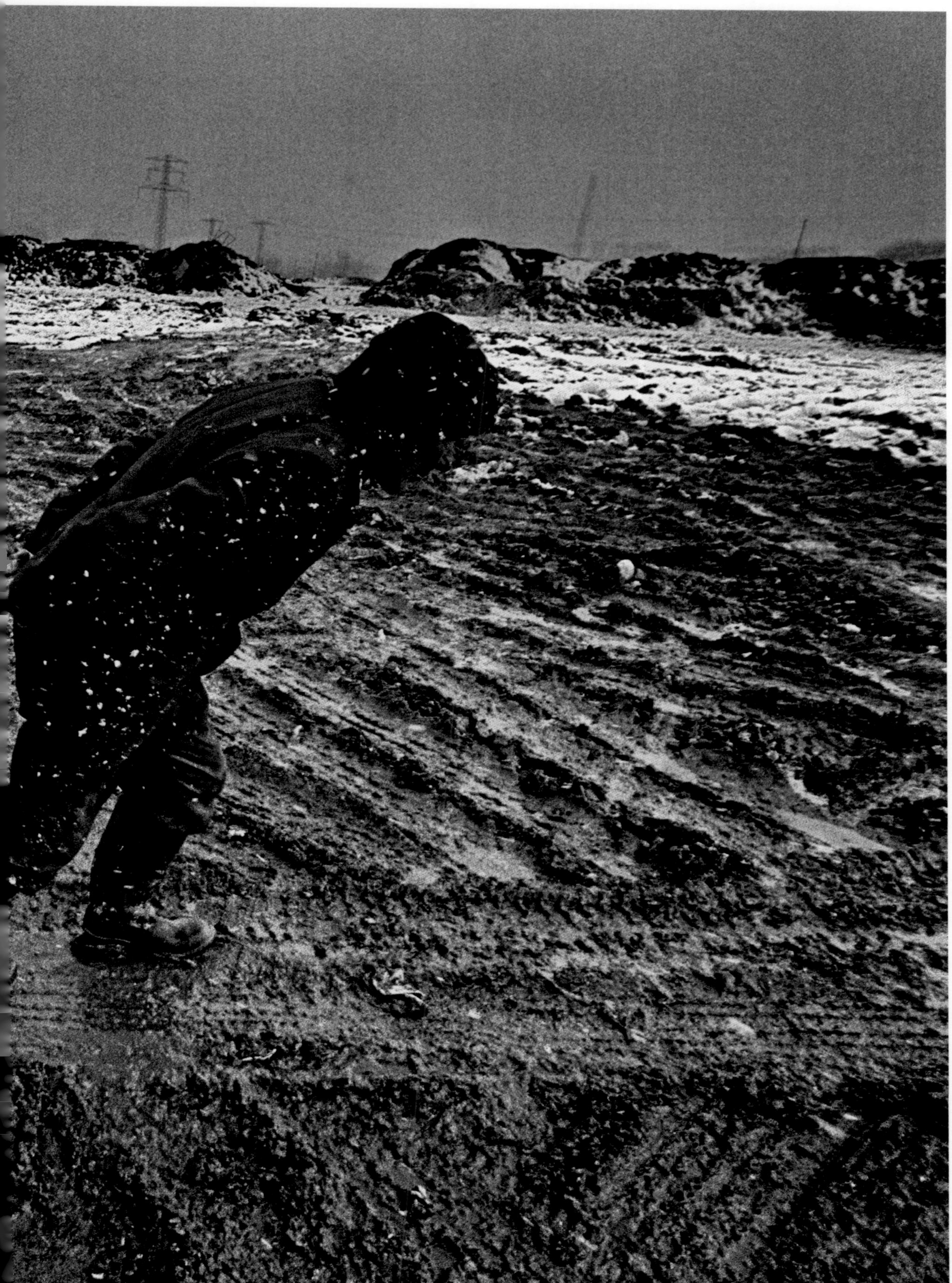

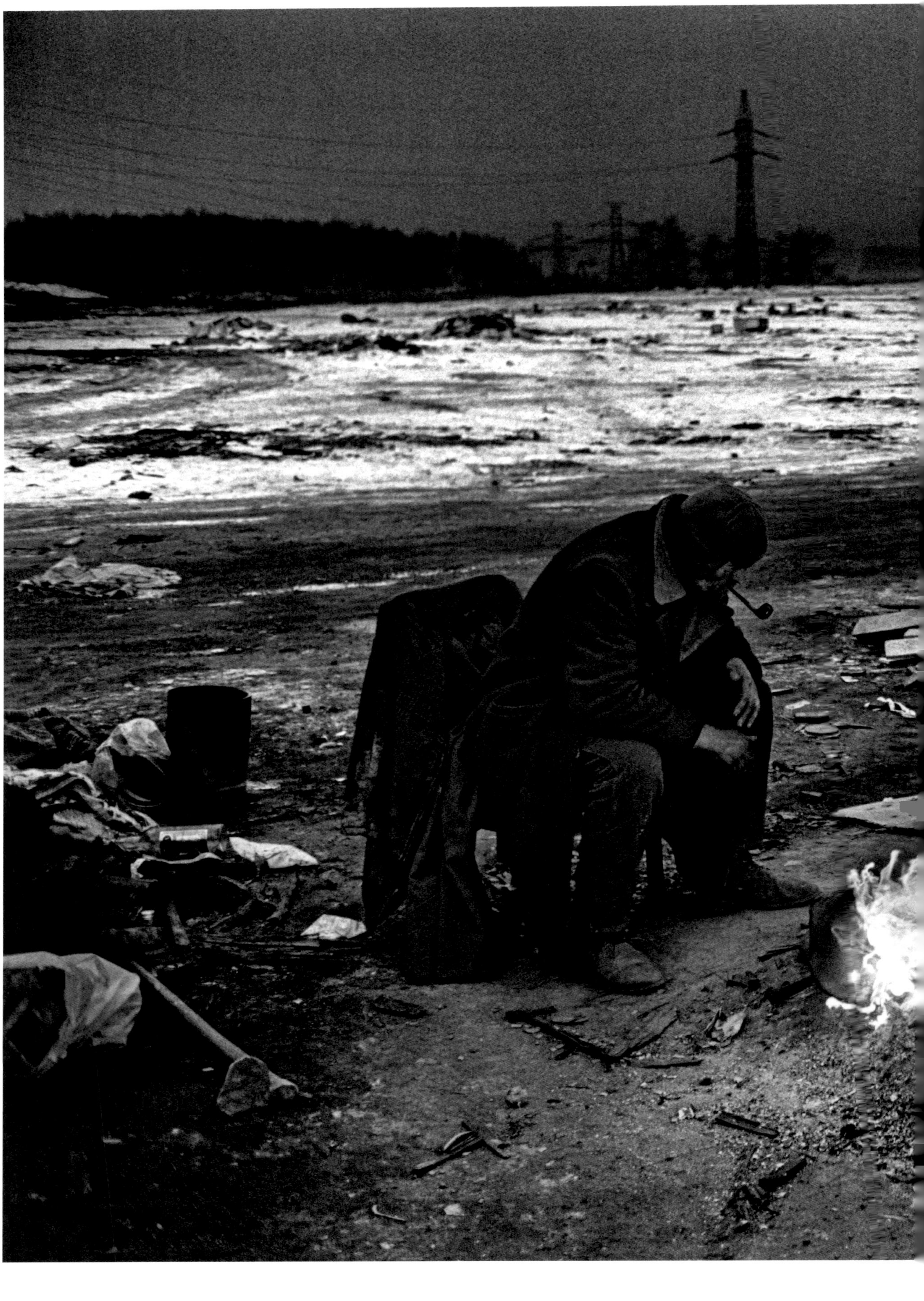

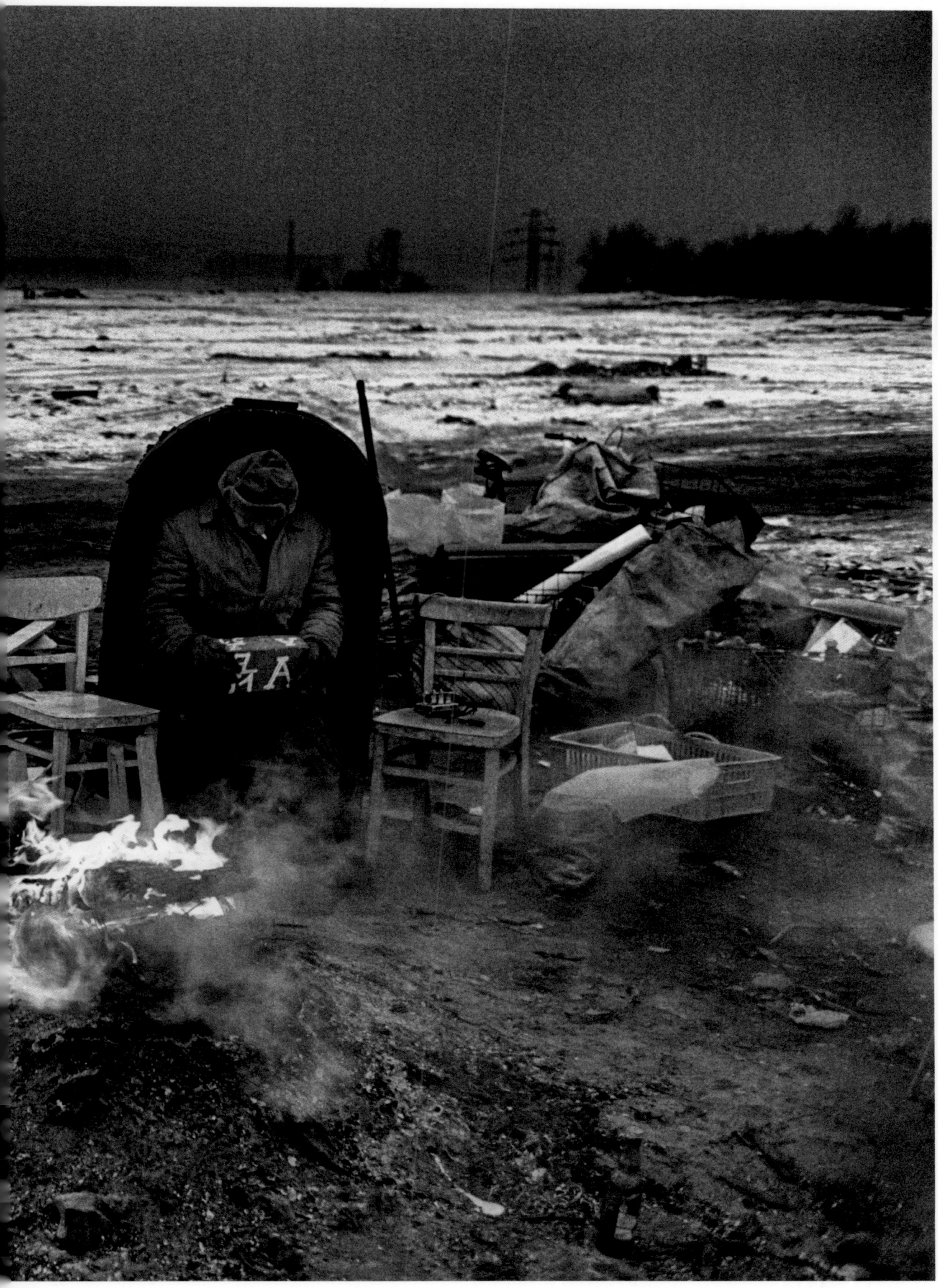

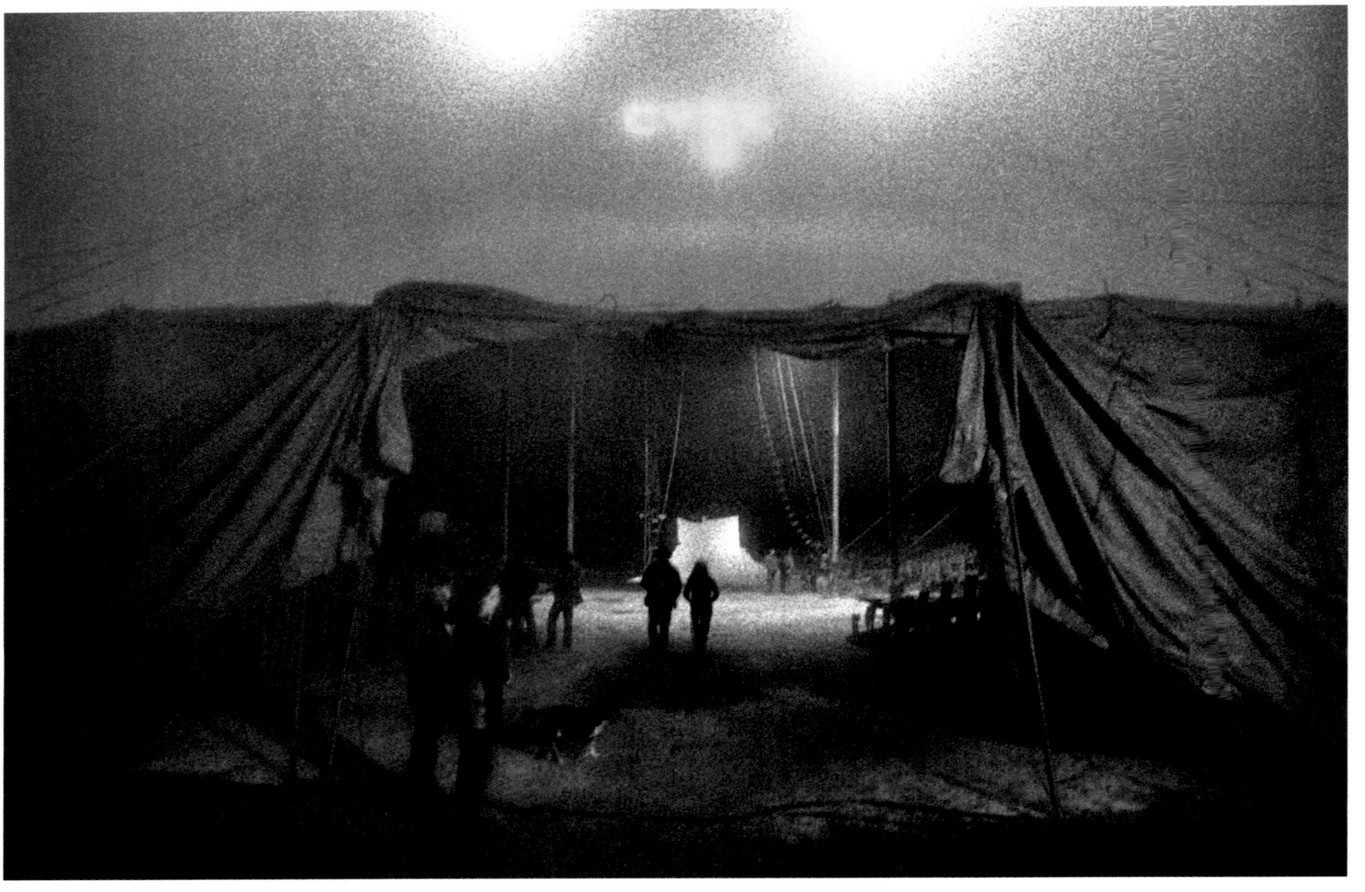

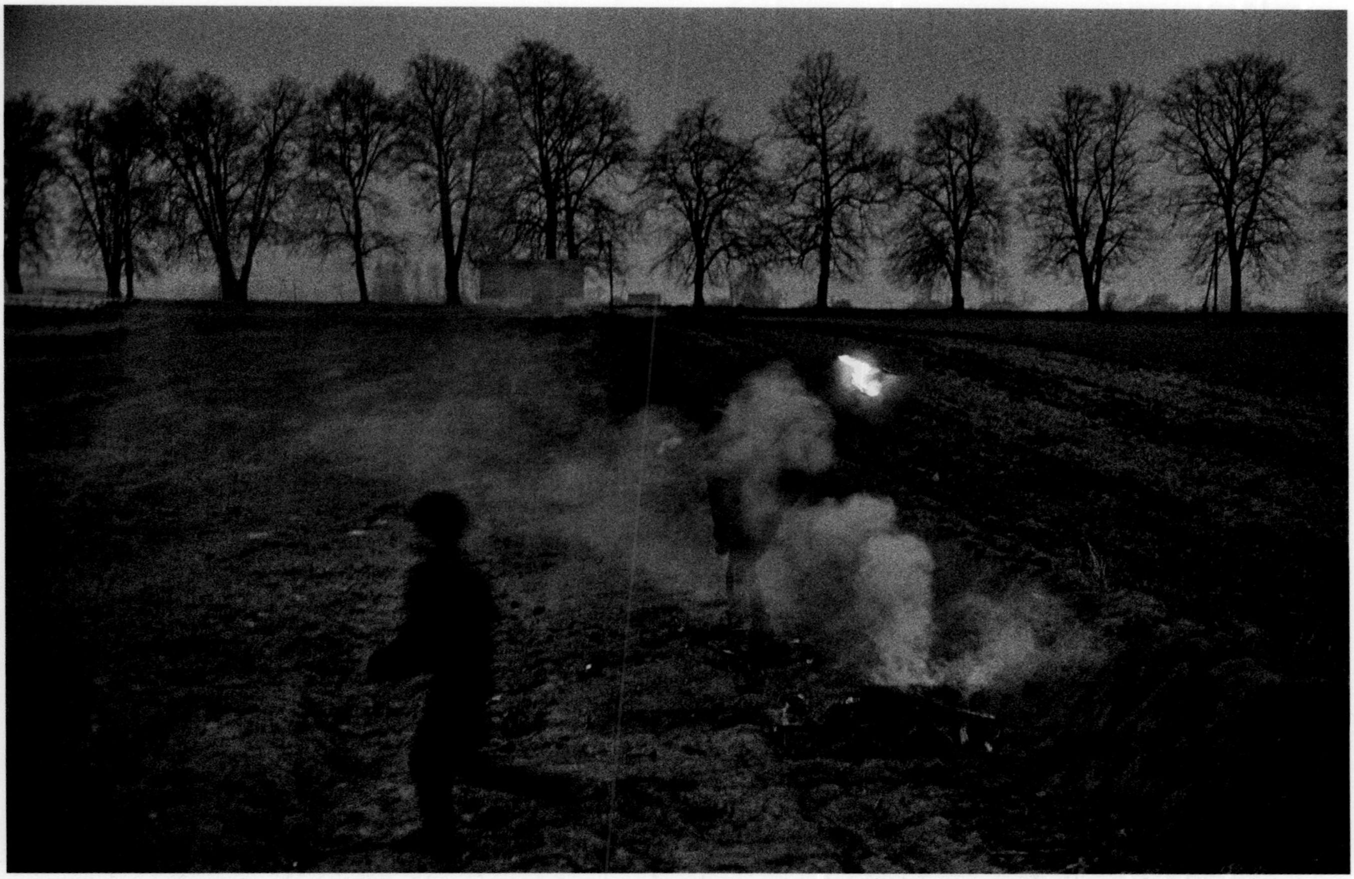

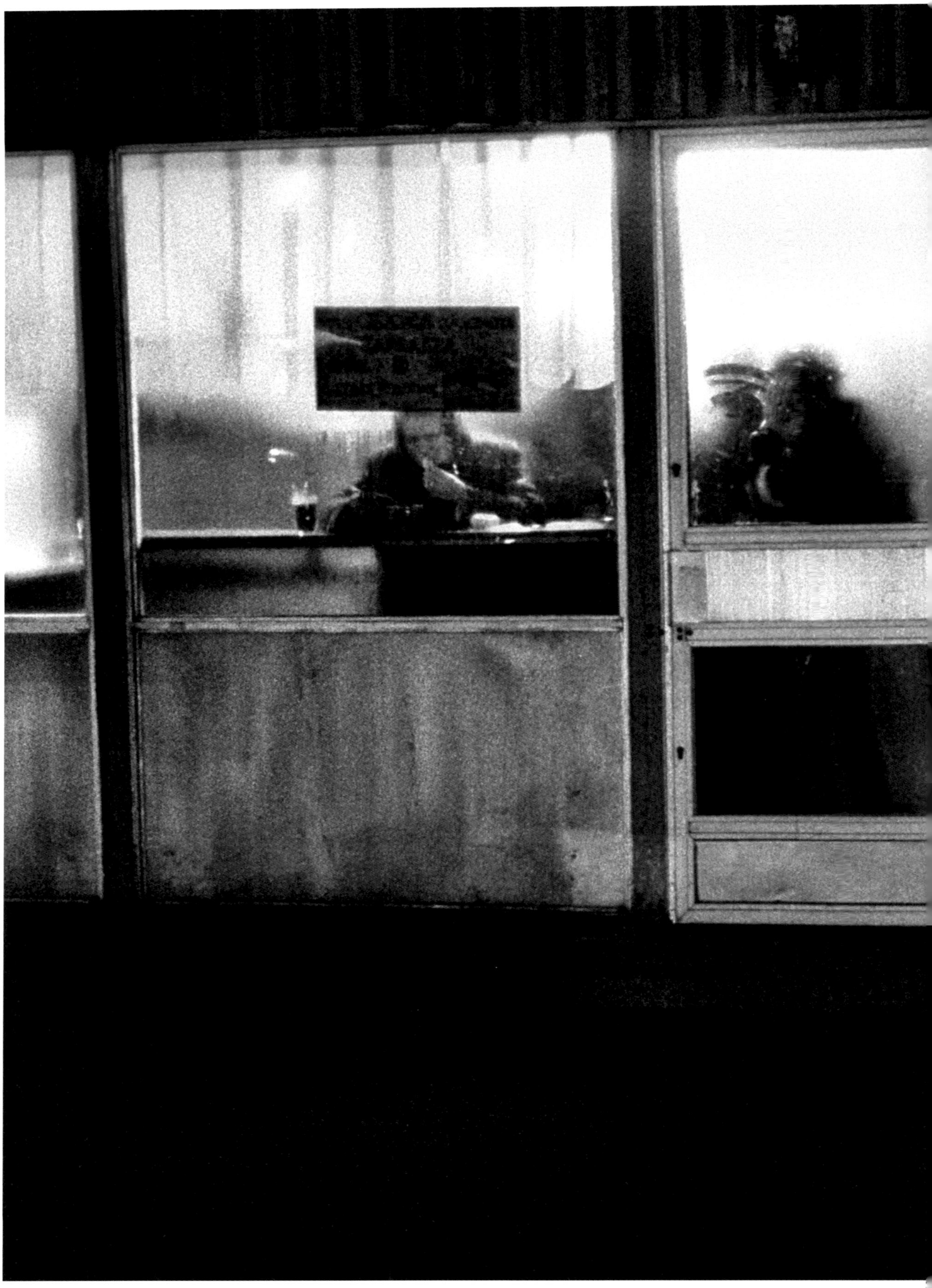

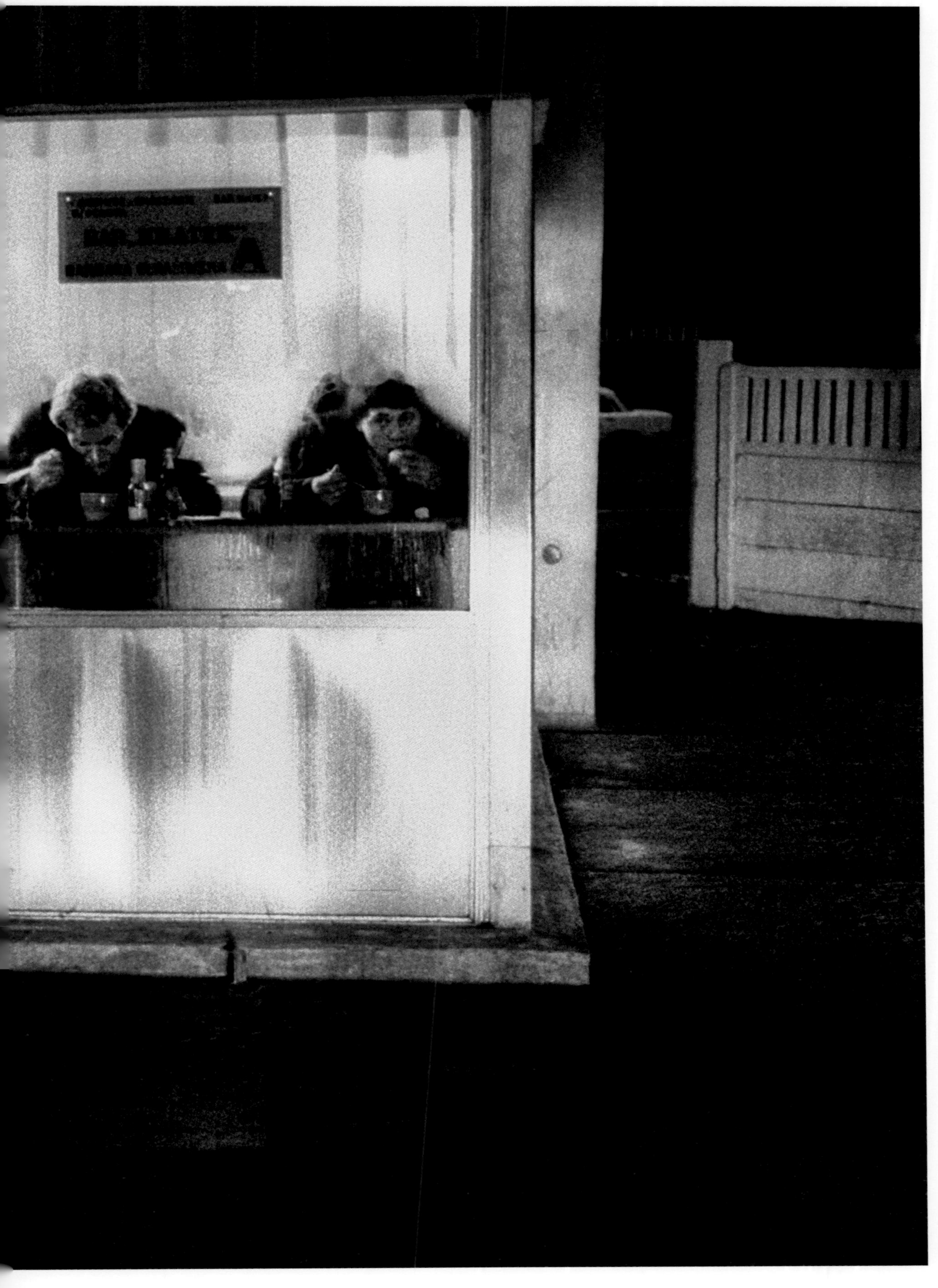

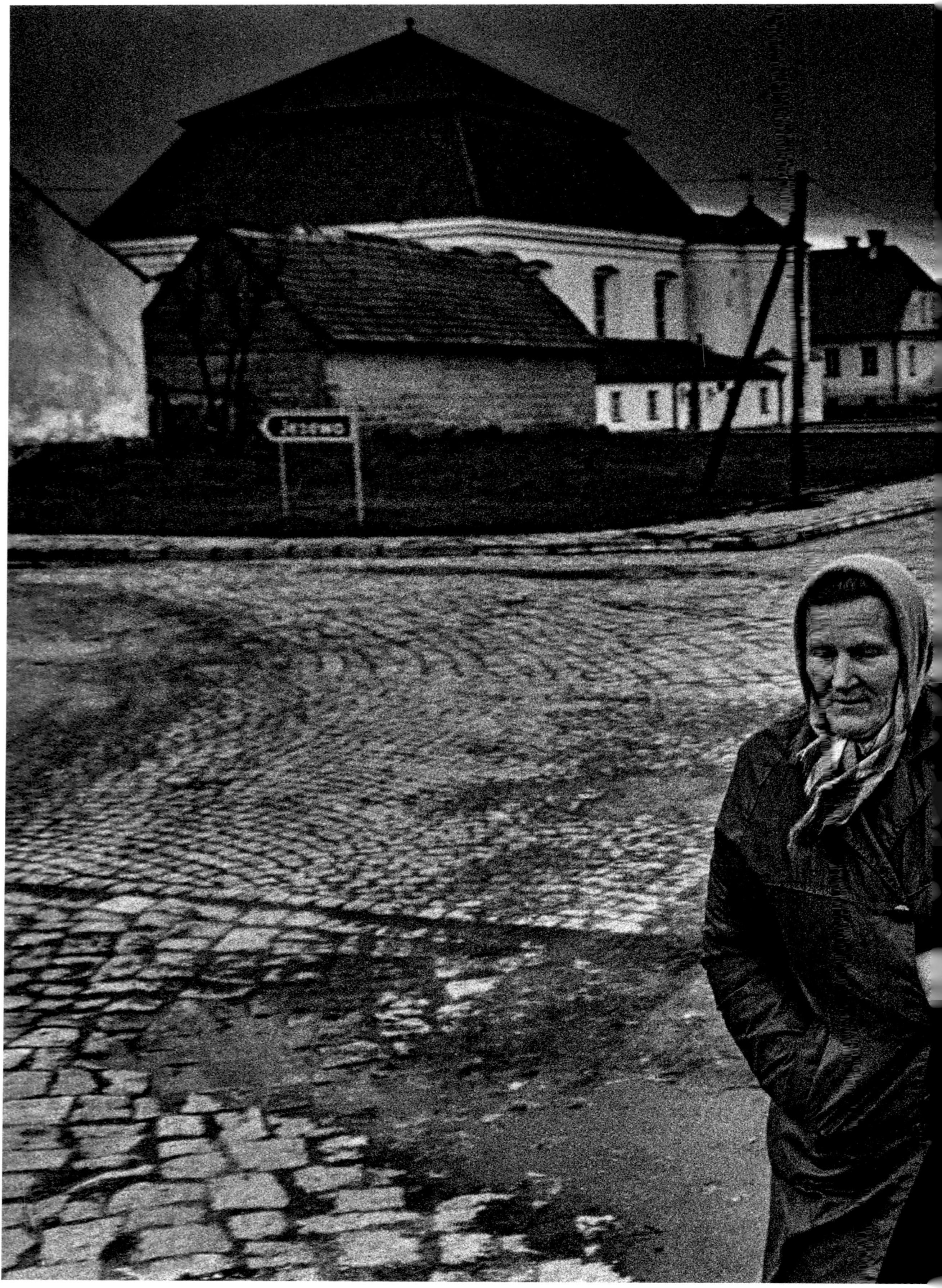

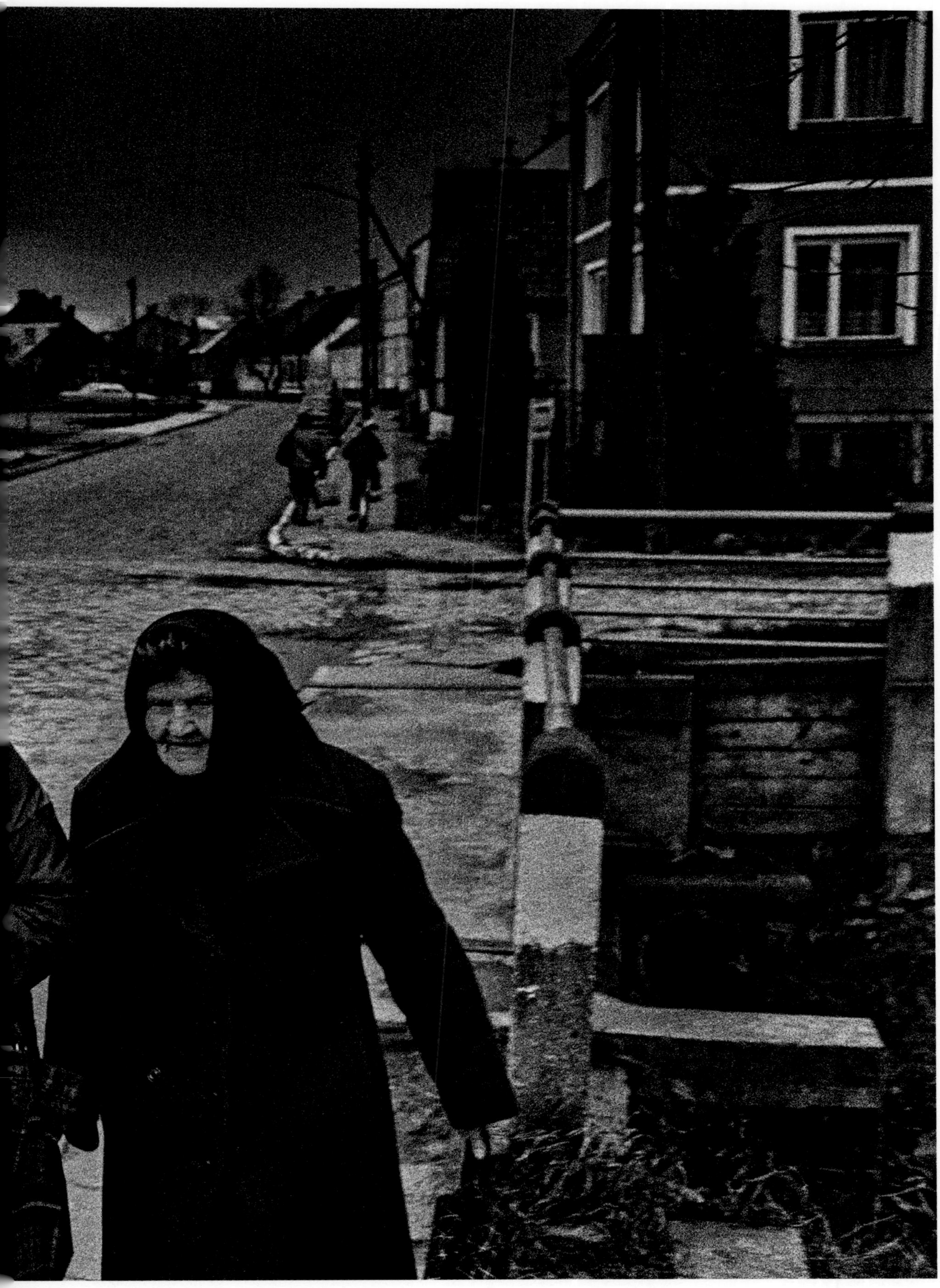

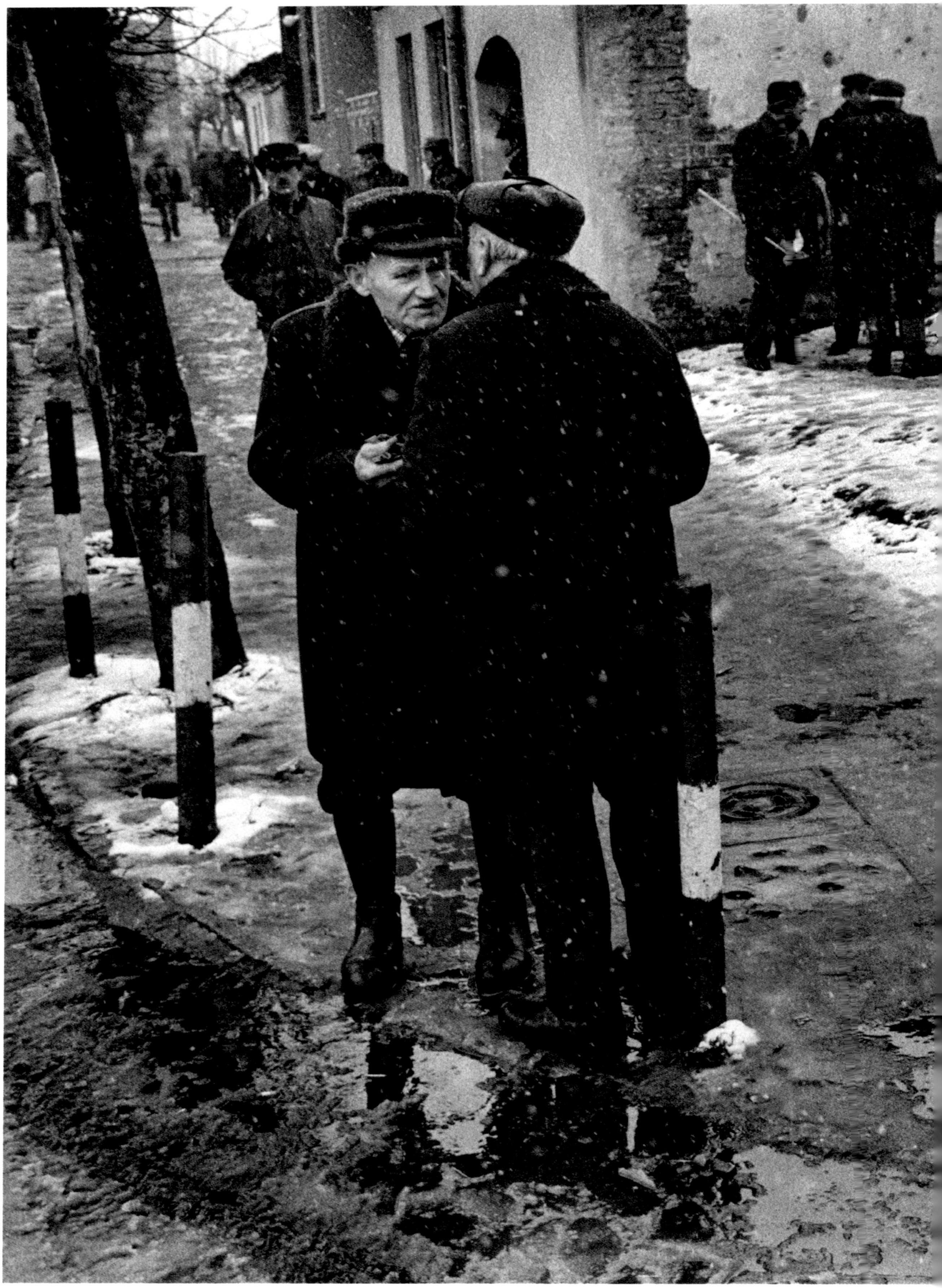

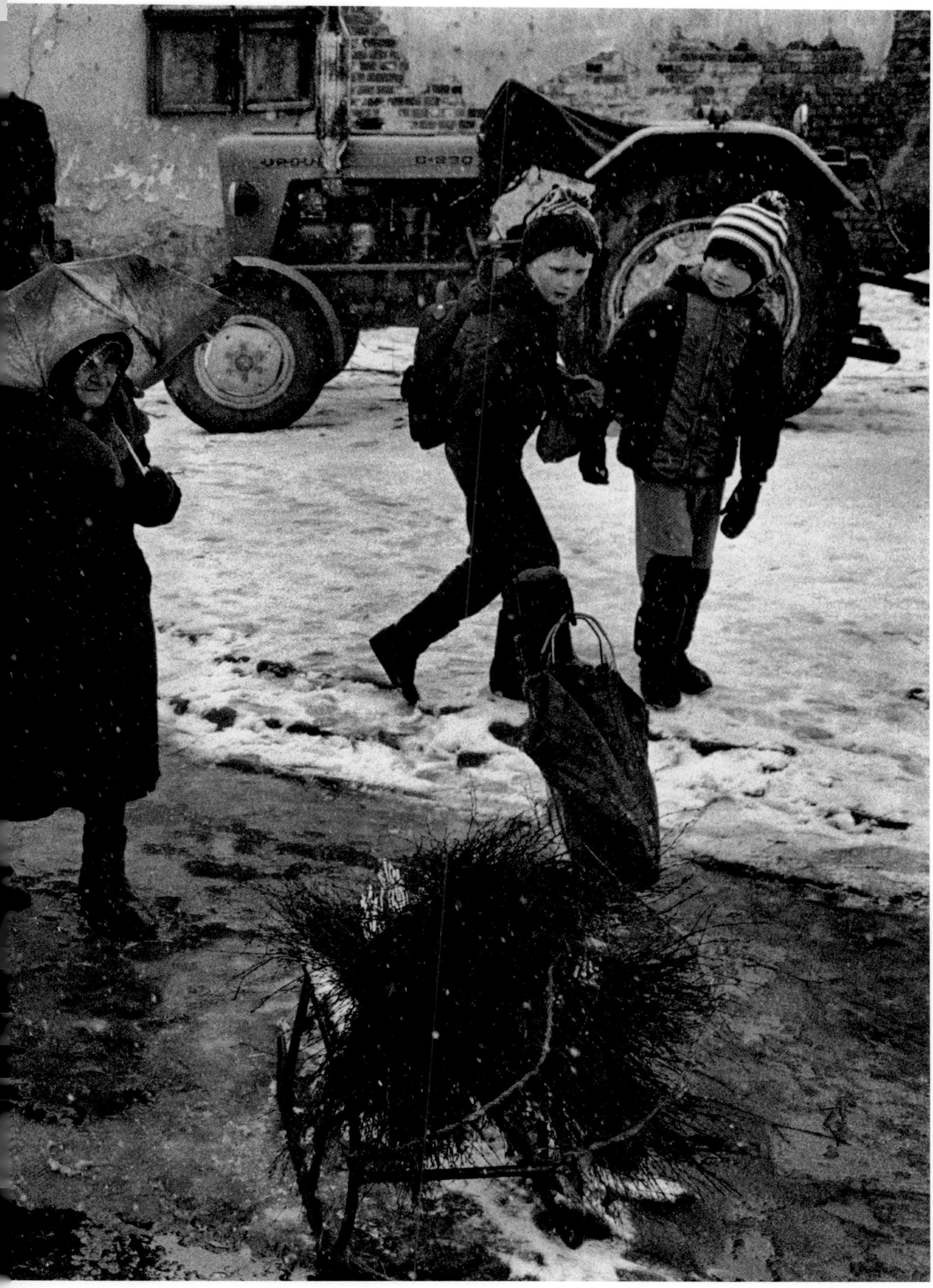

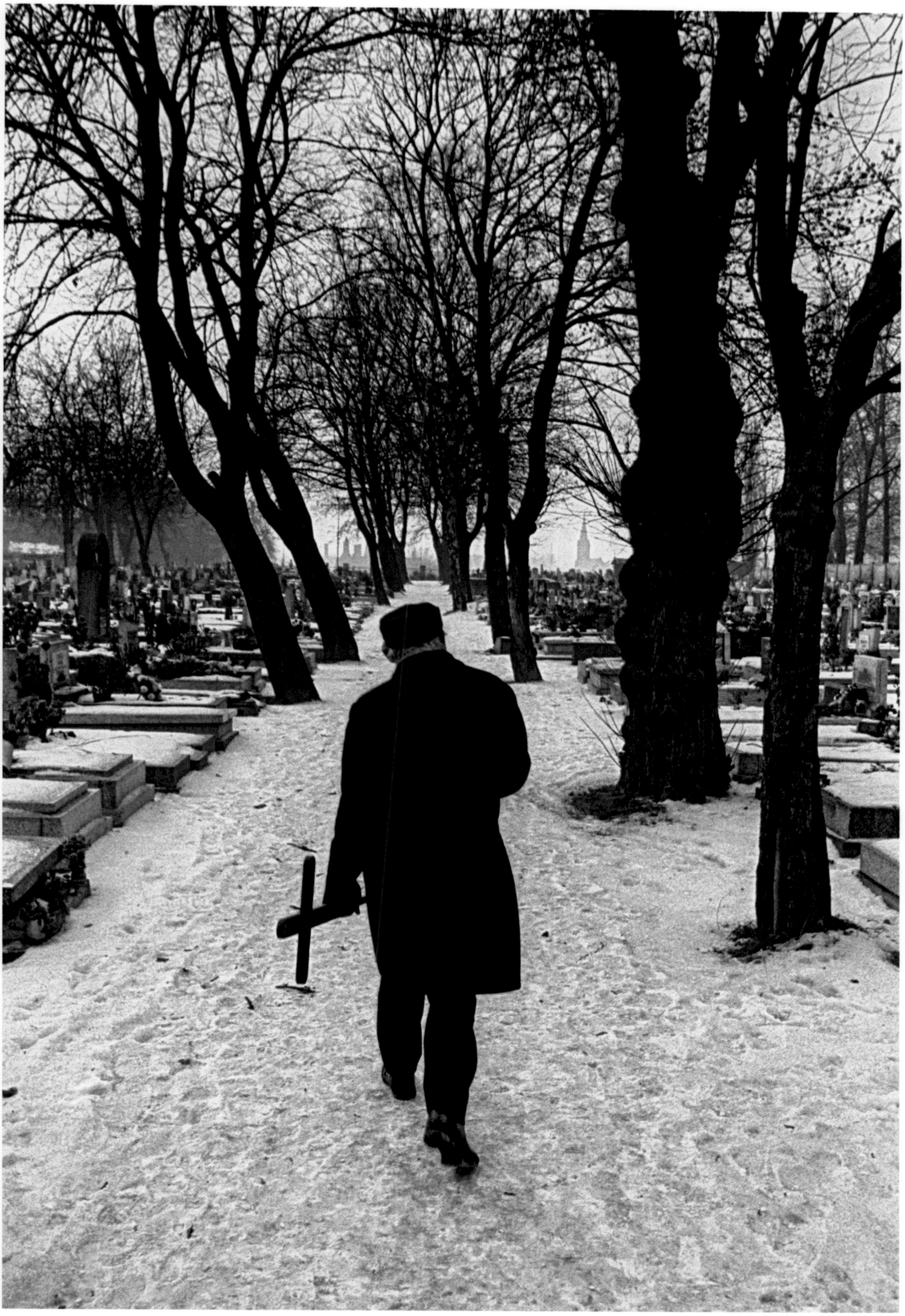

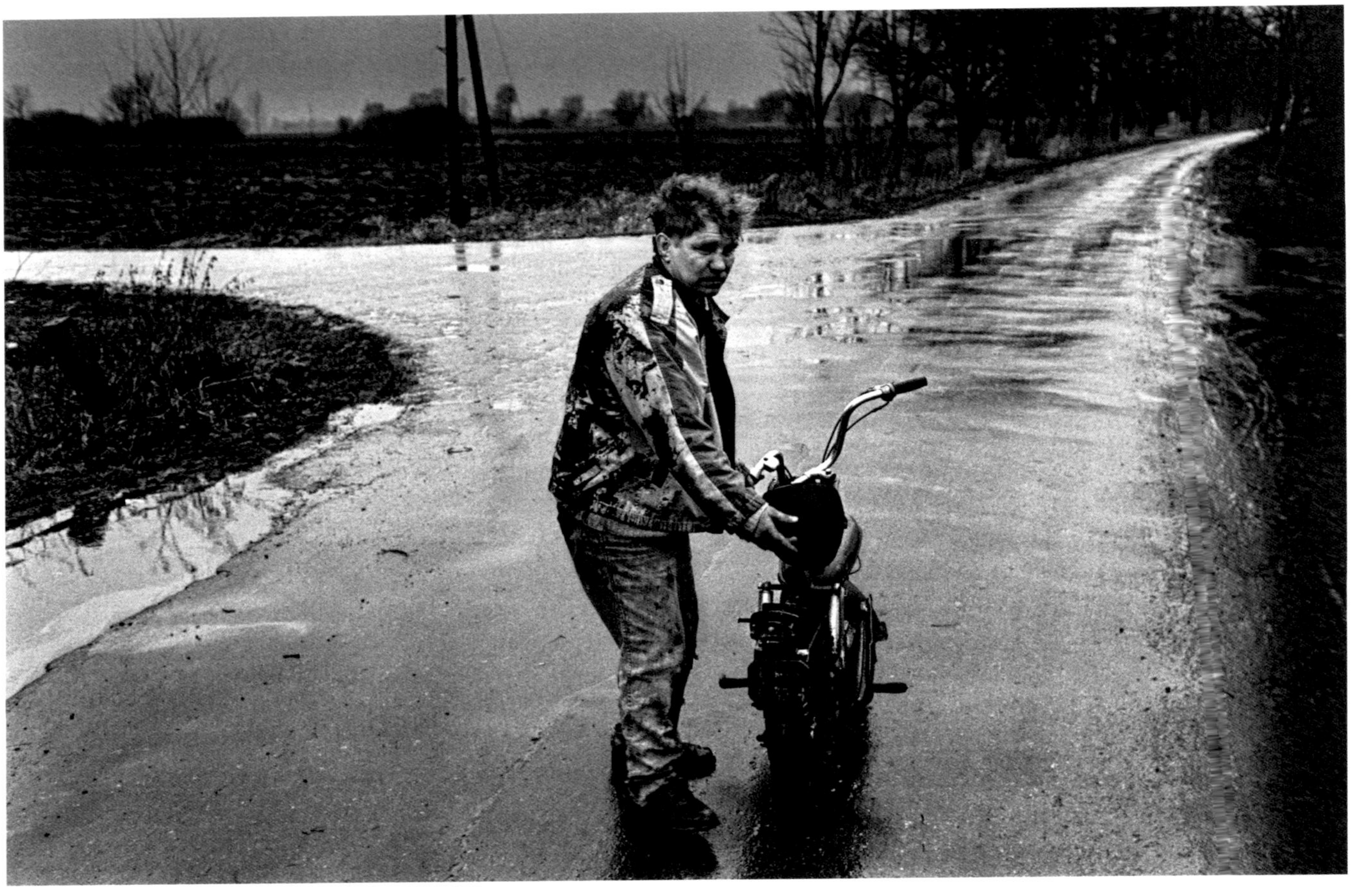

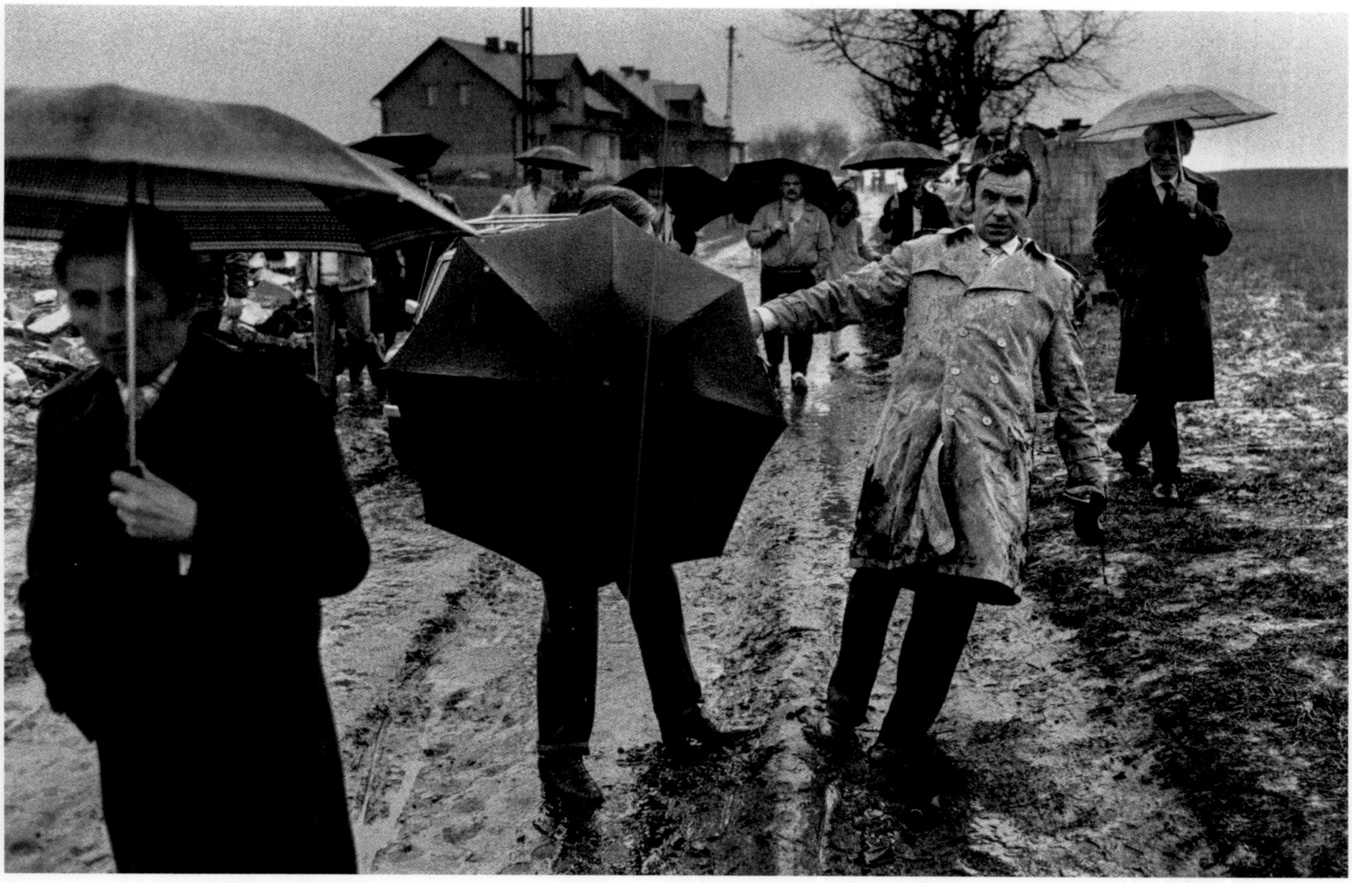

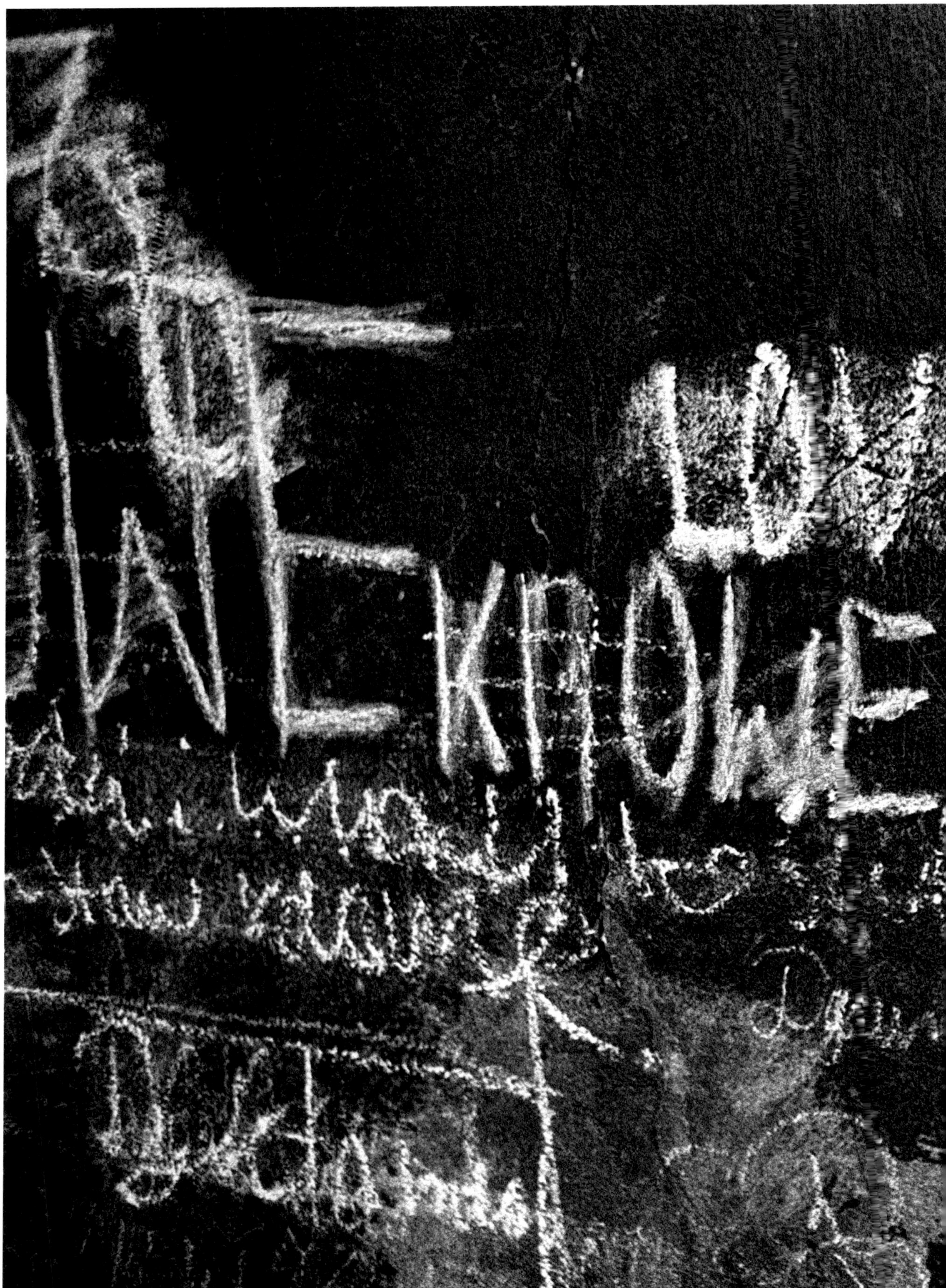

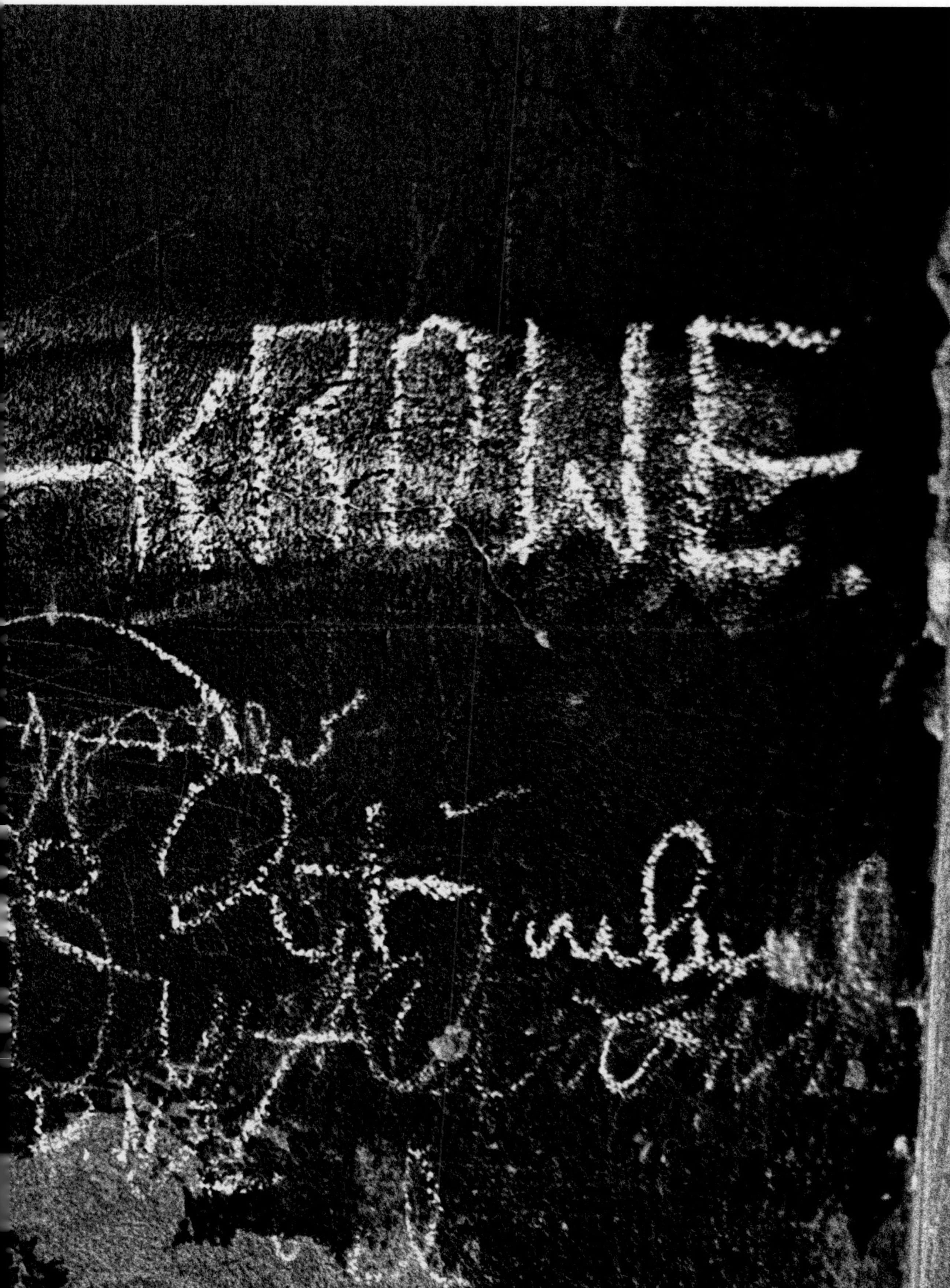
KRONE

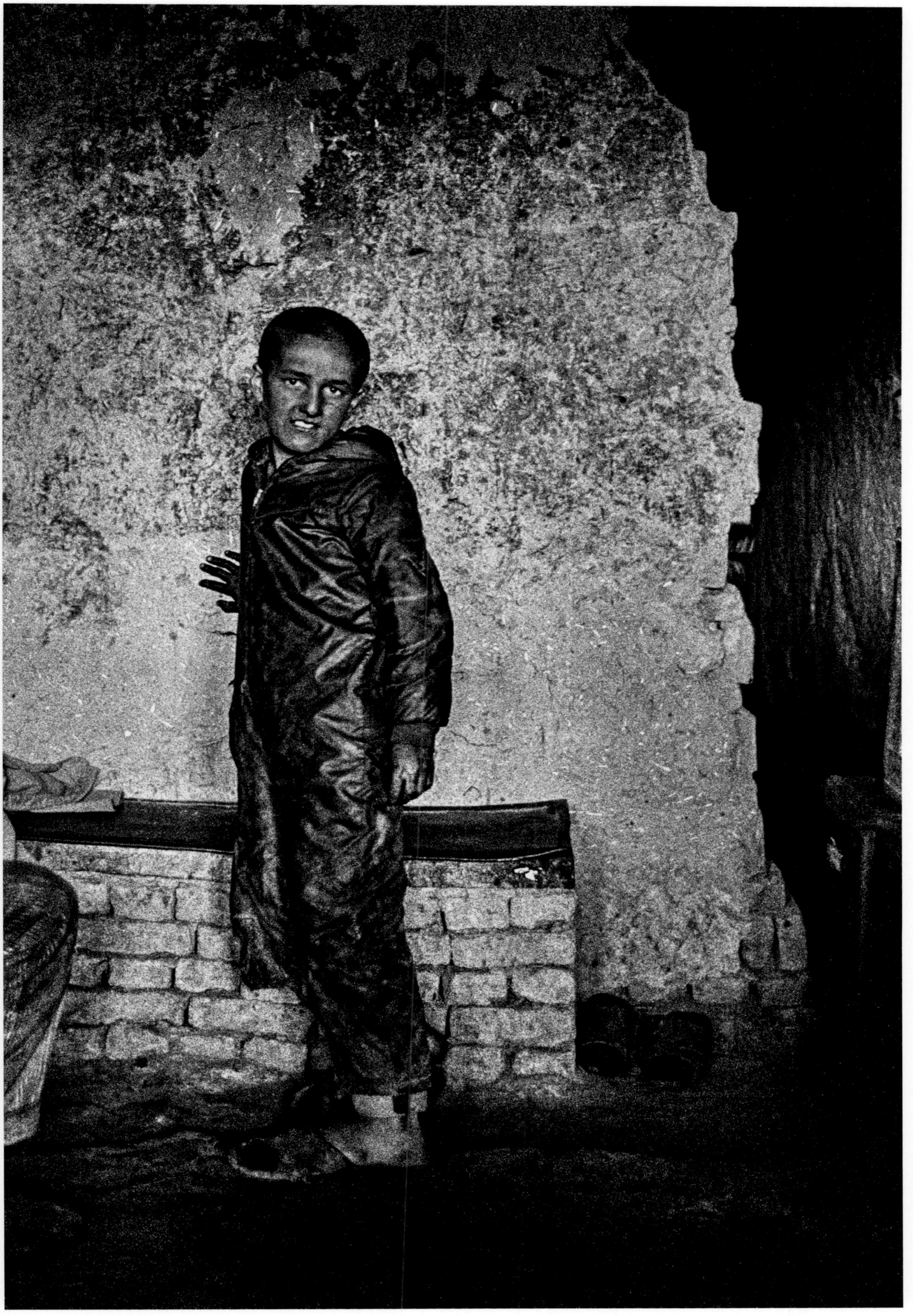

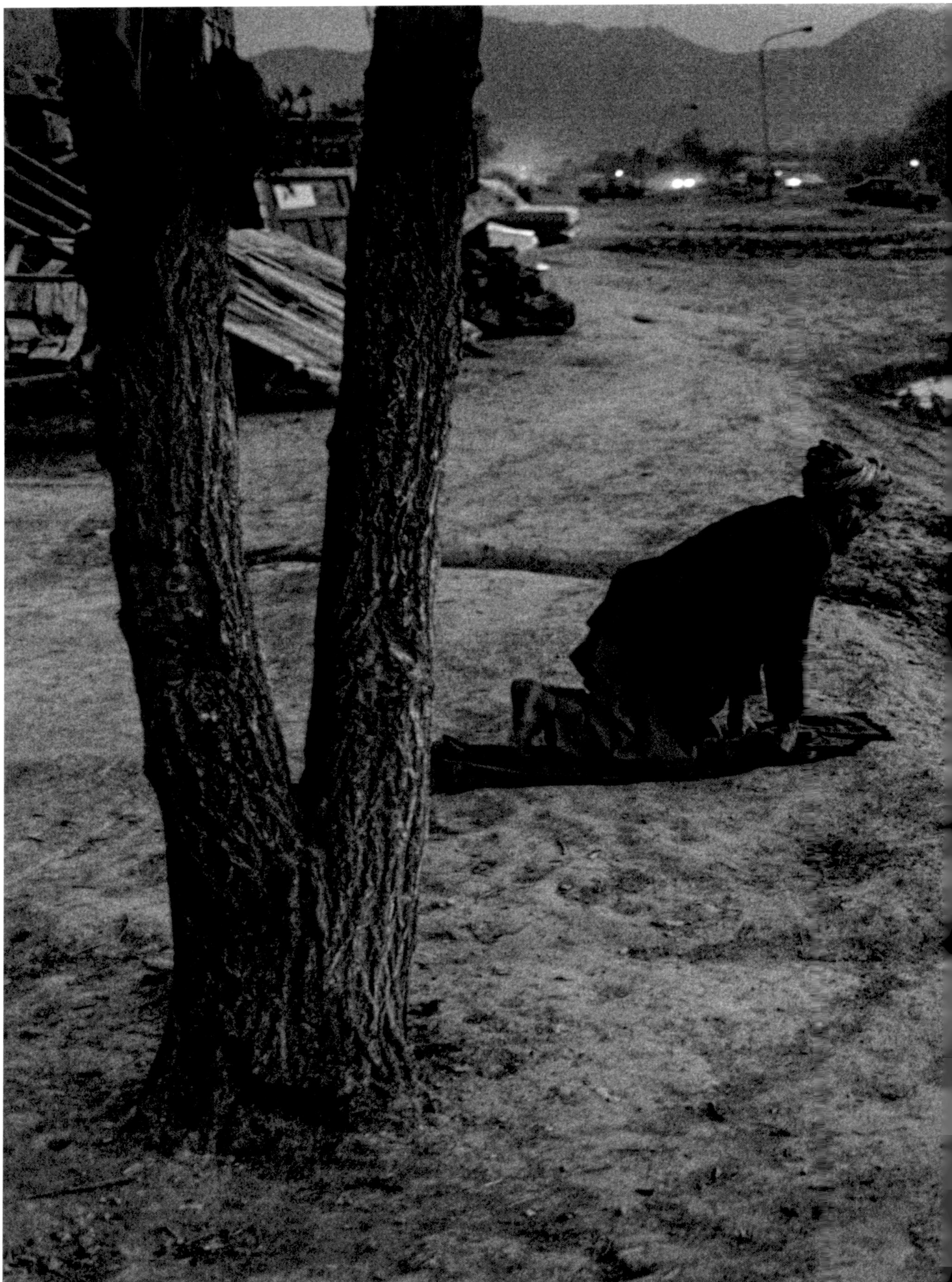

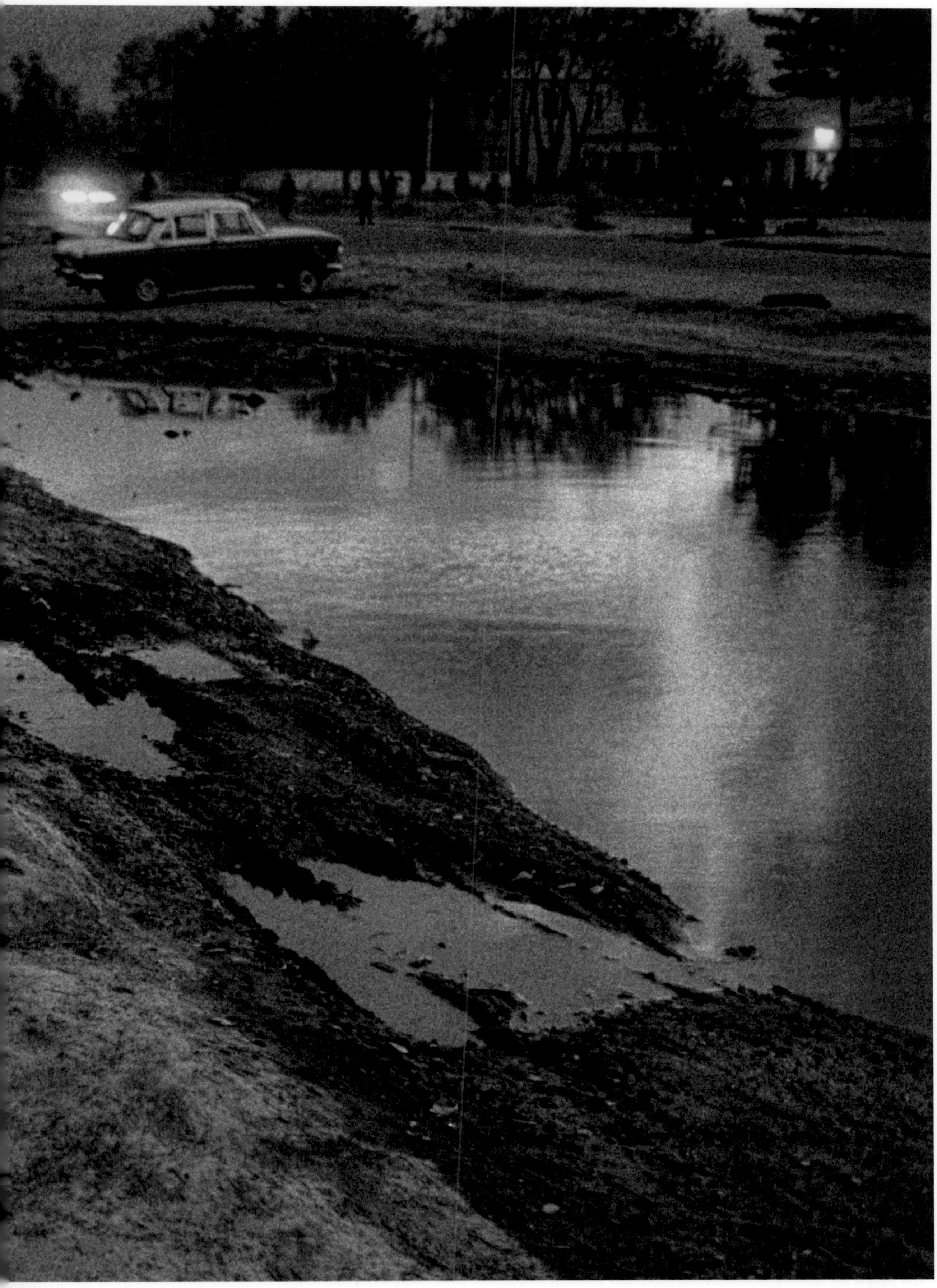

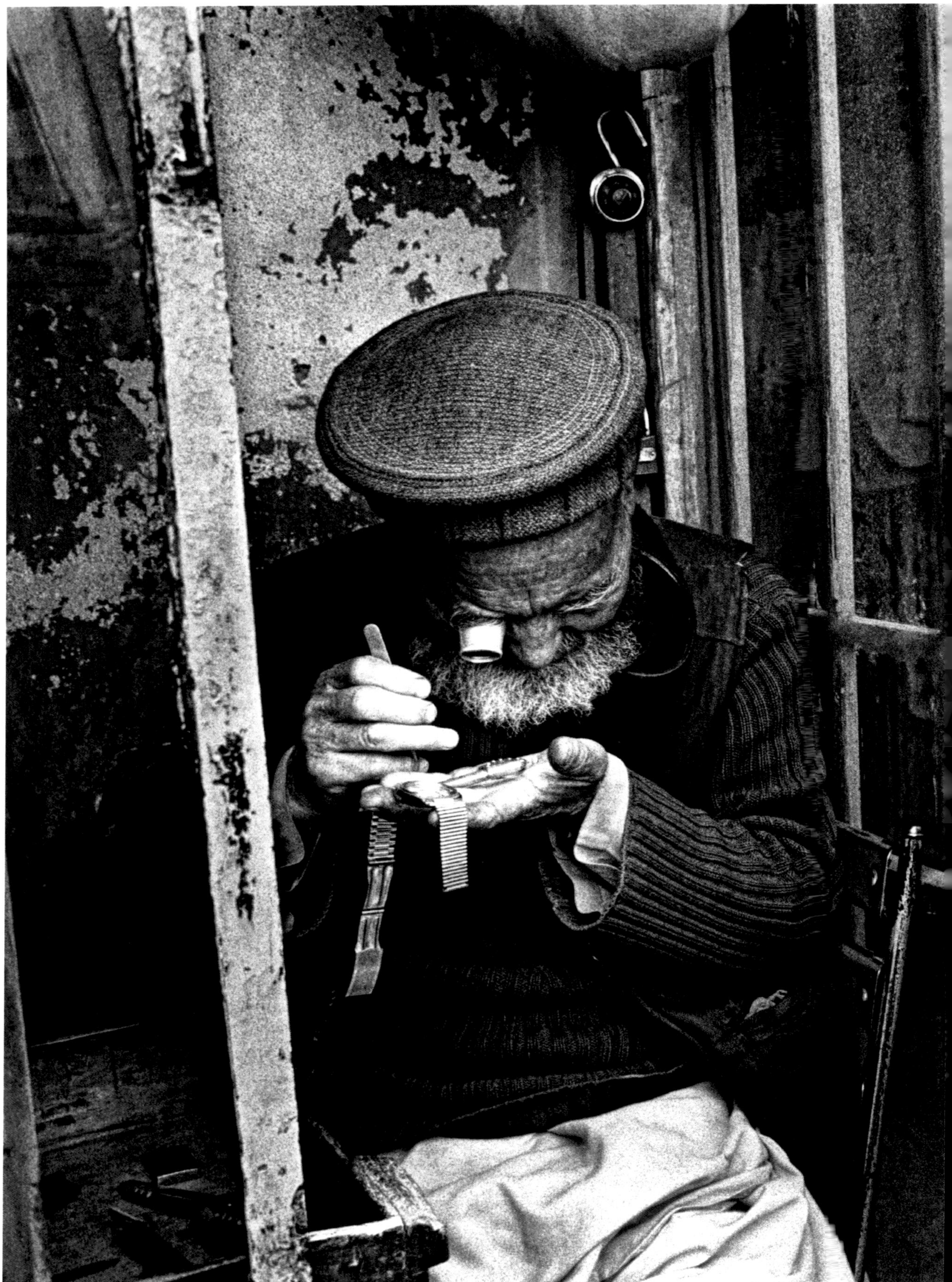

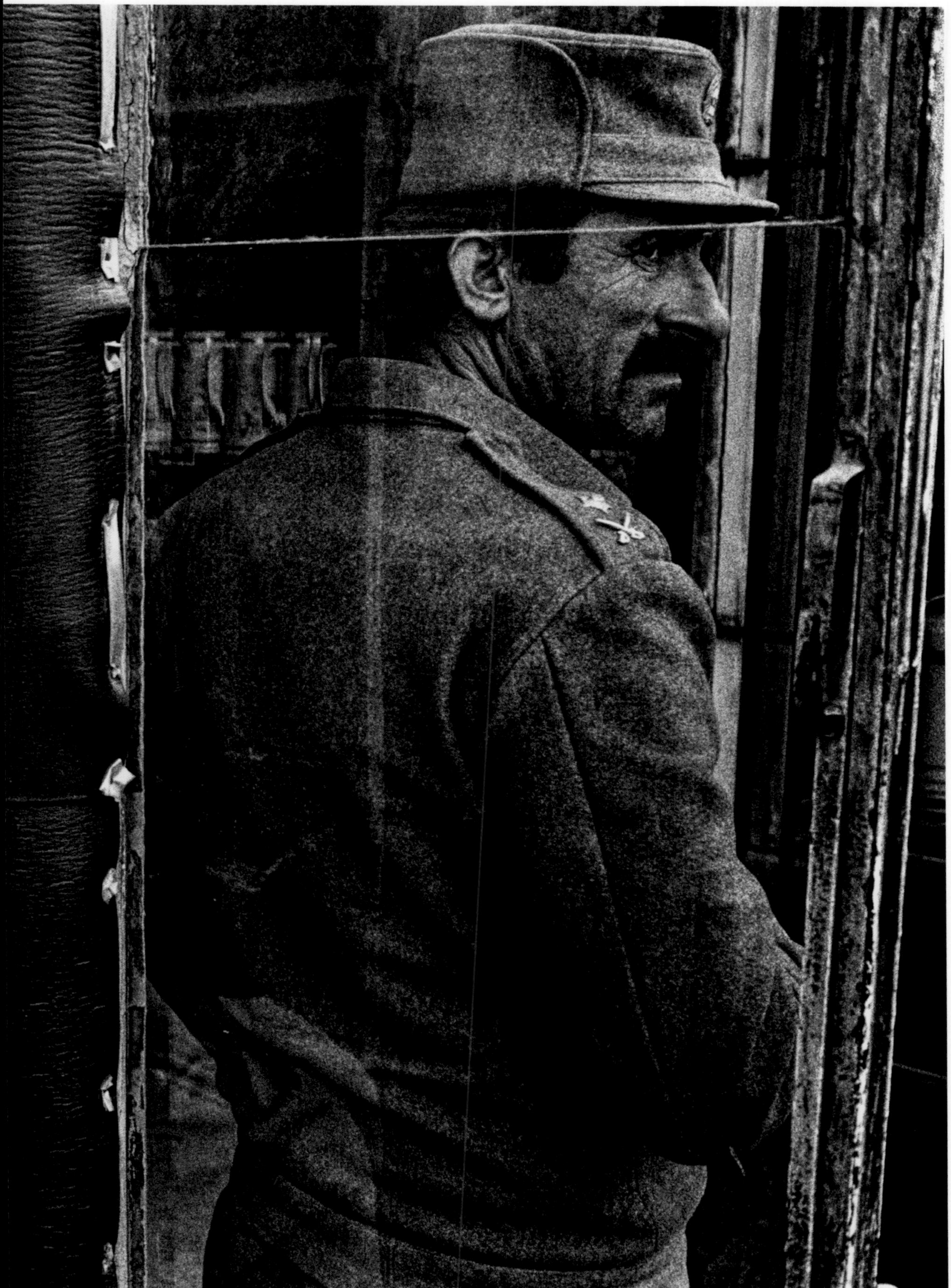

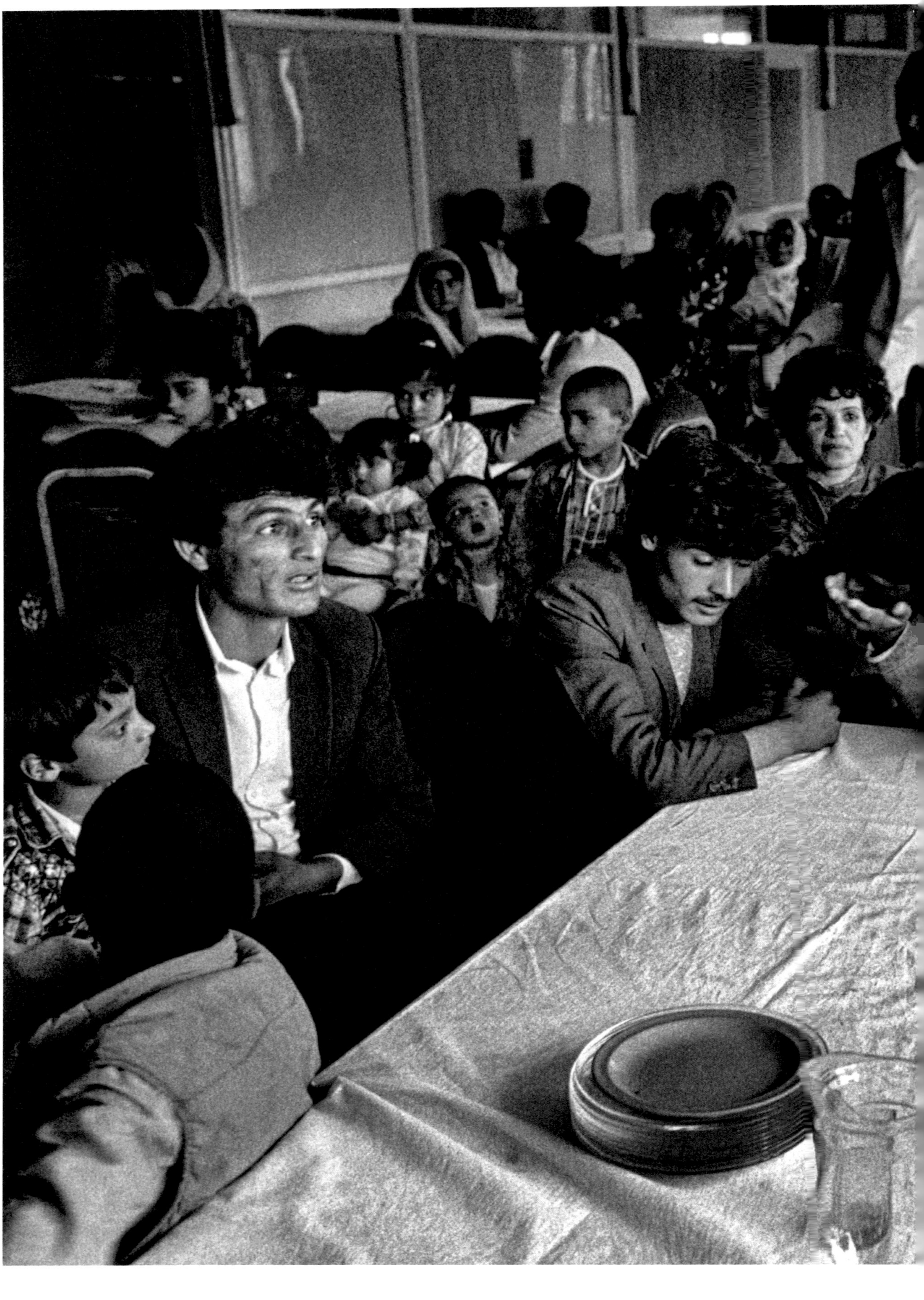

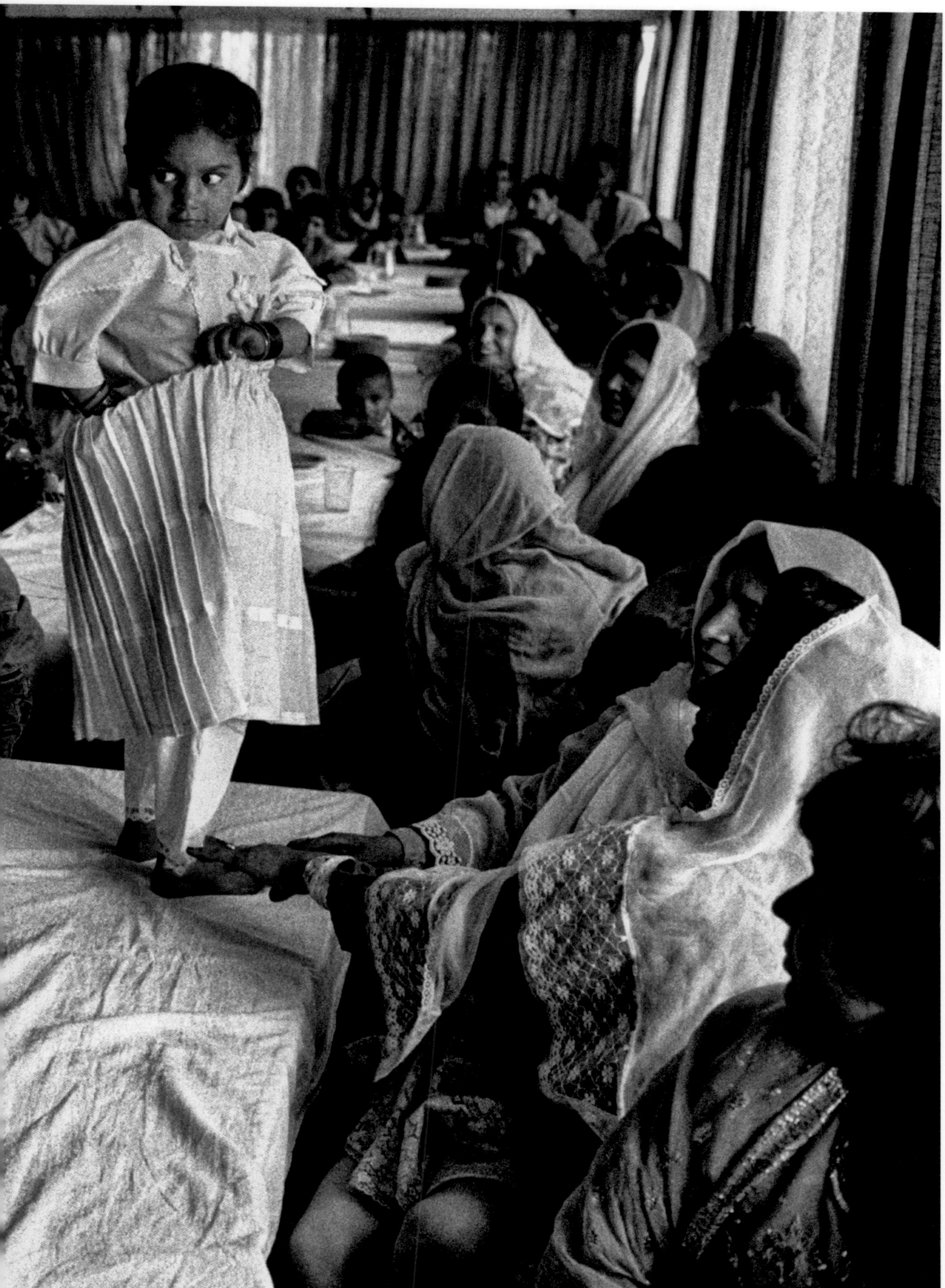

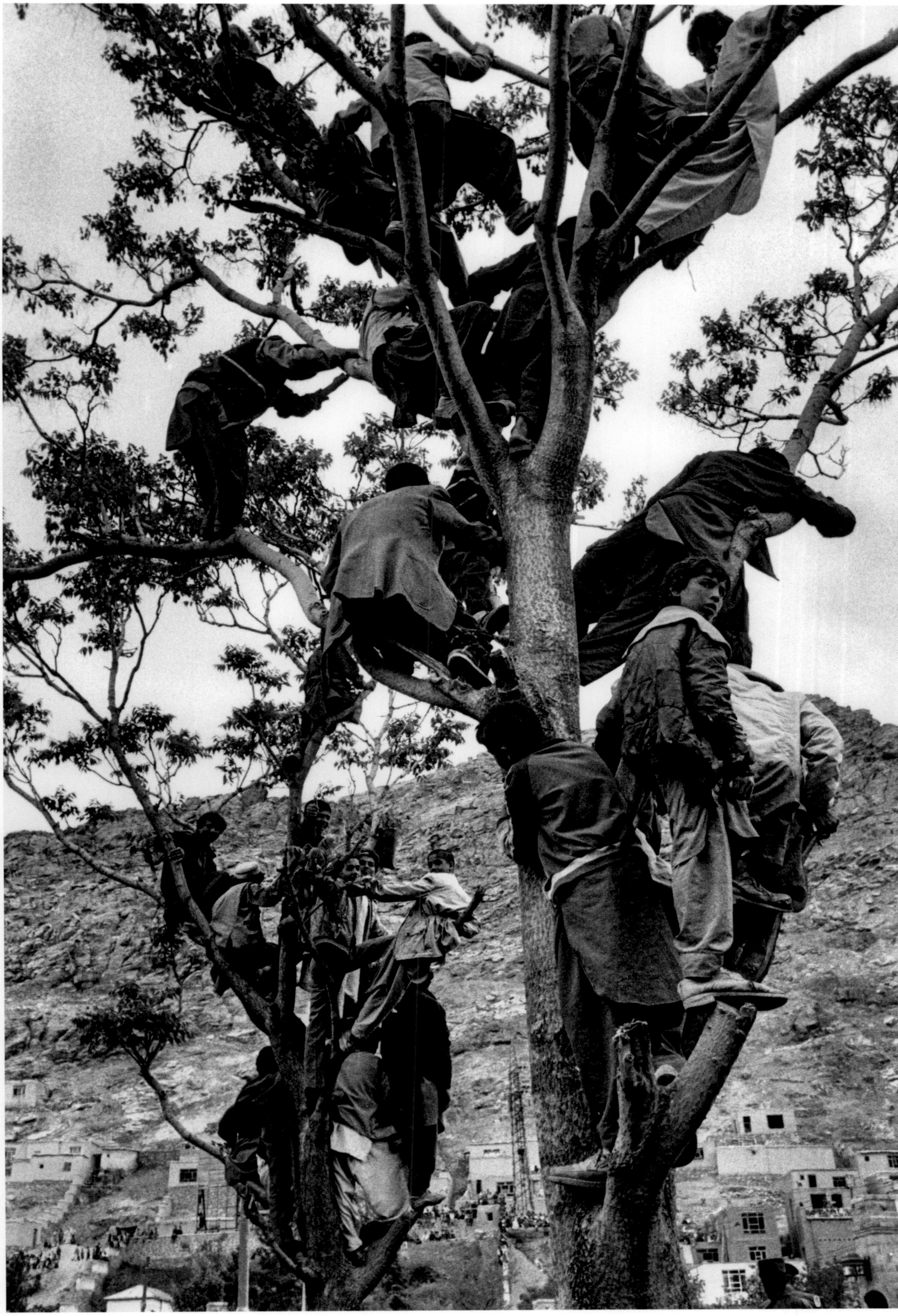

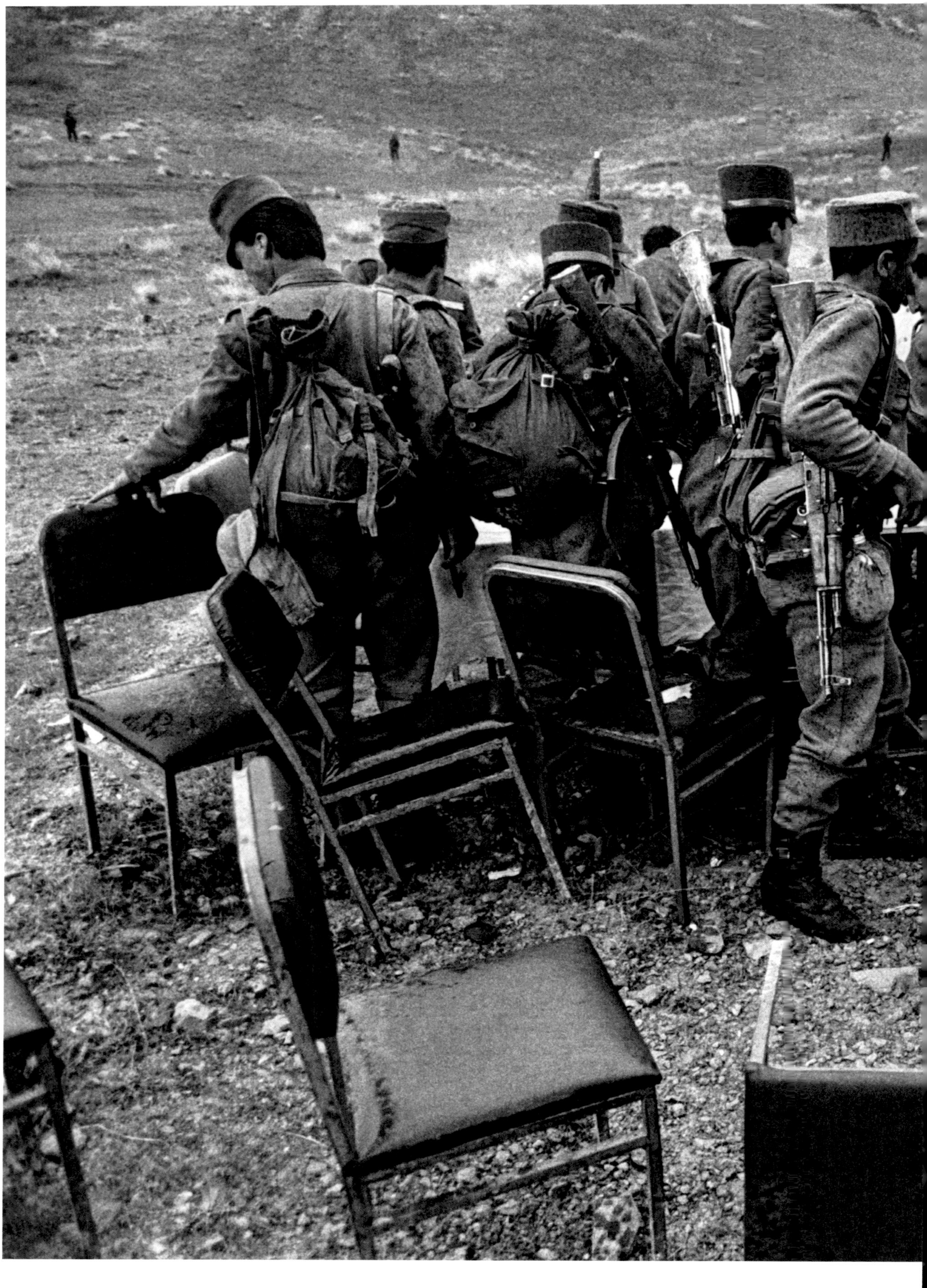

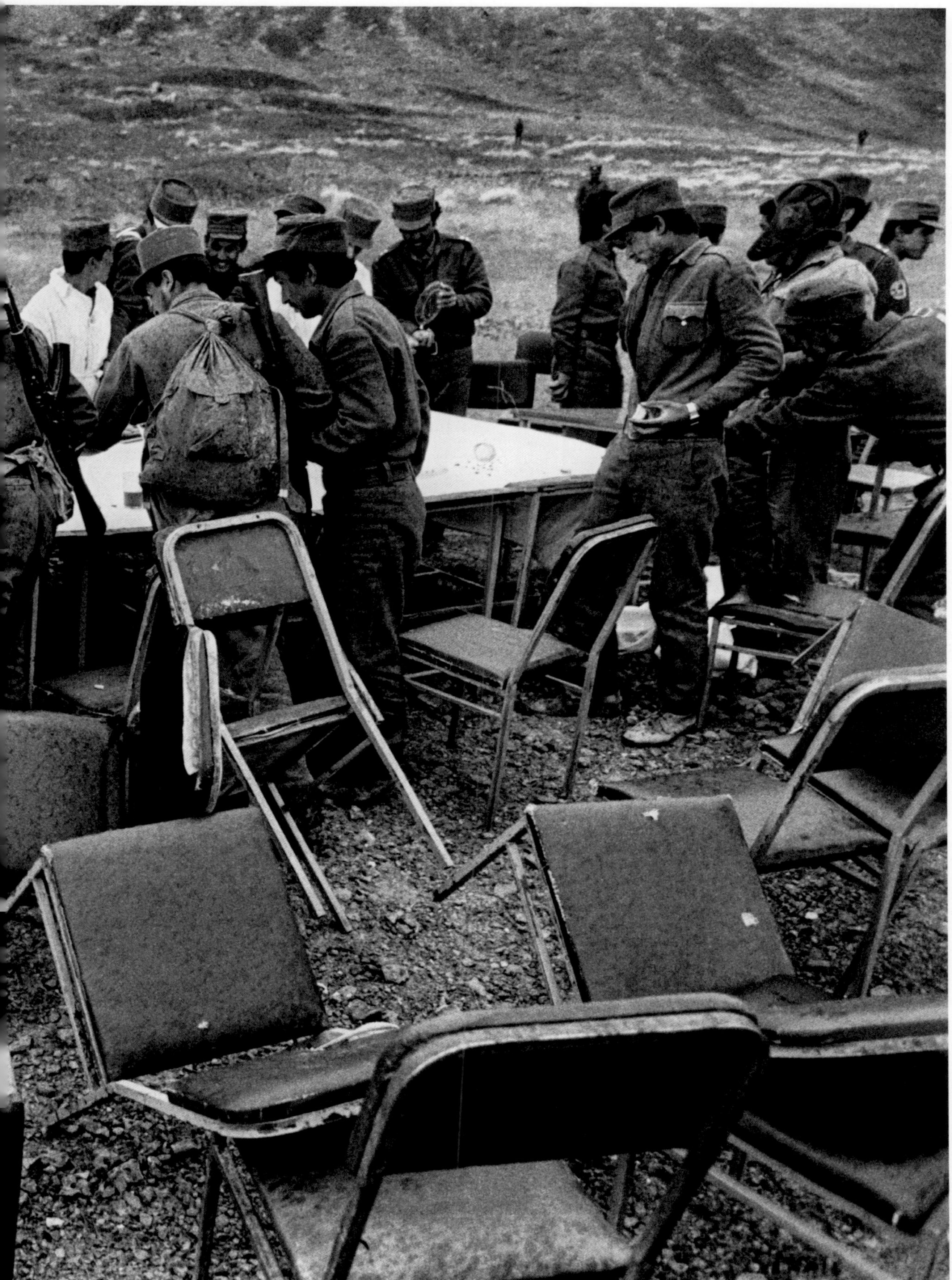

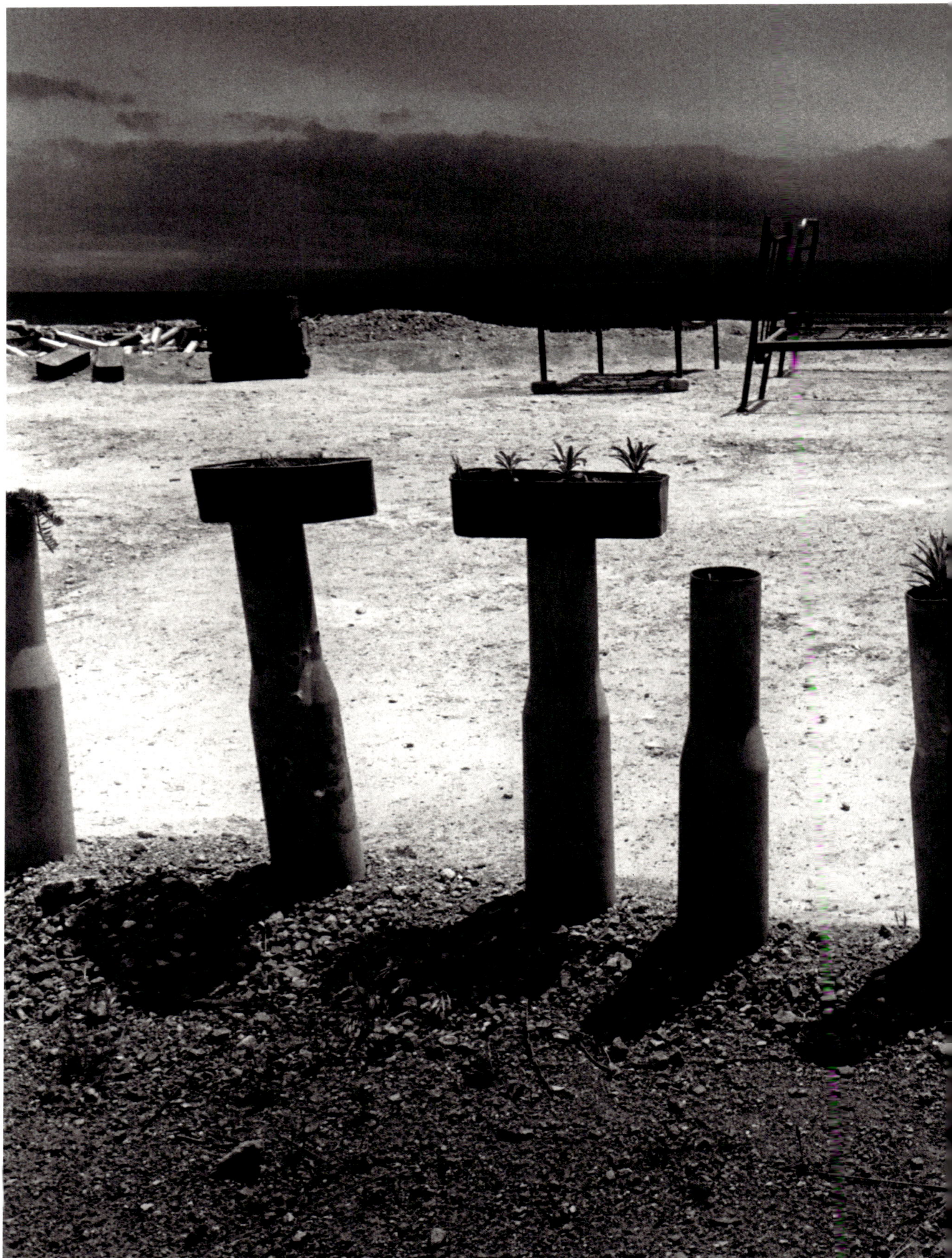

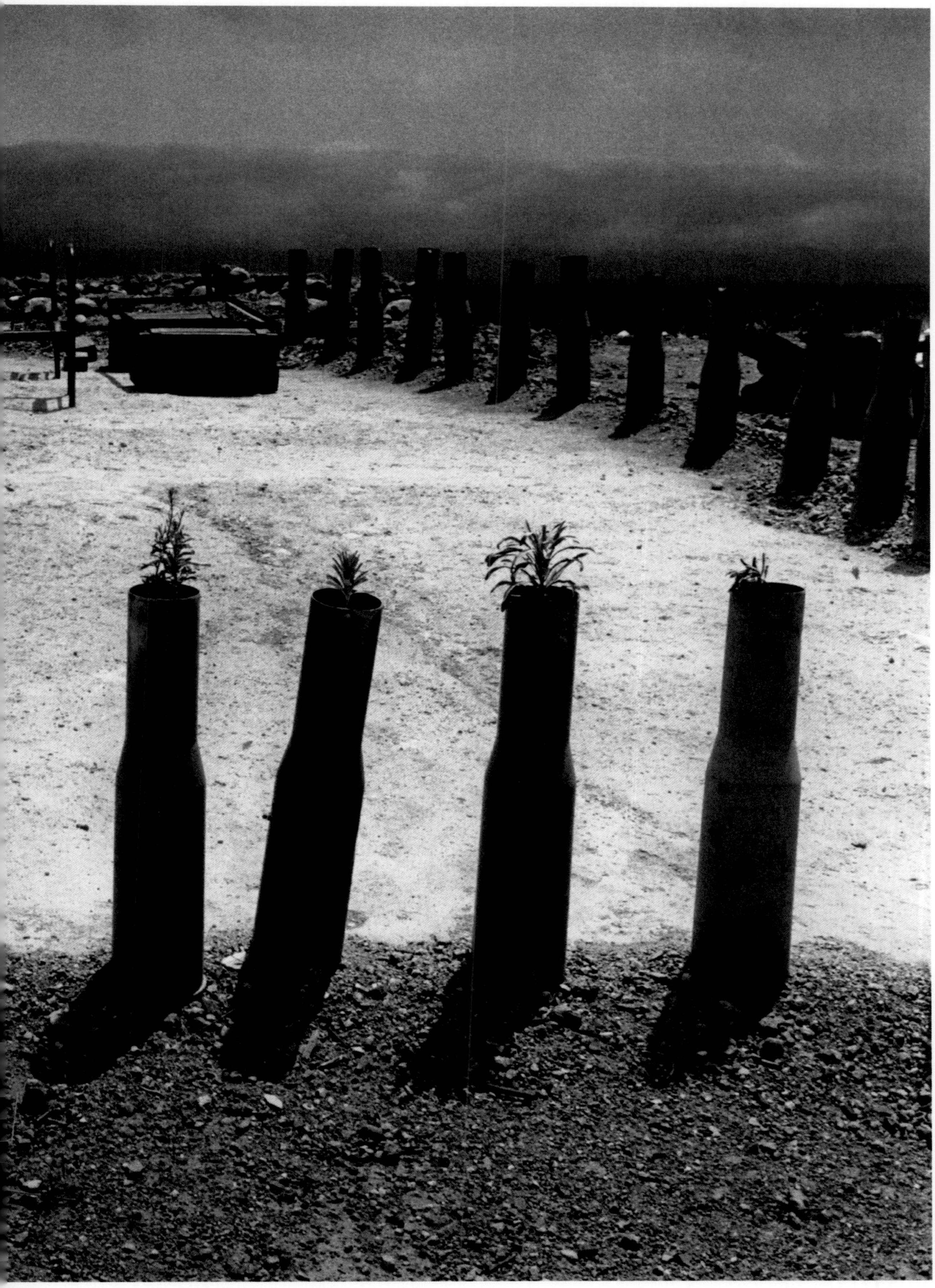

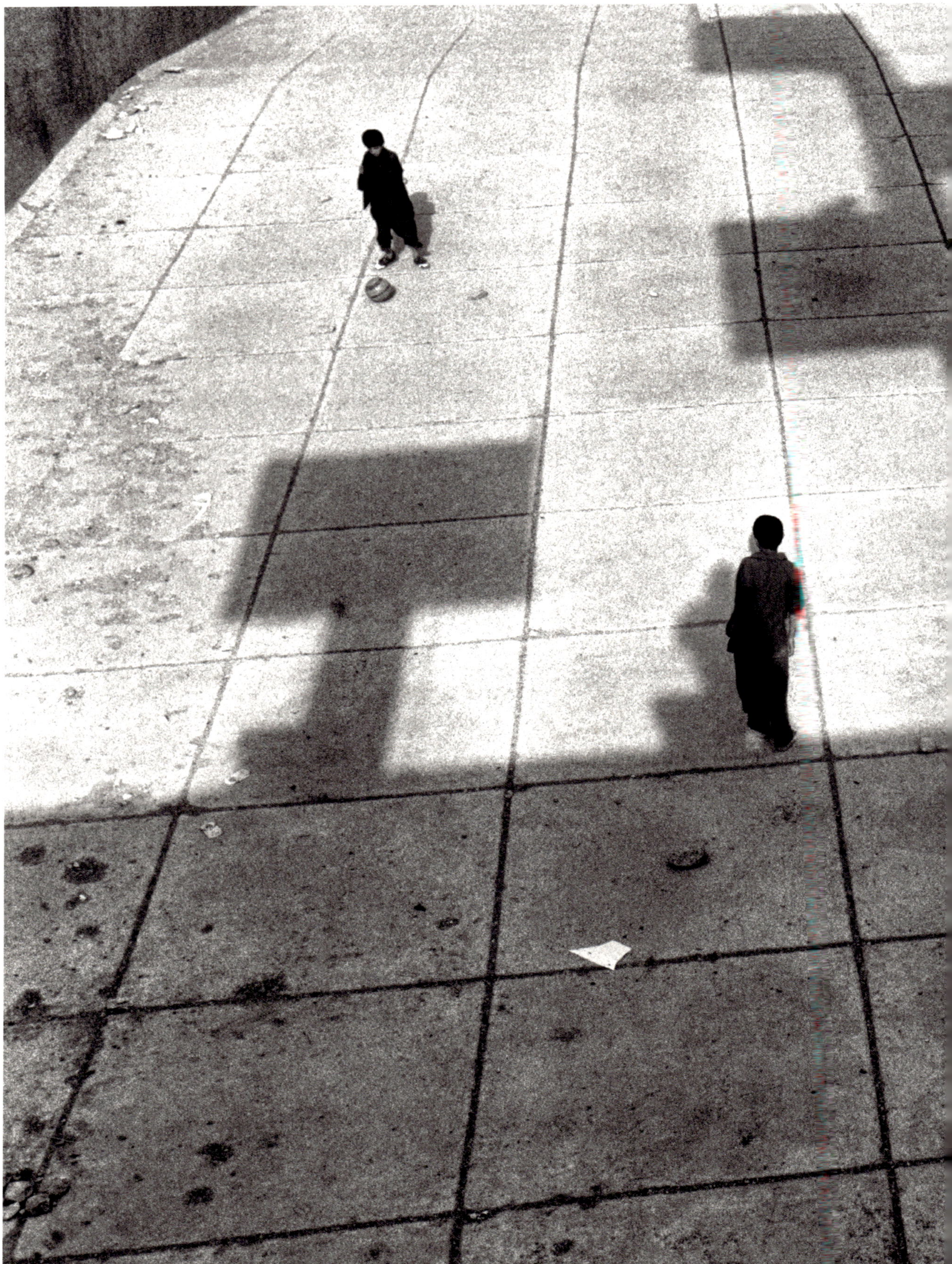

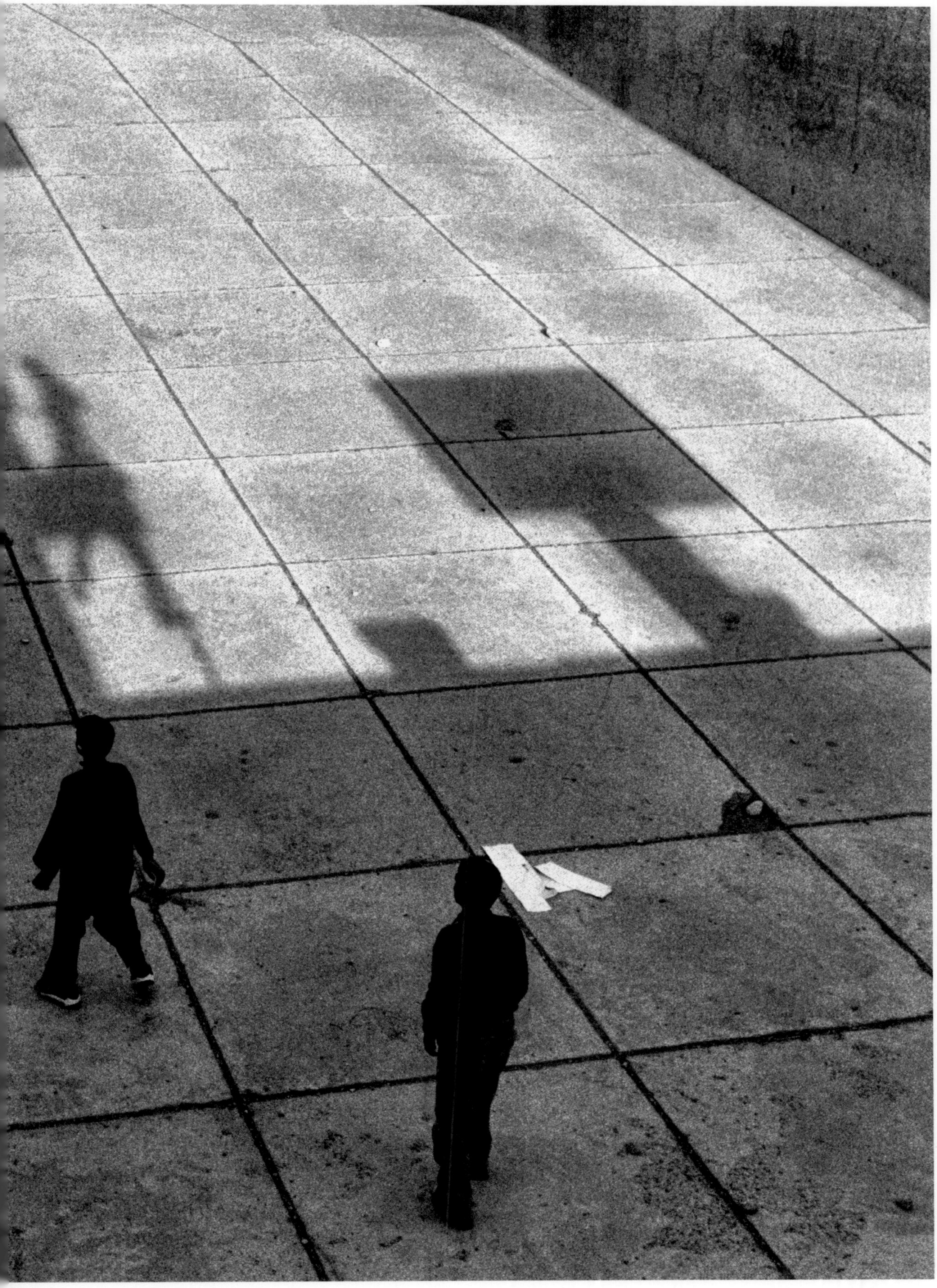

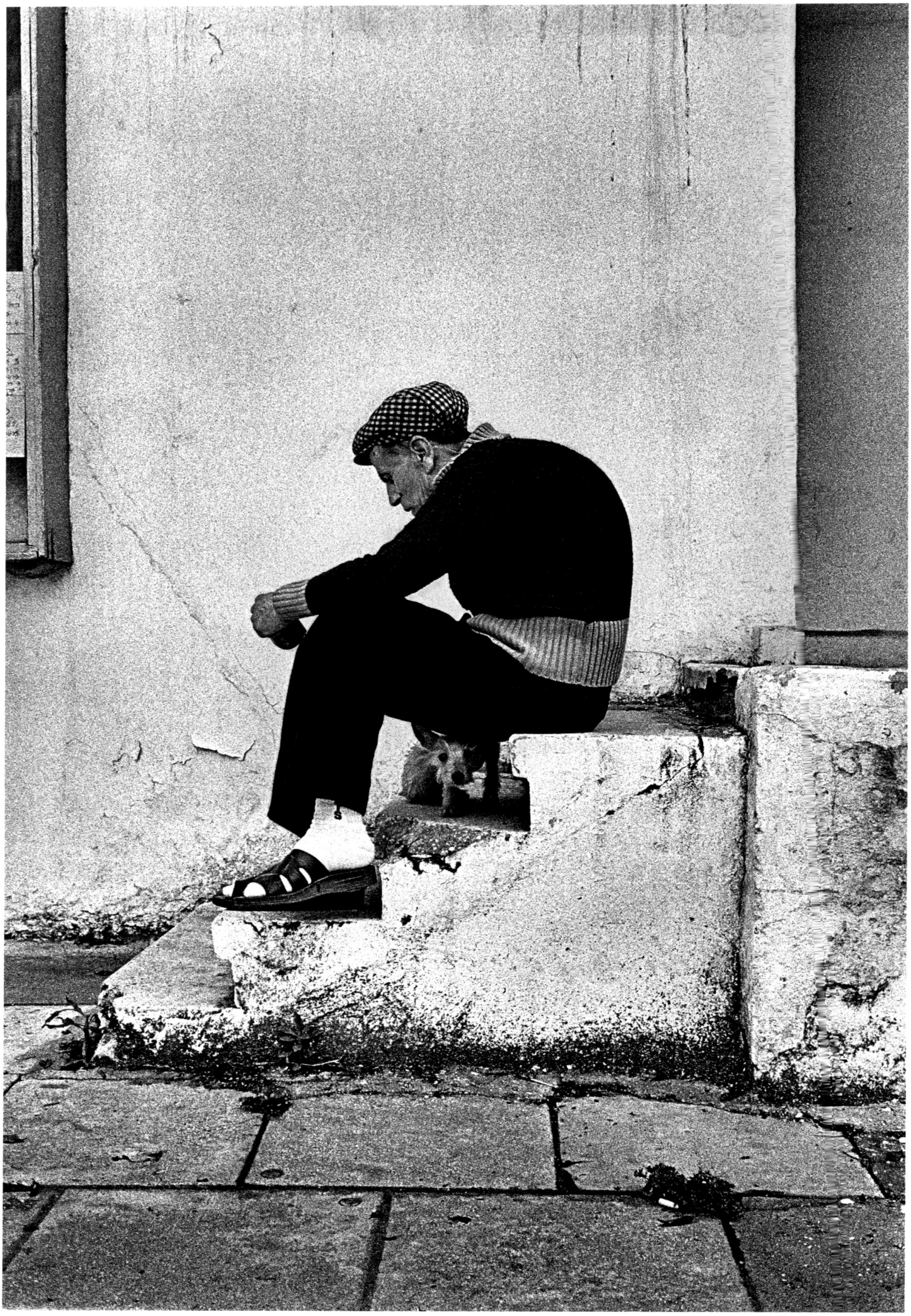

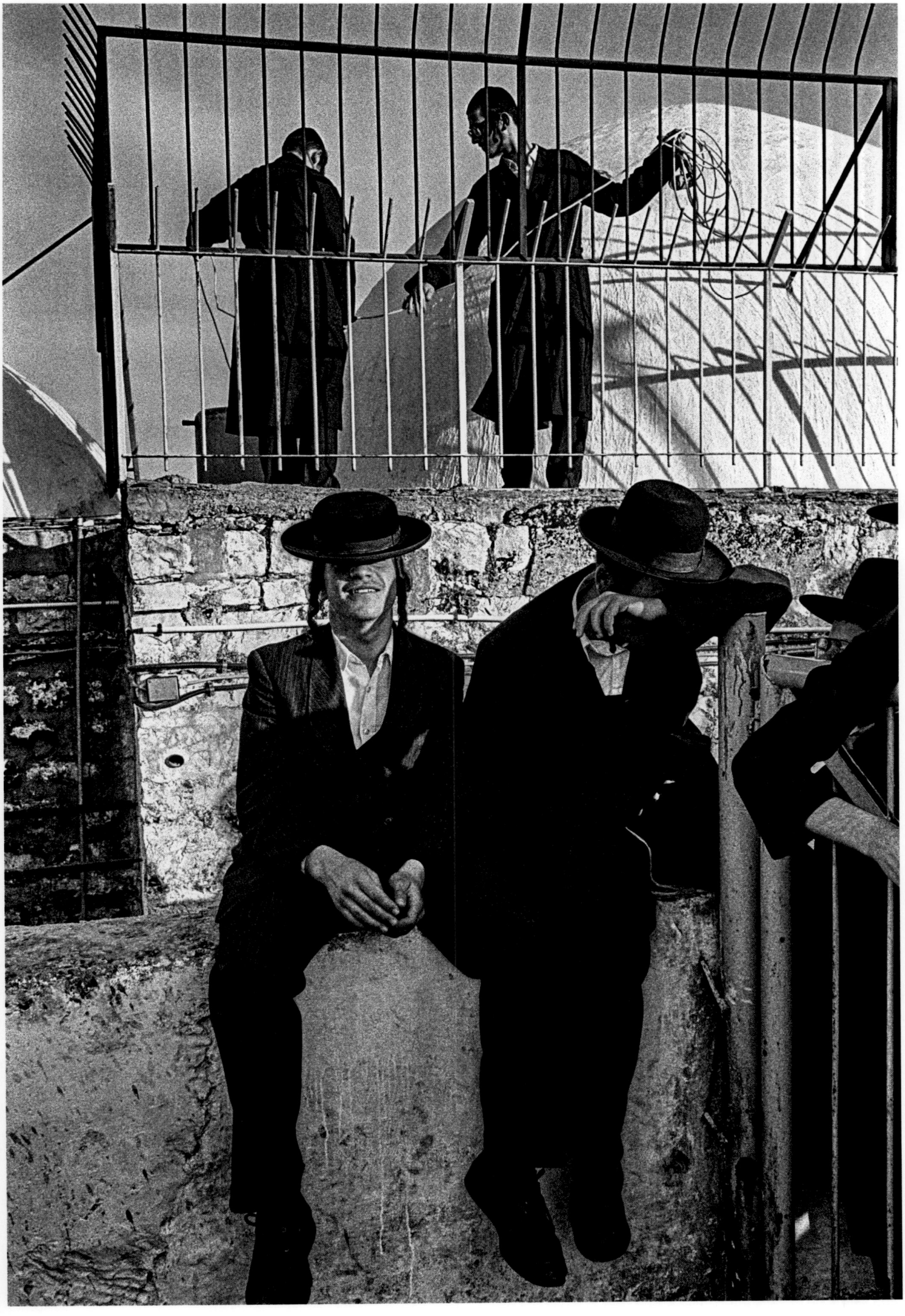

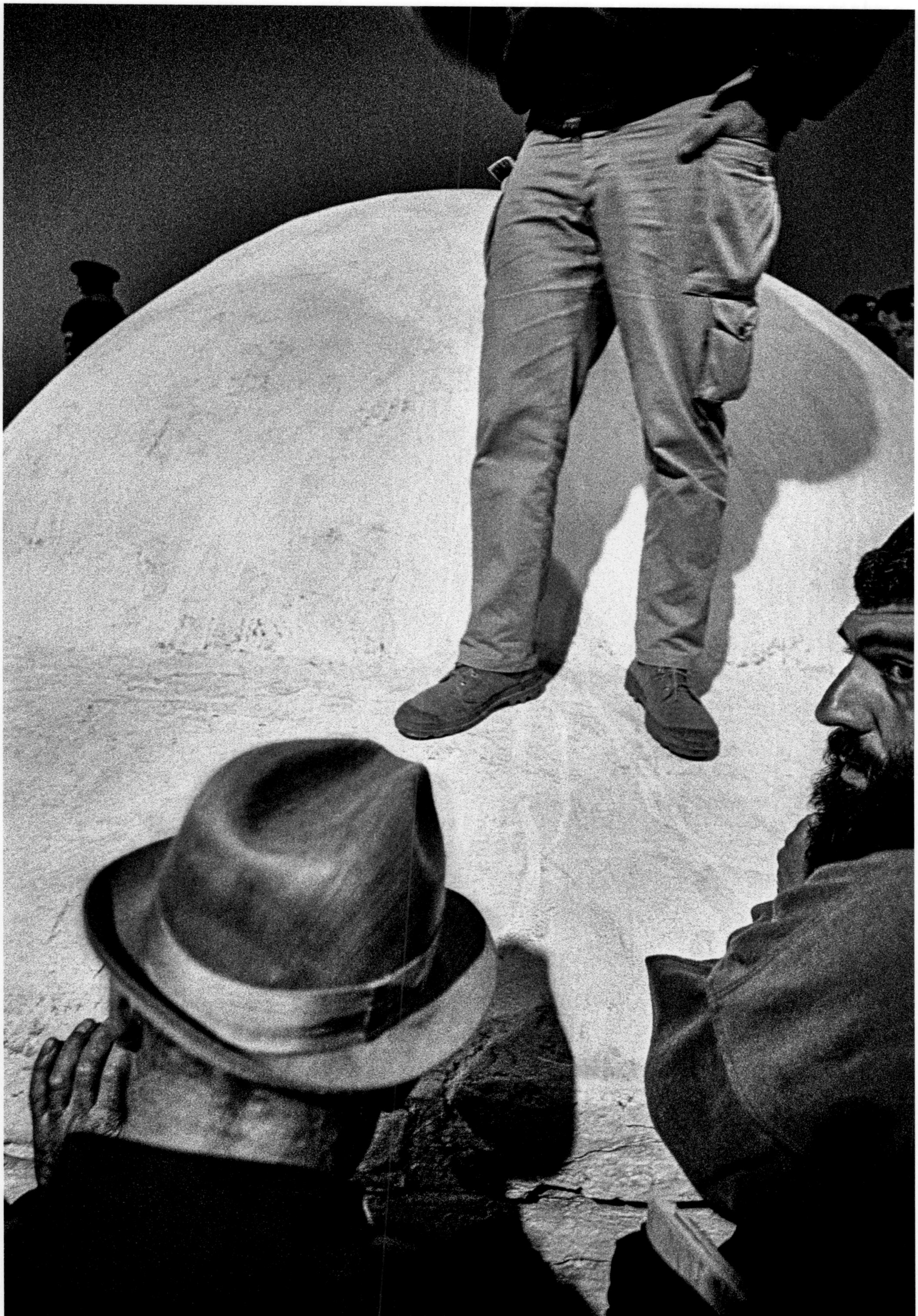

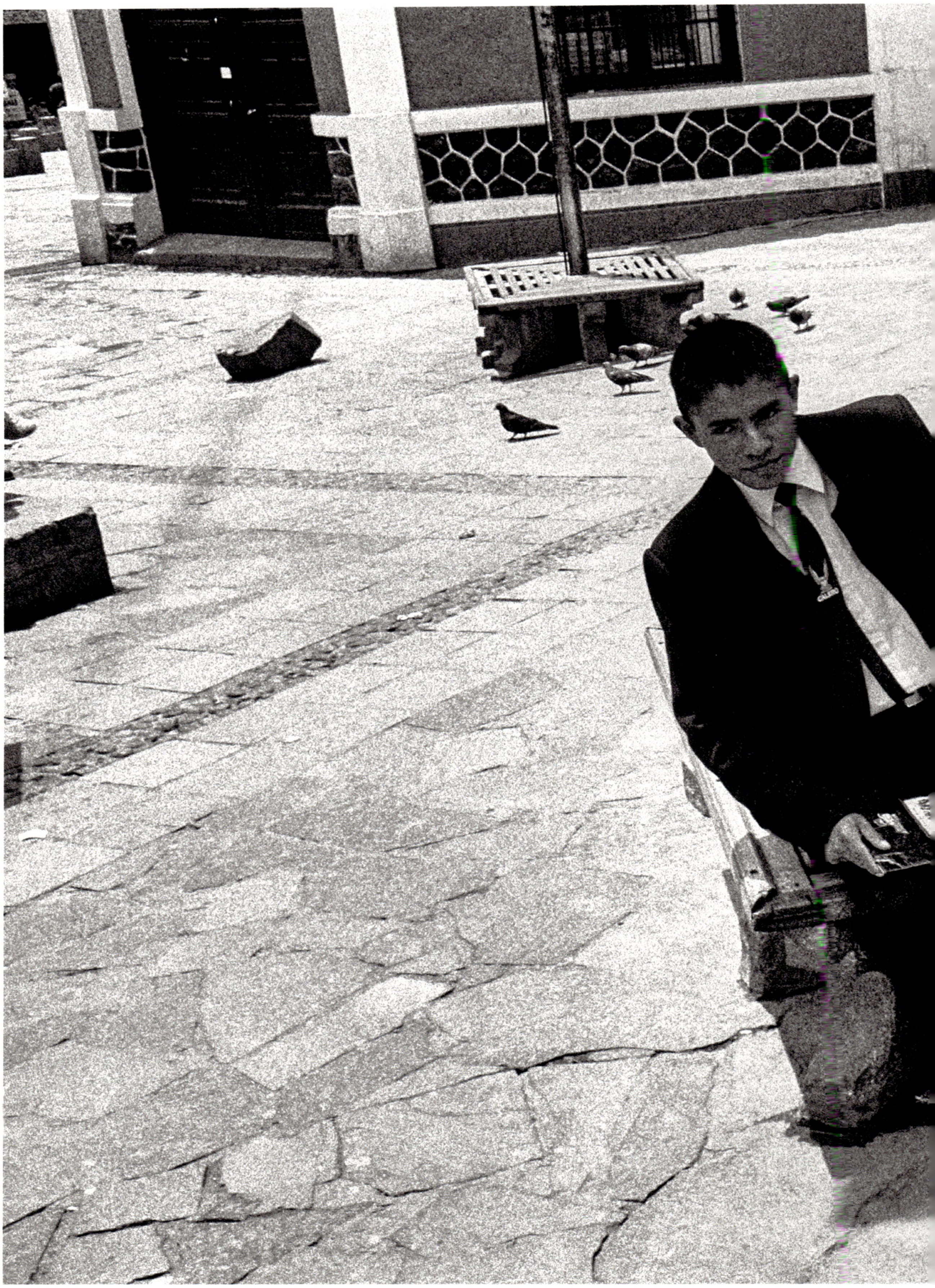

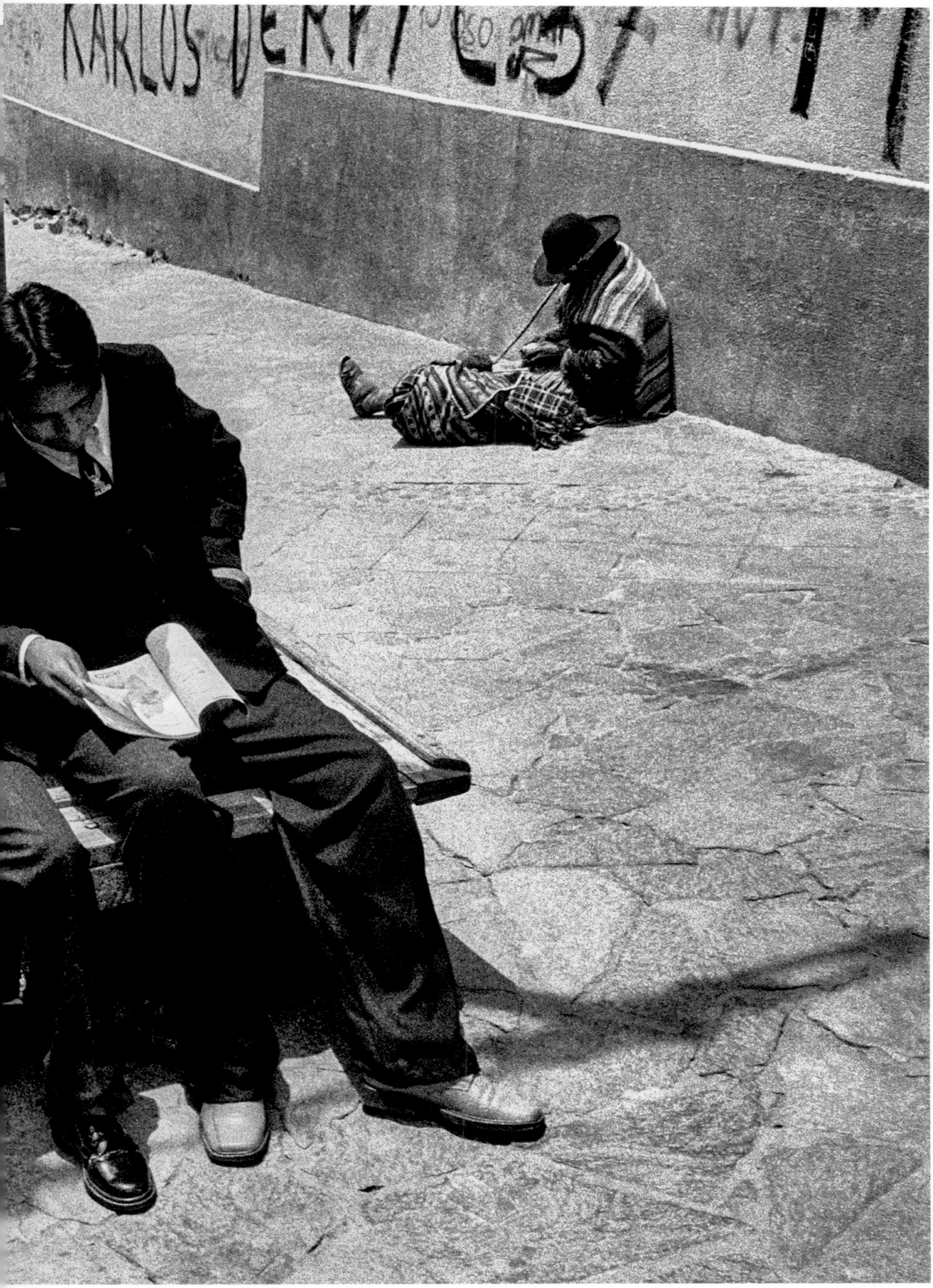
KARLOS

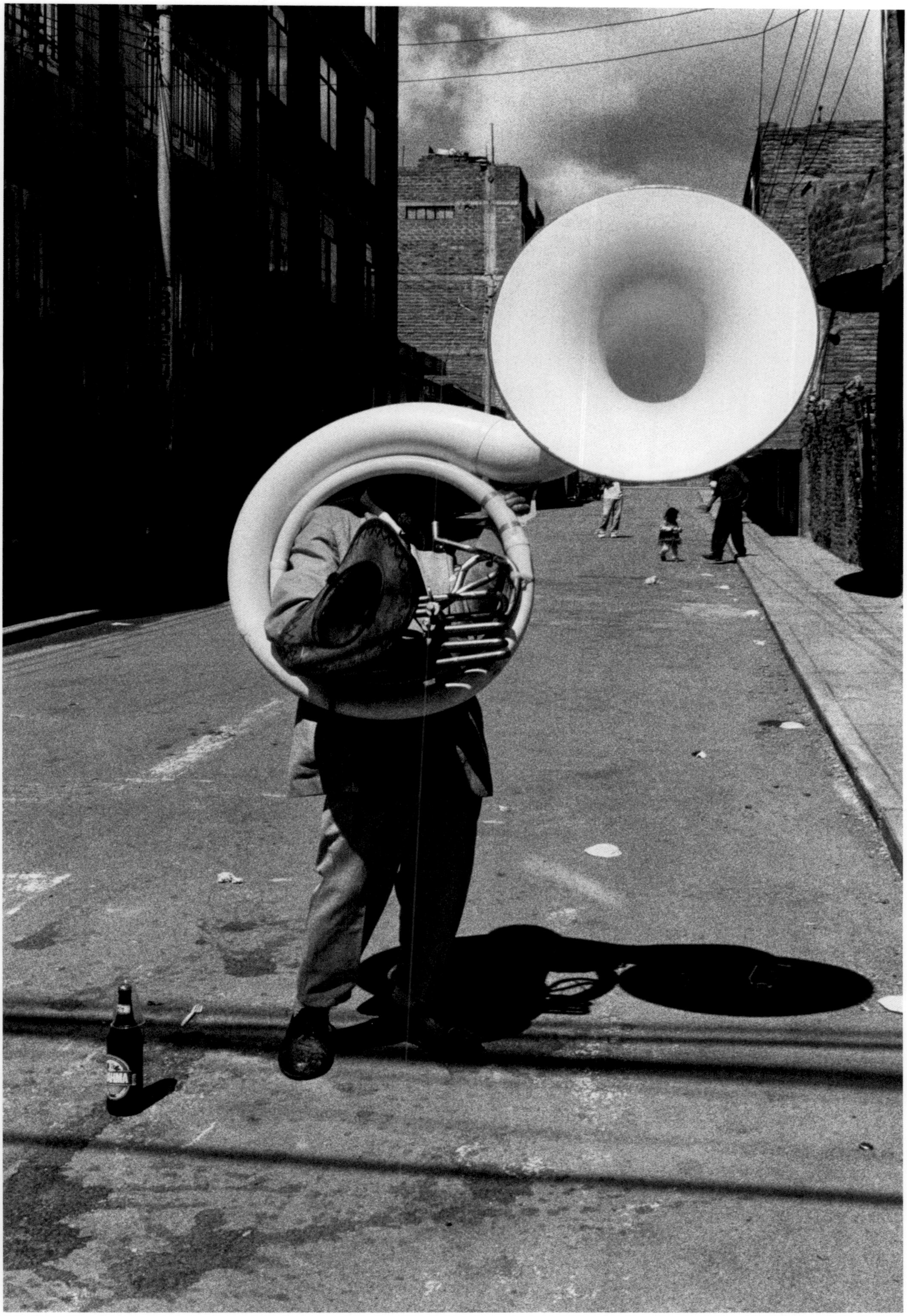

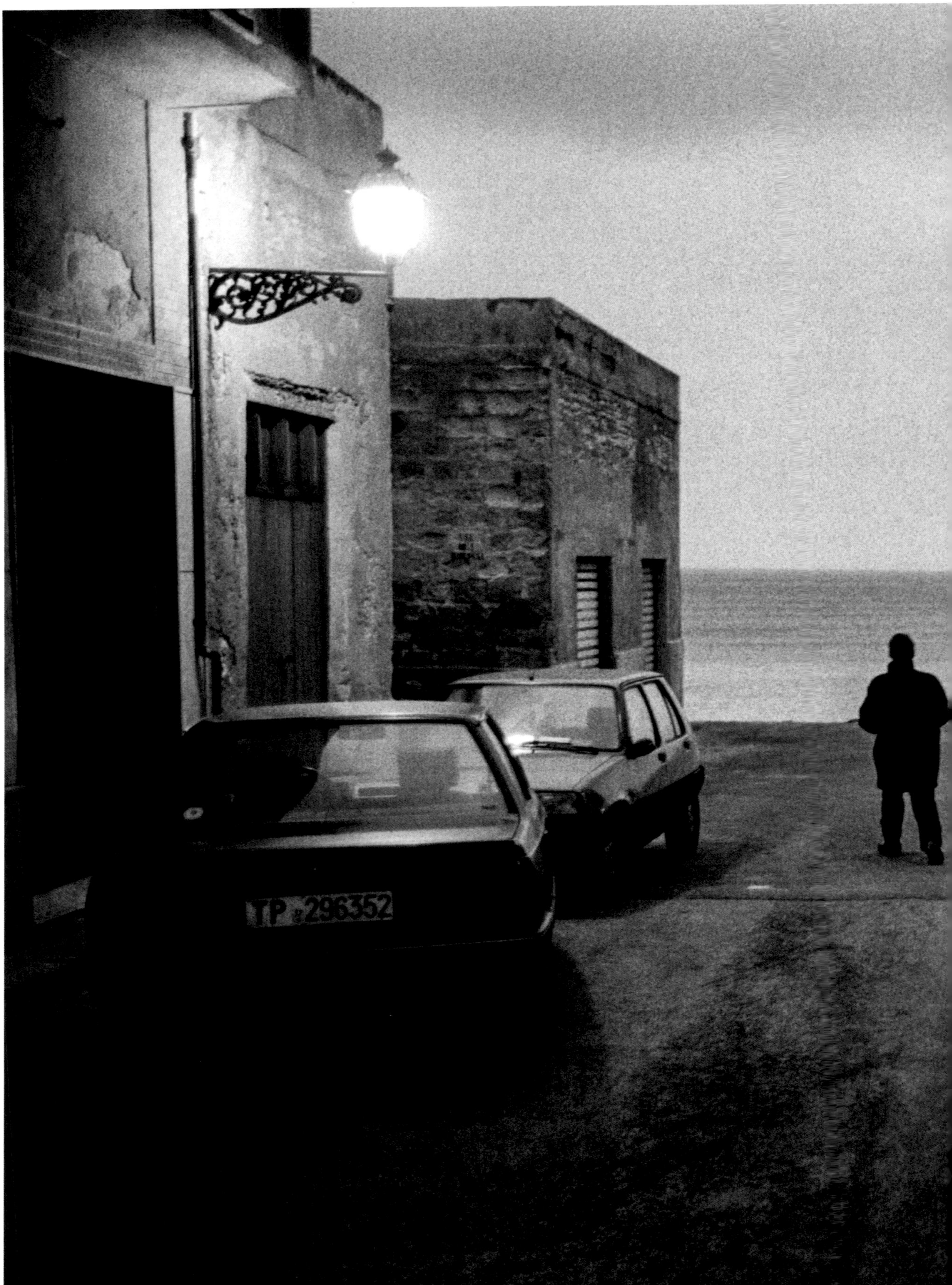
TP 296352

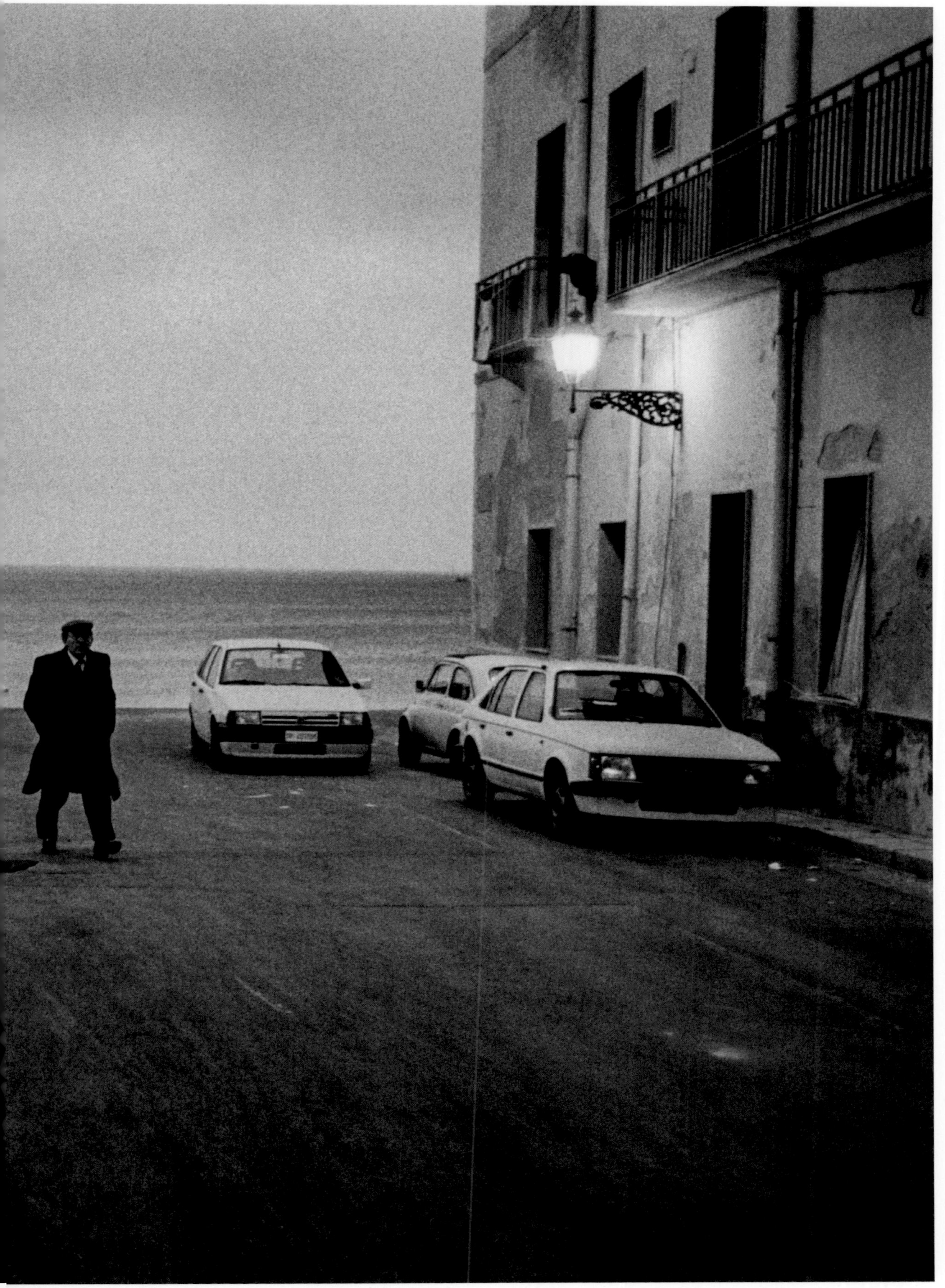

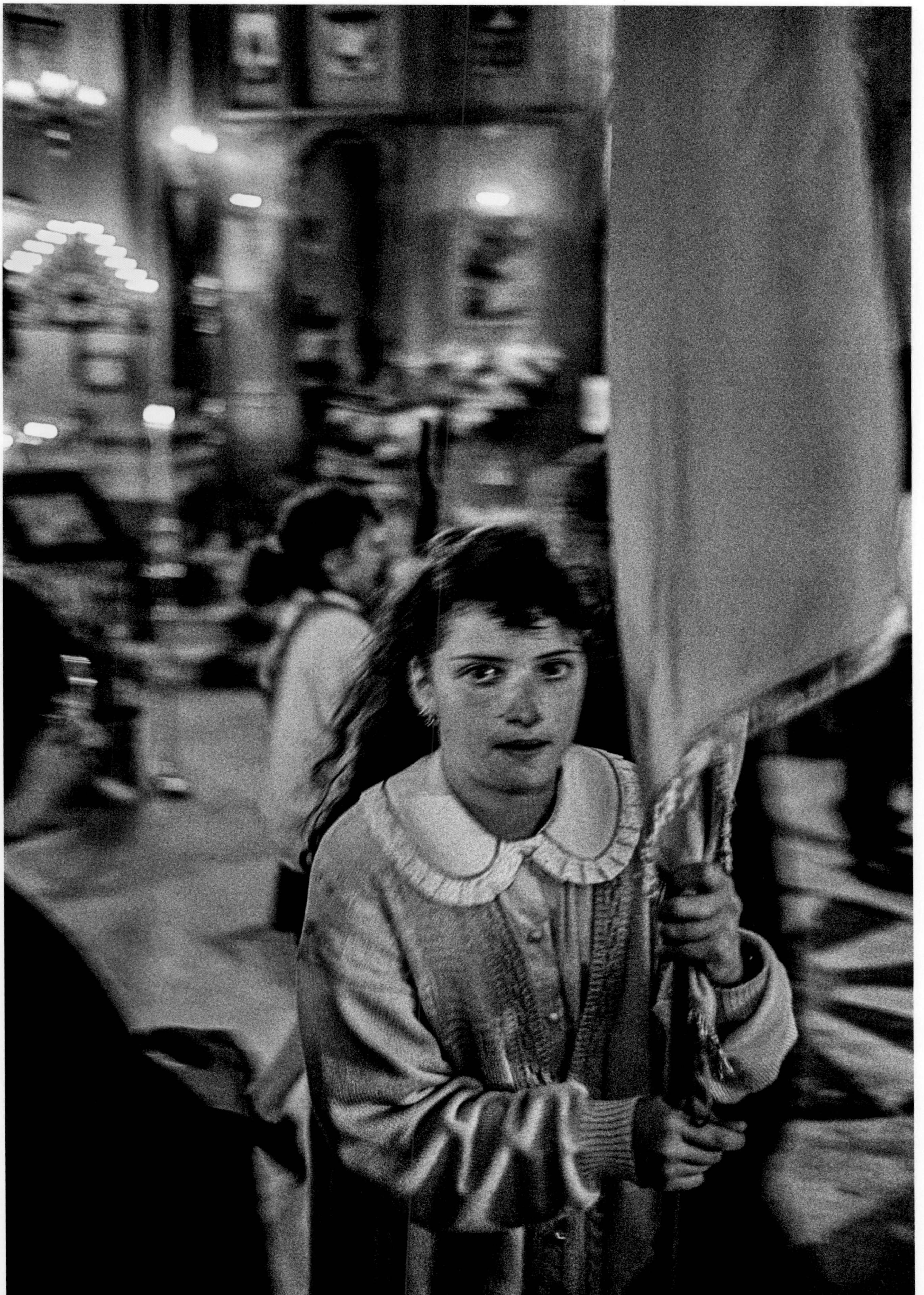

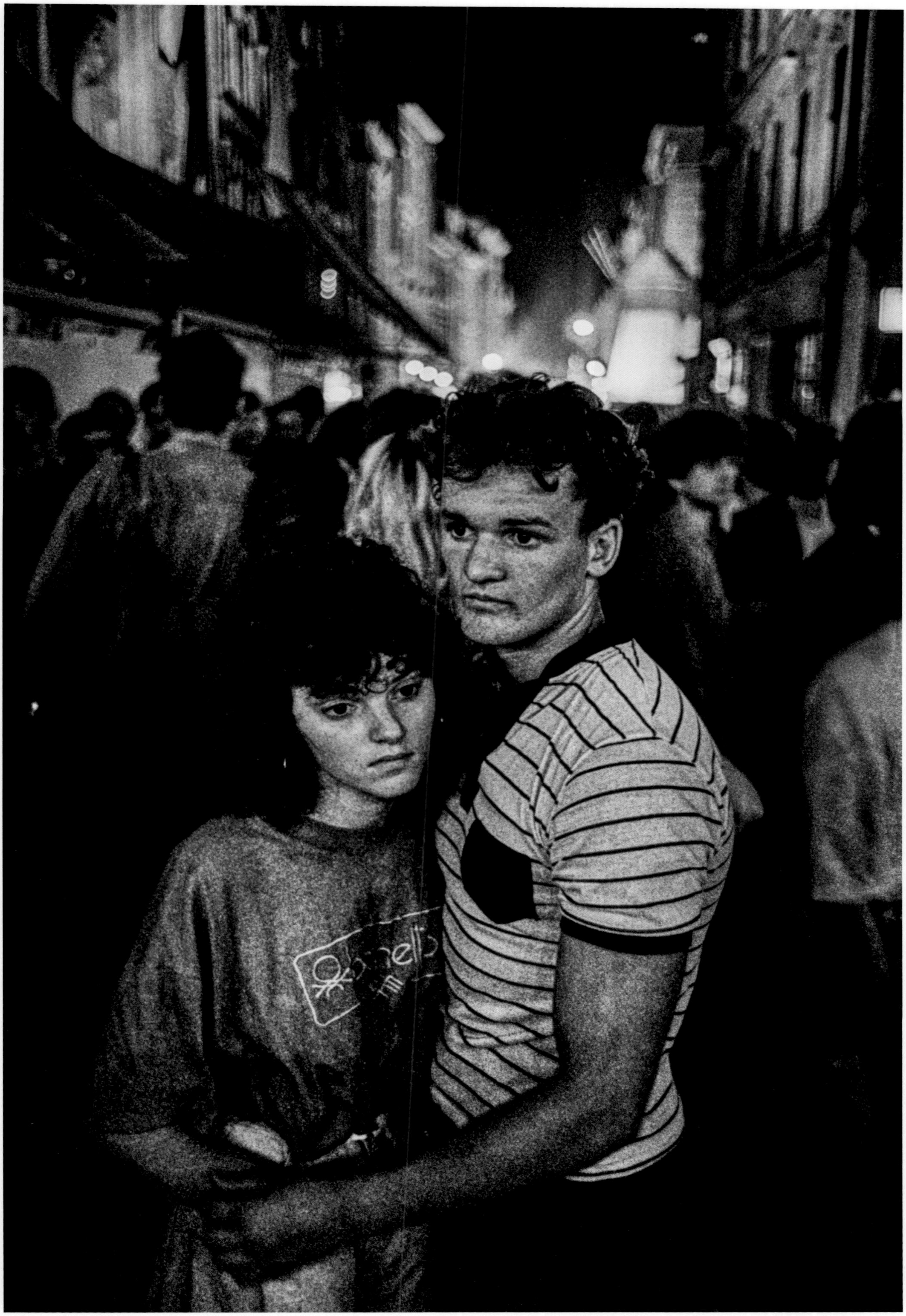

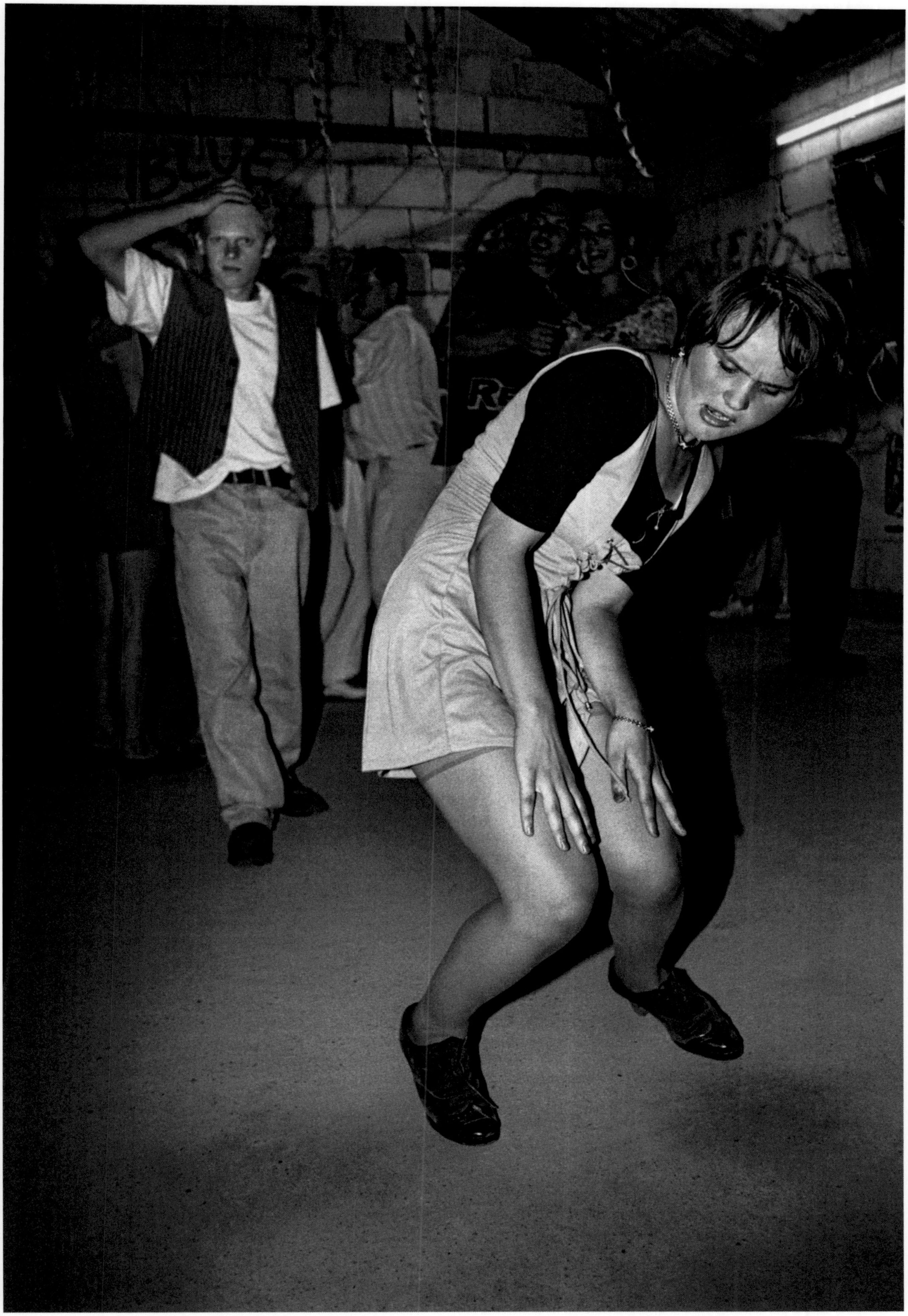

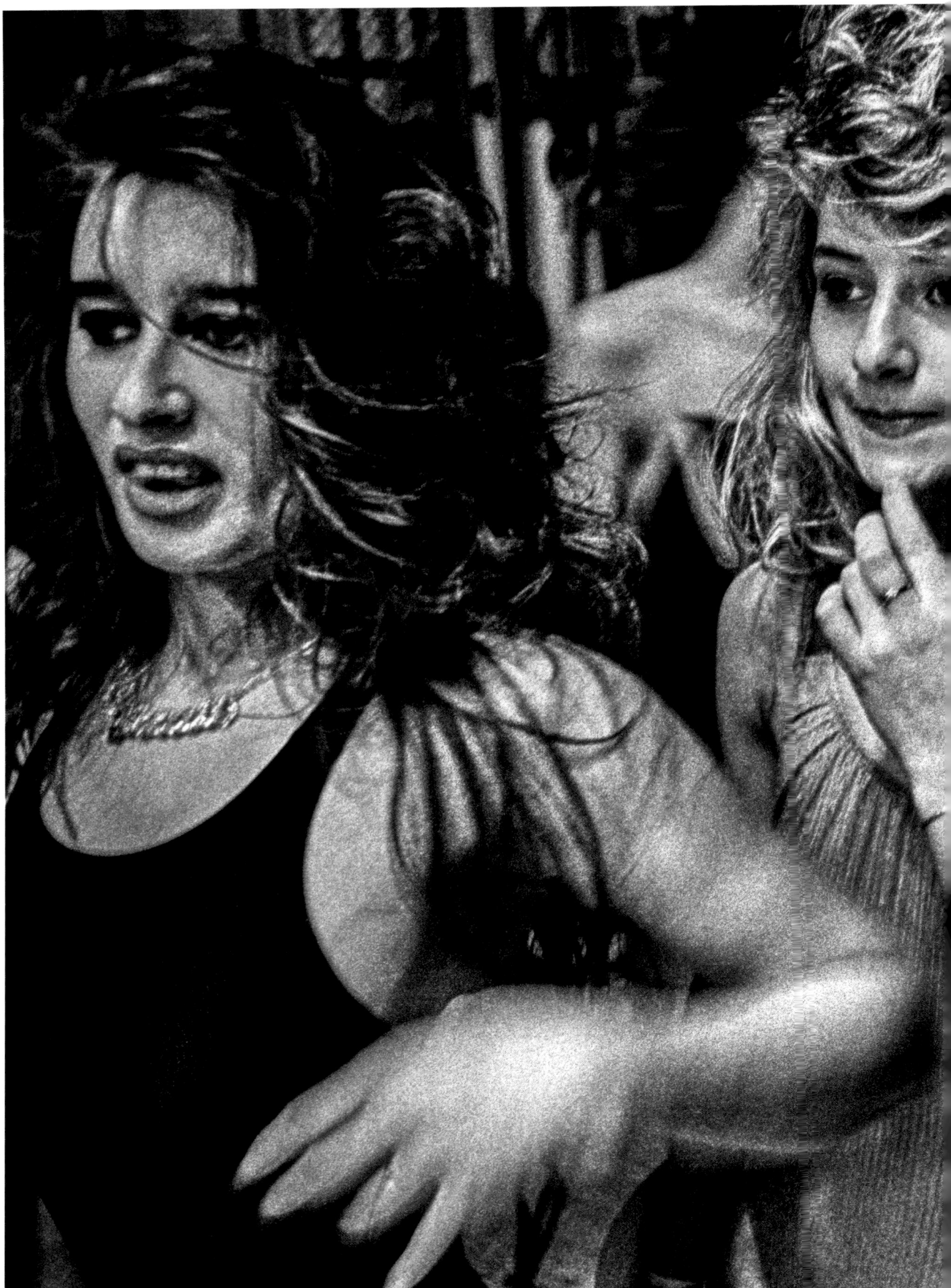

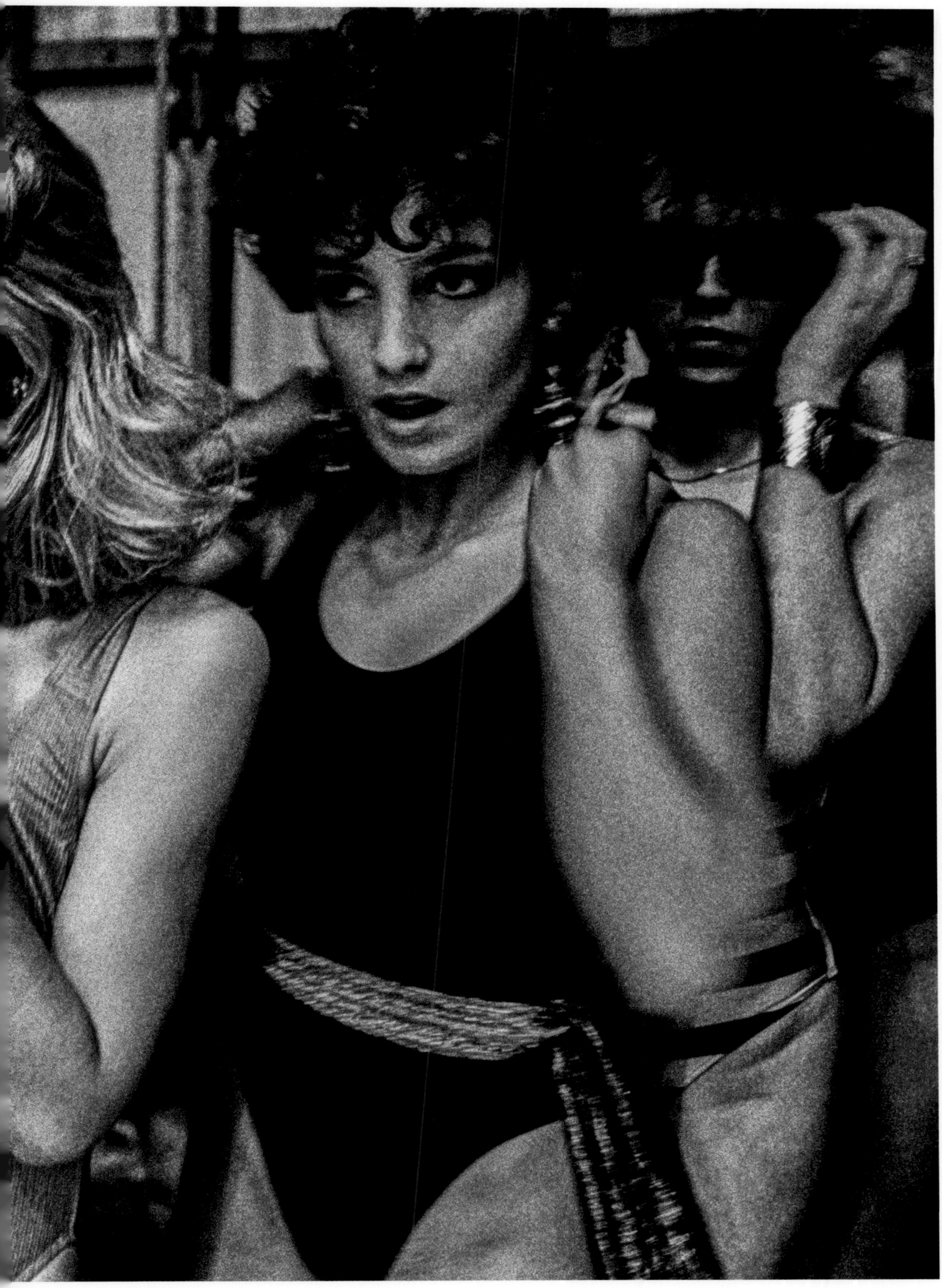

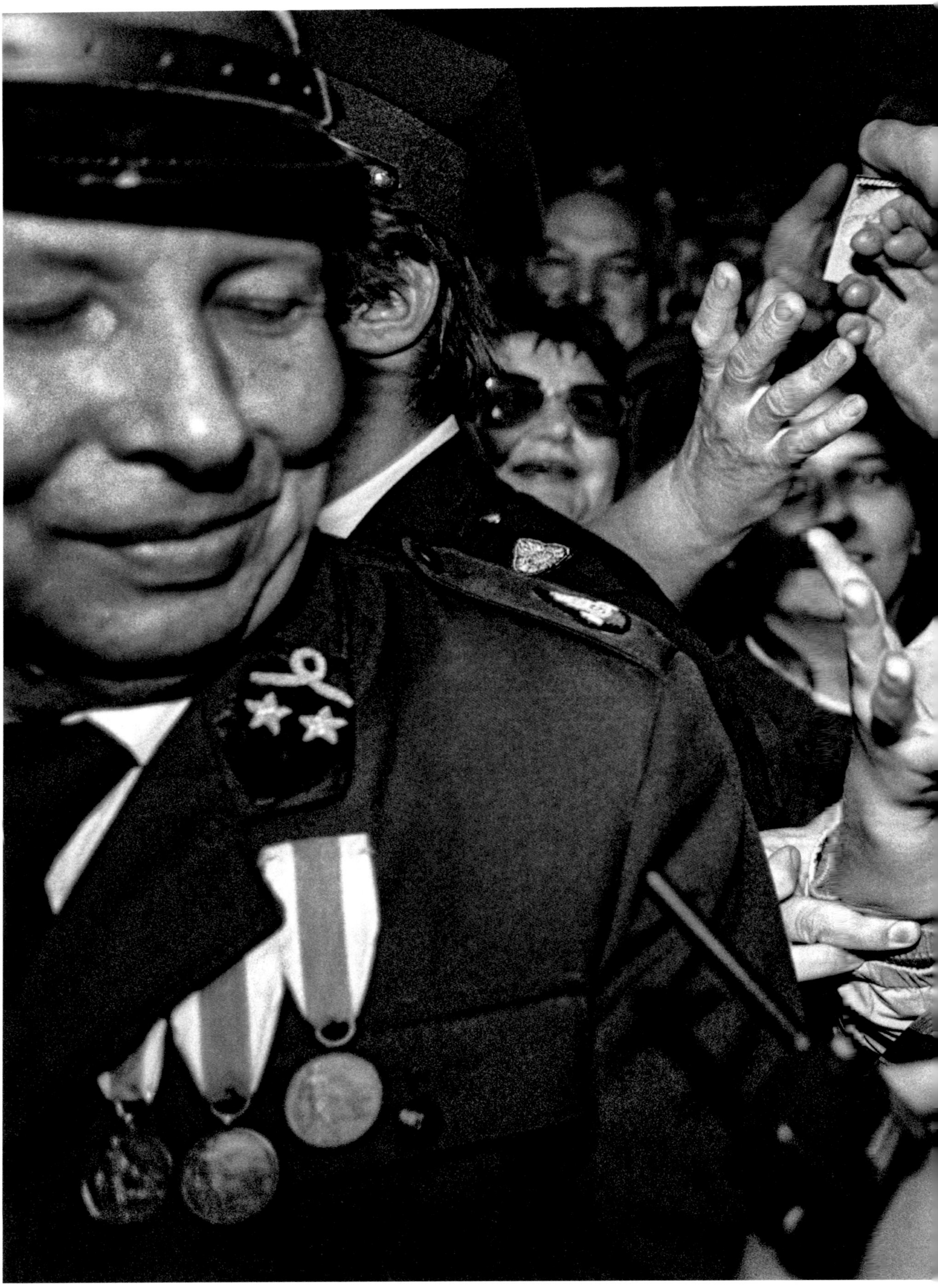

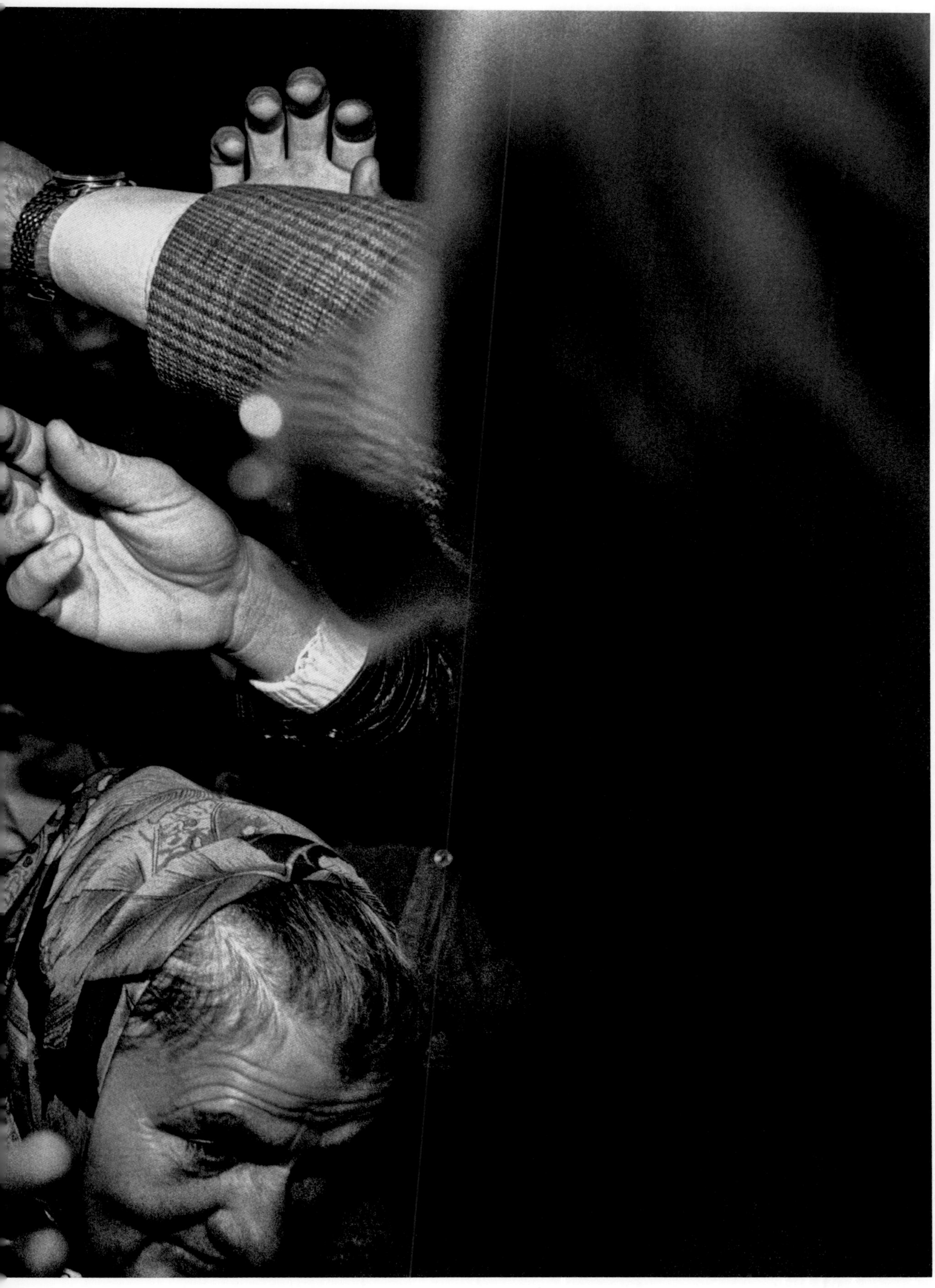

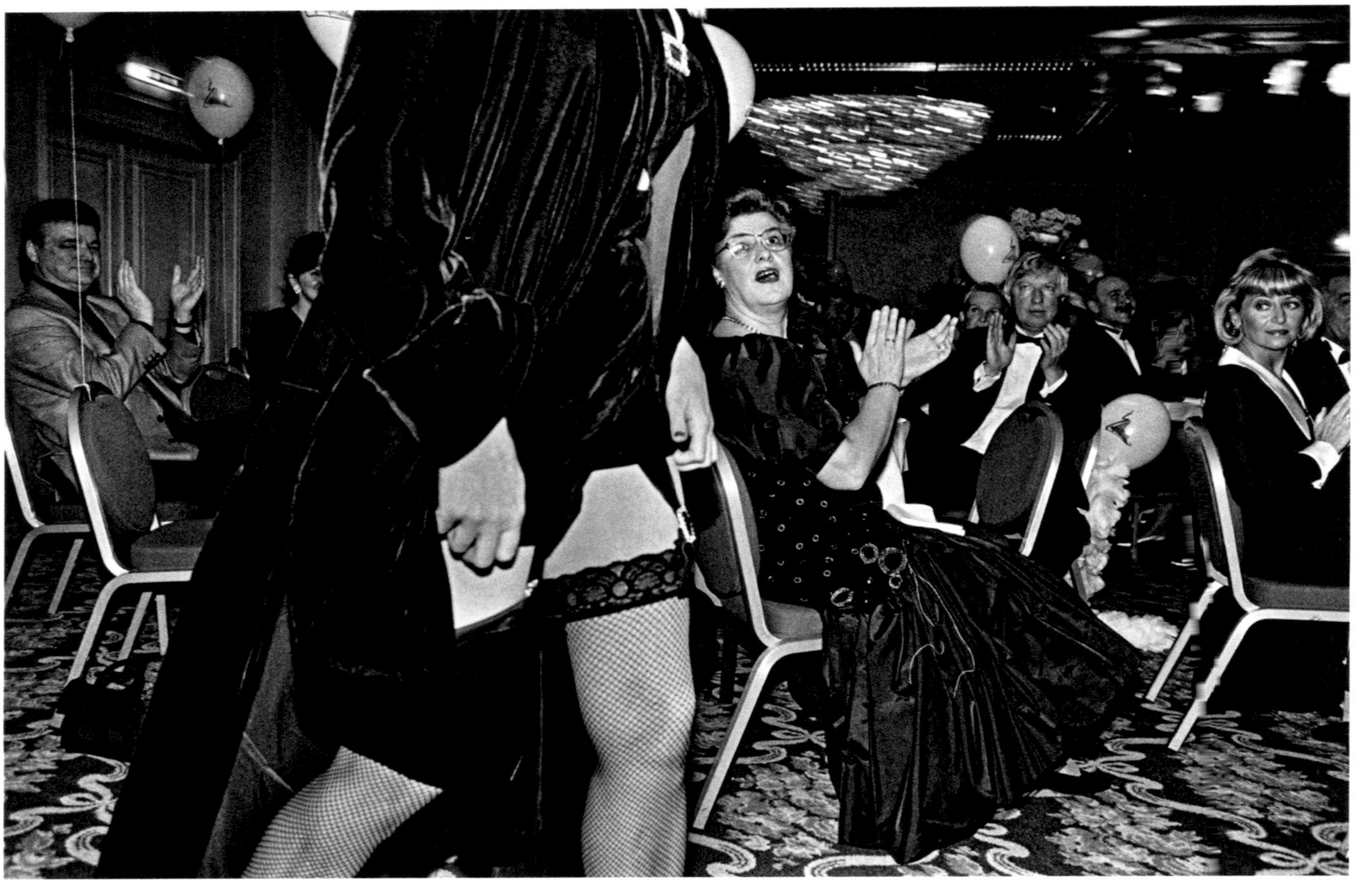

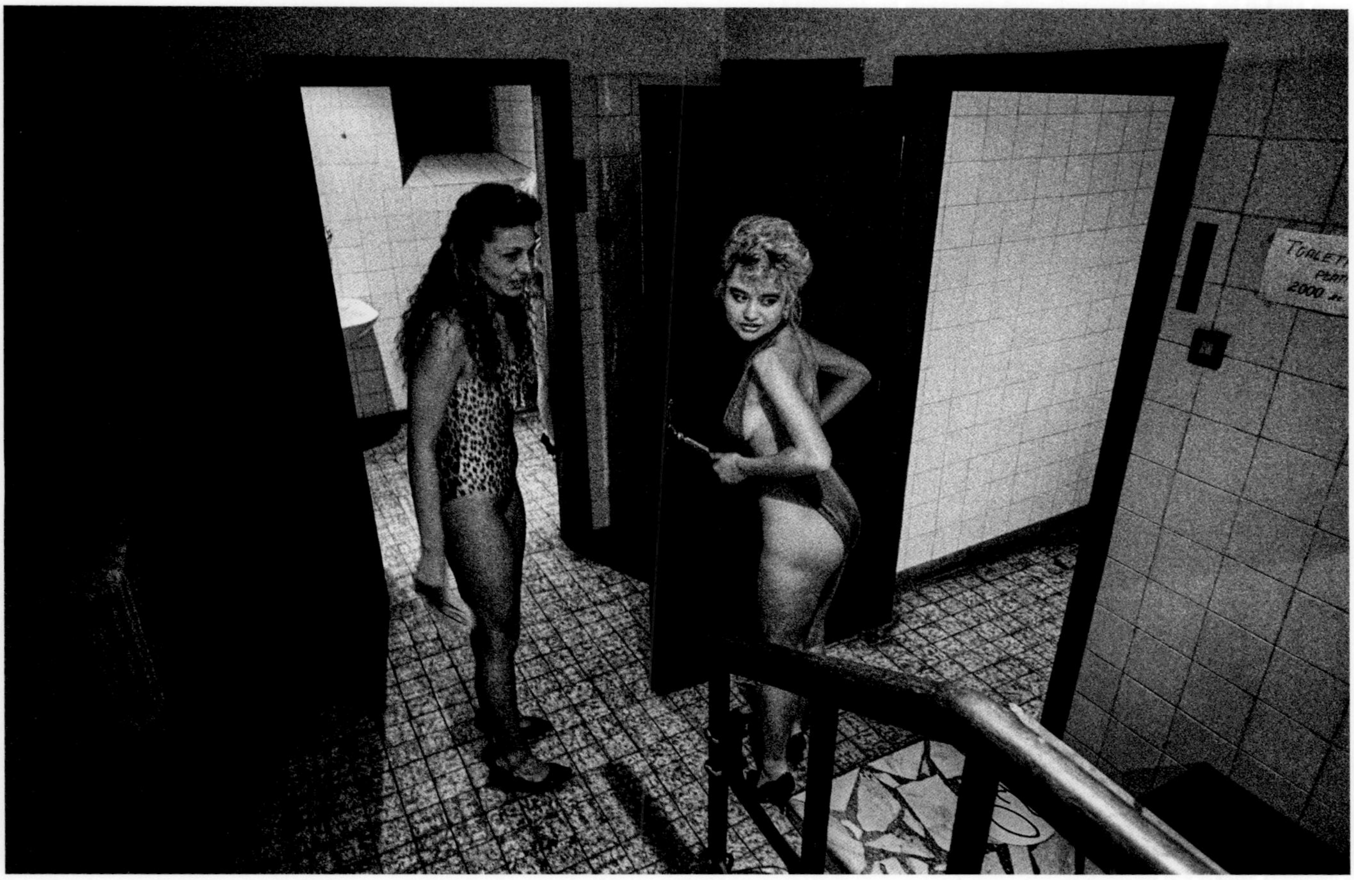

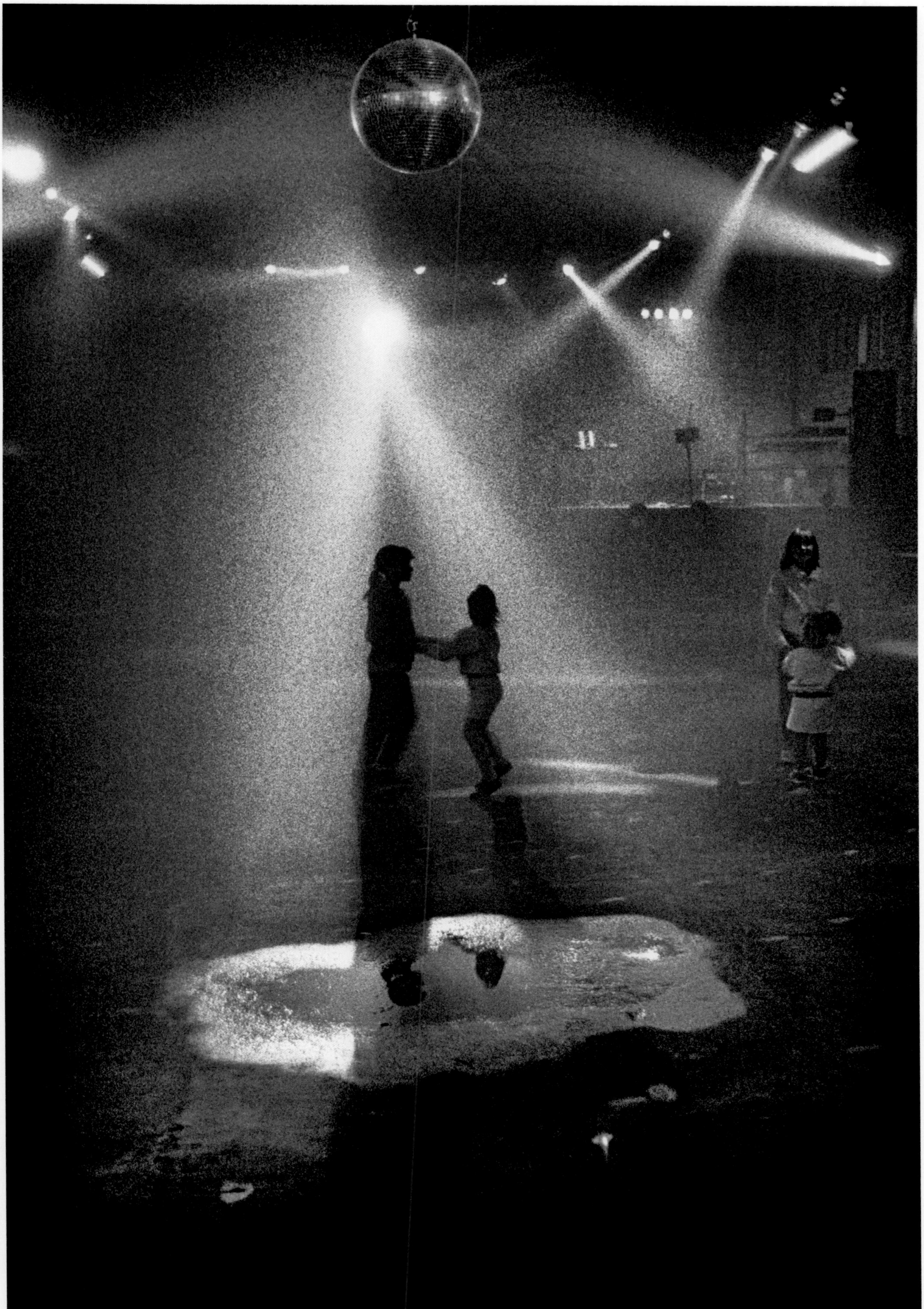

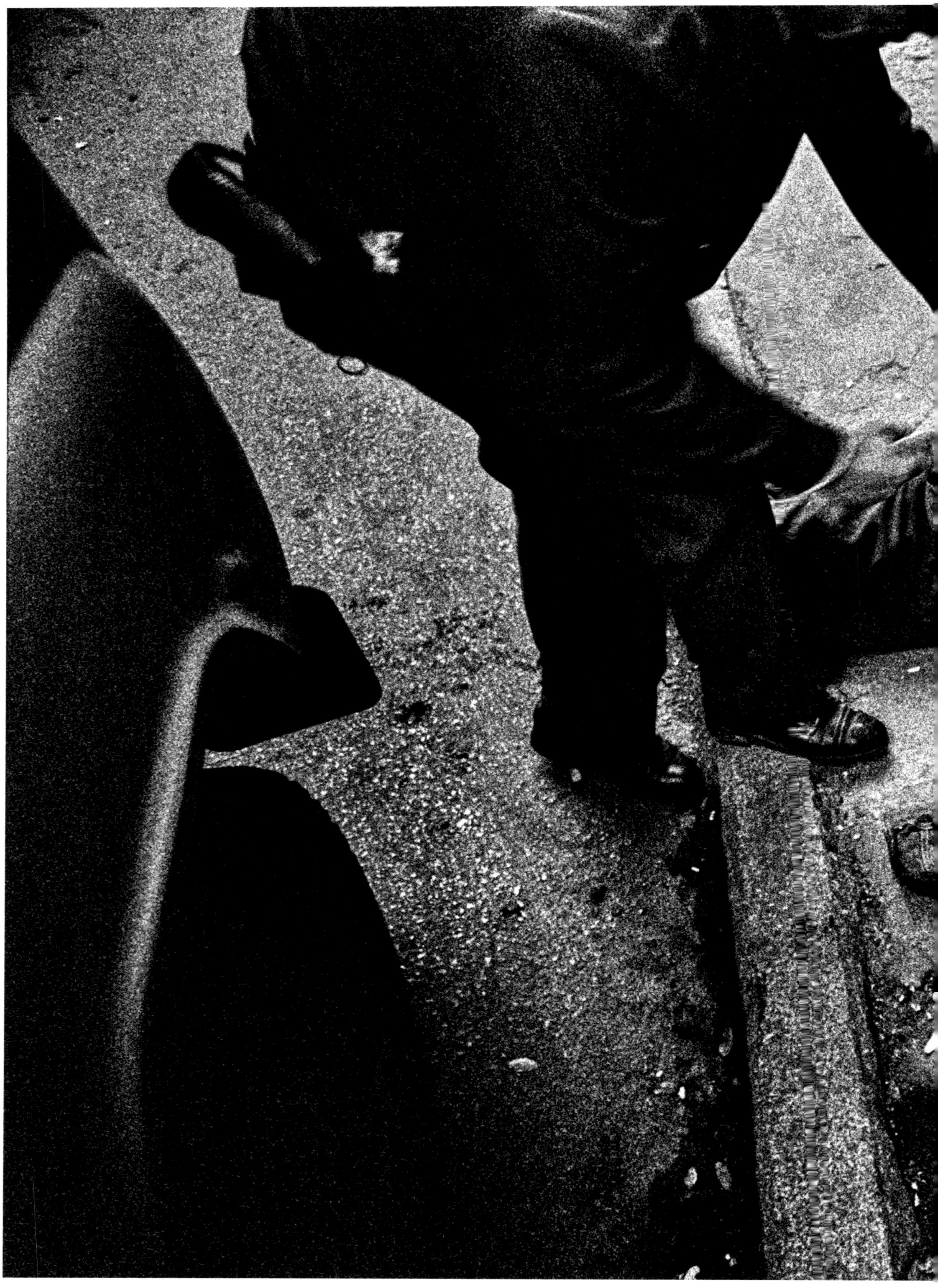

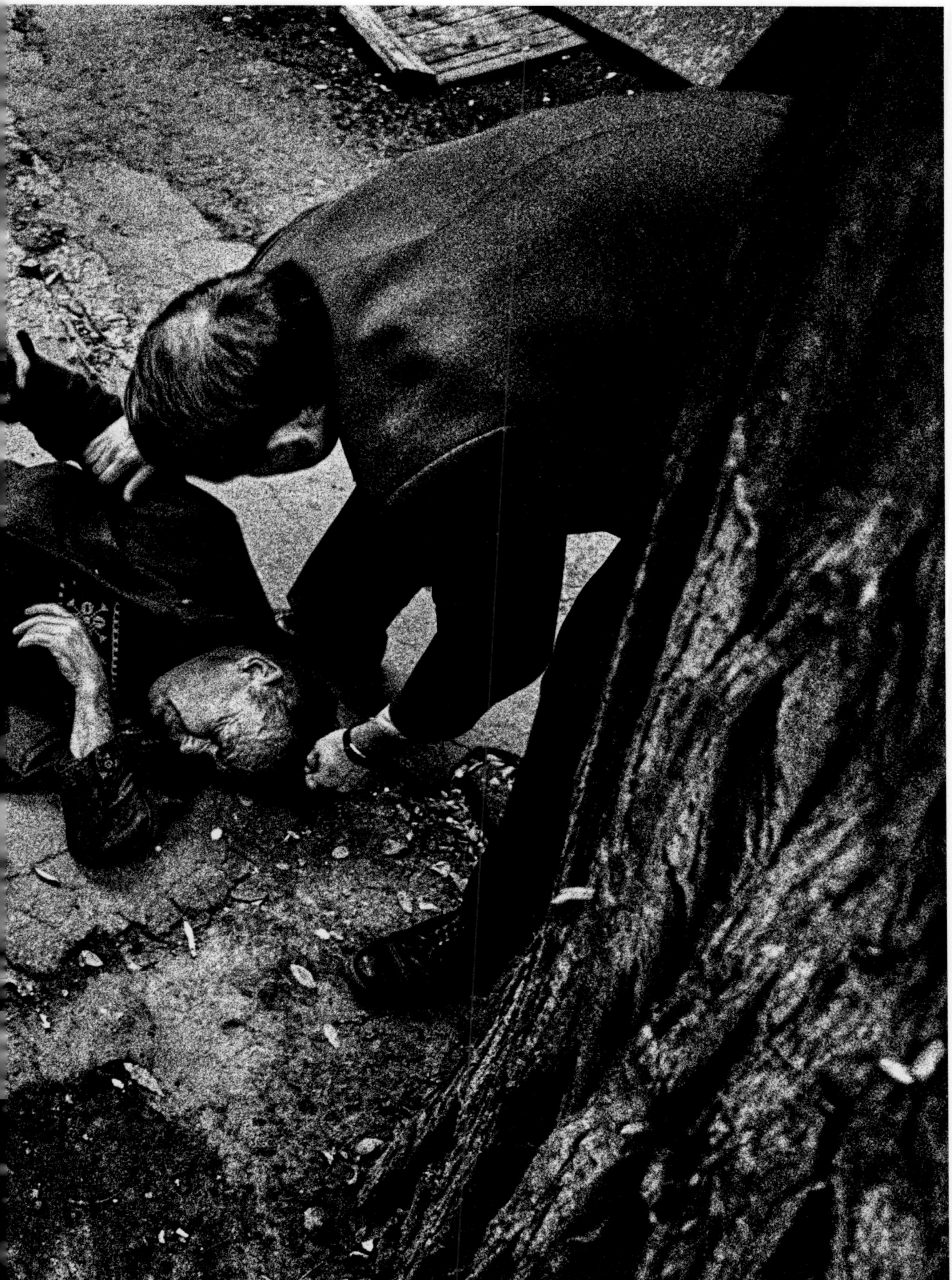

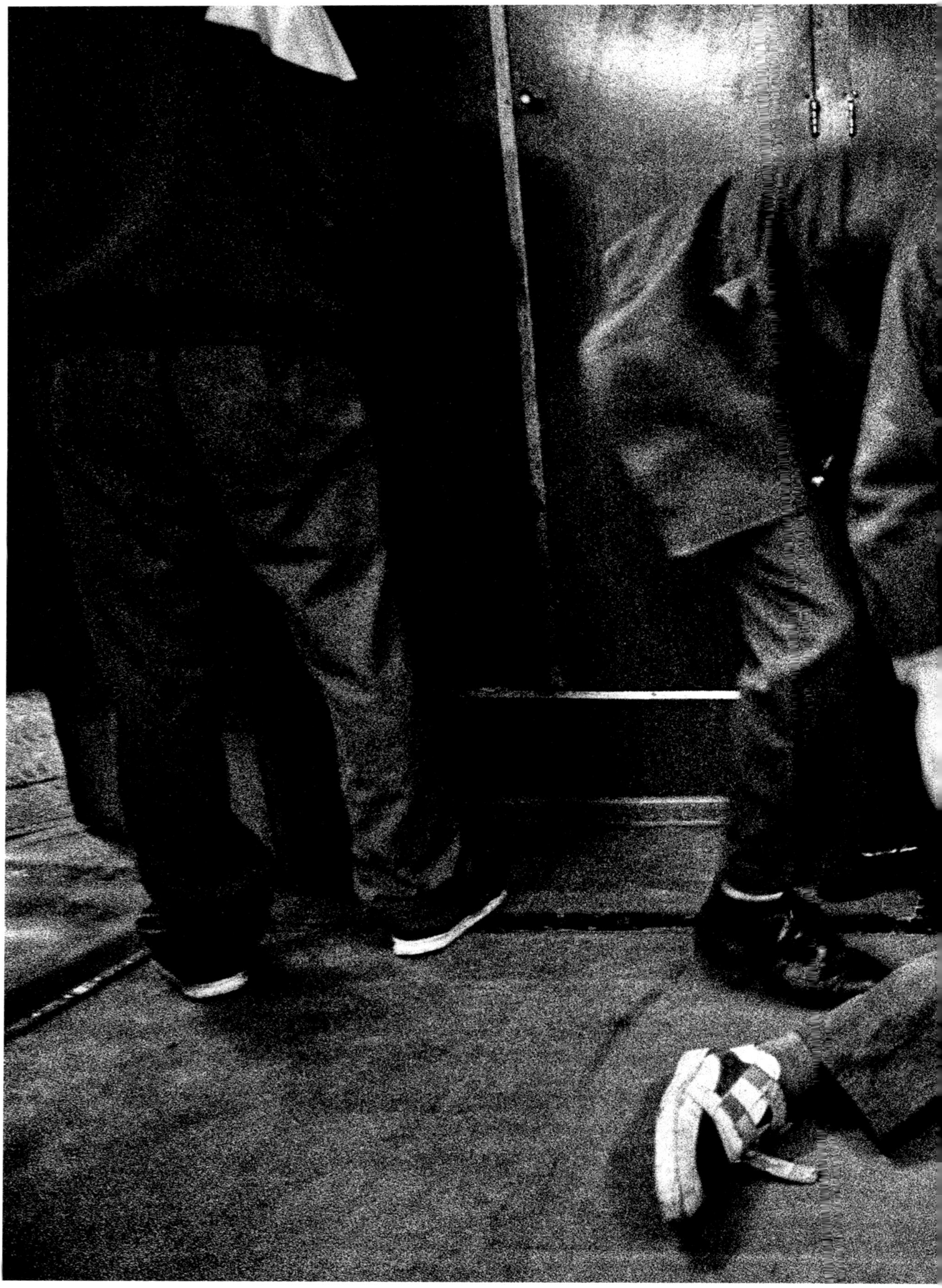

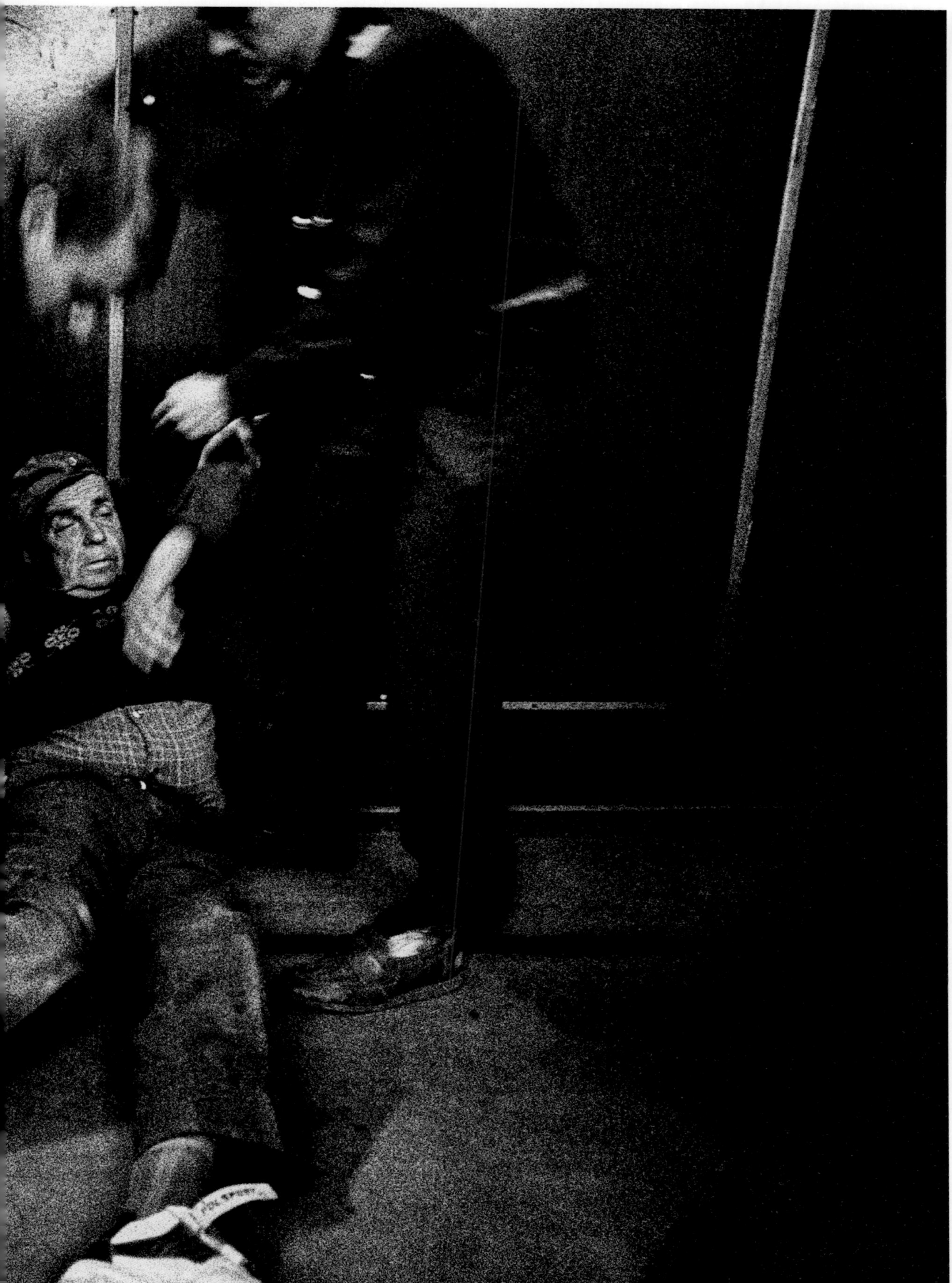

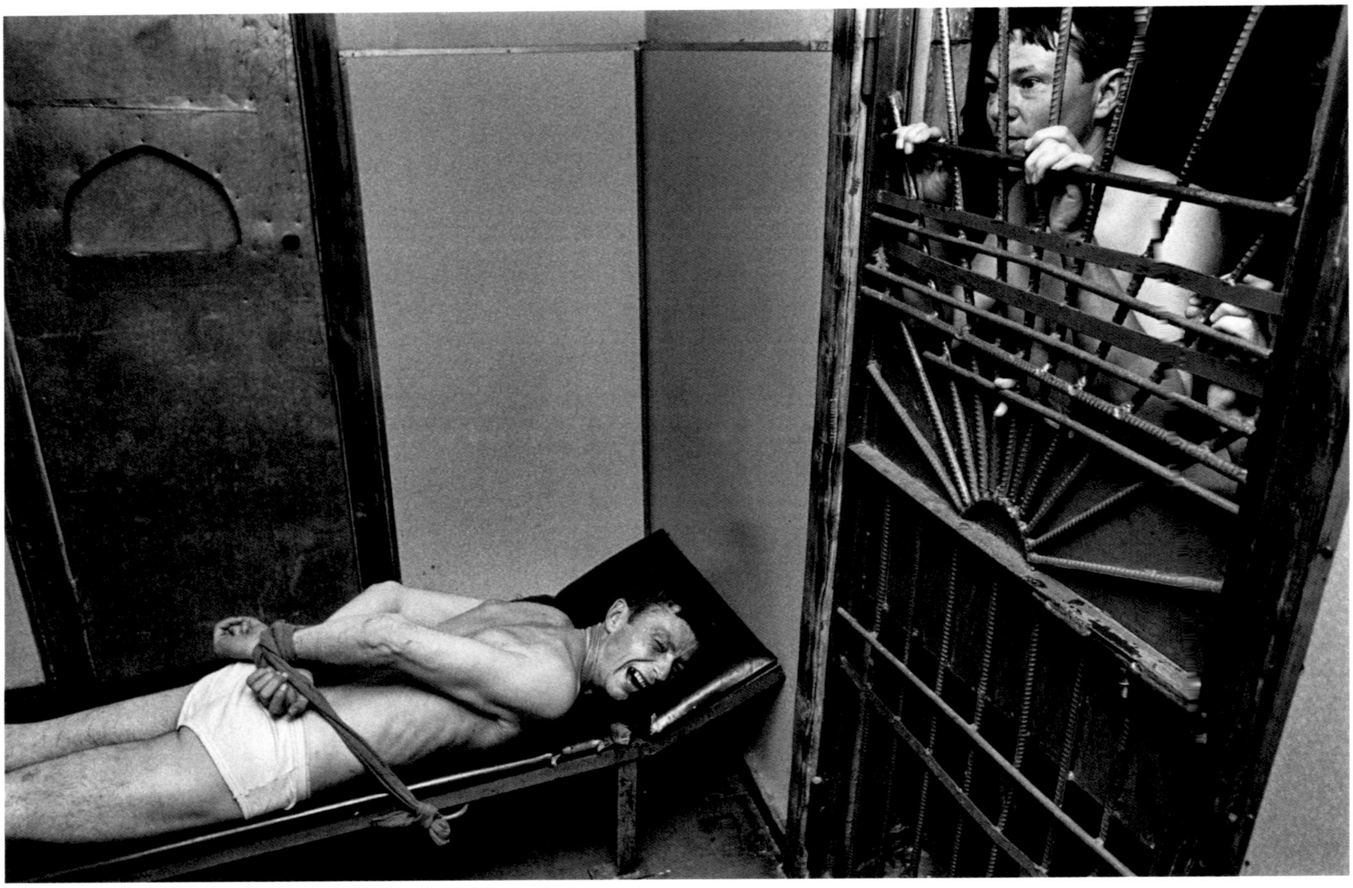

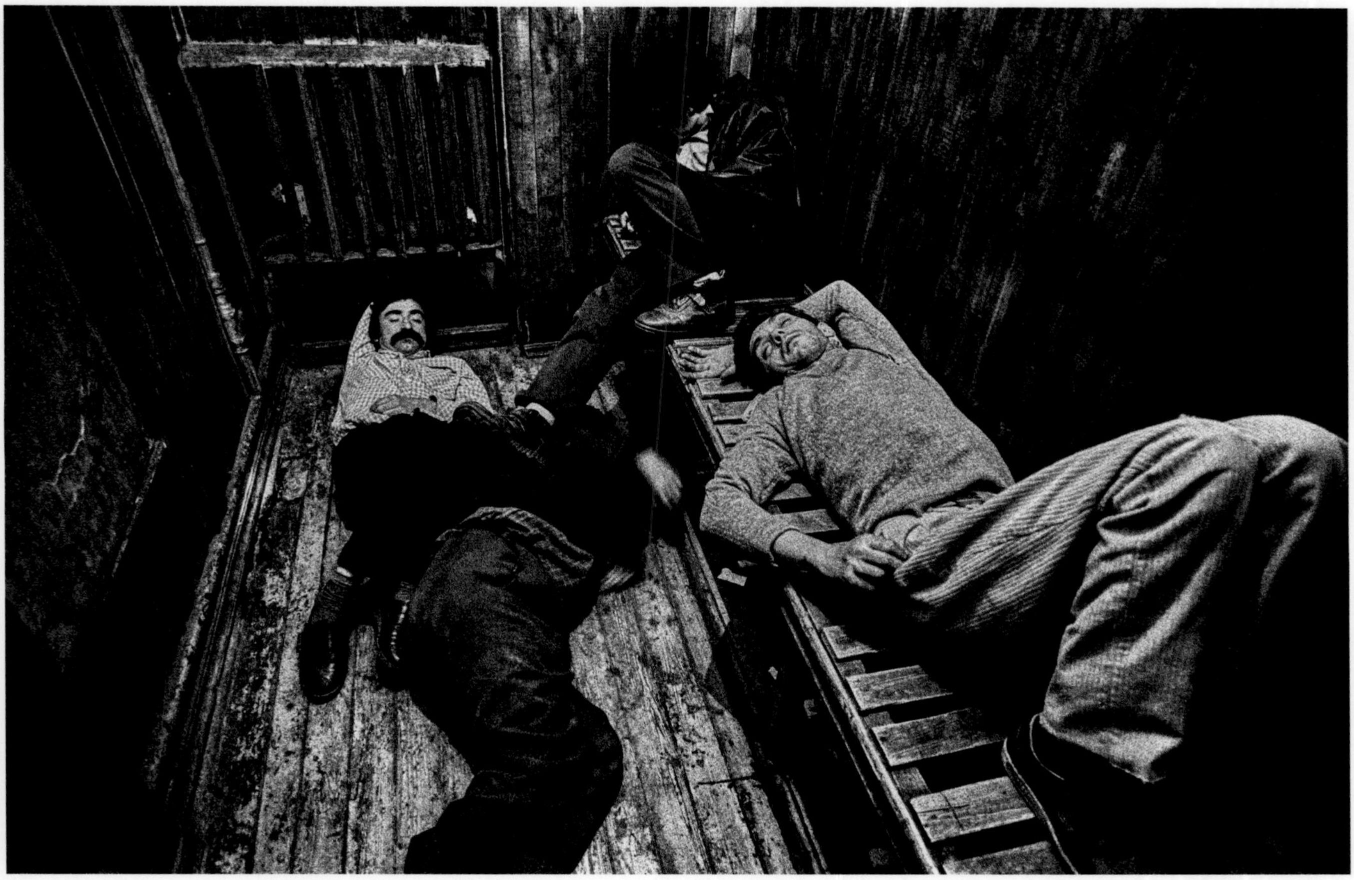

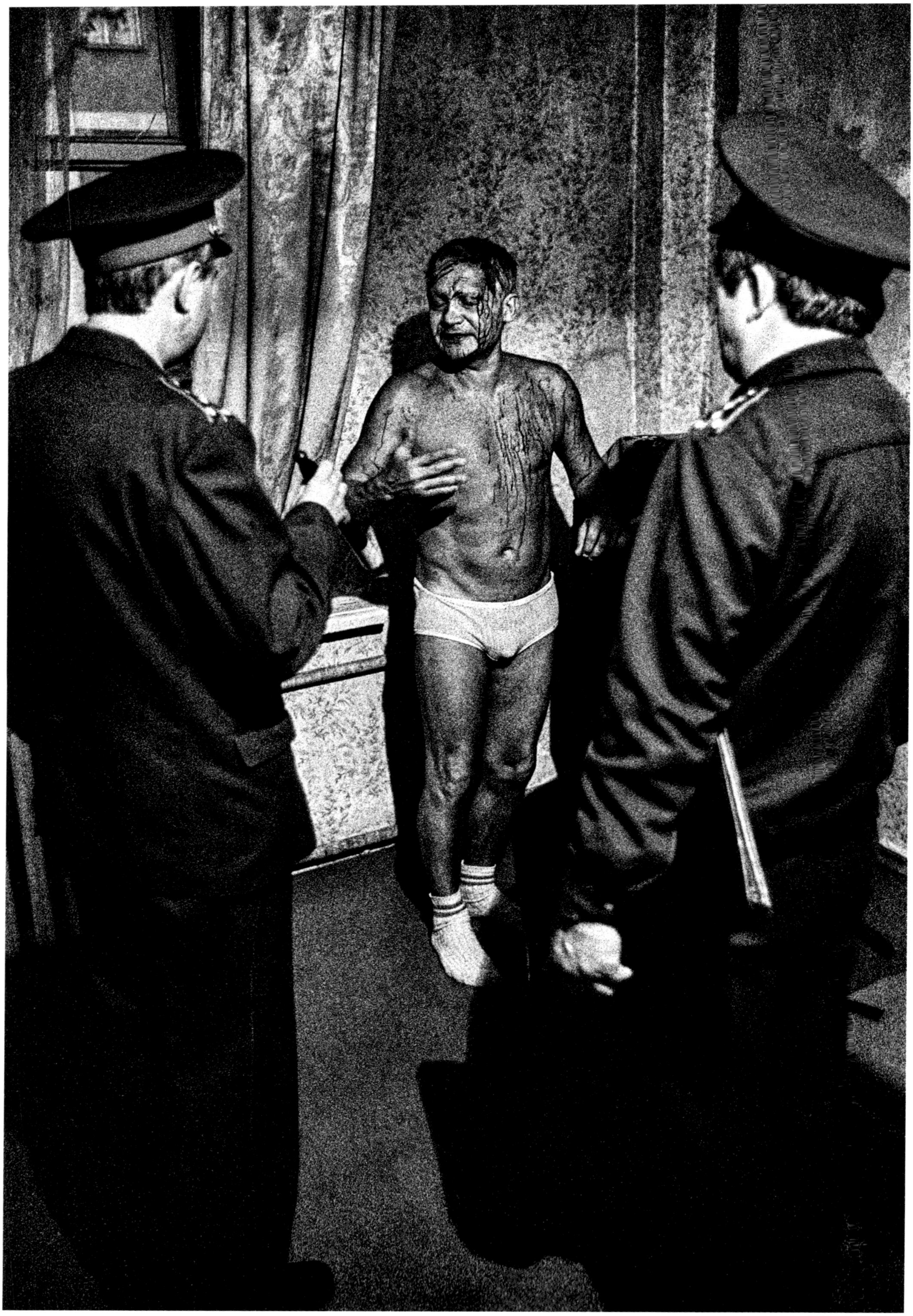

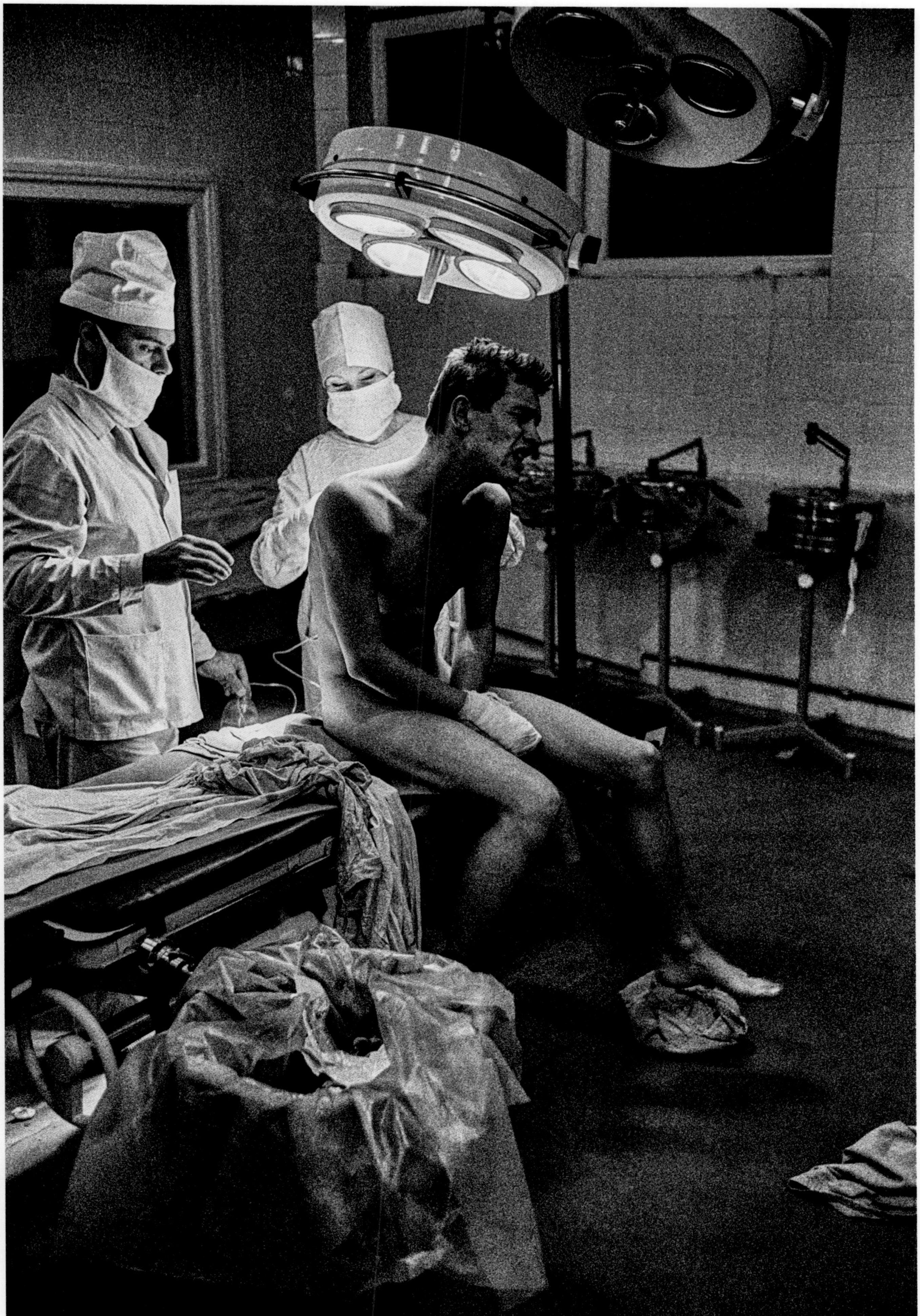

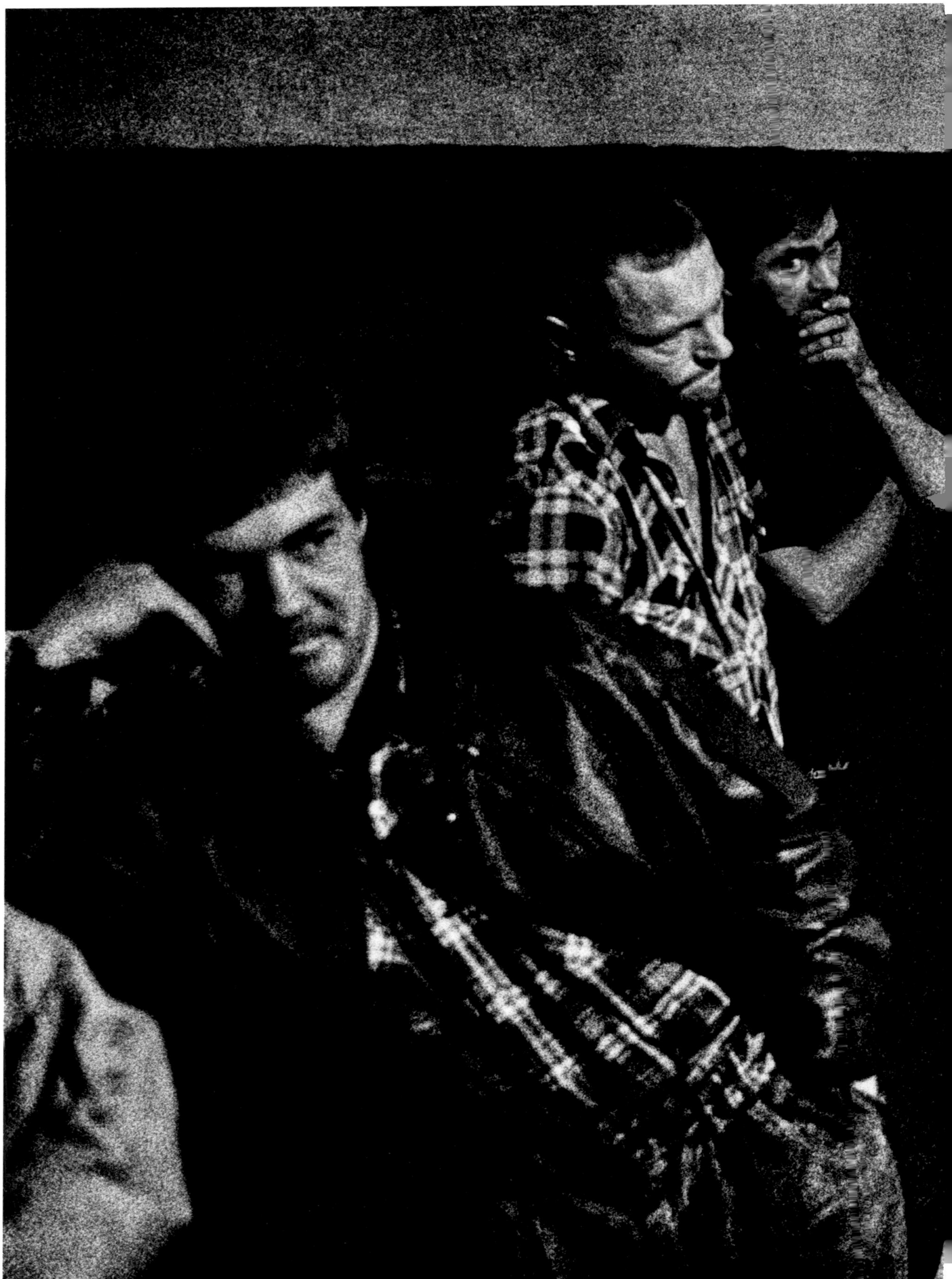

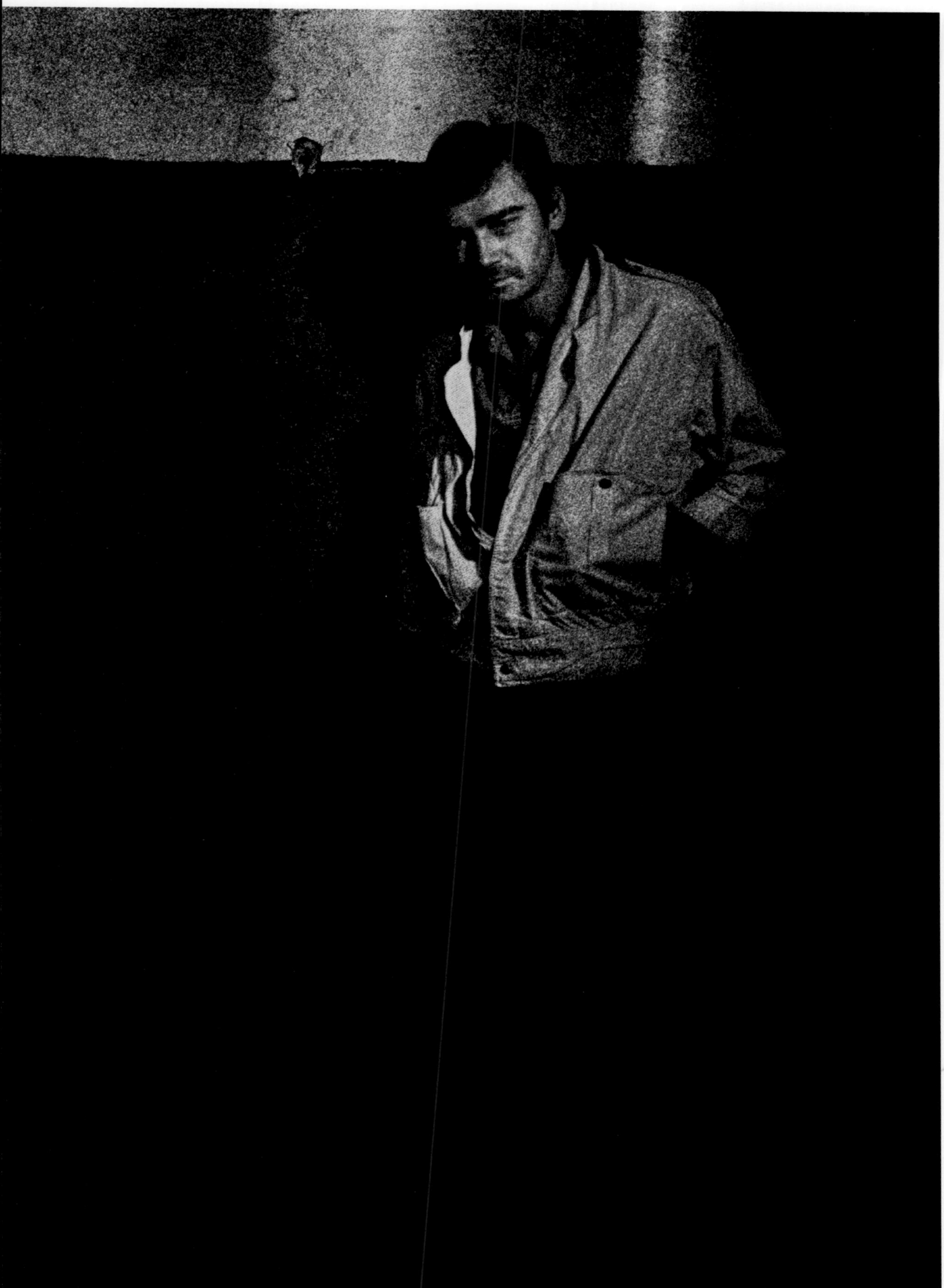

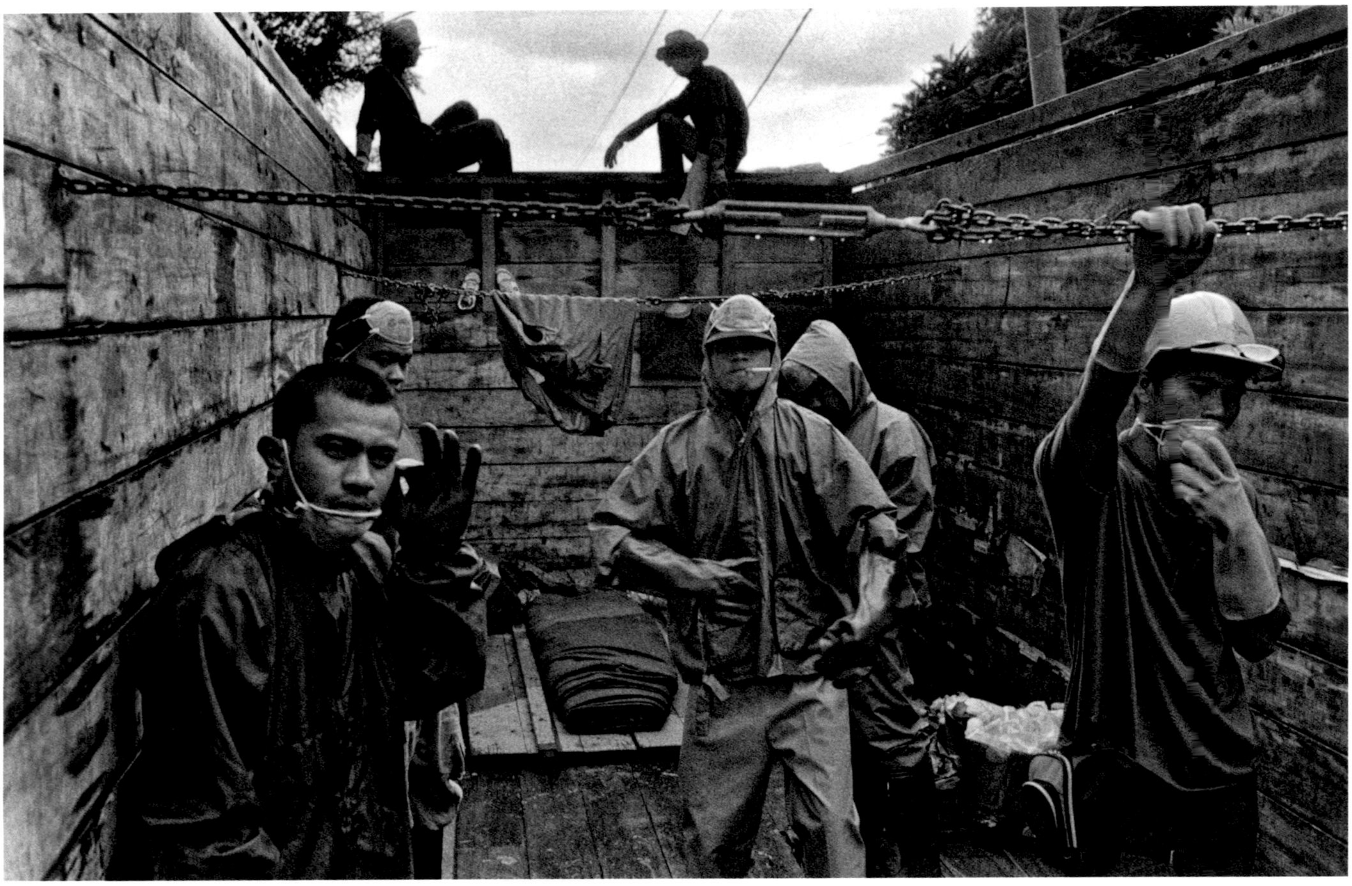

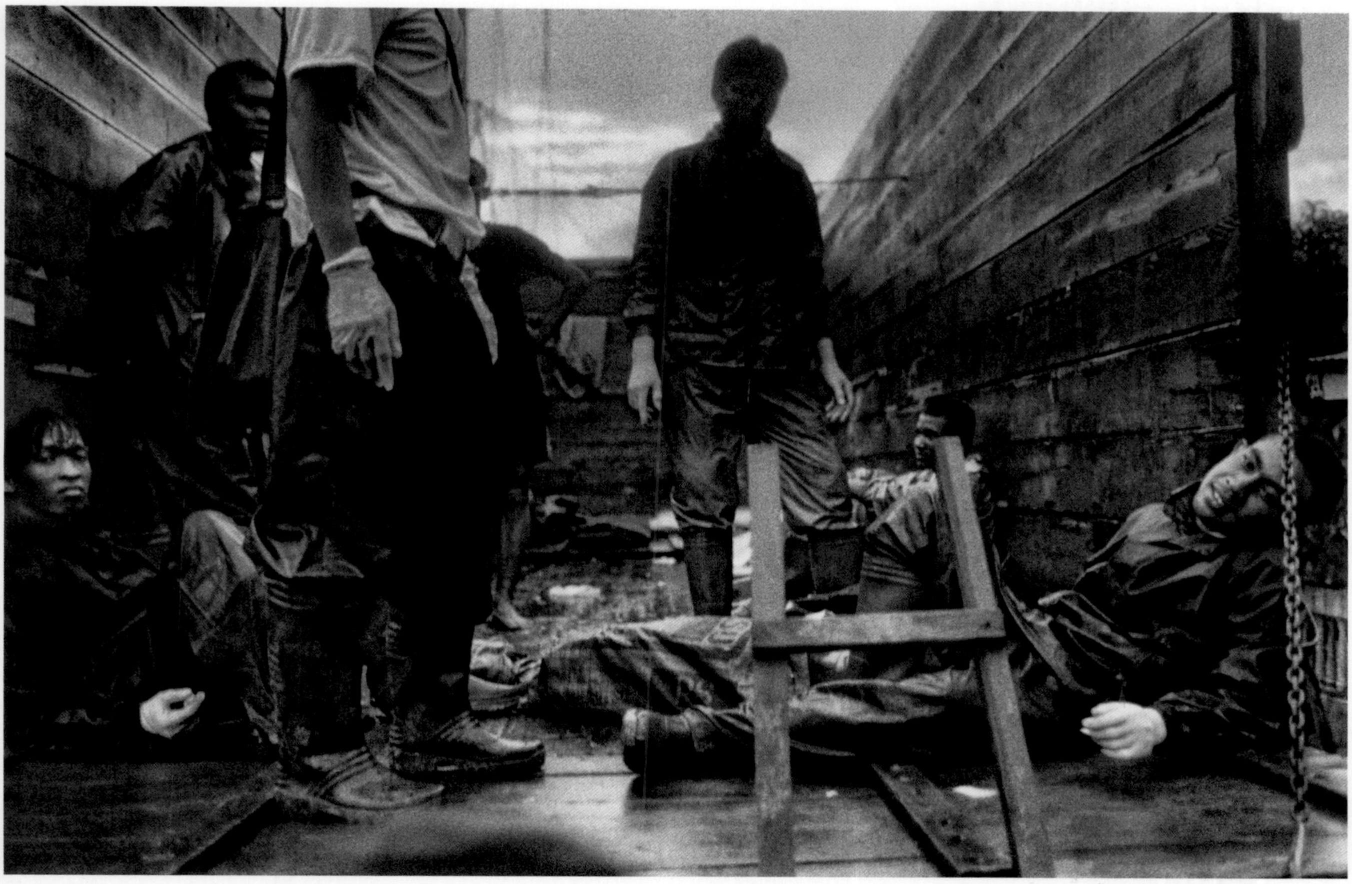

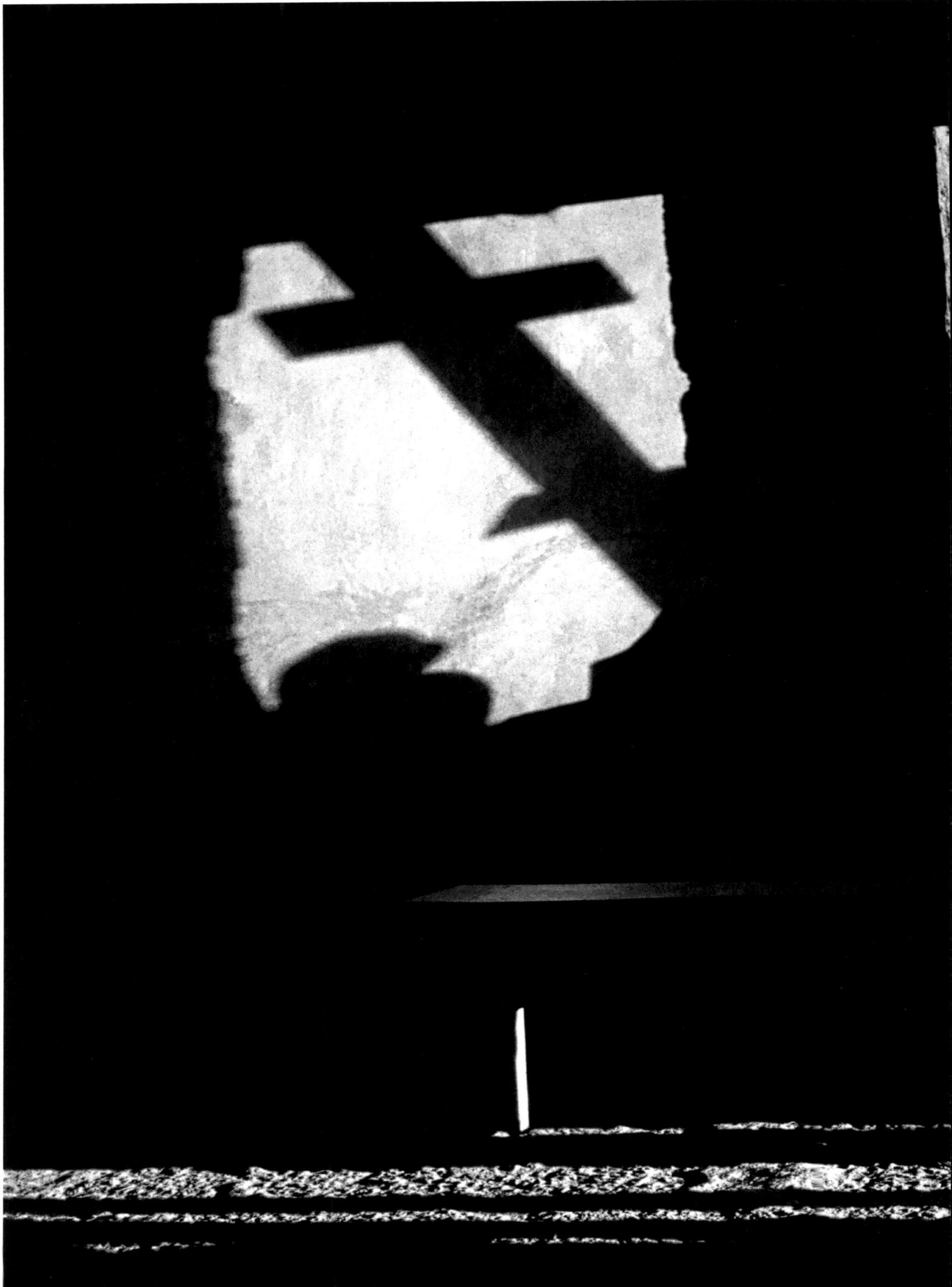

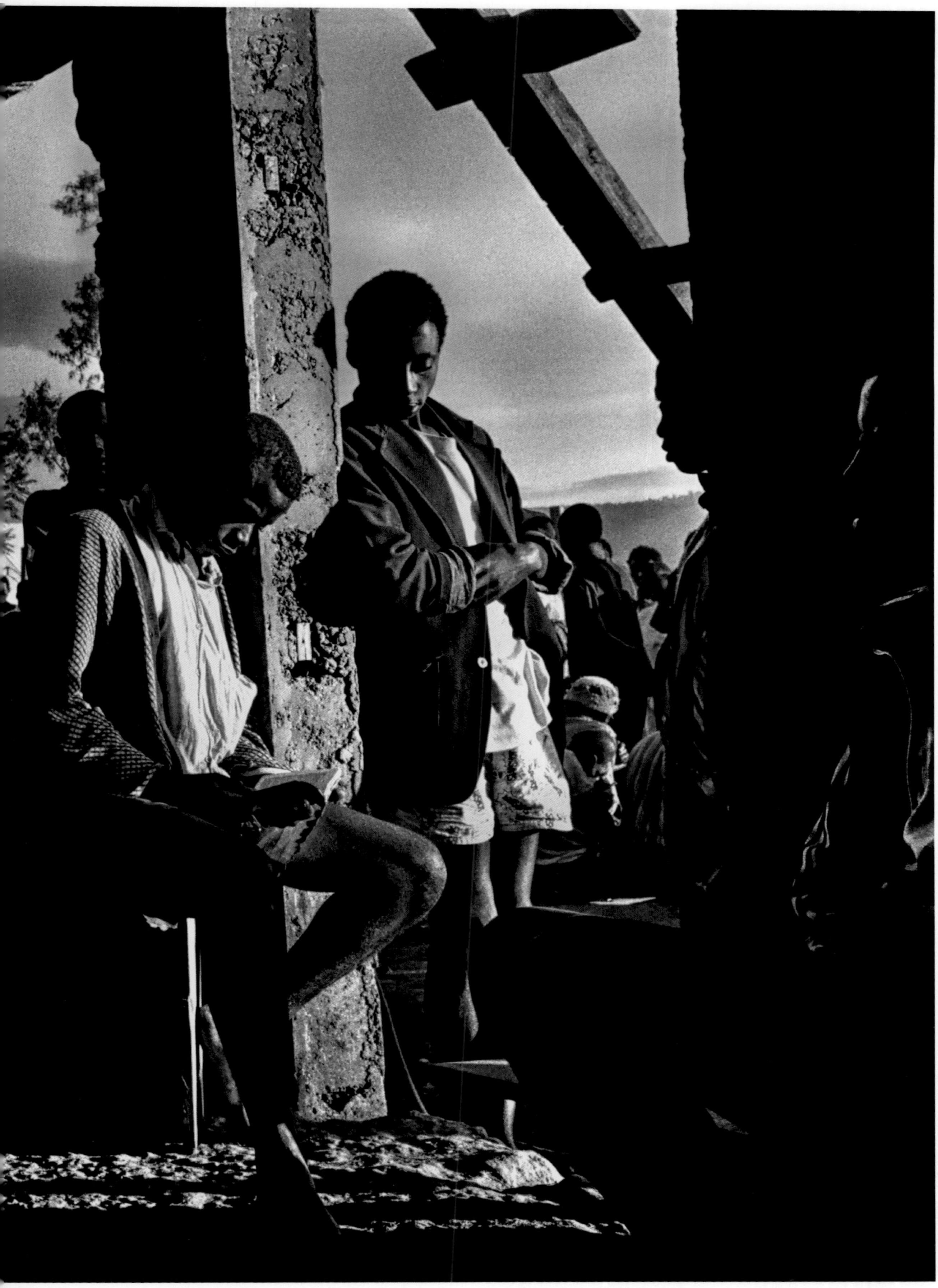

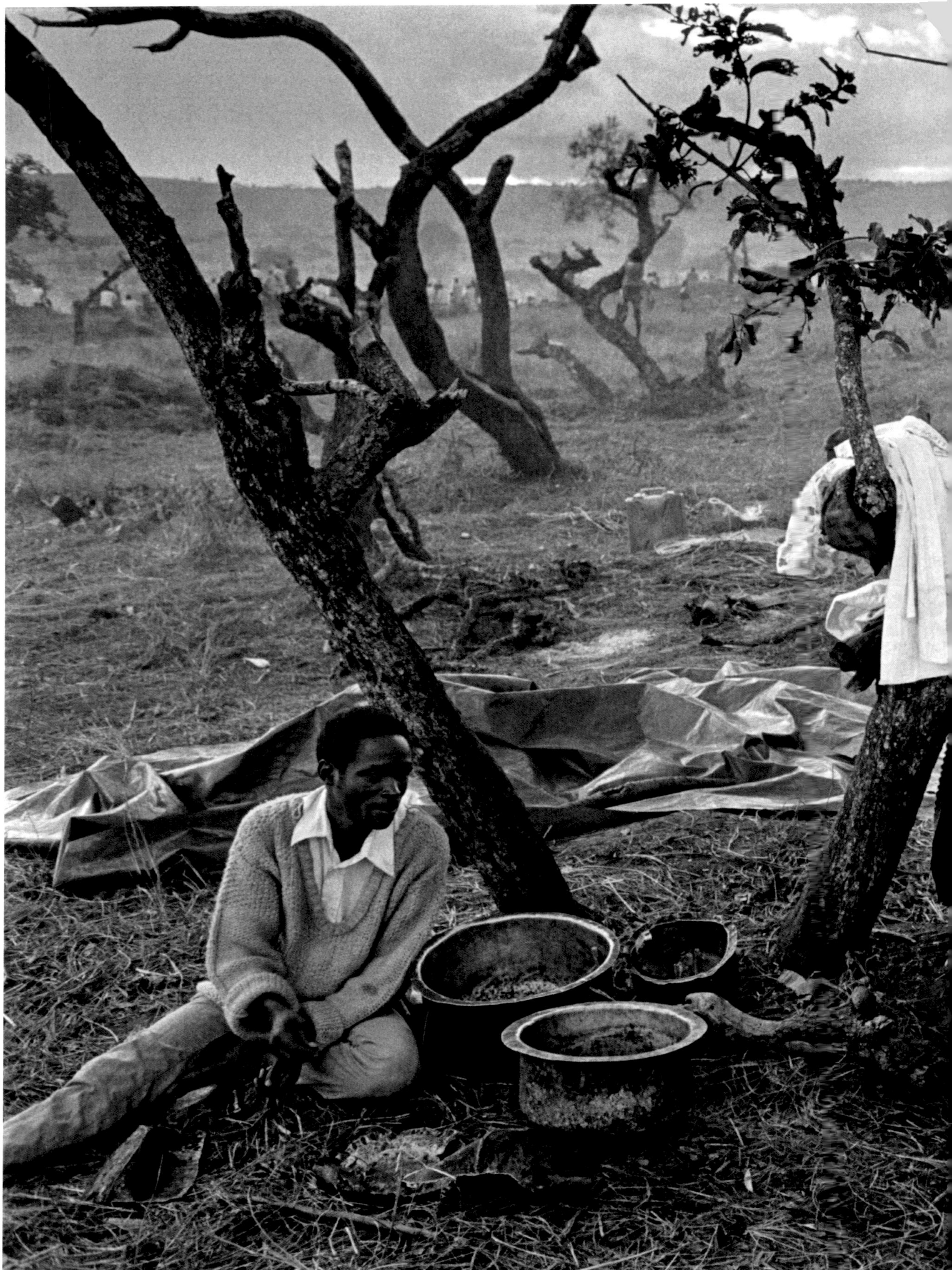

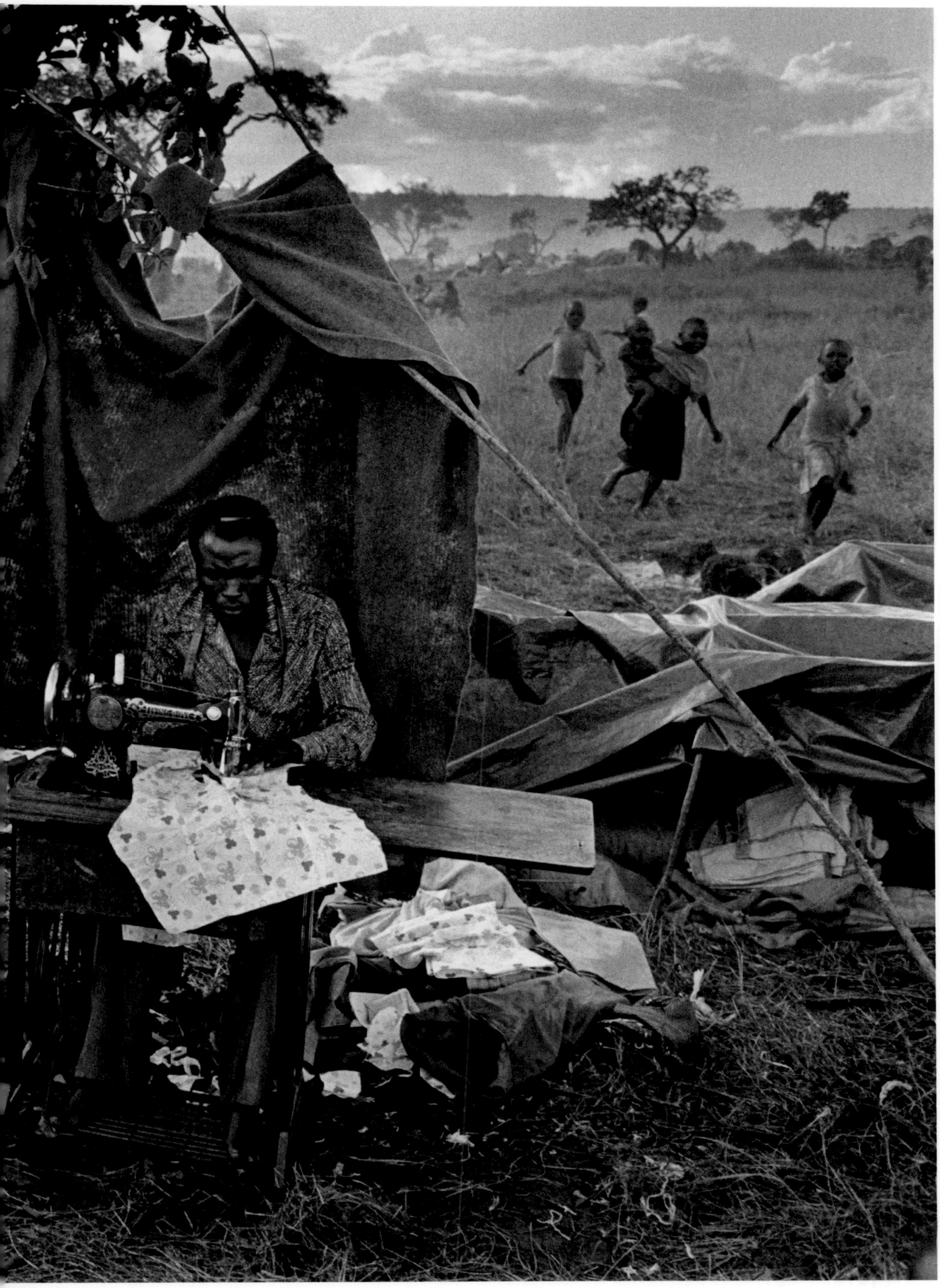

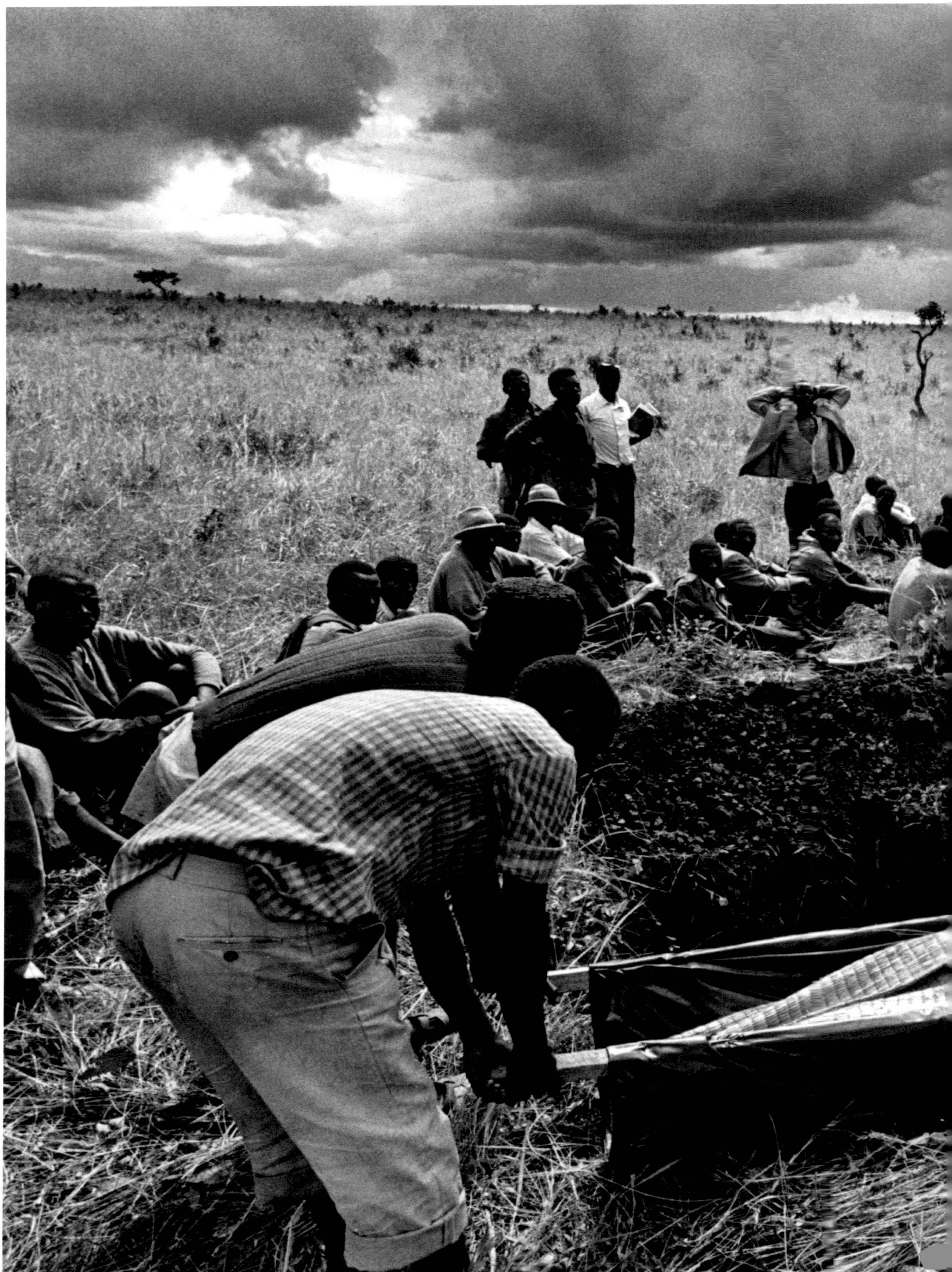

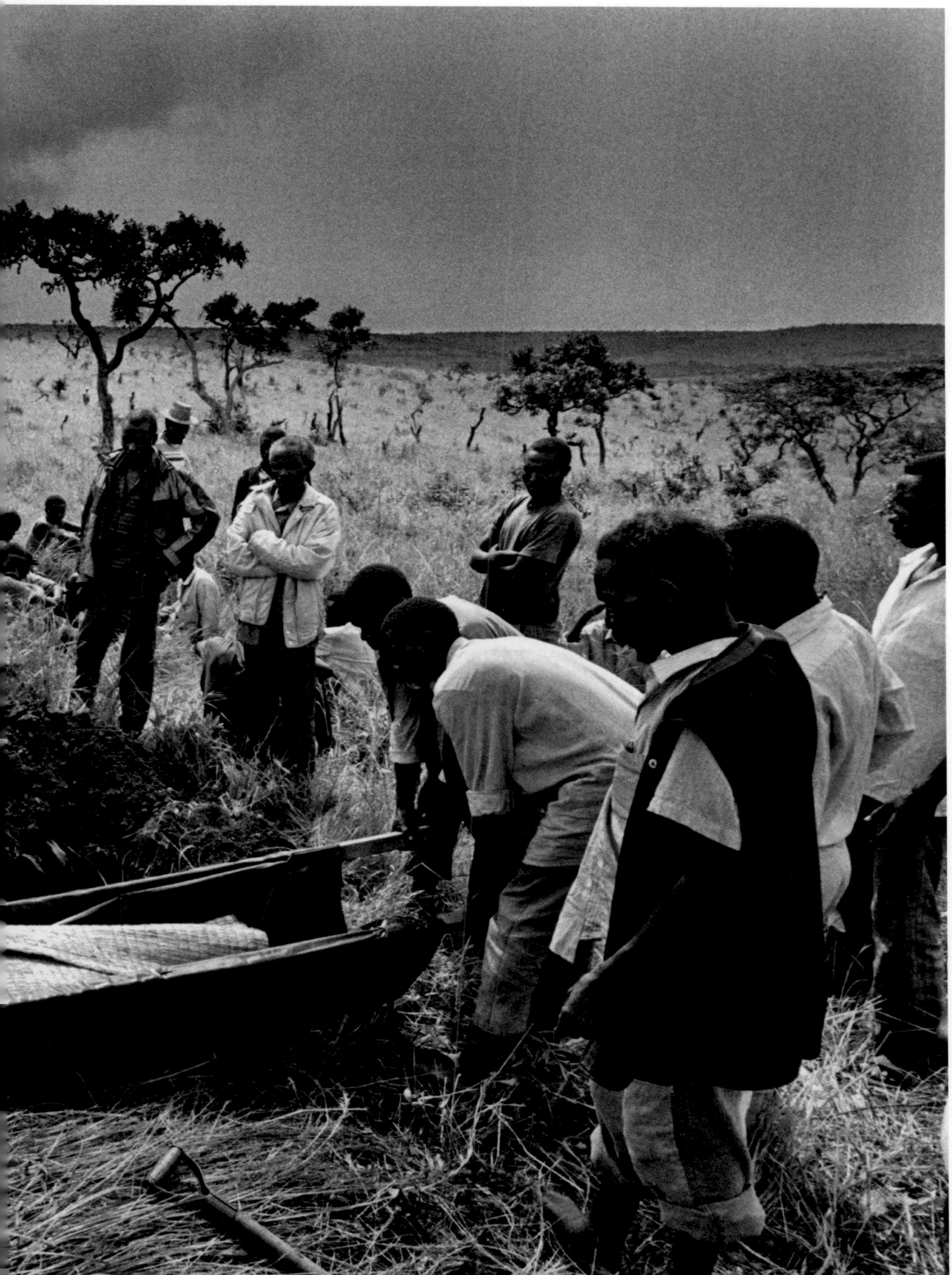

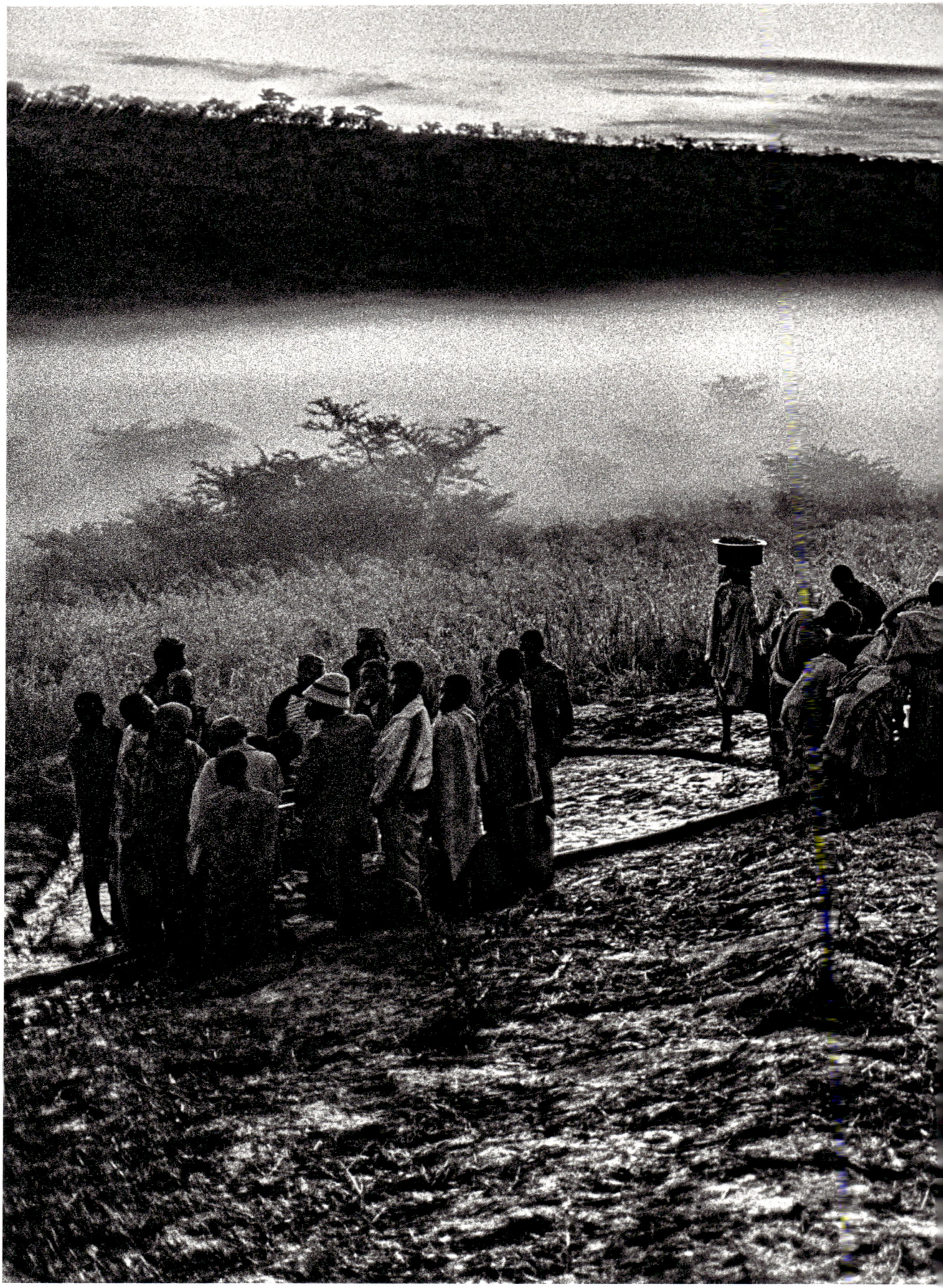

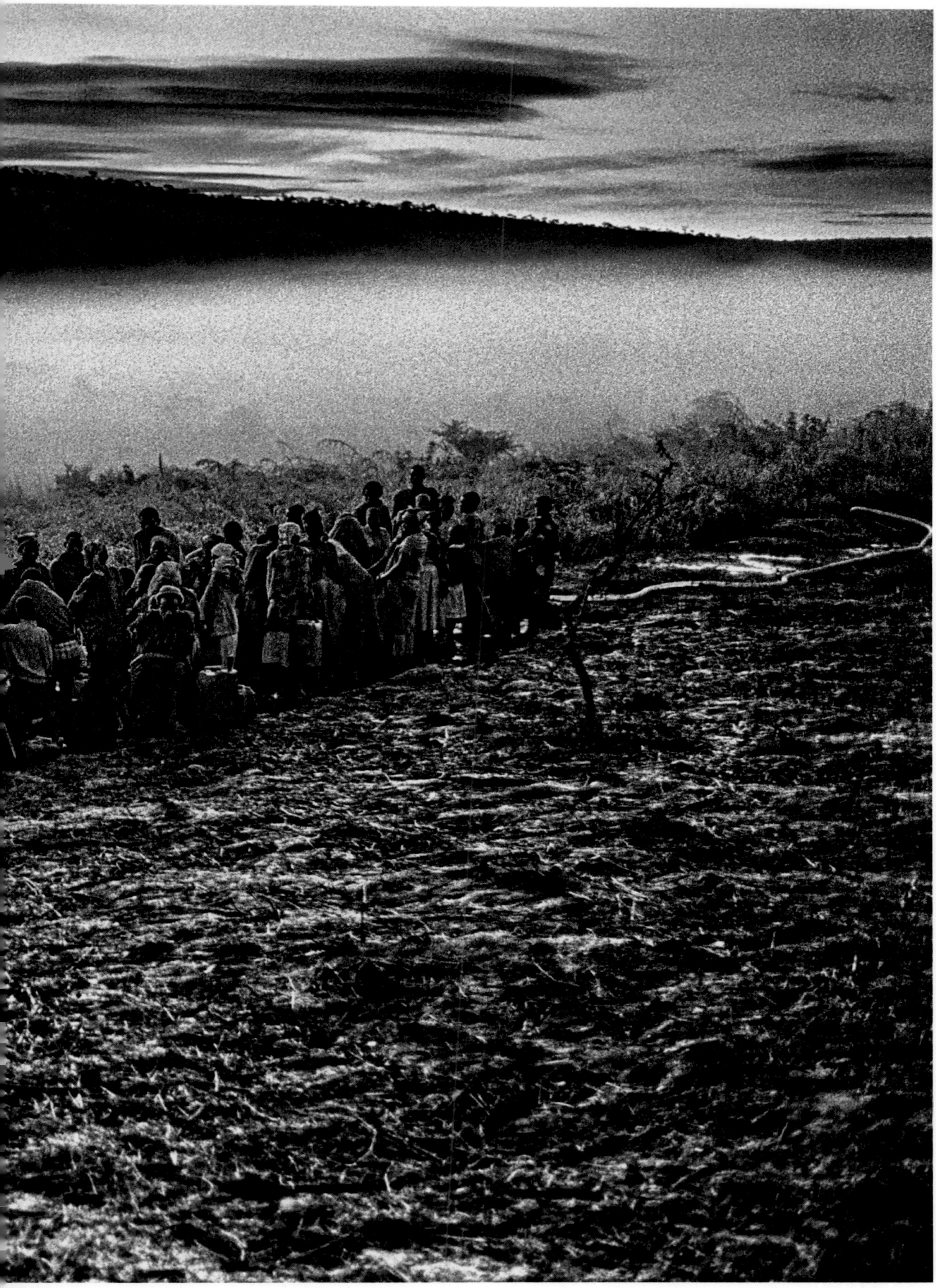

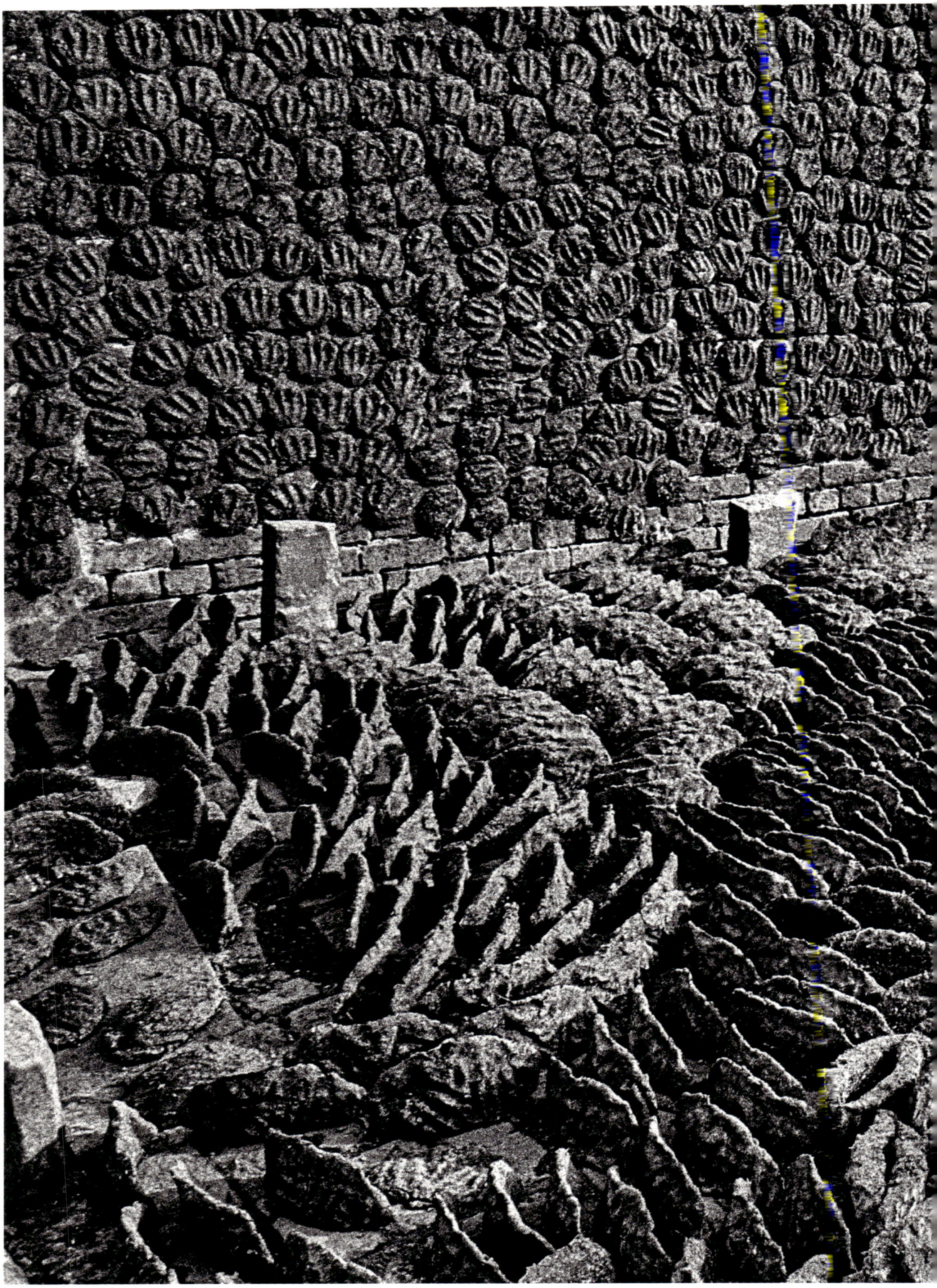

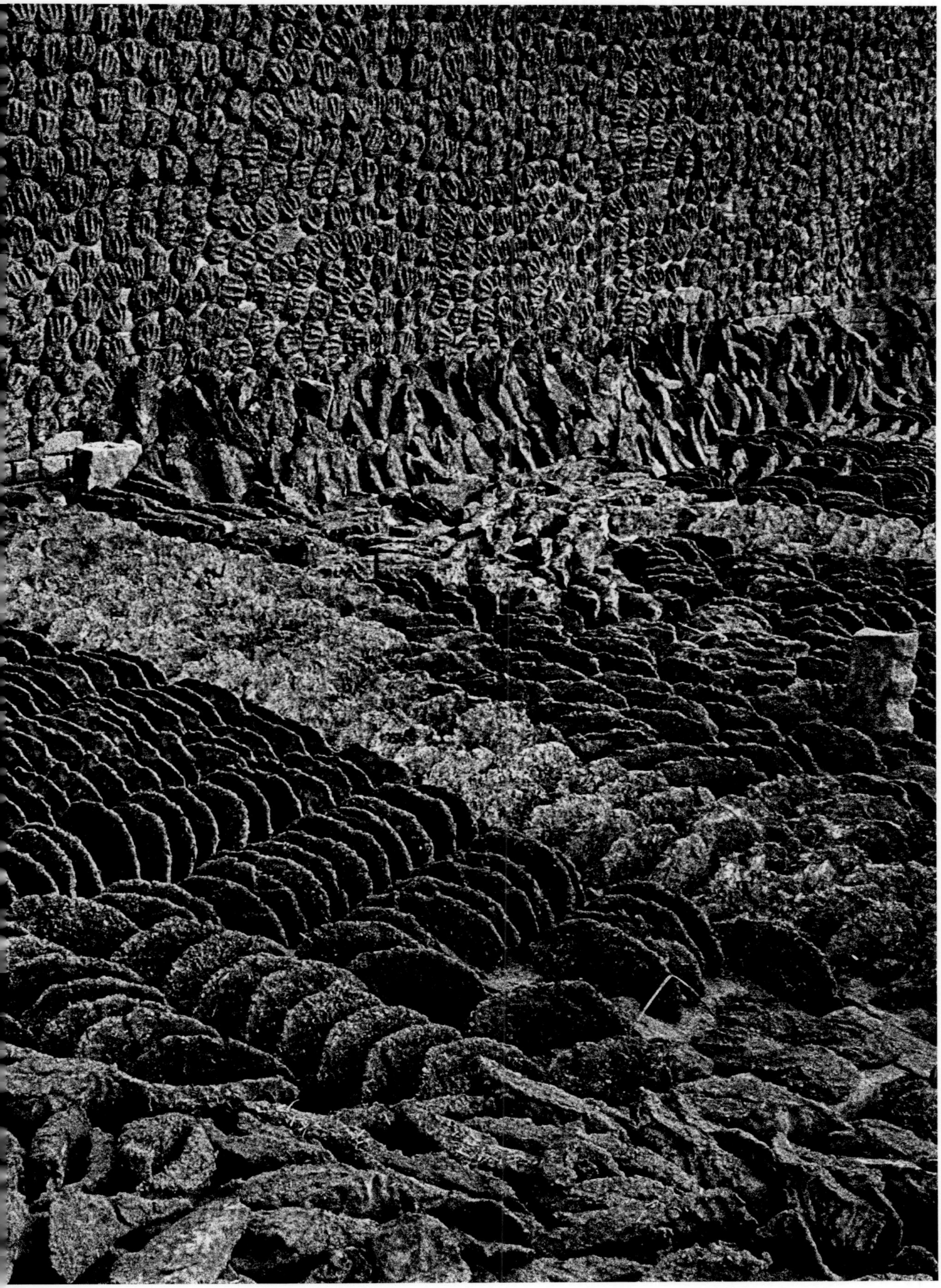

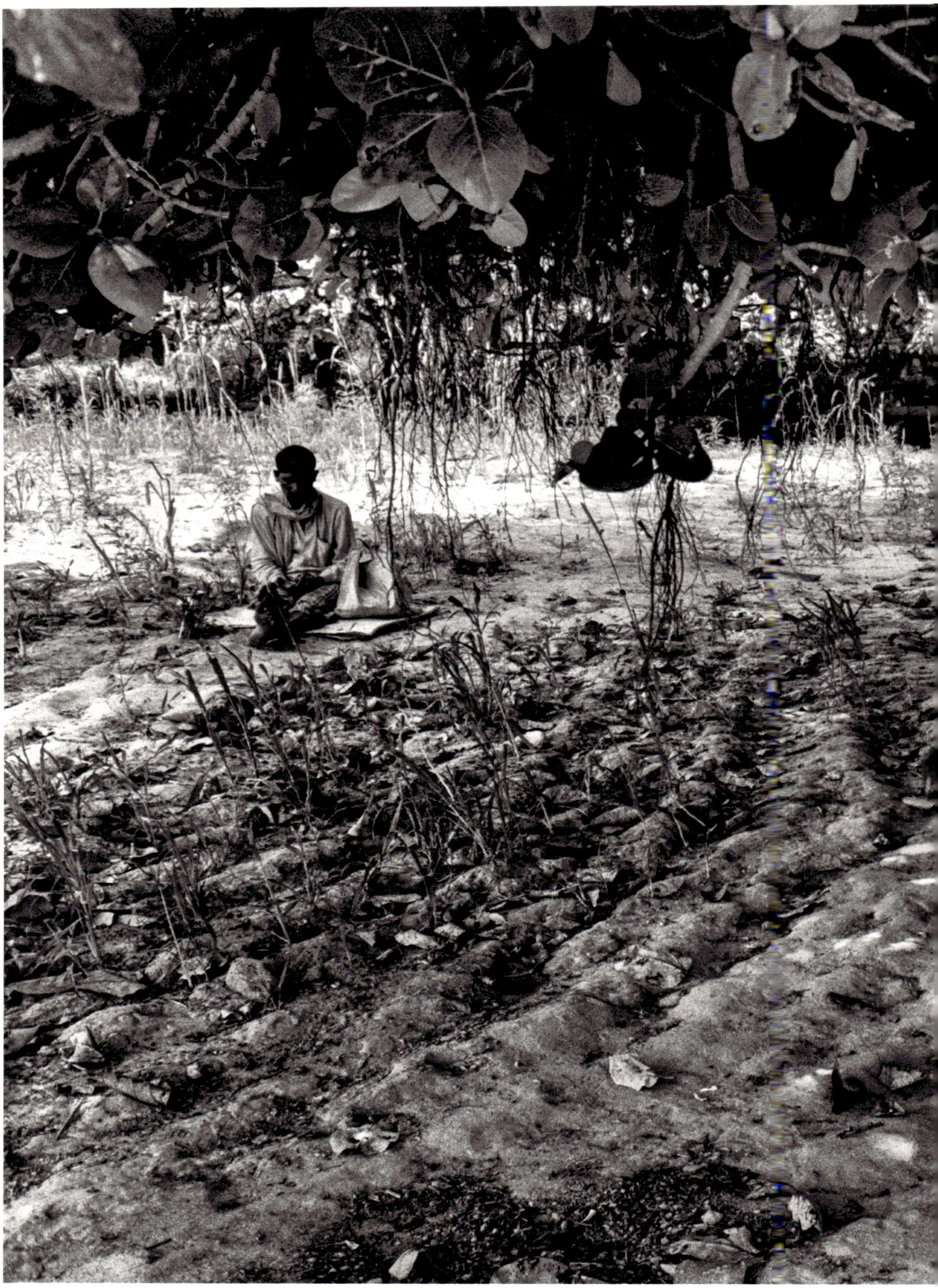

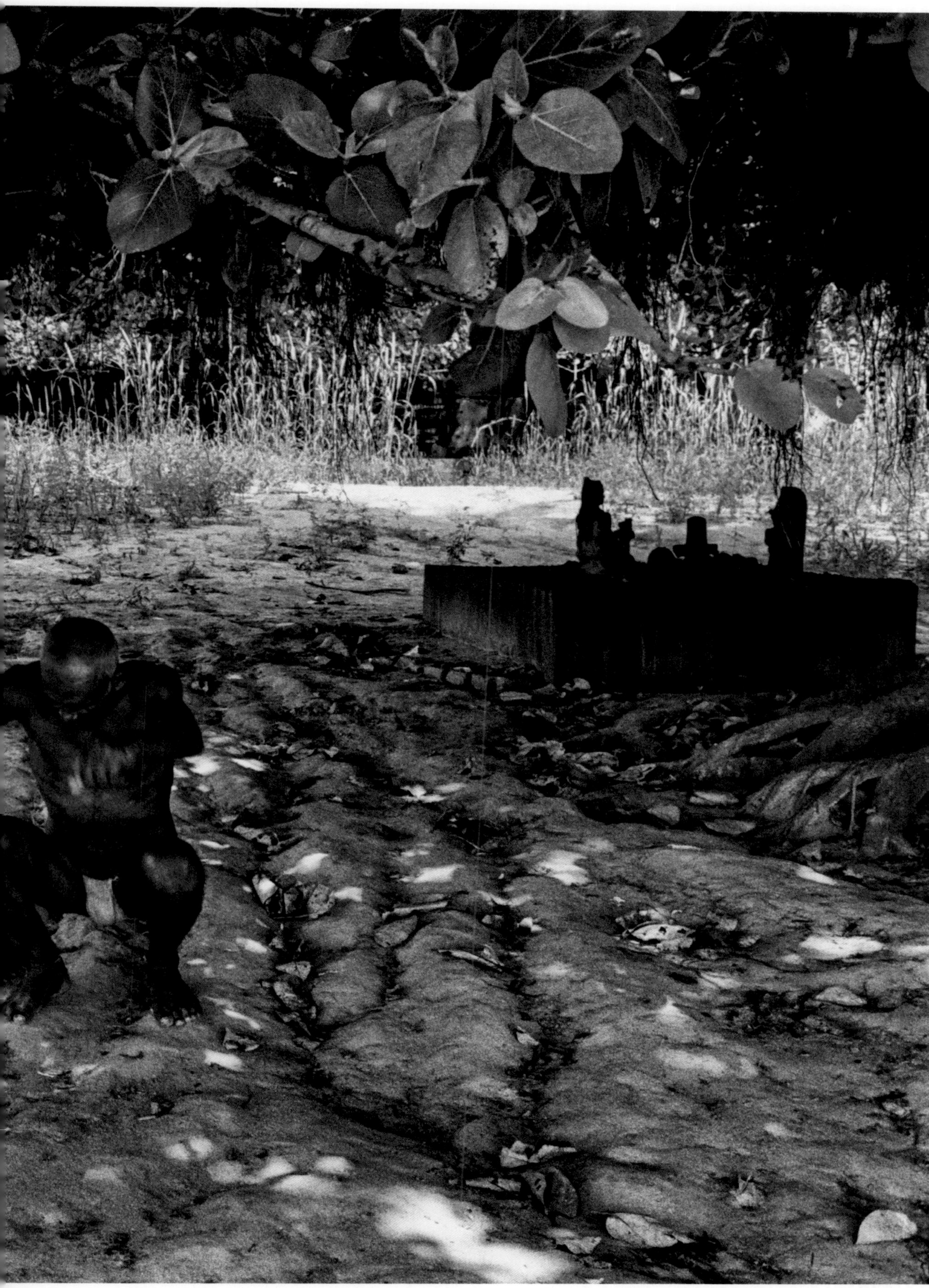

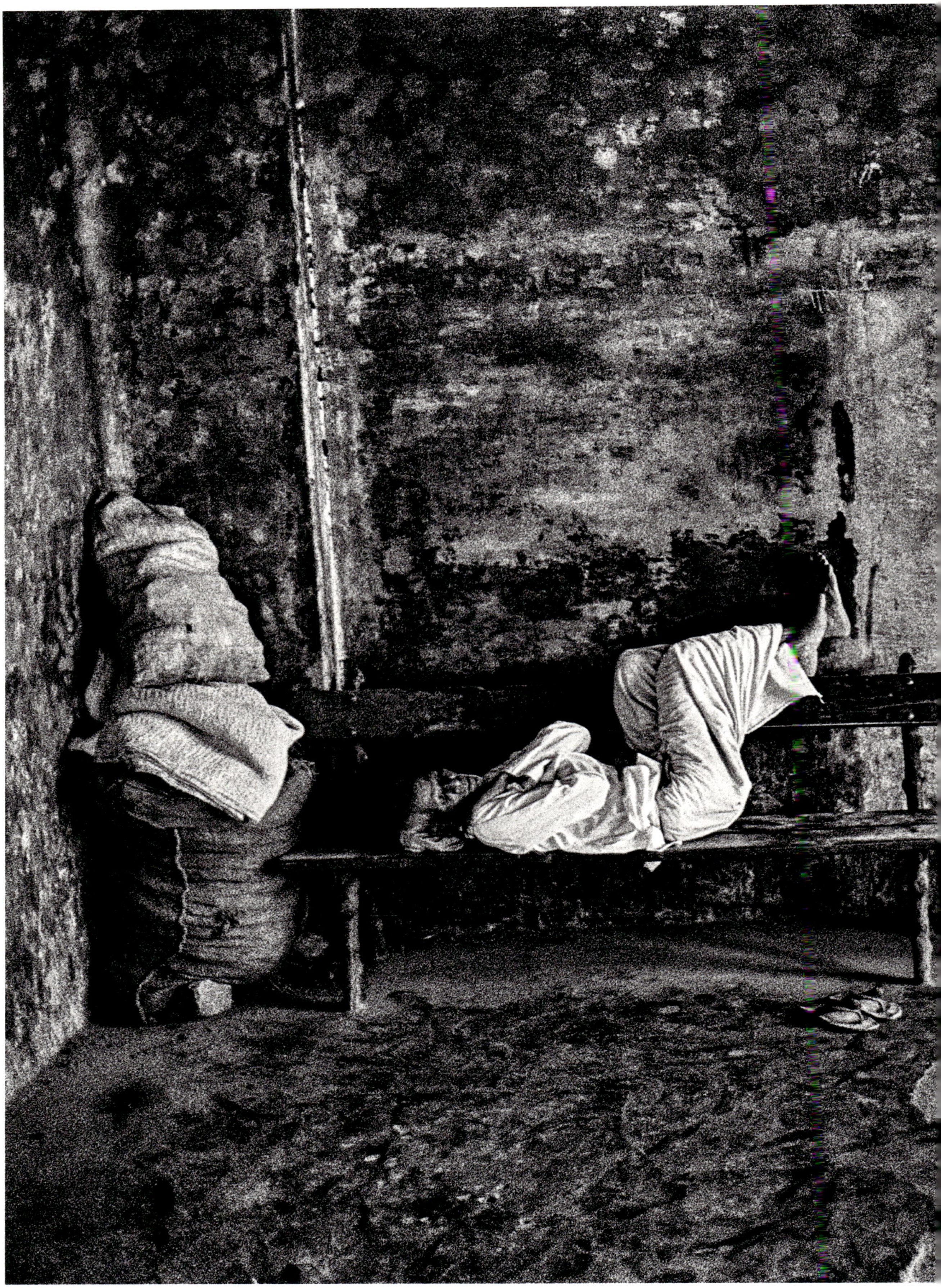

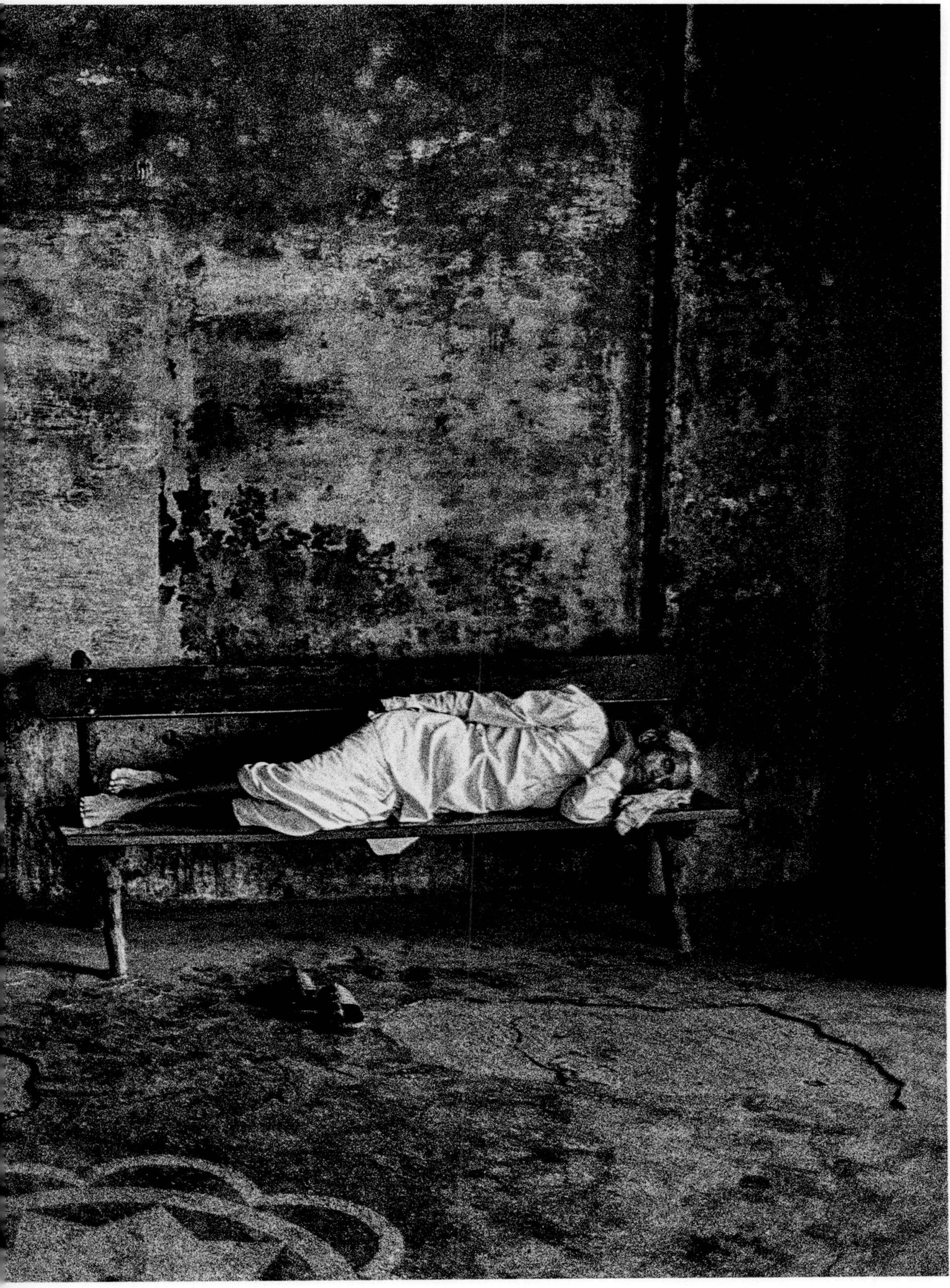

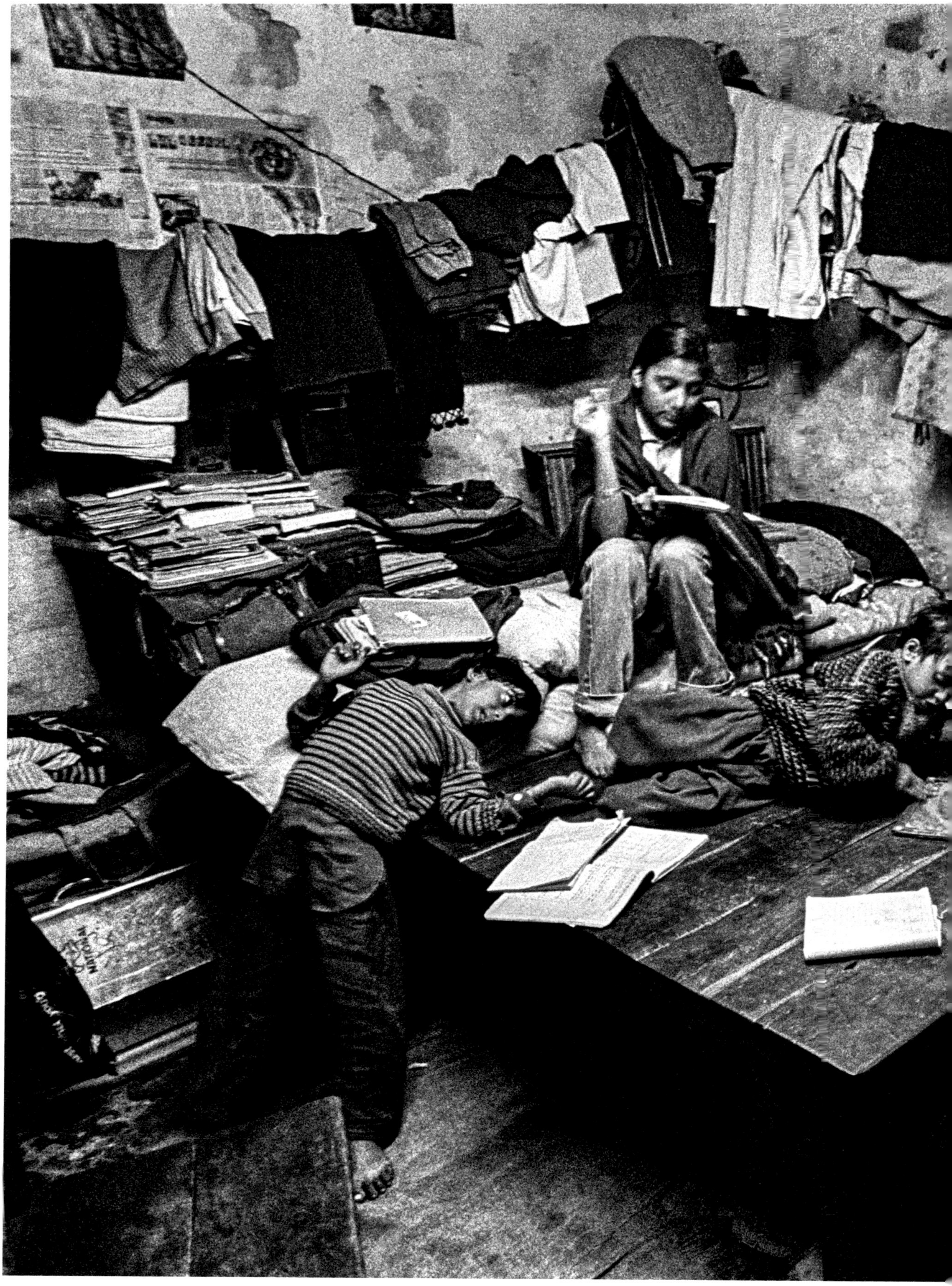

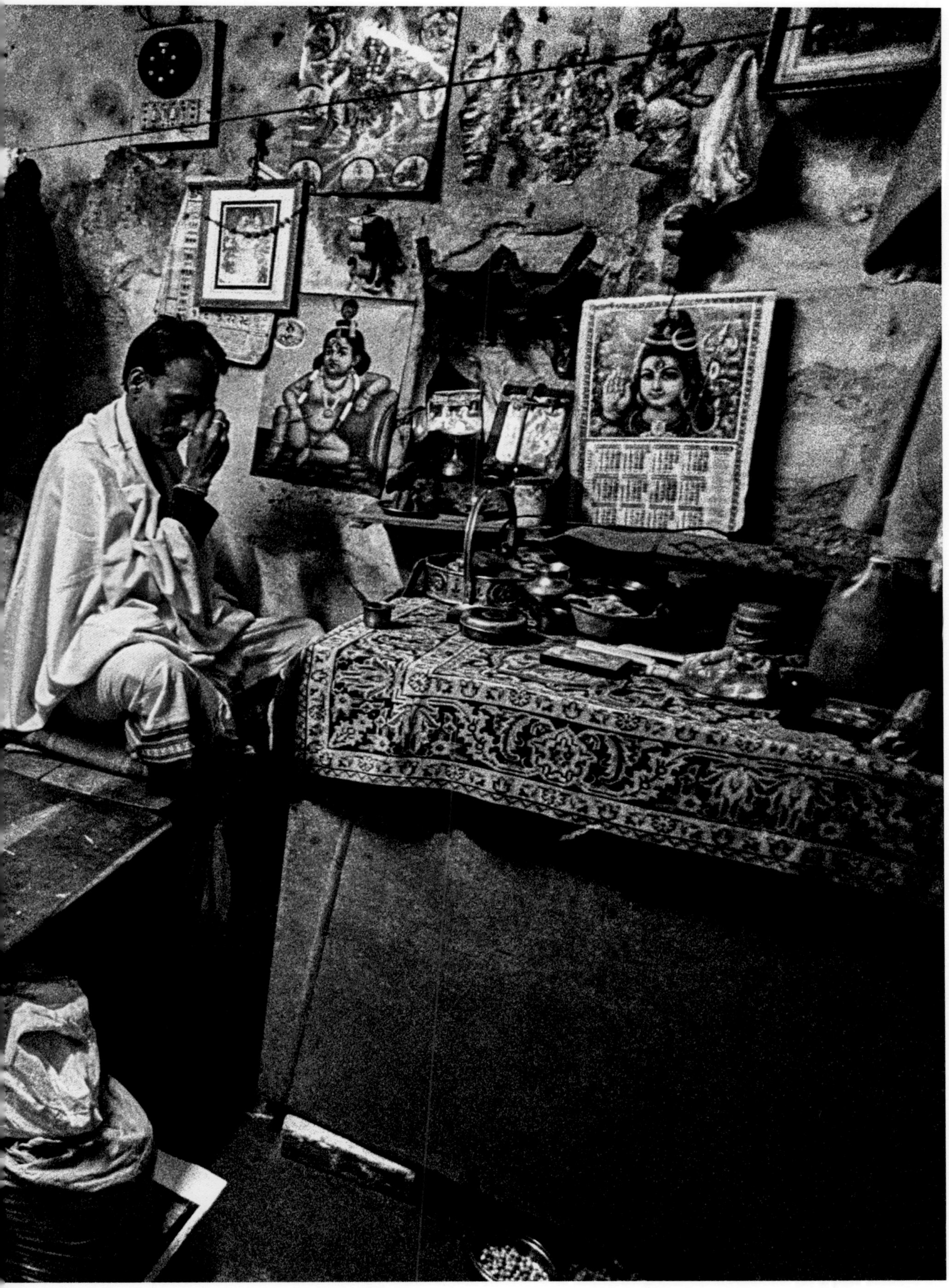

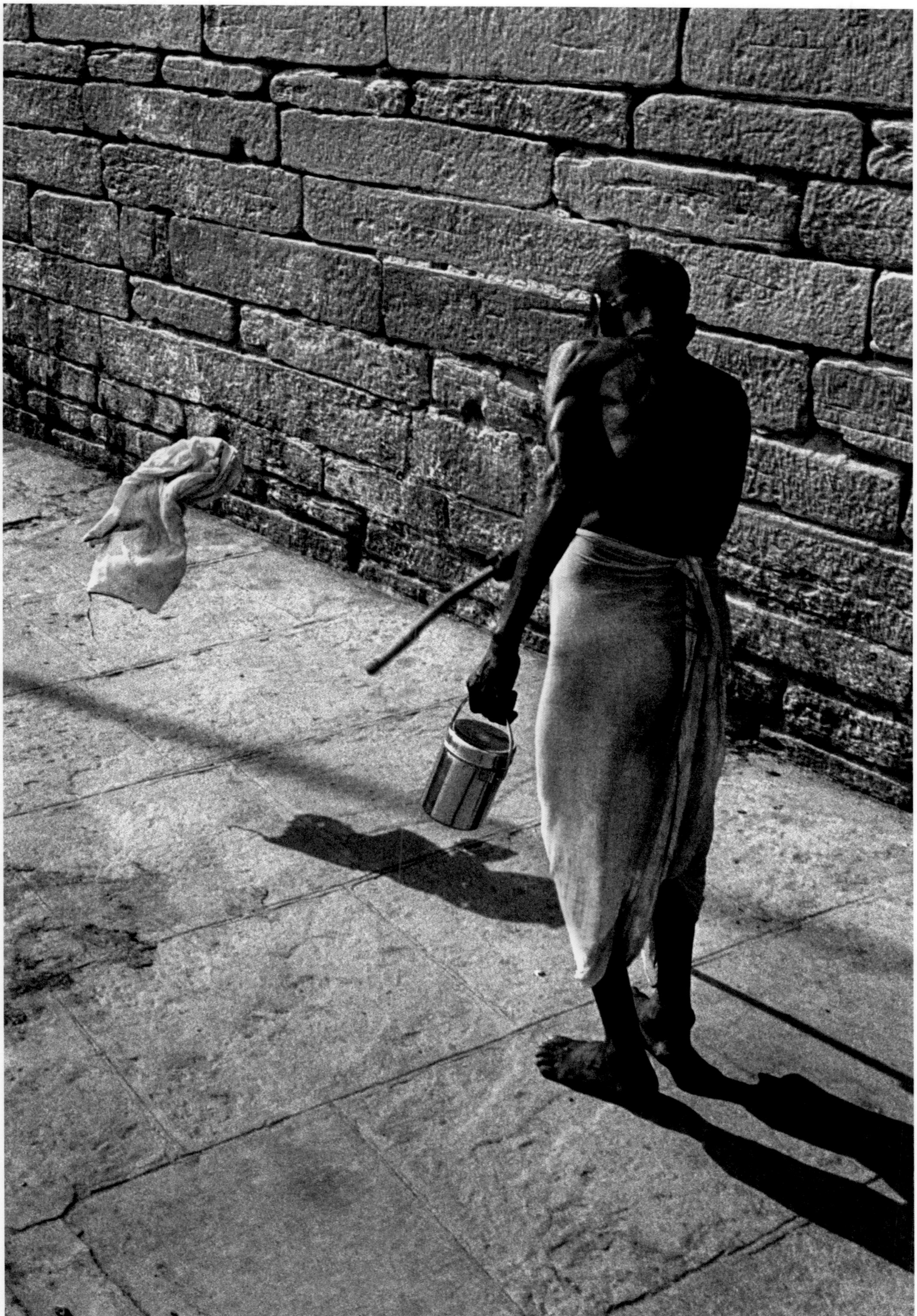

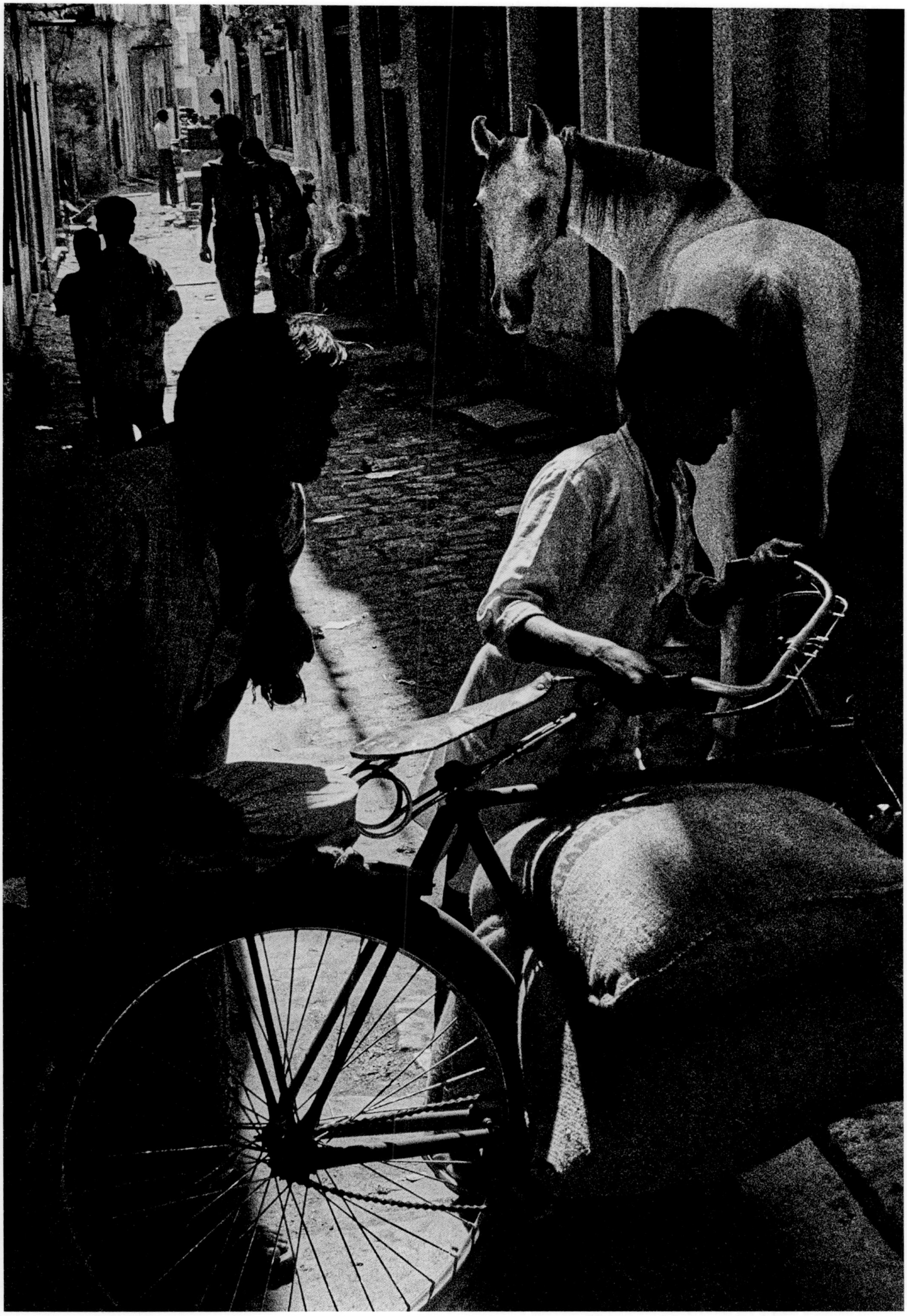

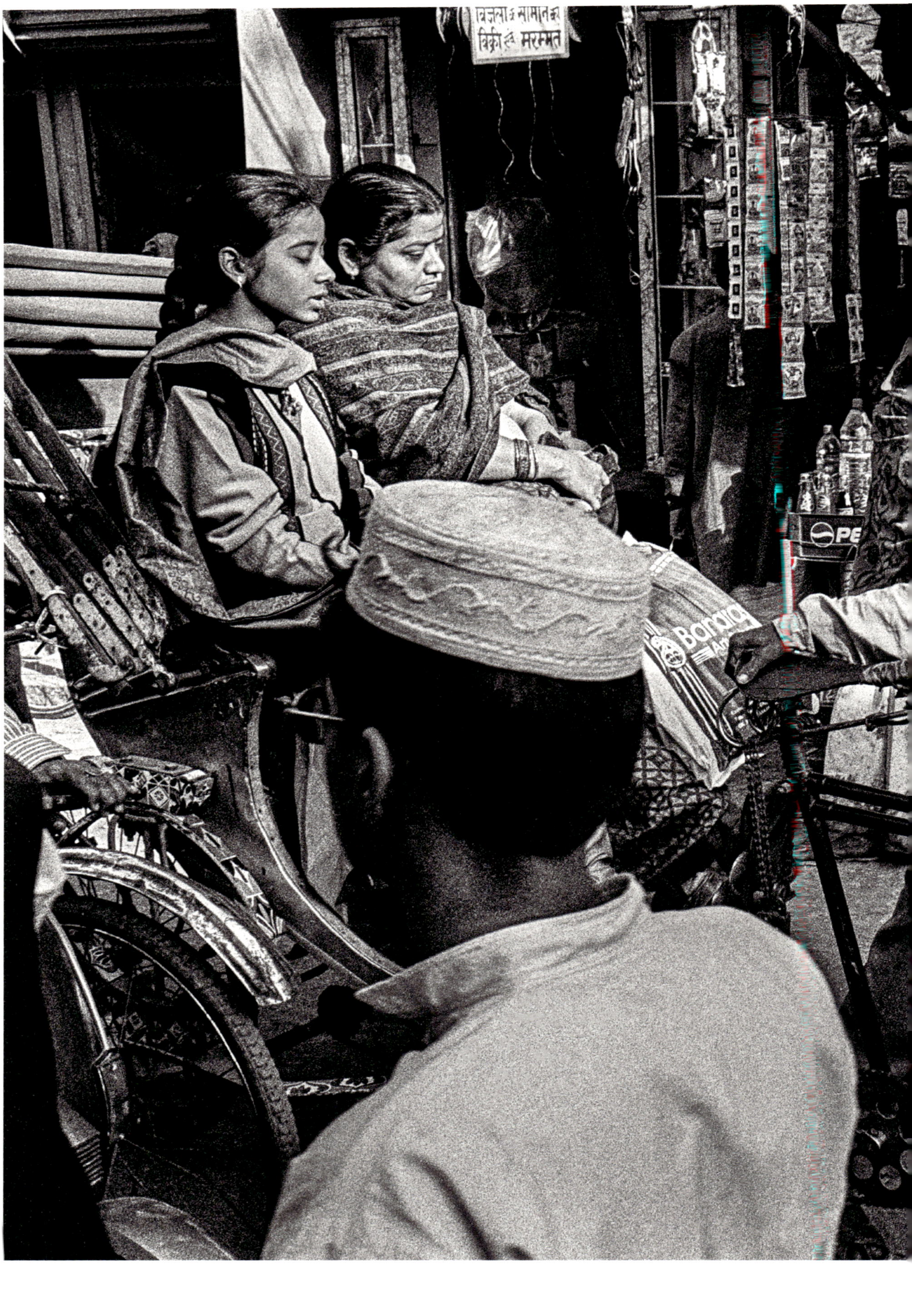
बिजली के सामान की
बिक्री एवं मरम्मत

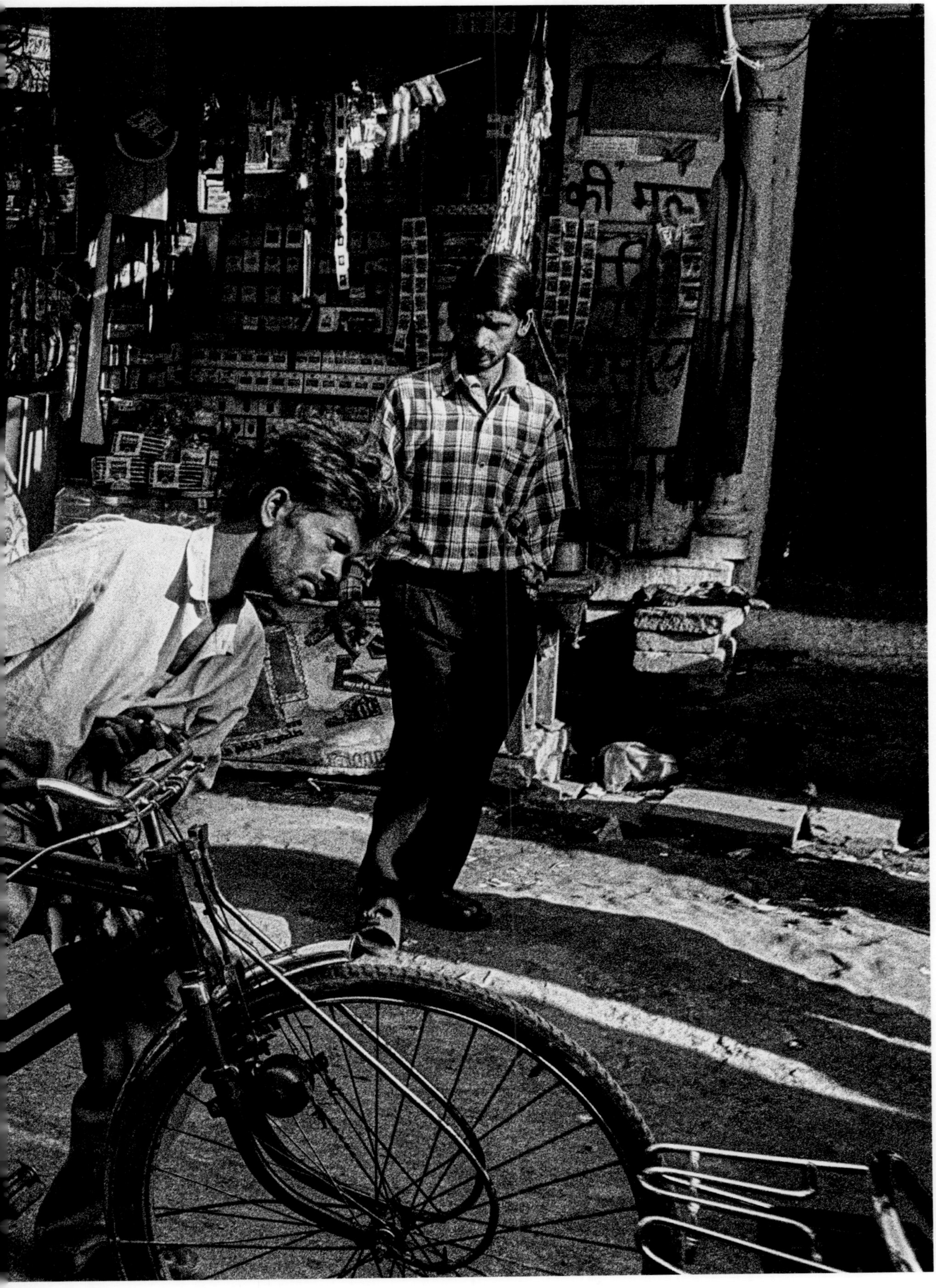

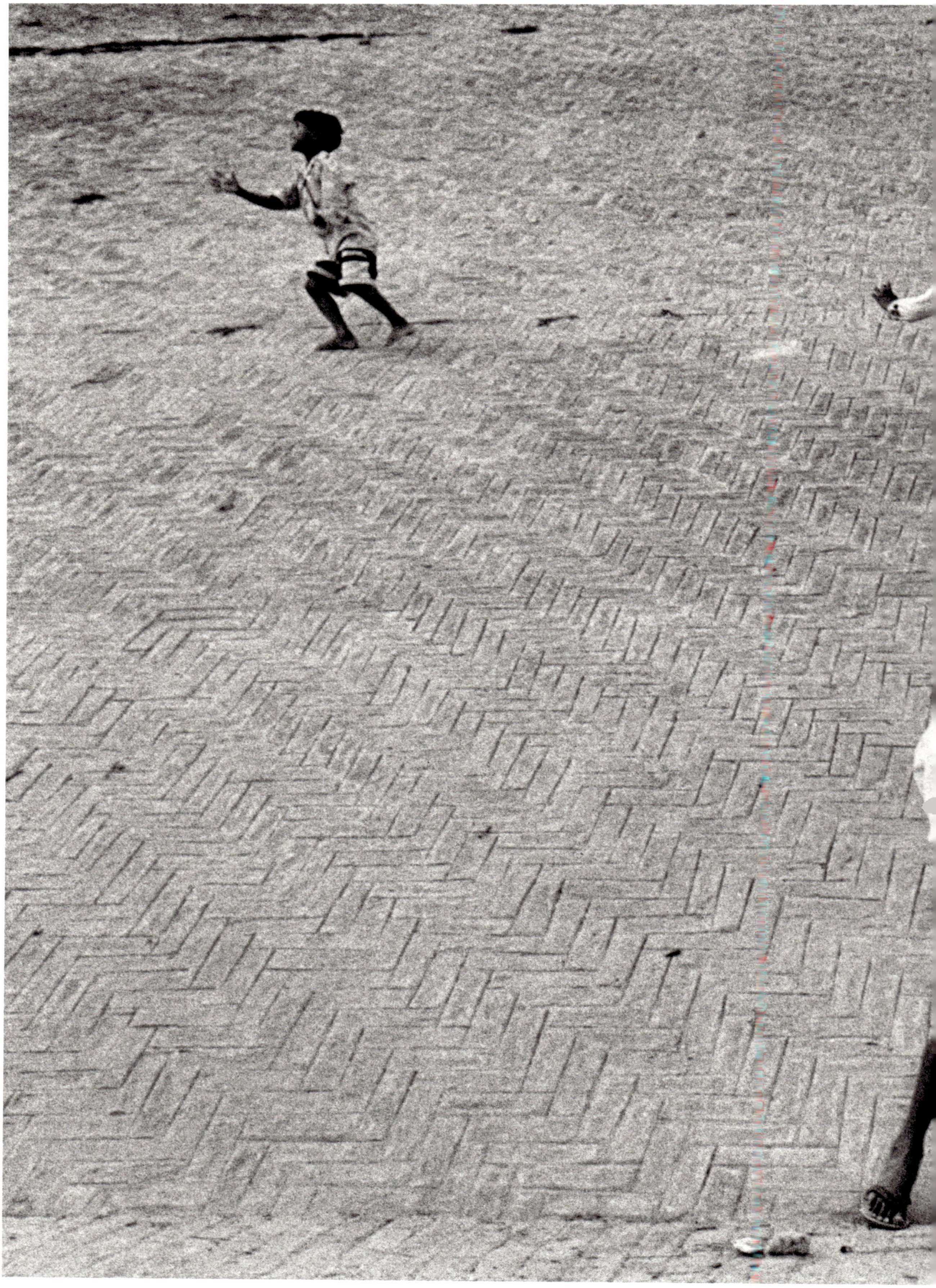

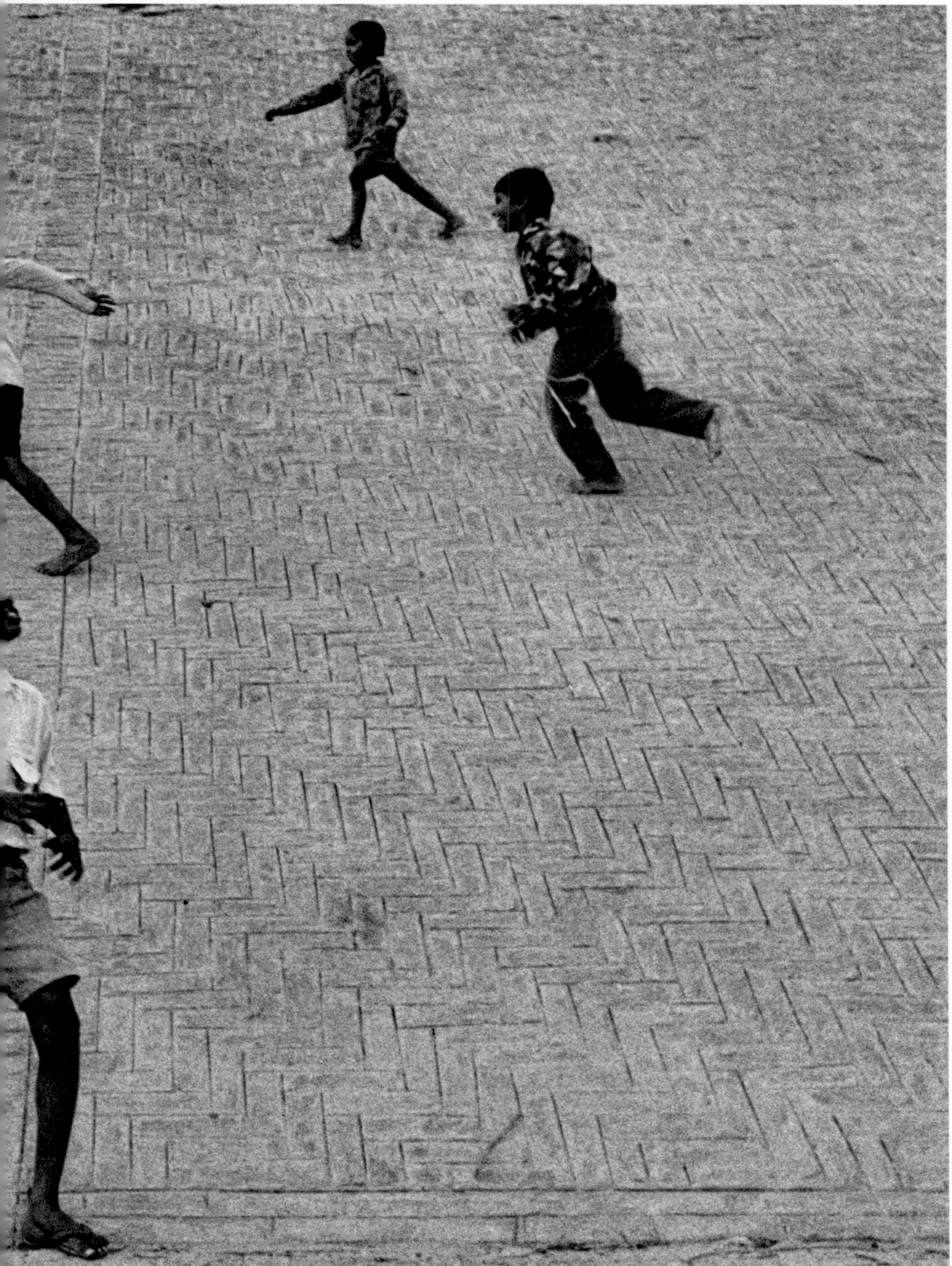

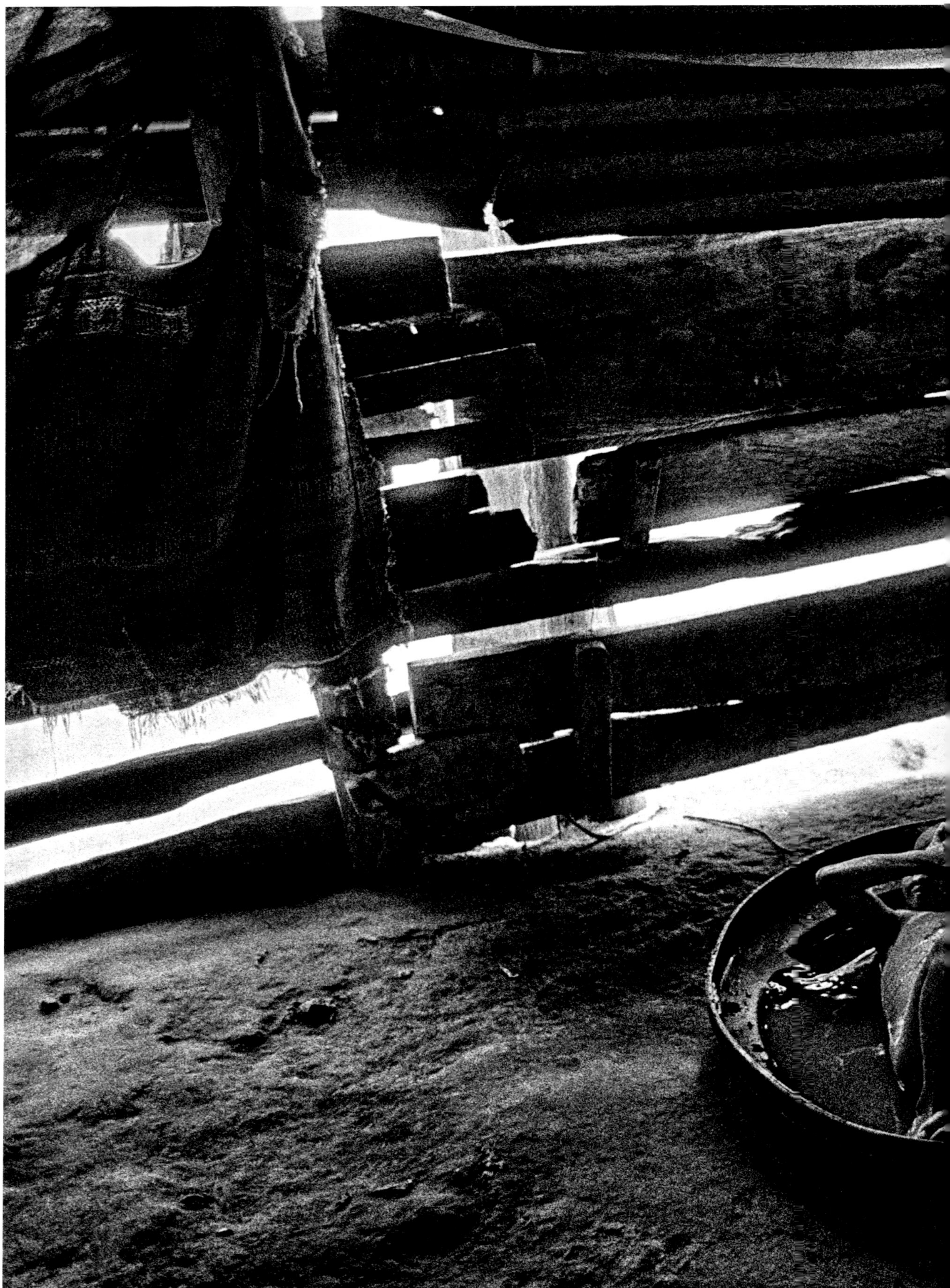

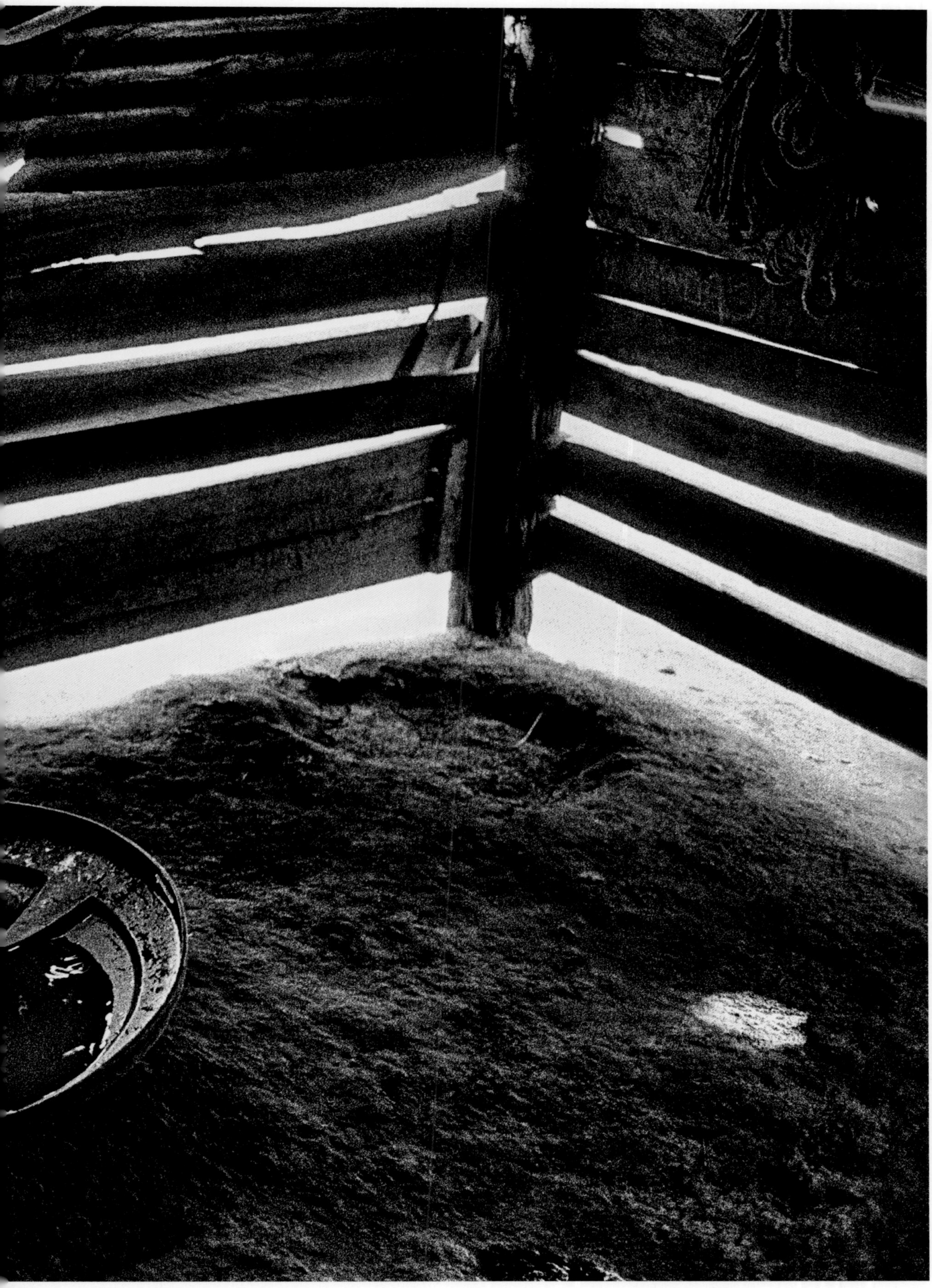

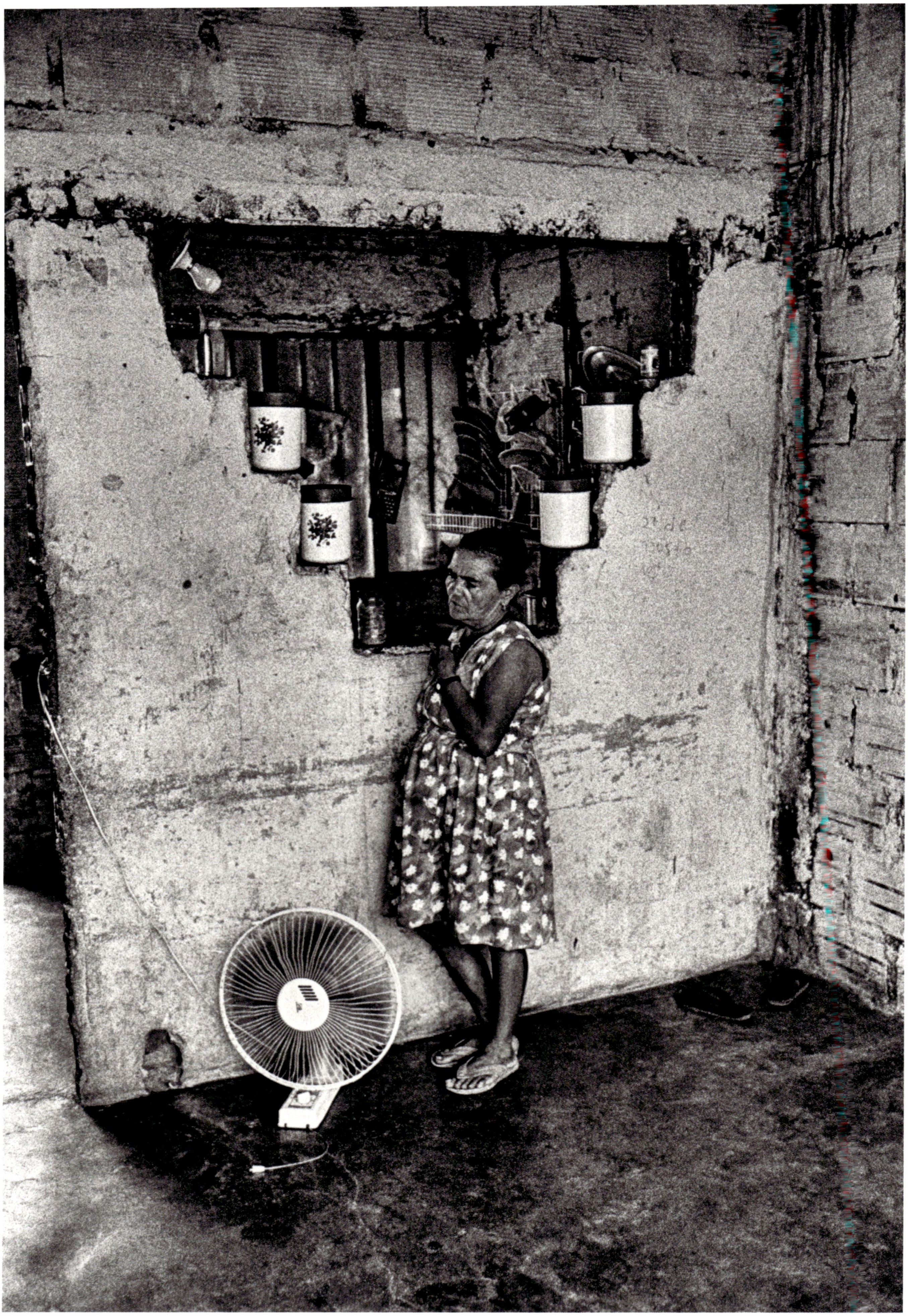

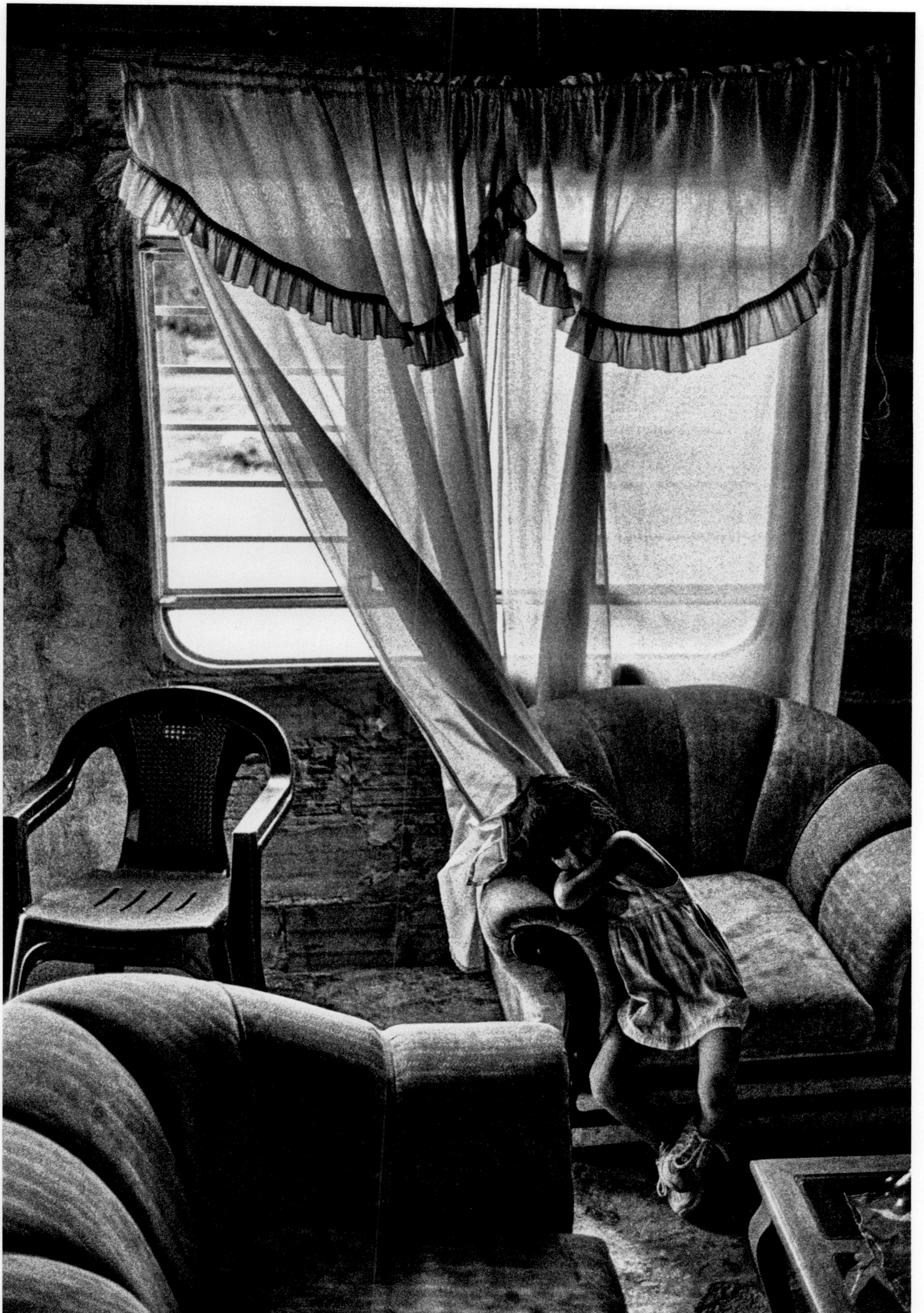

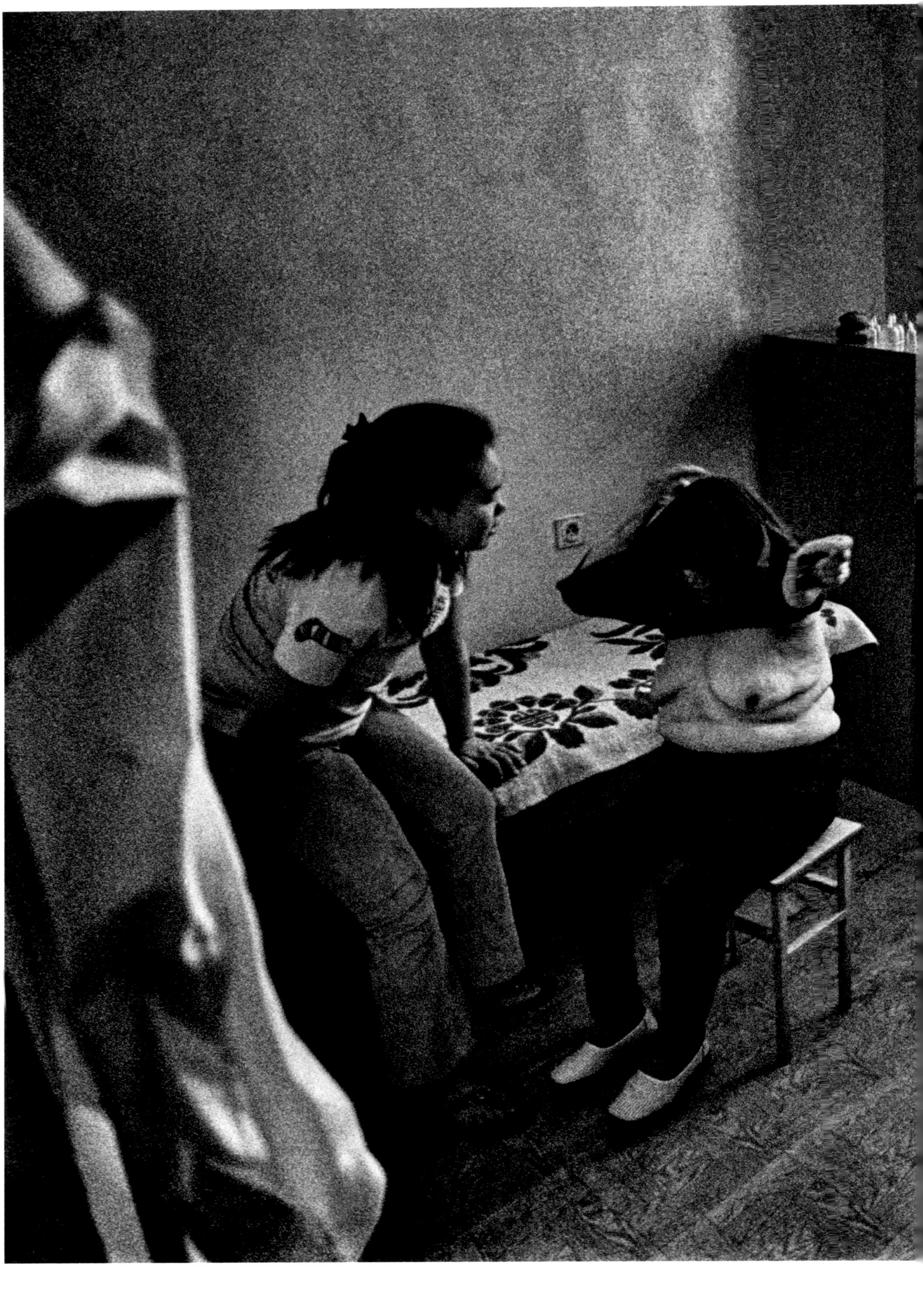

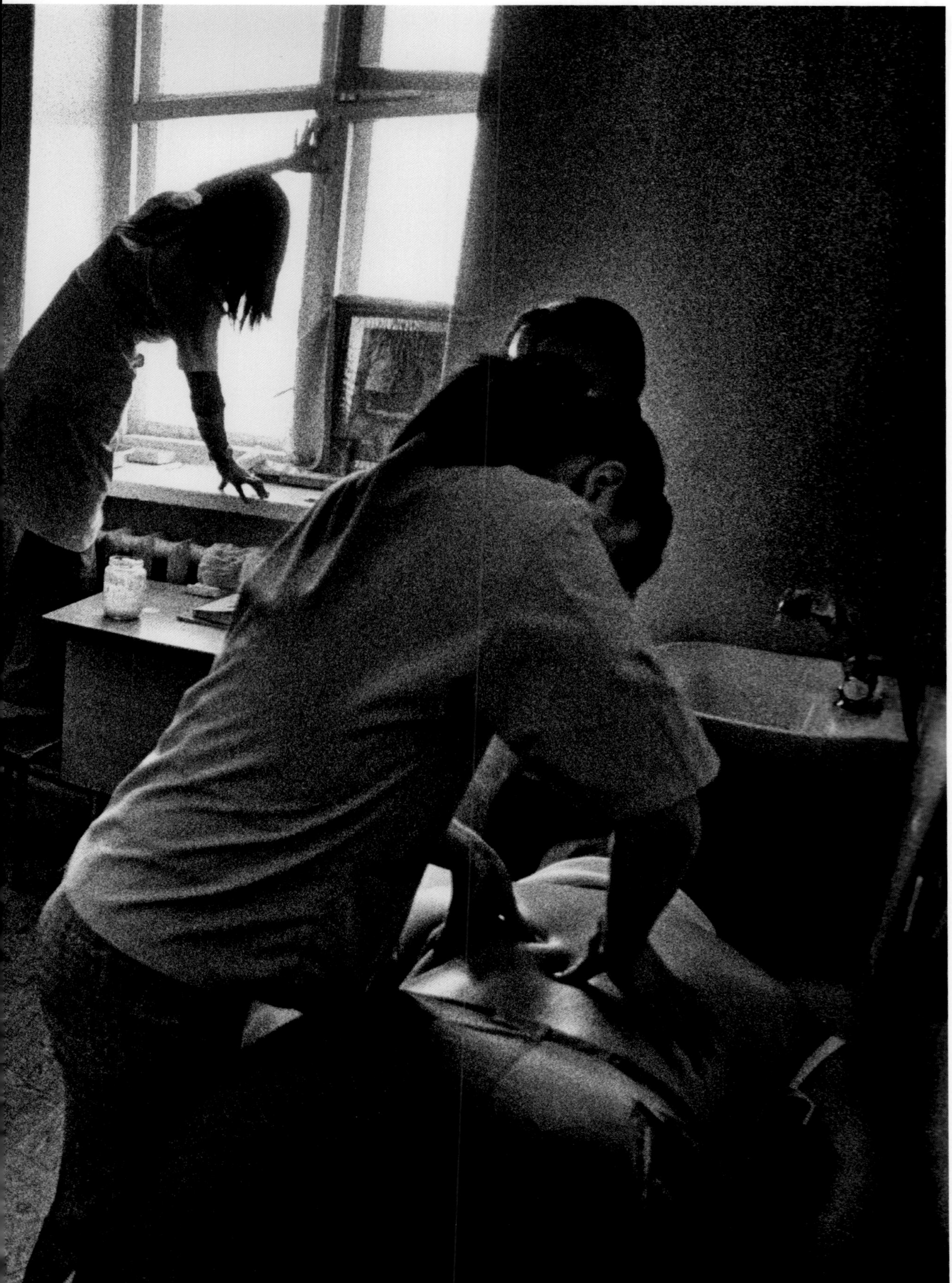

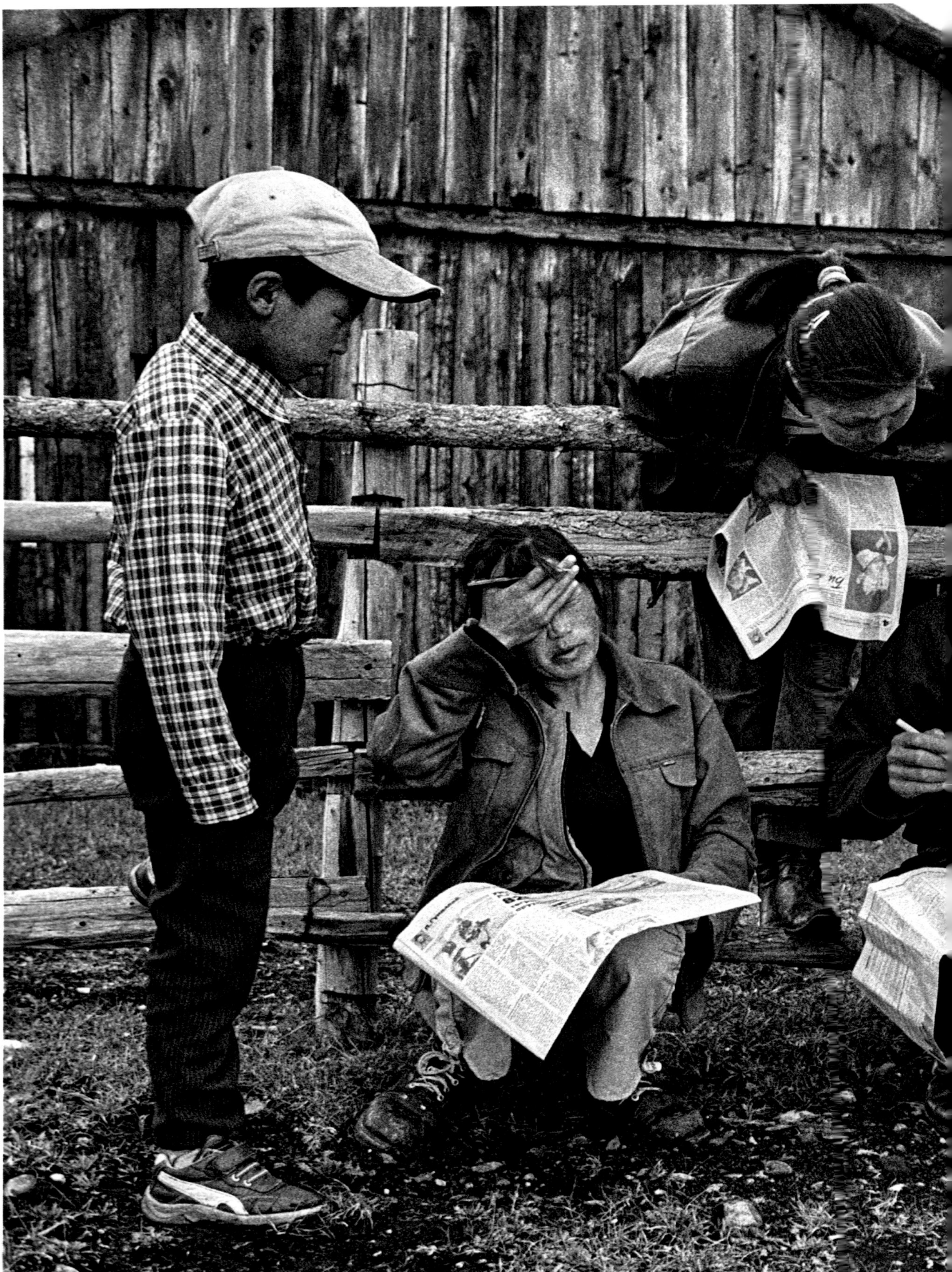

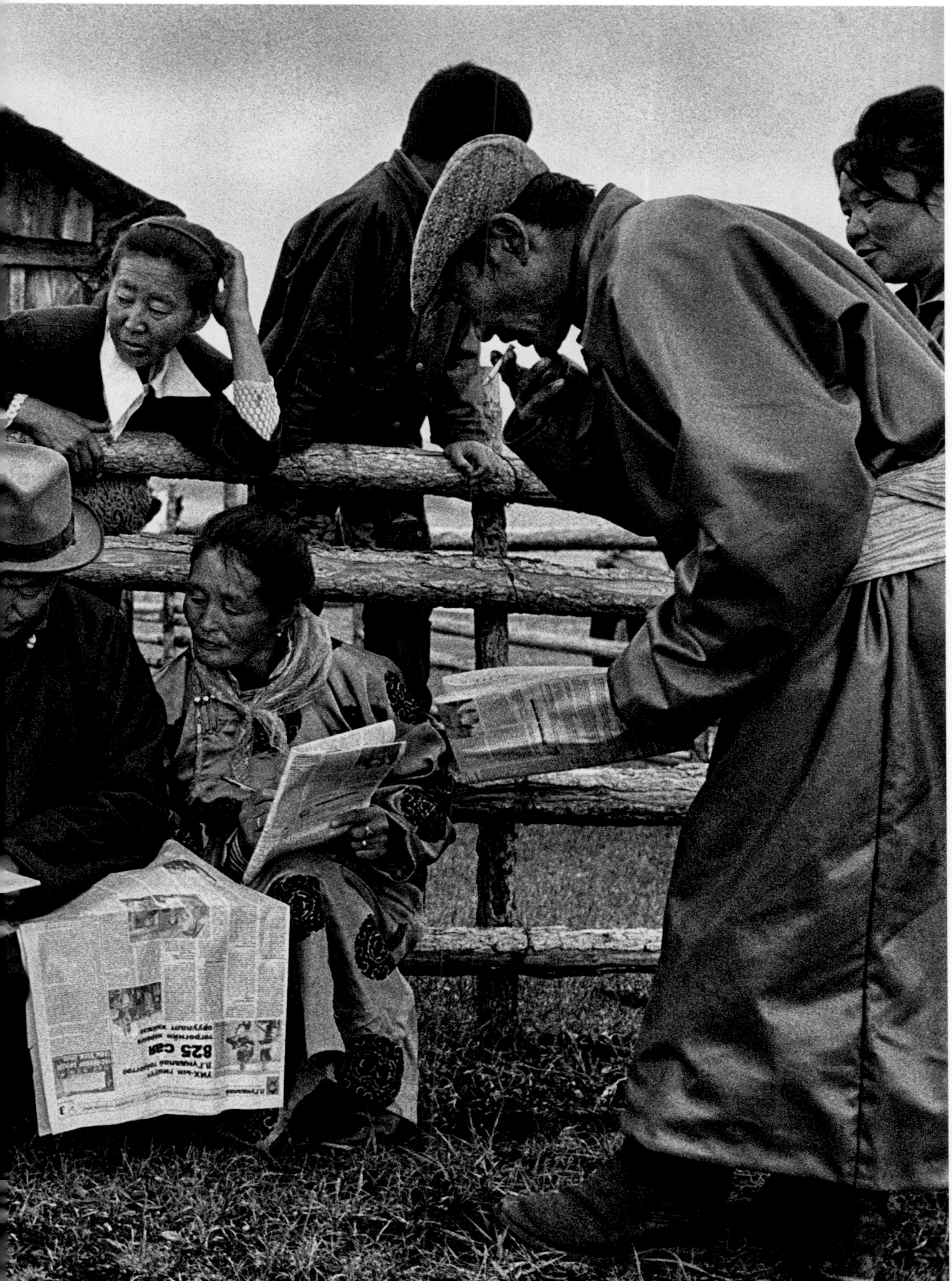

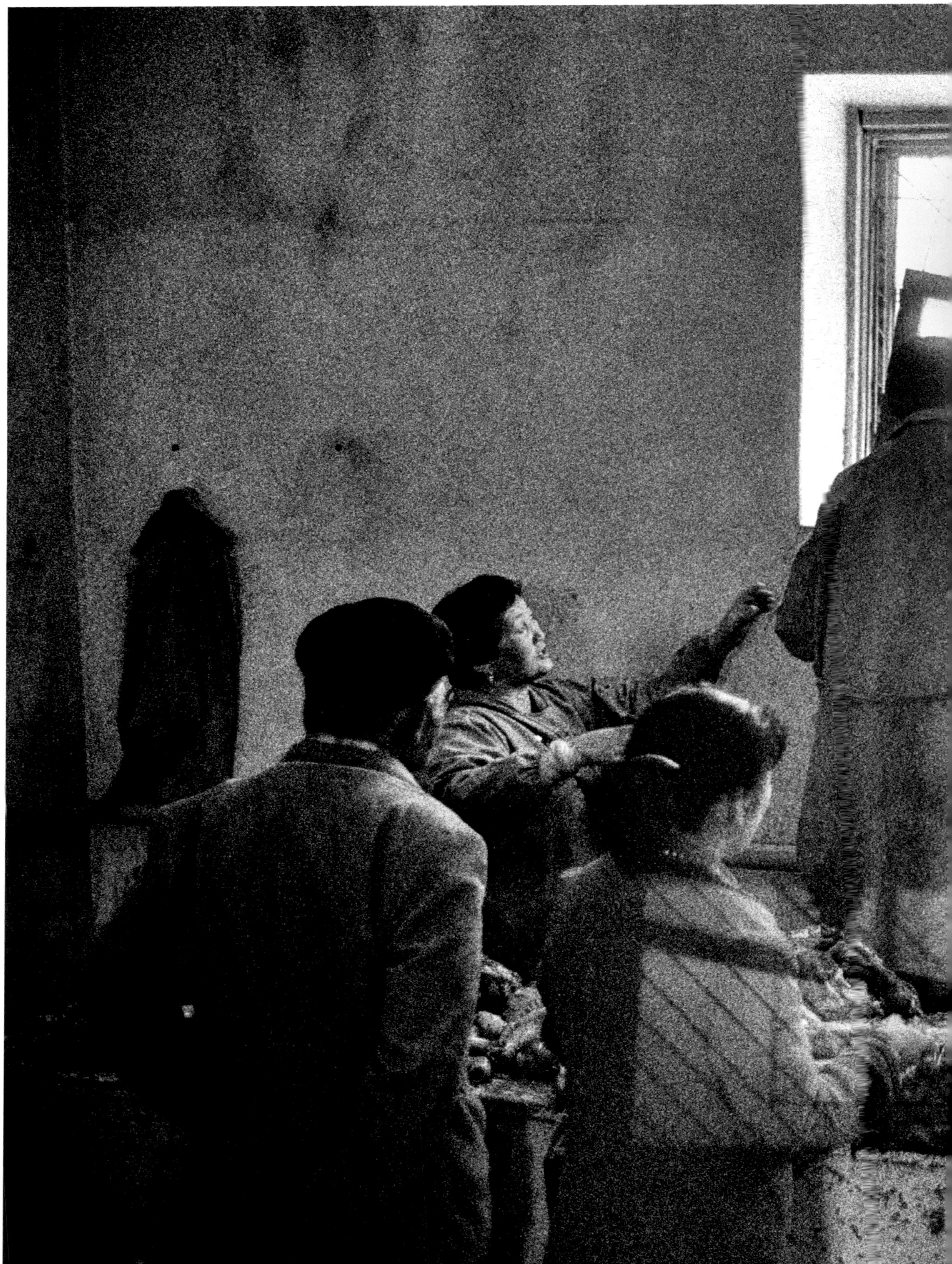

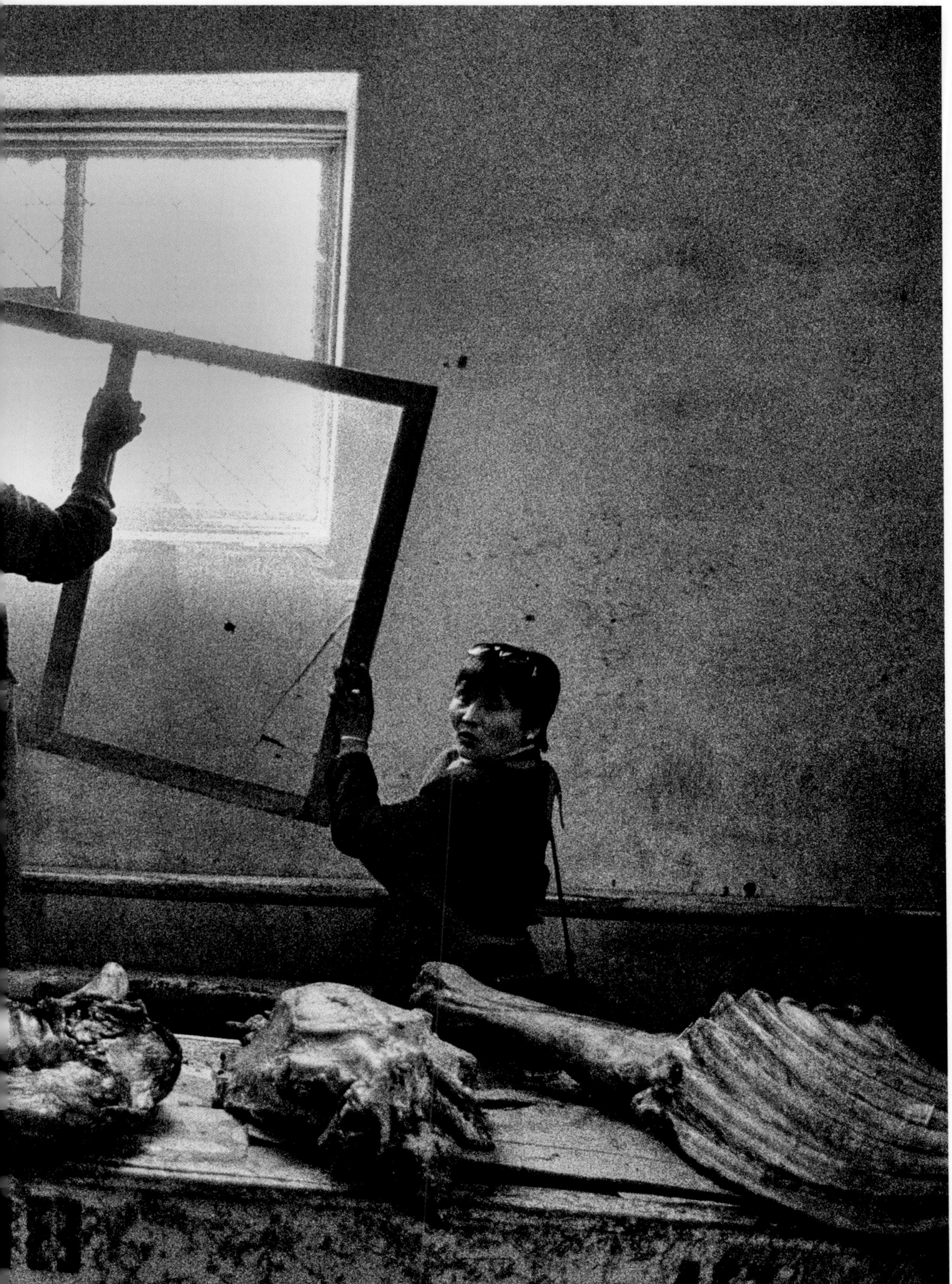

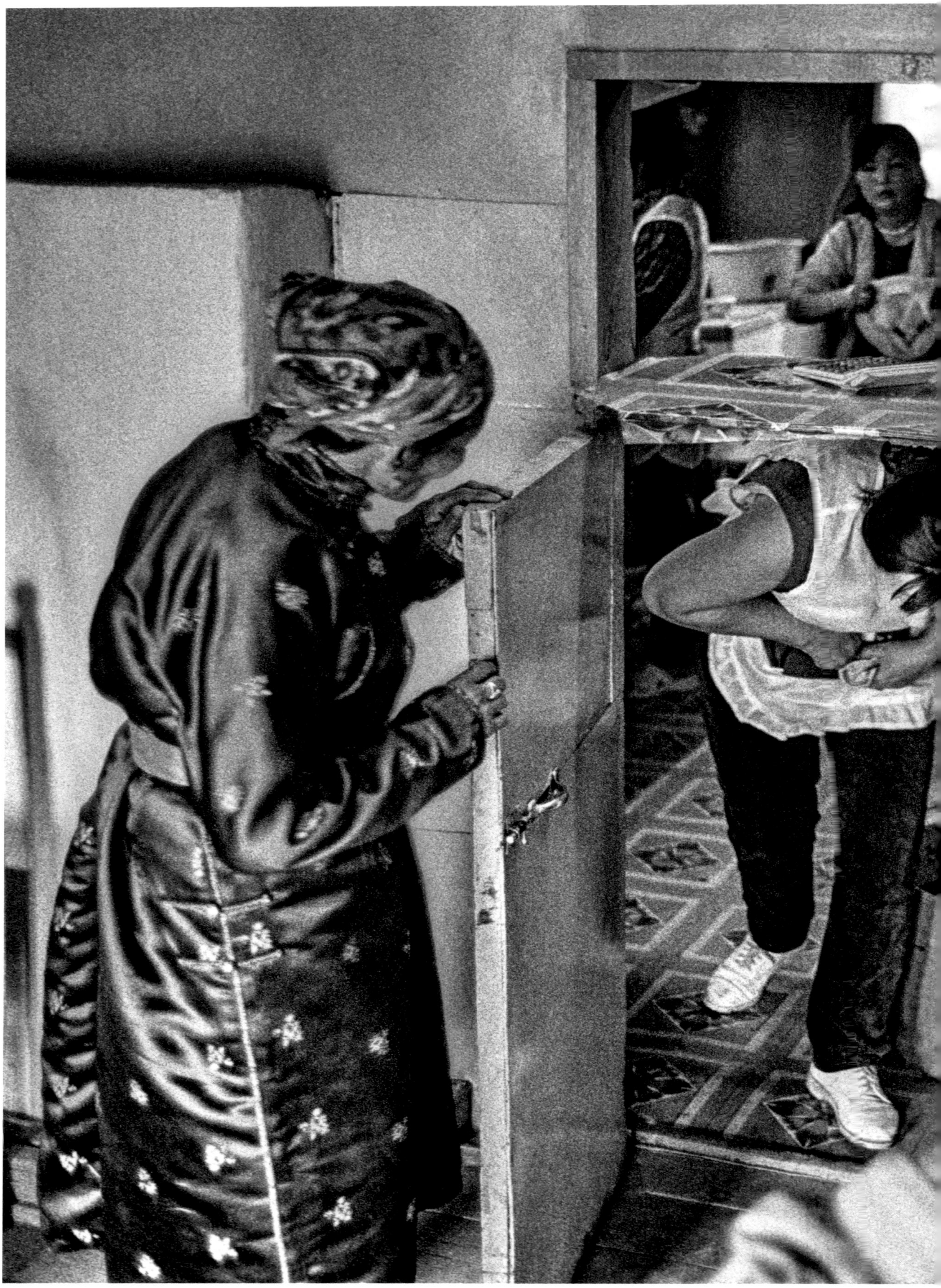

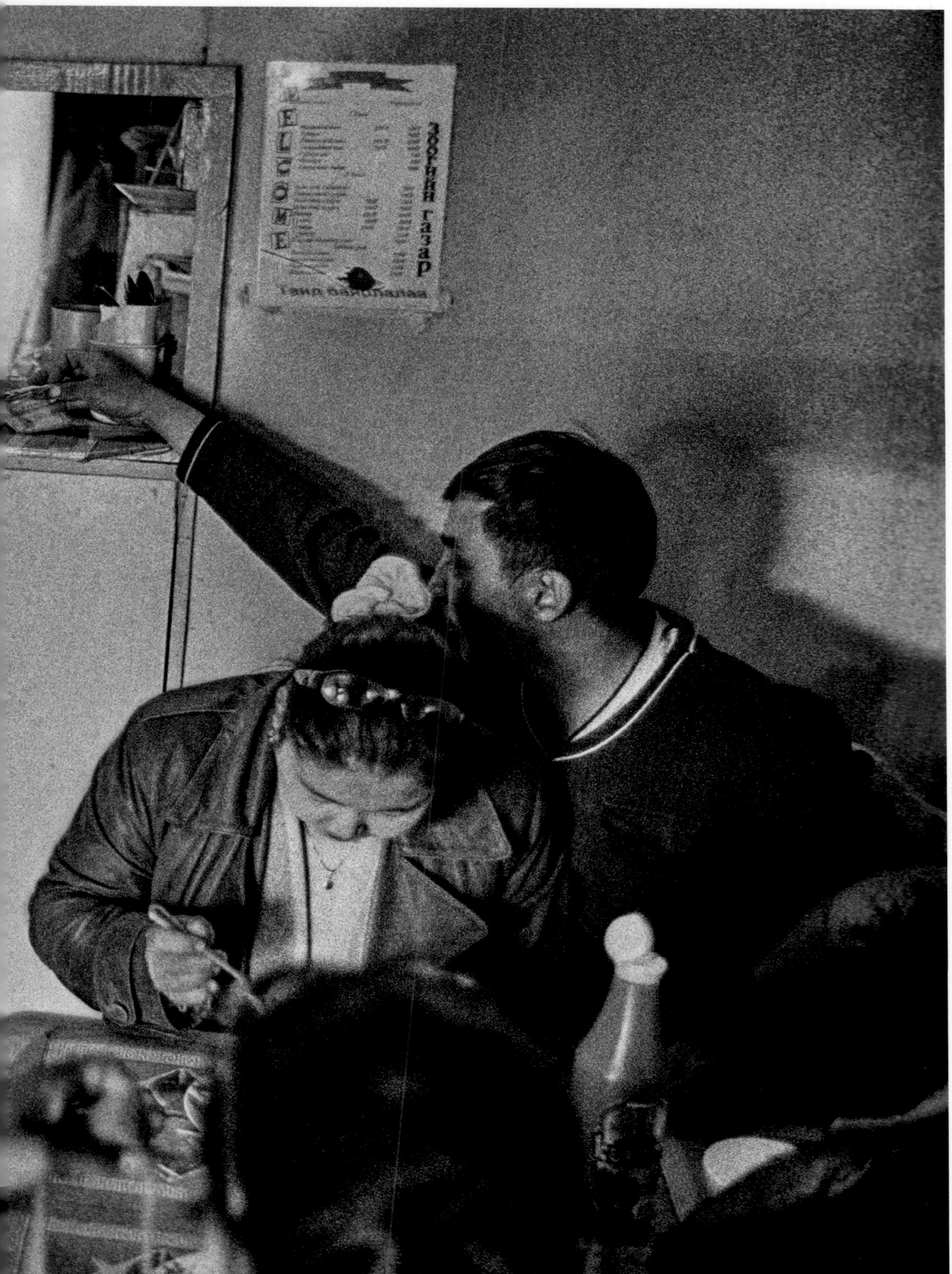
ELCOME
зоогийн газар

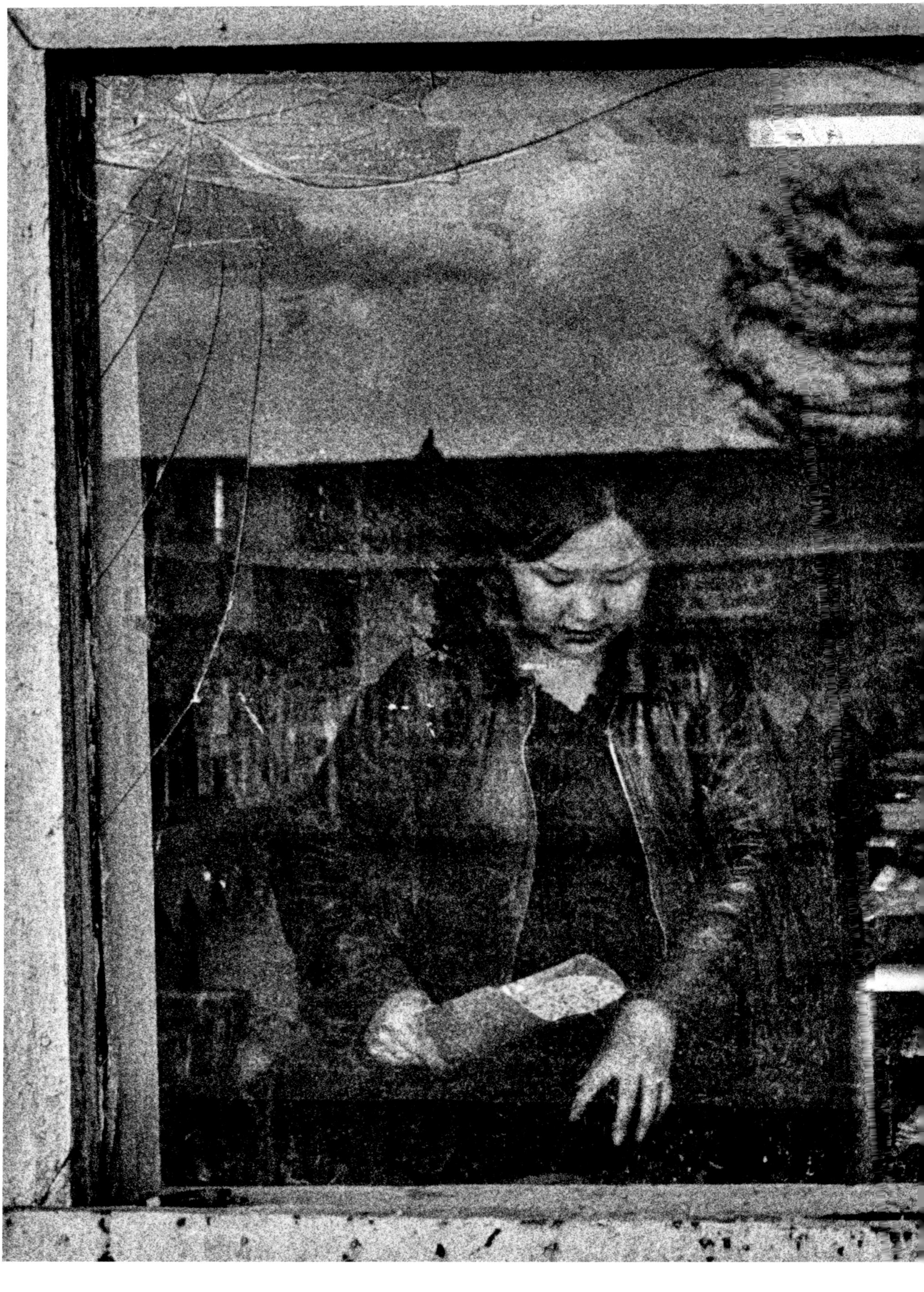

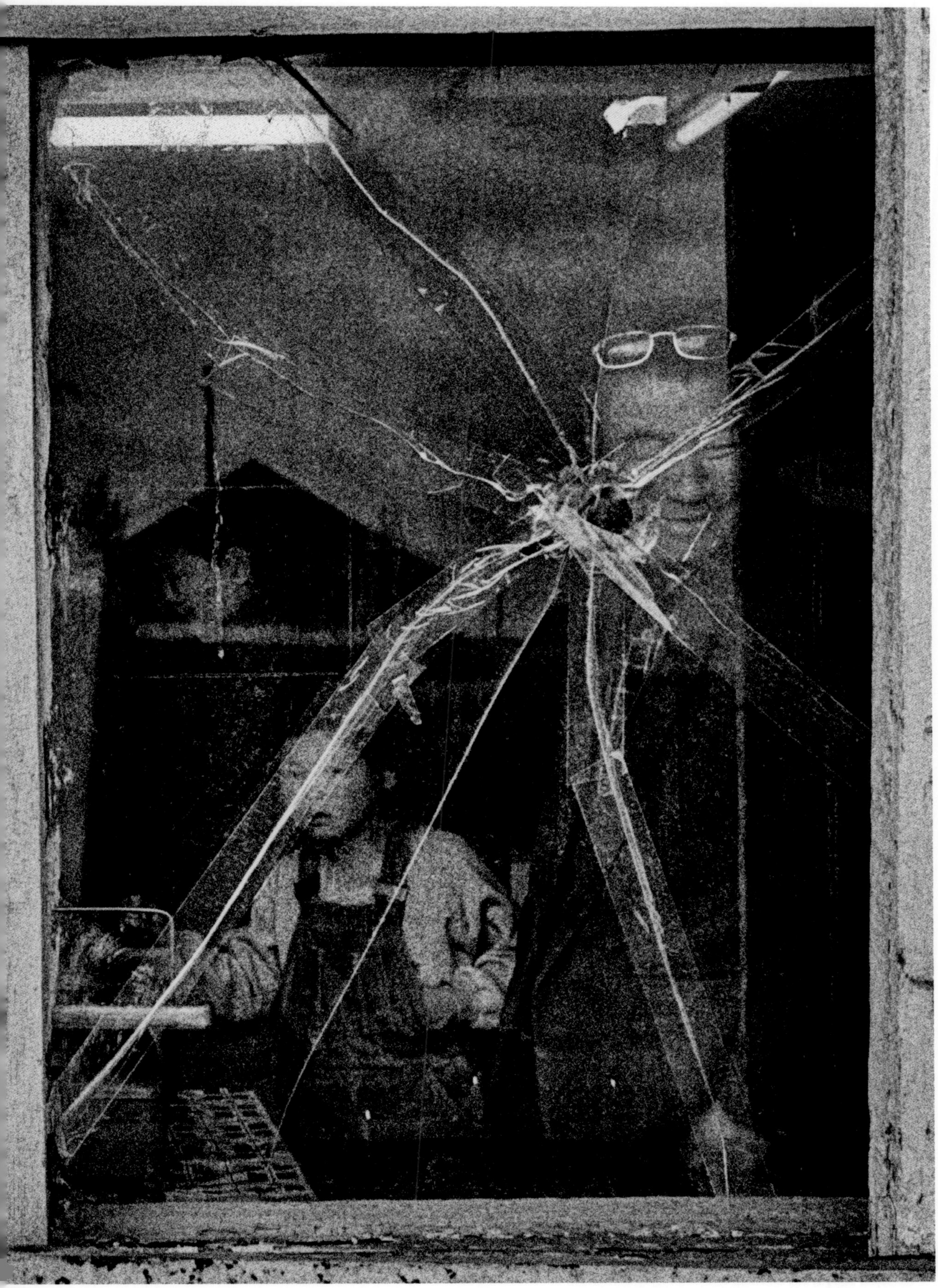

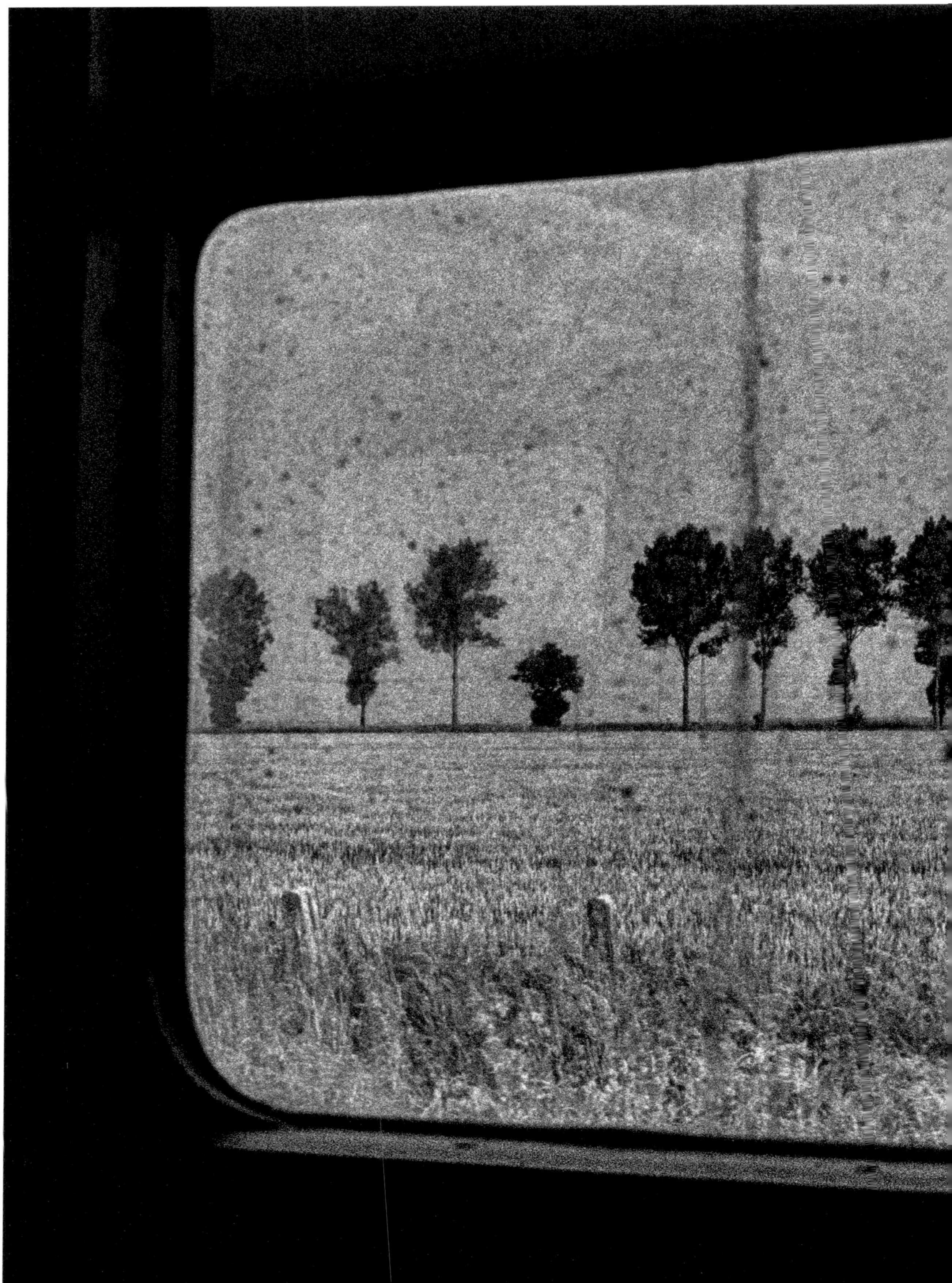

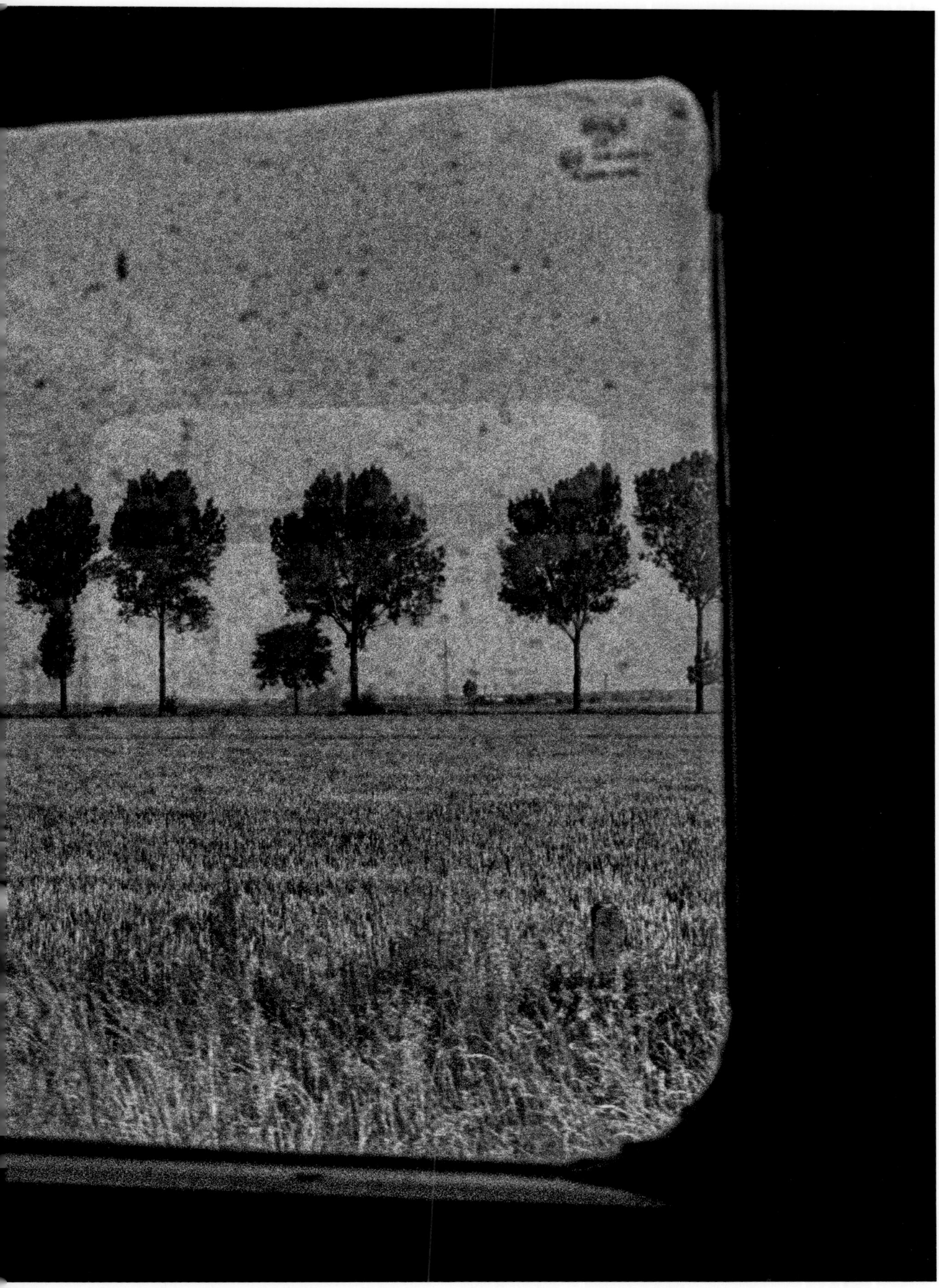

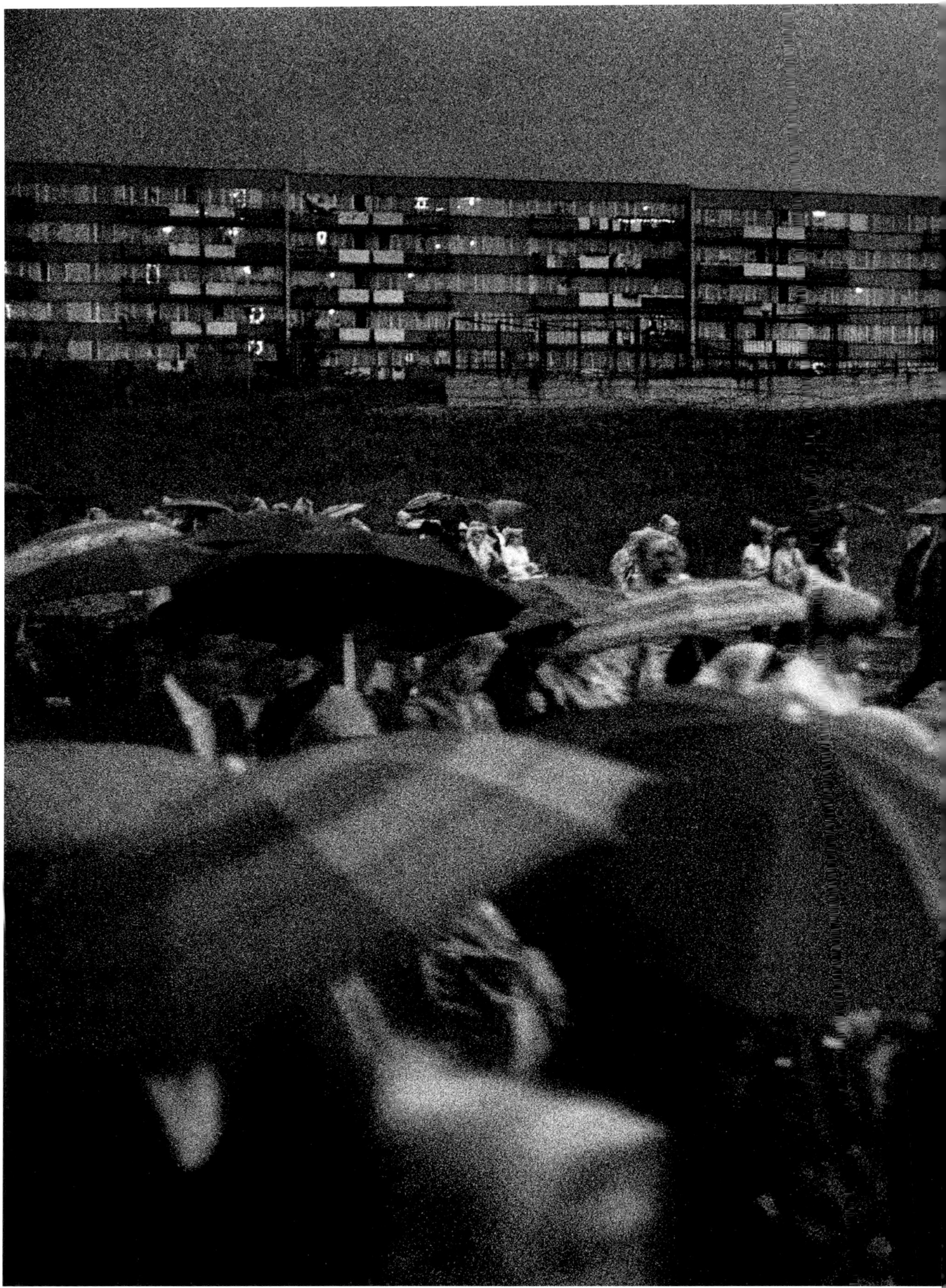

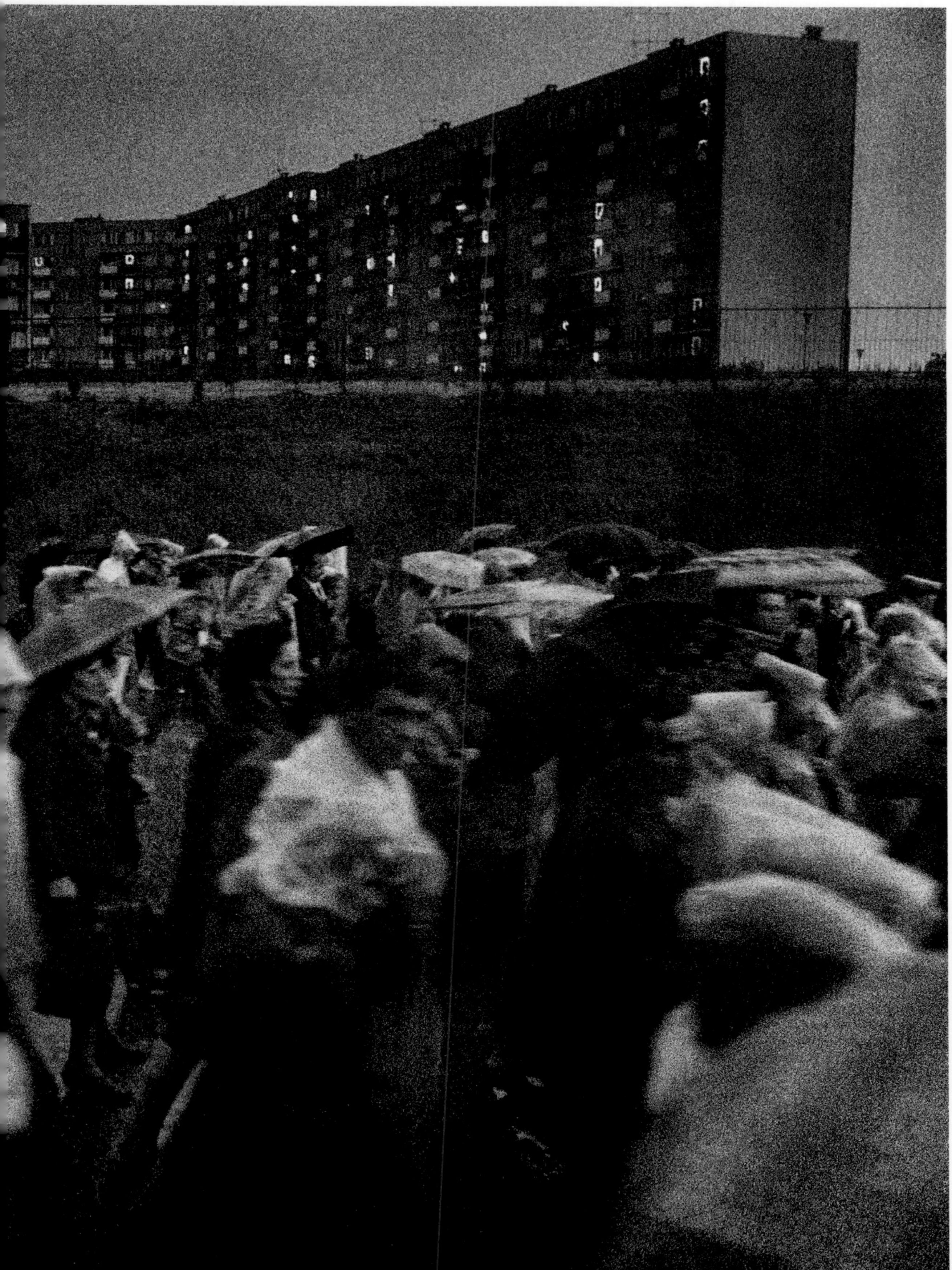

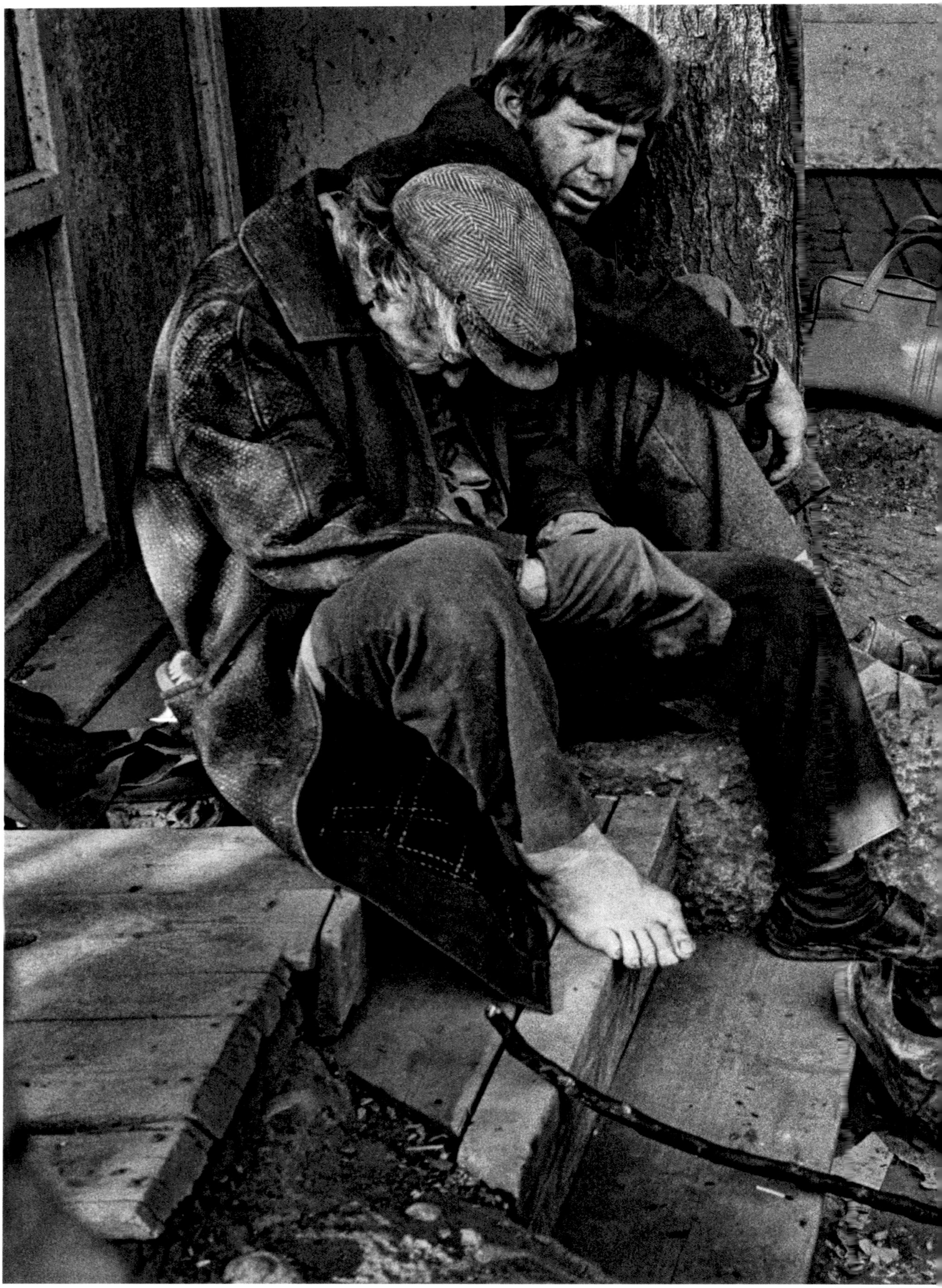

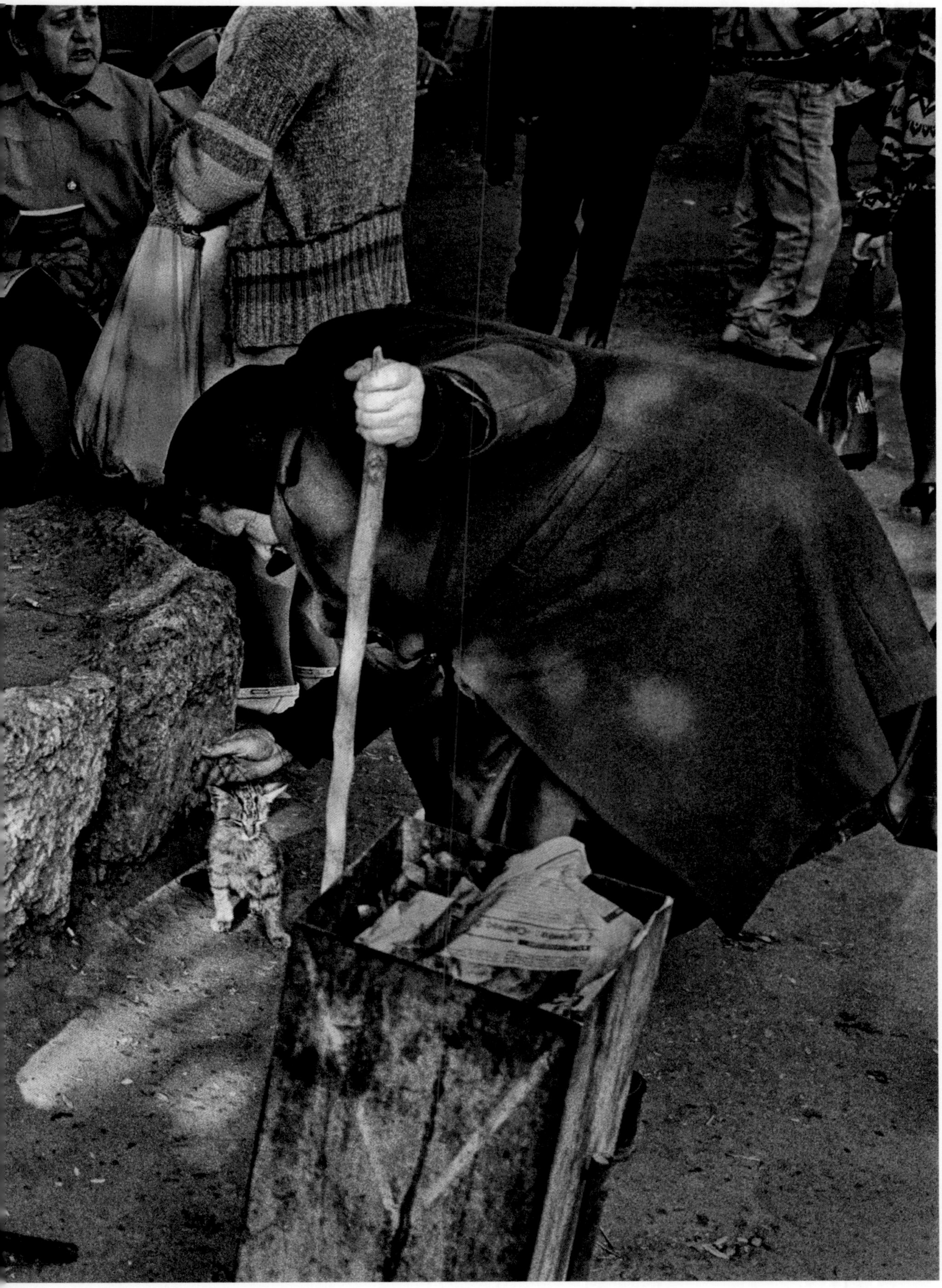

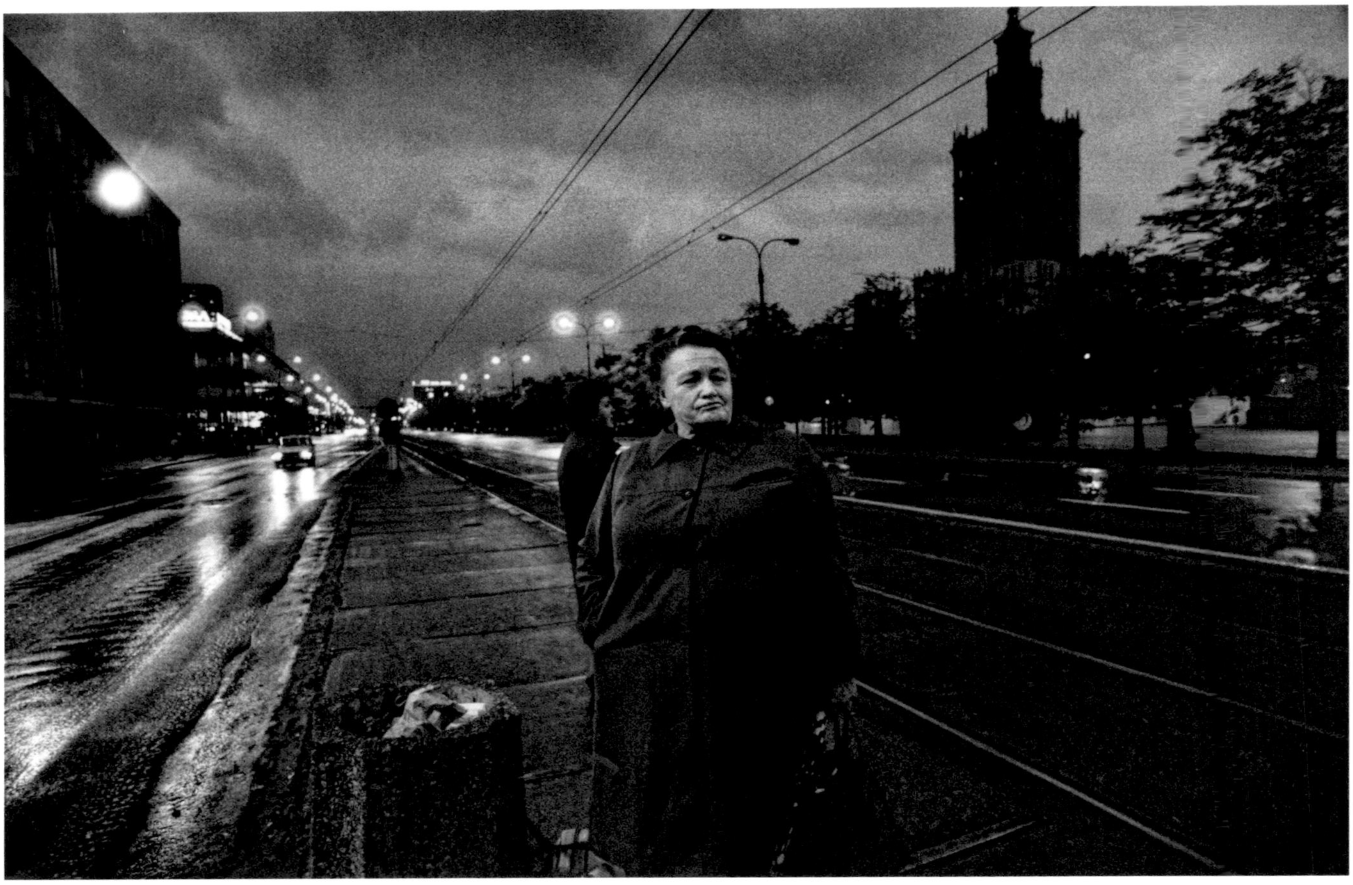

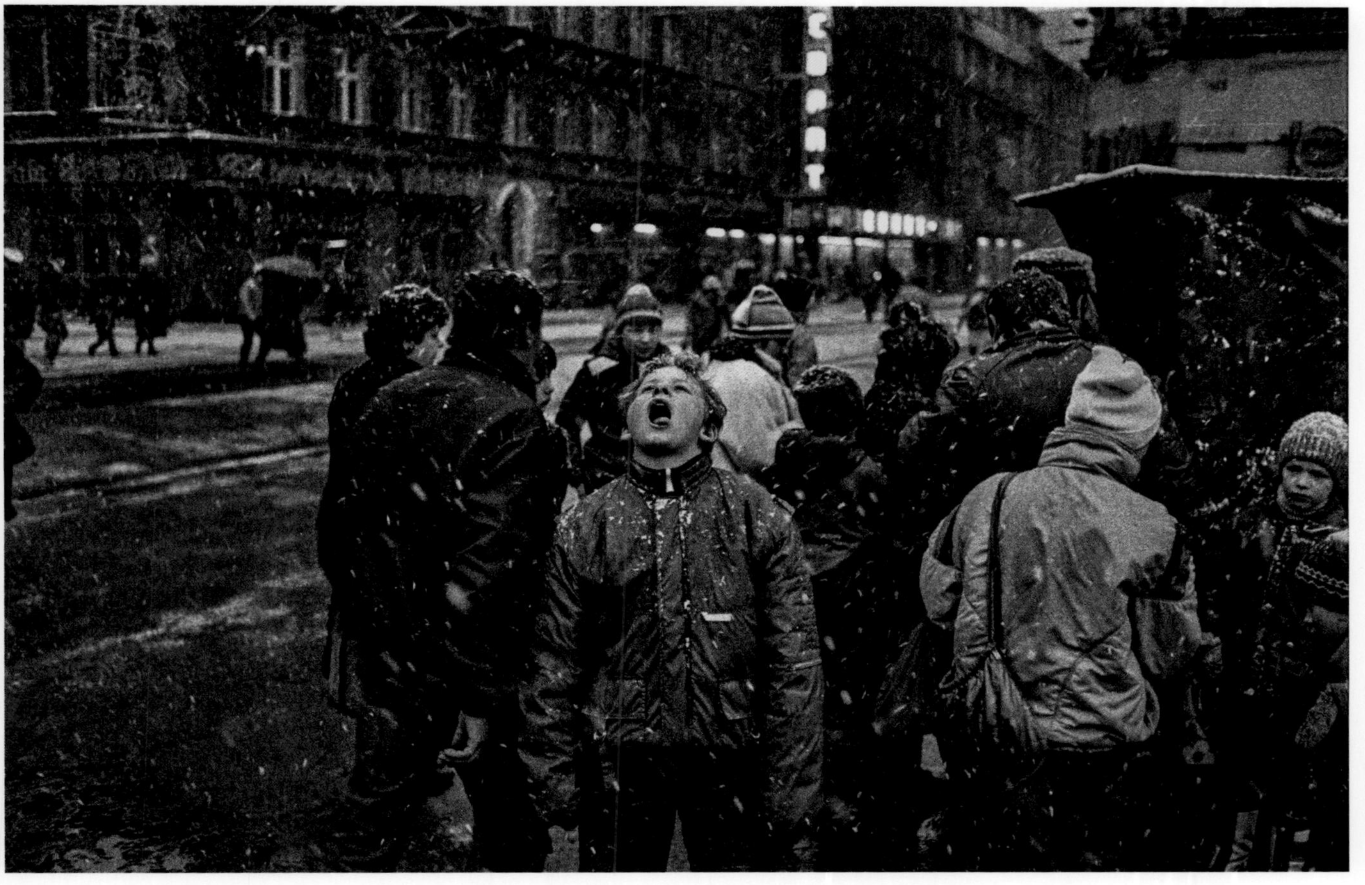

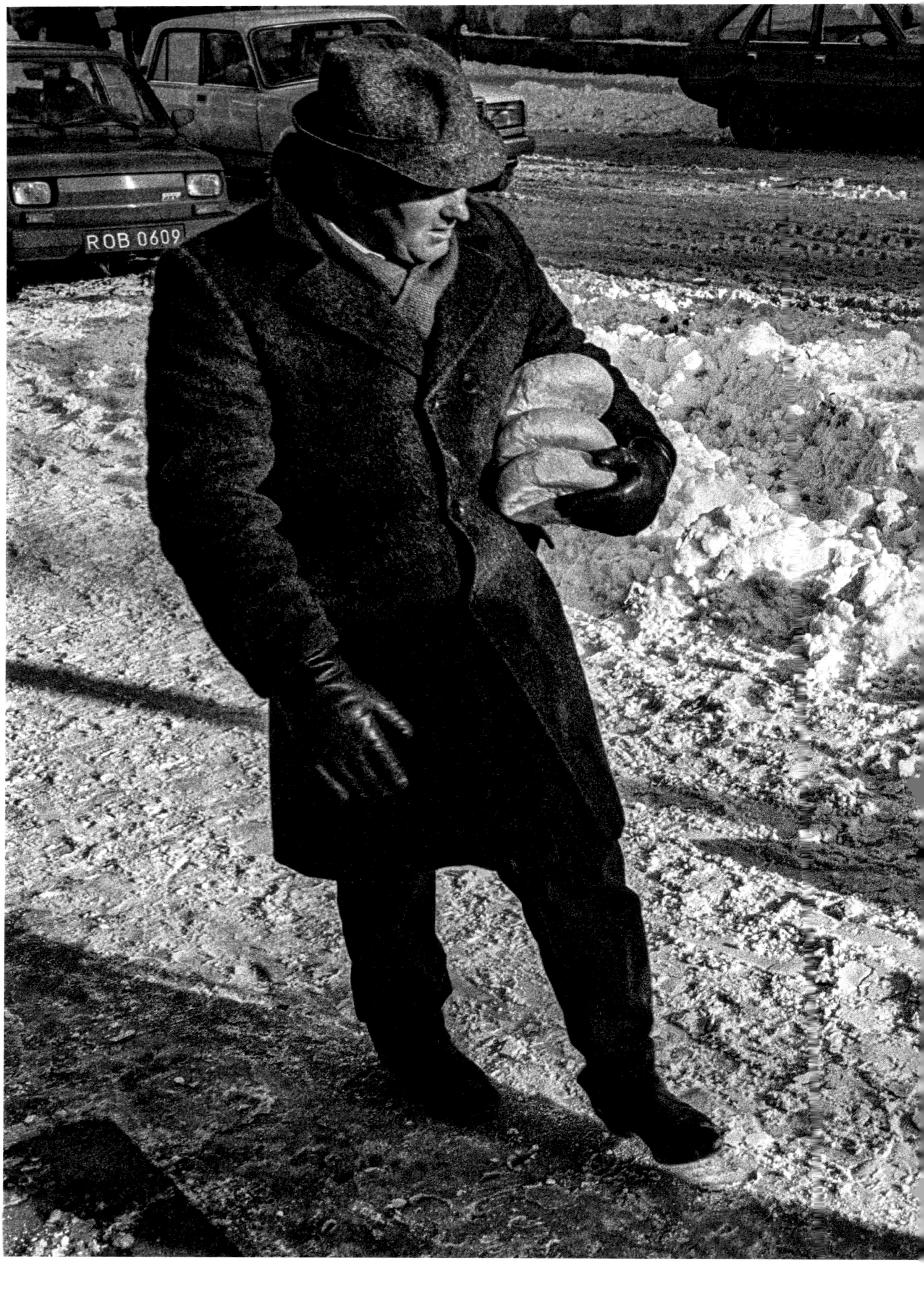
ROB 0609

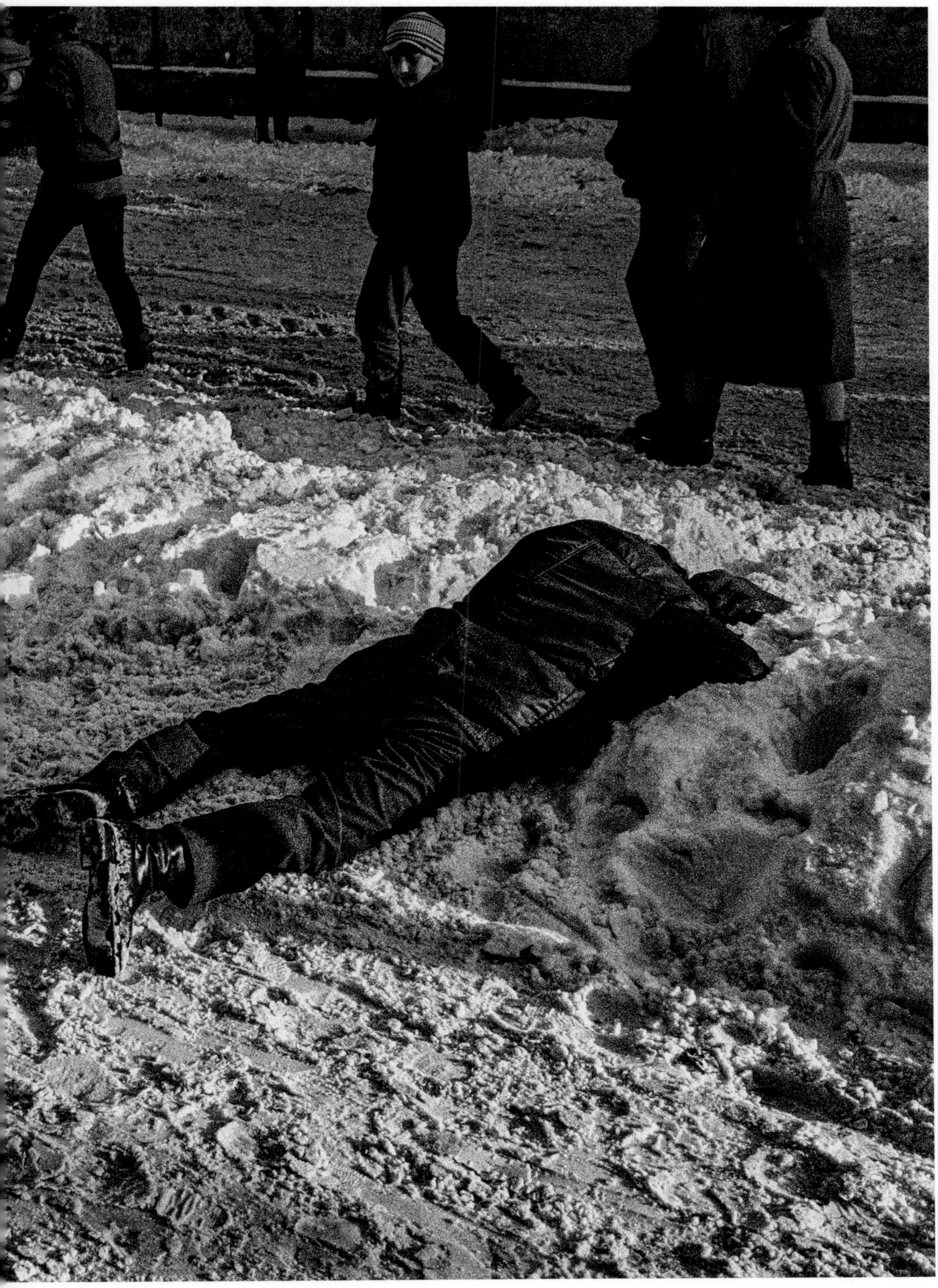

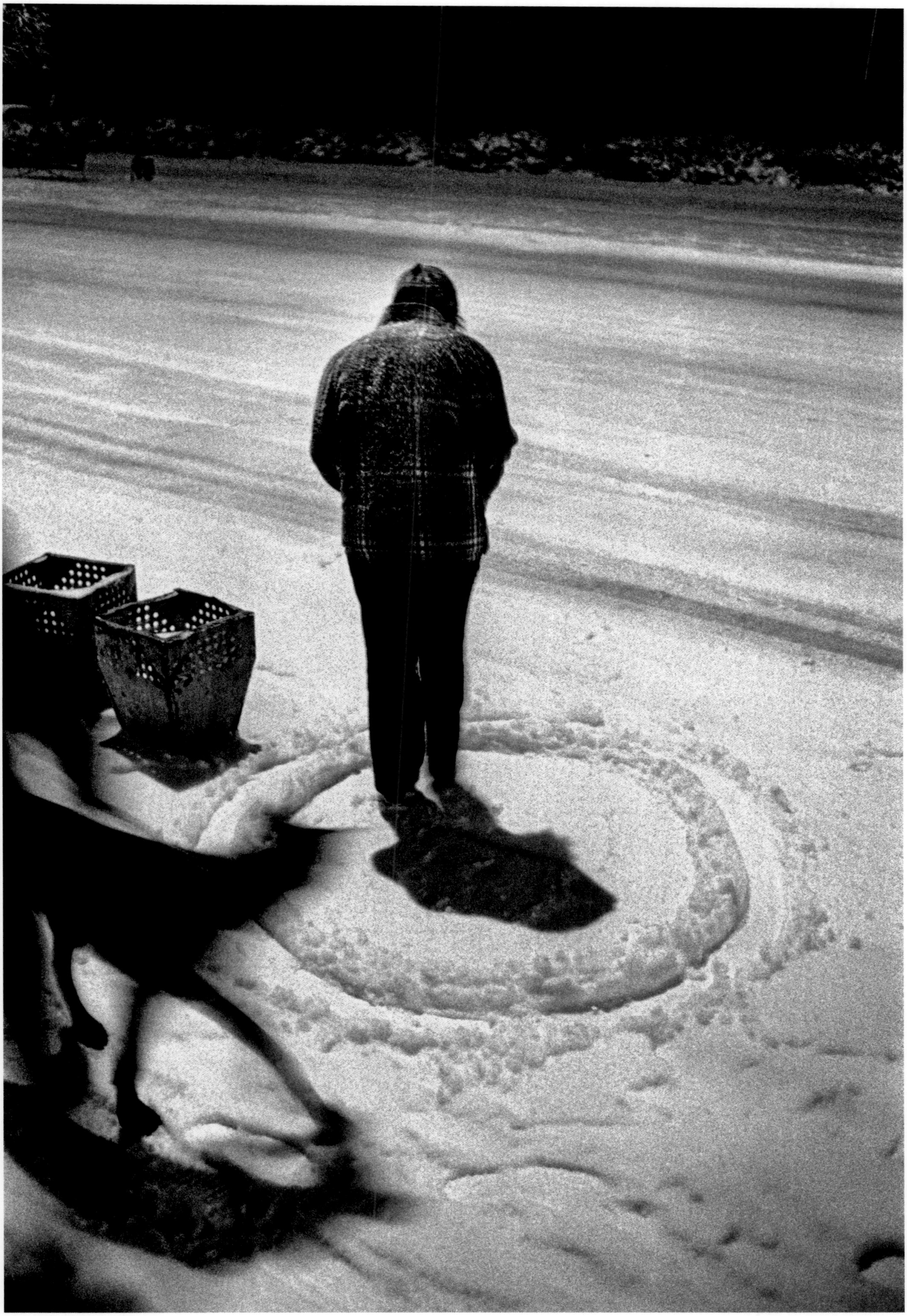

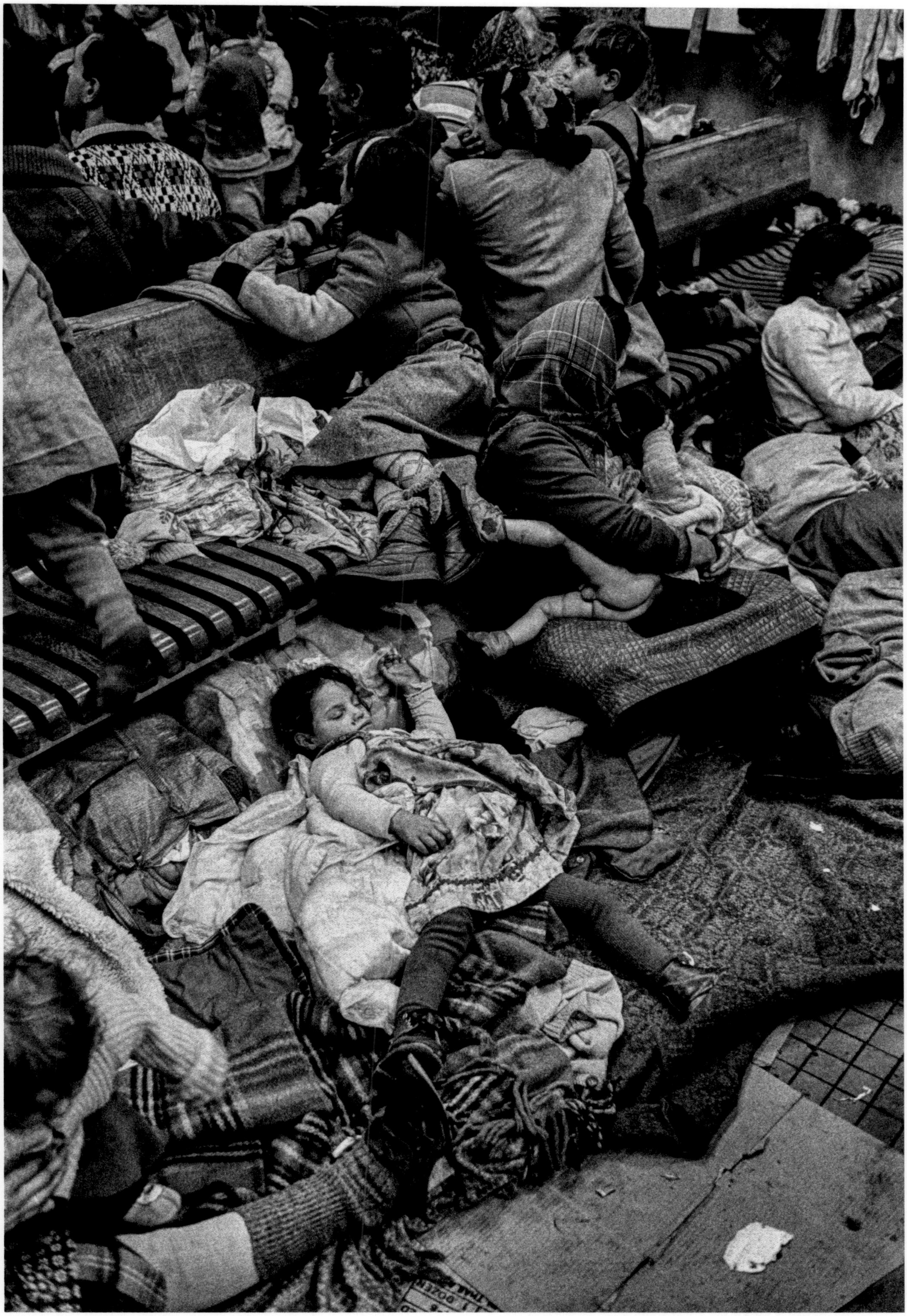

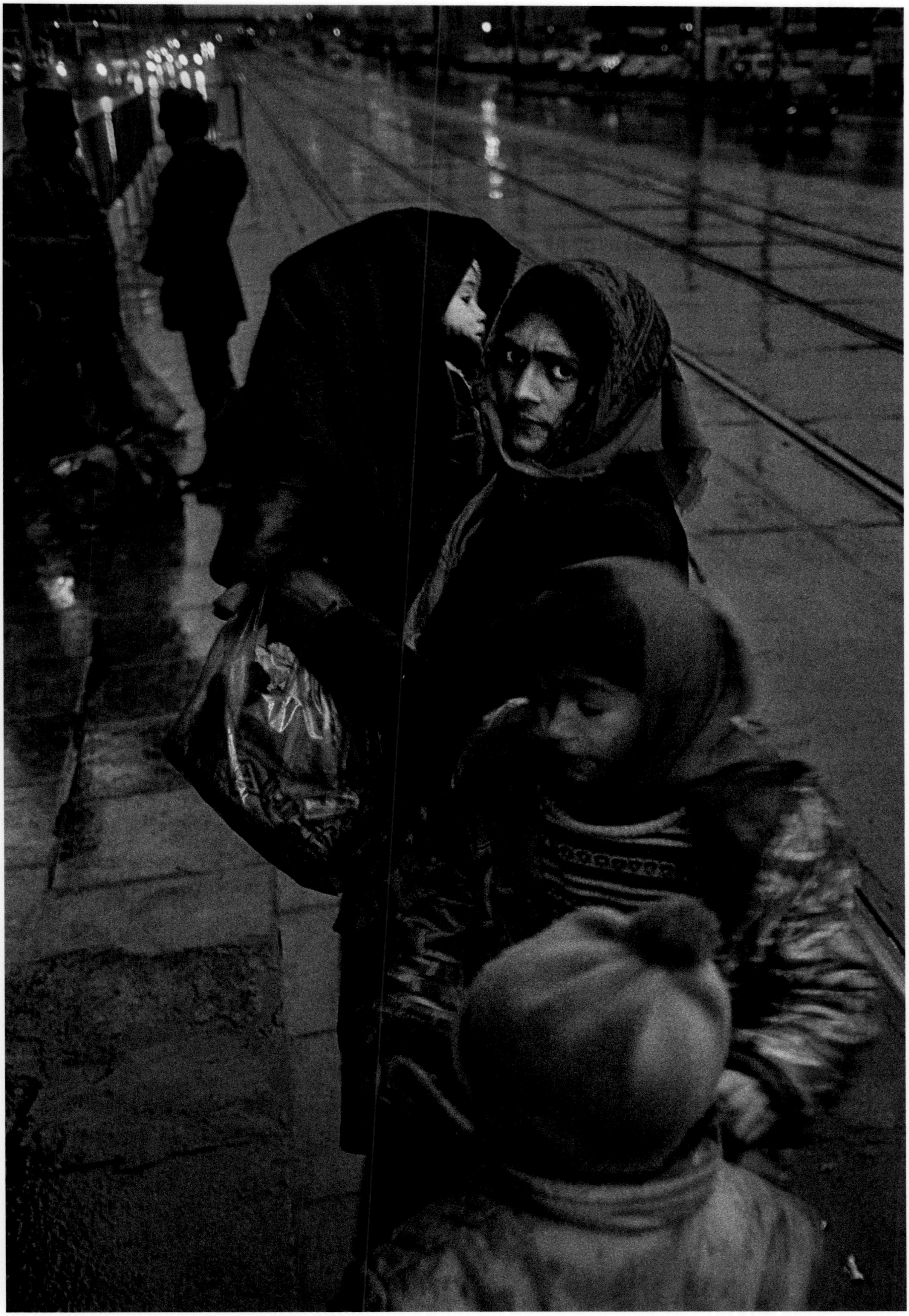

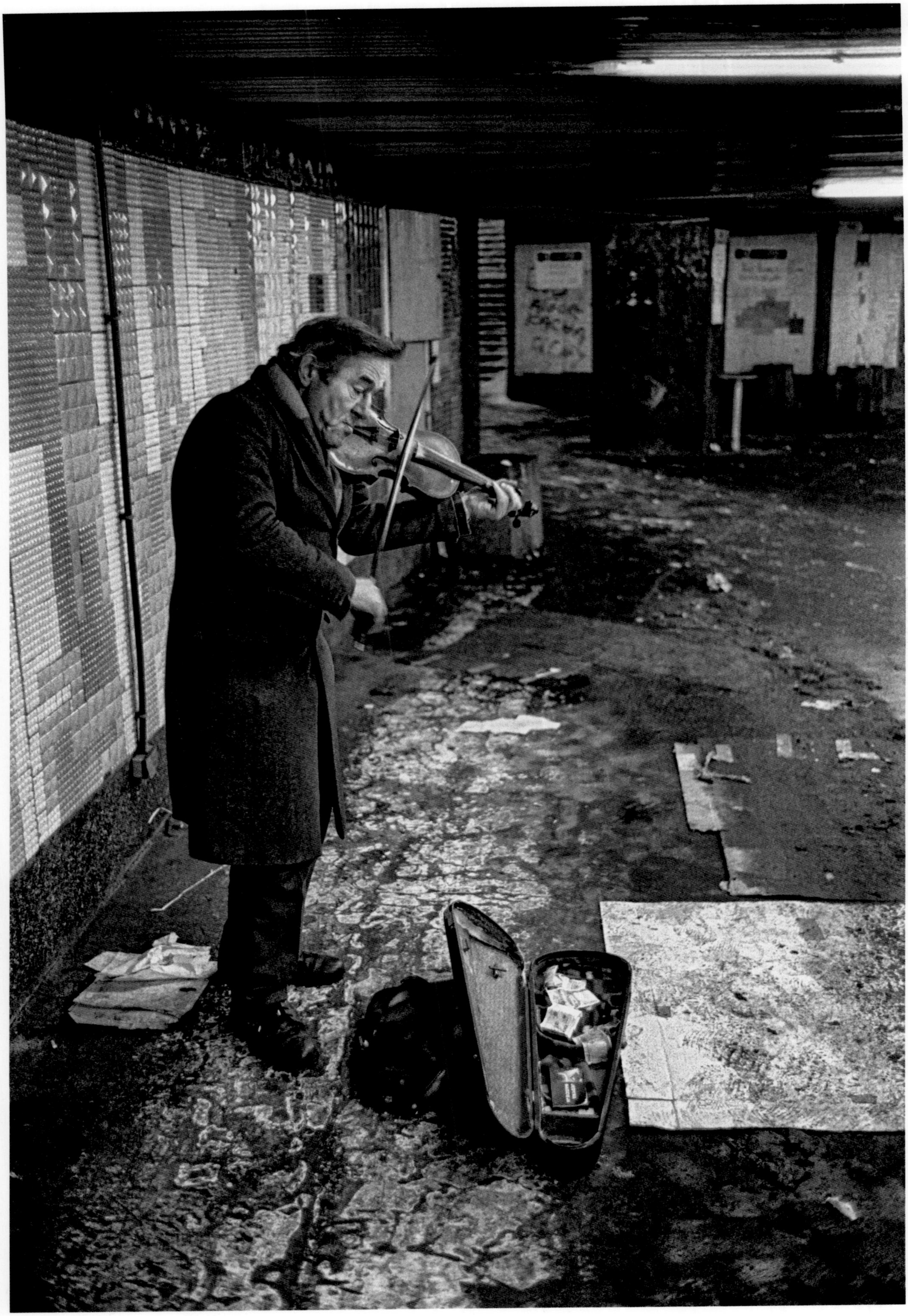

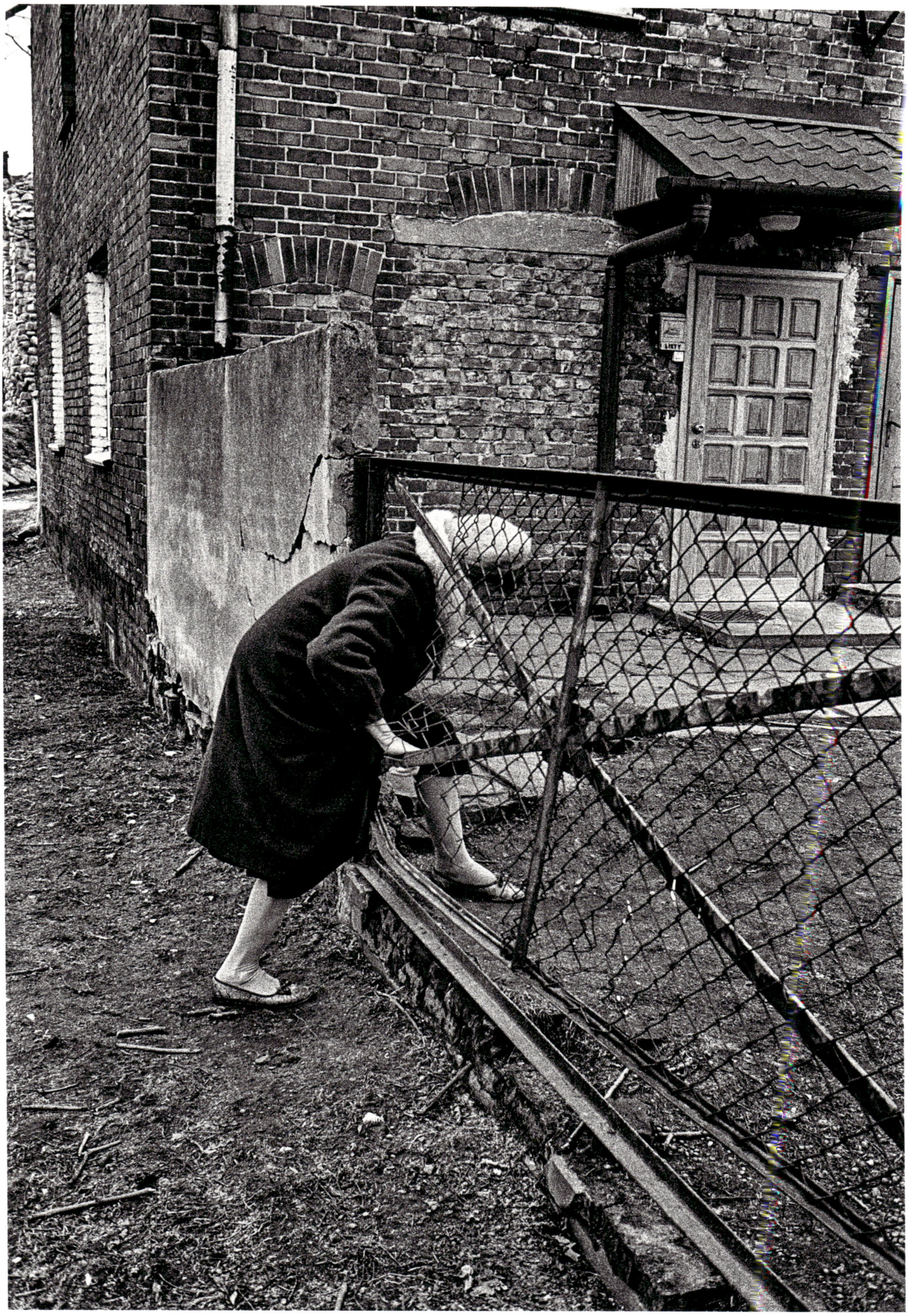

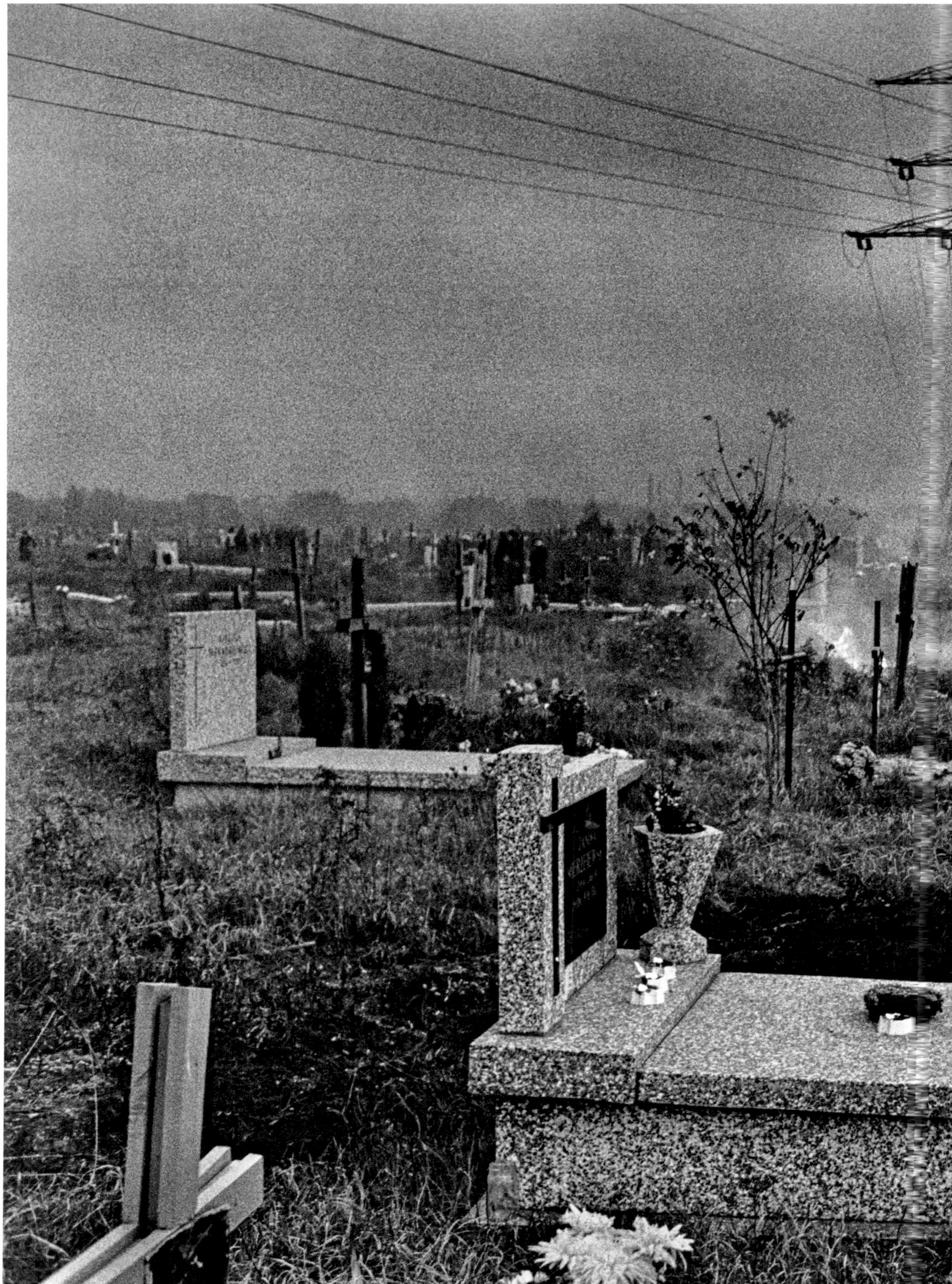

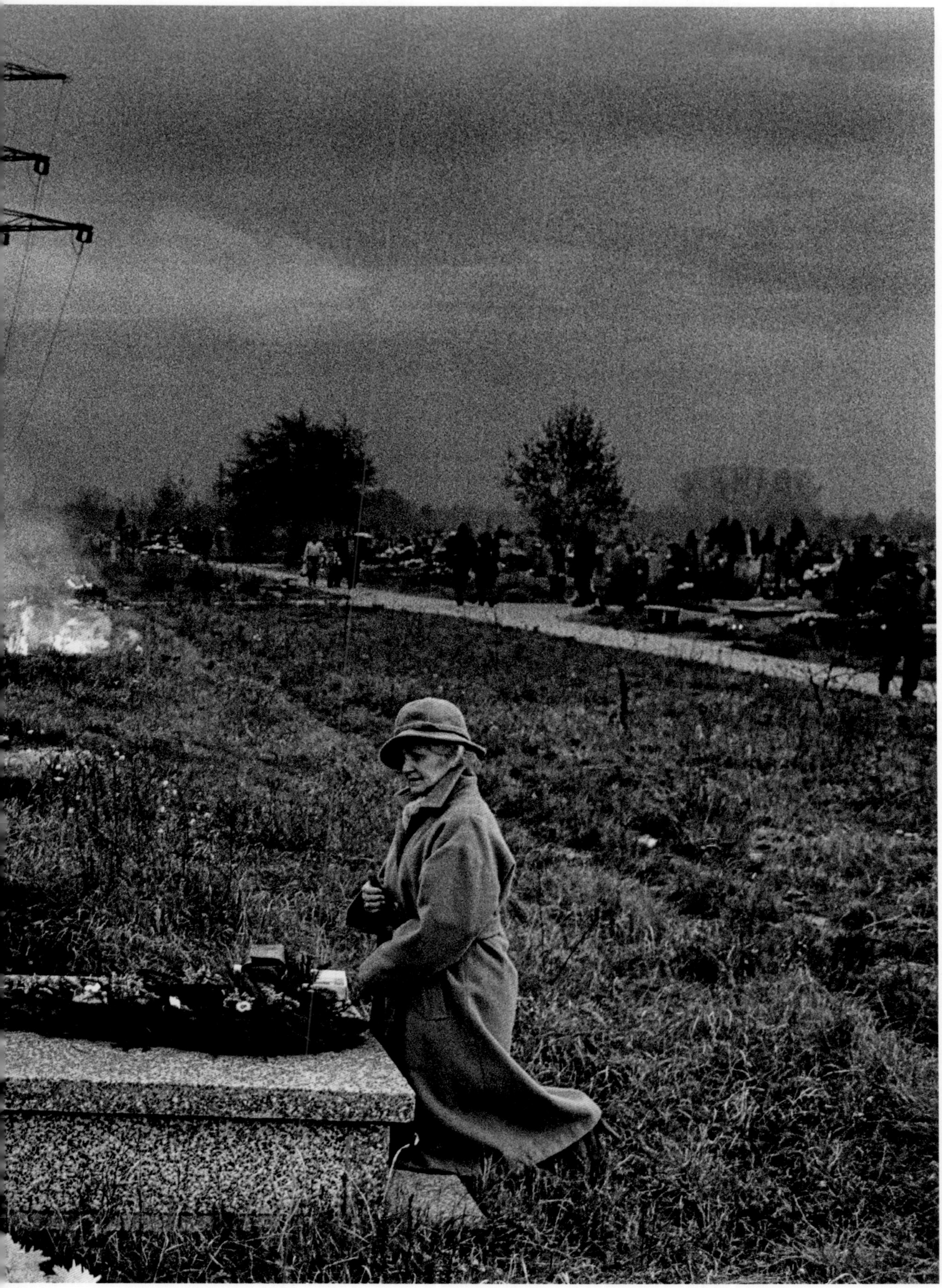

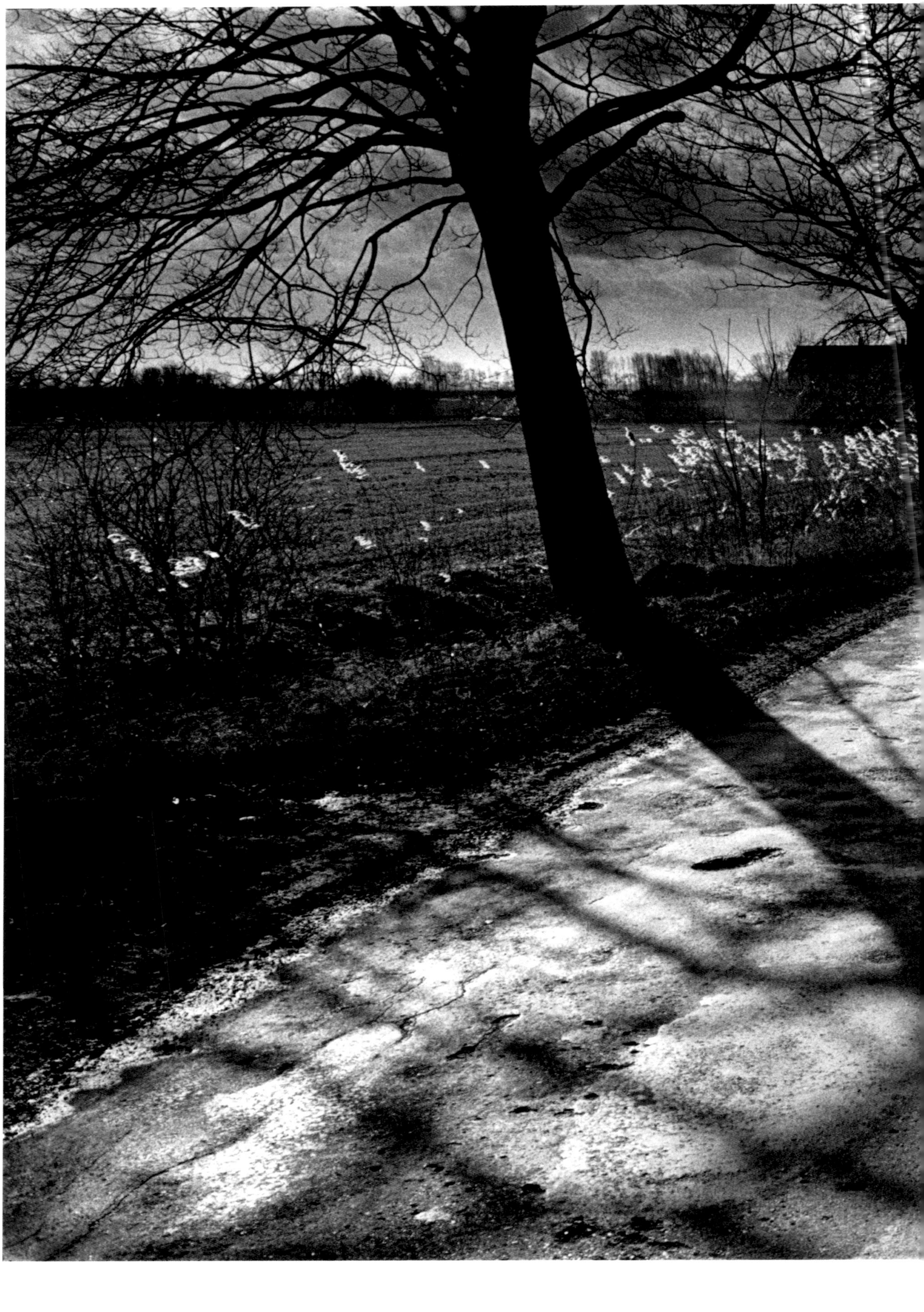

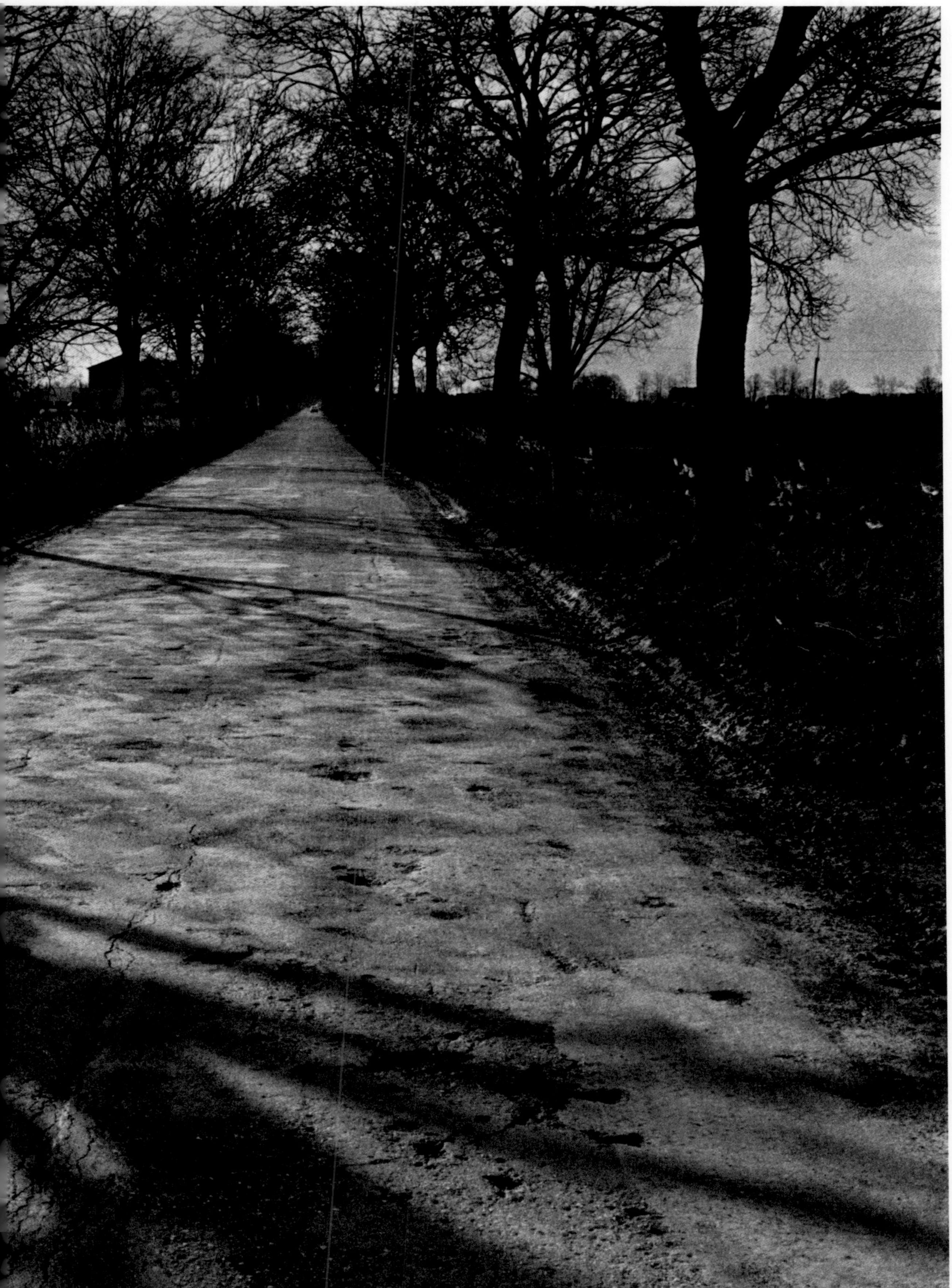

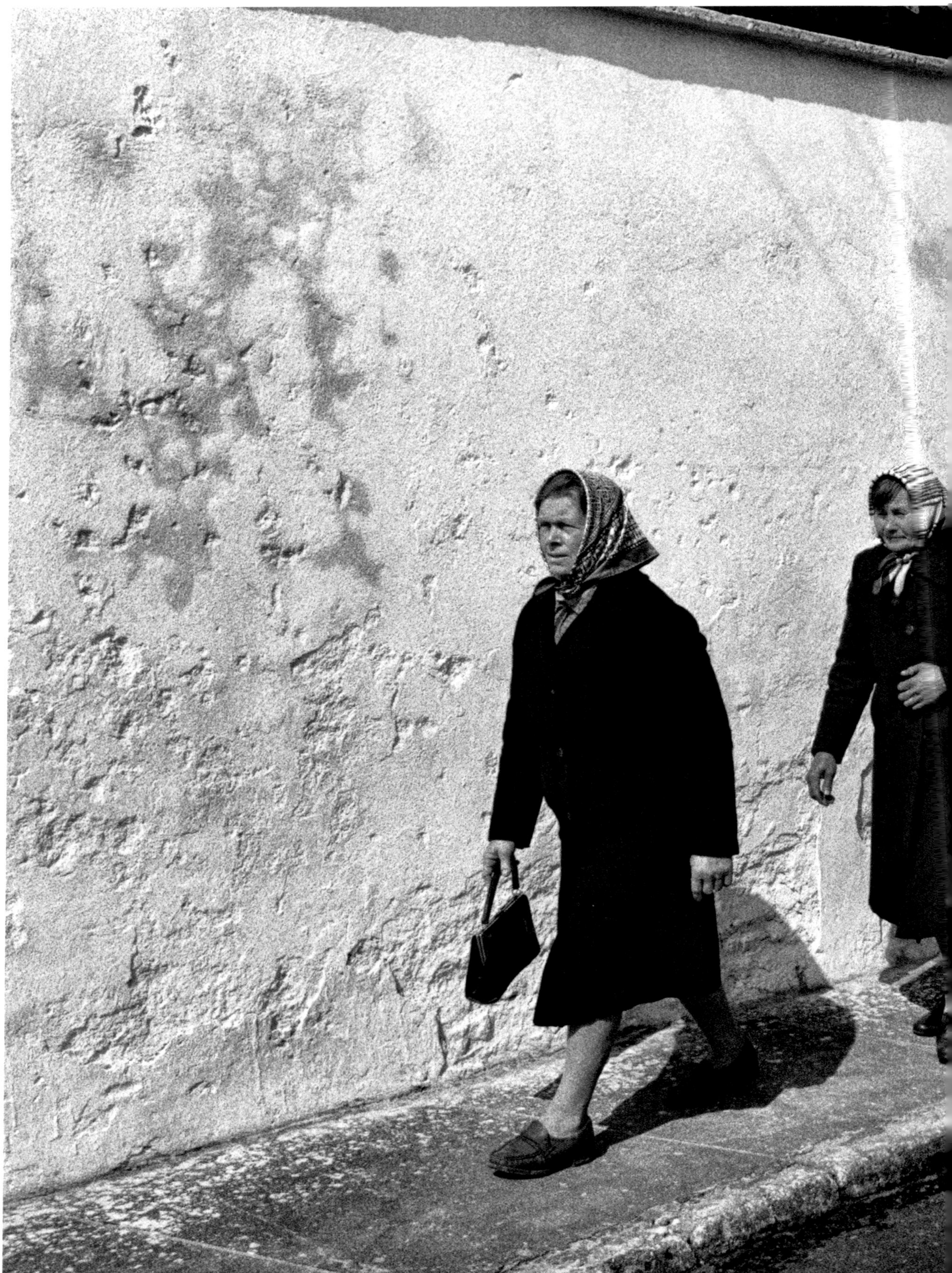

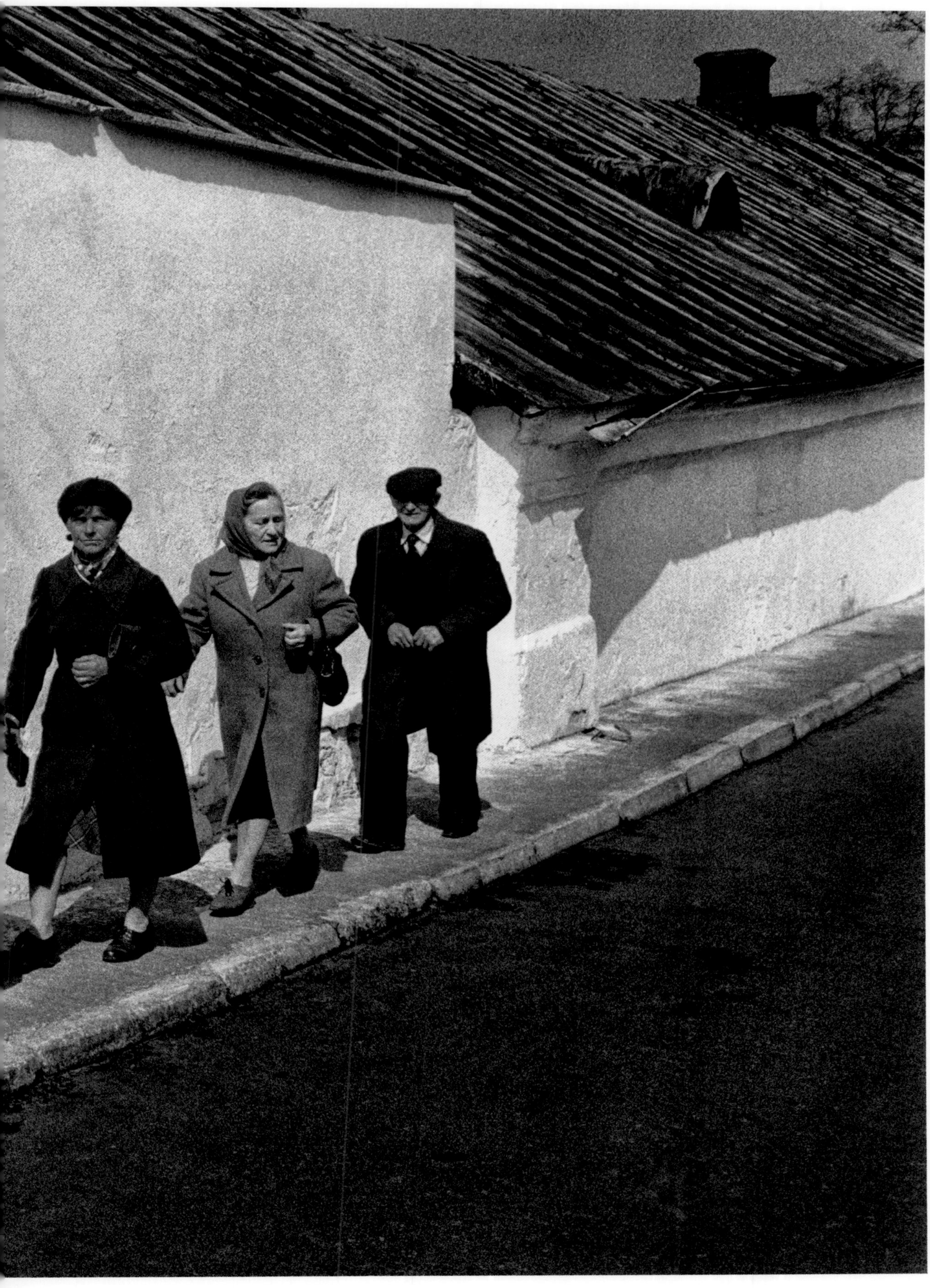

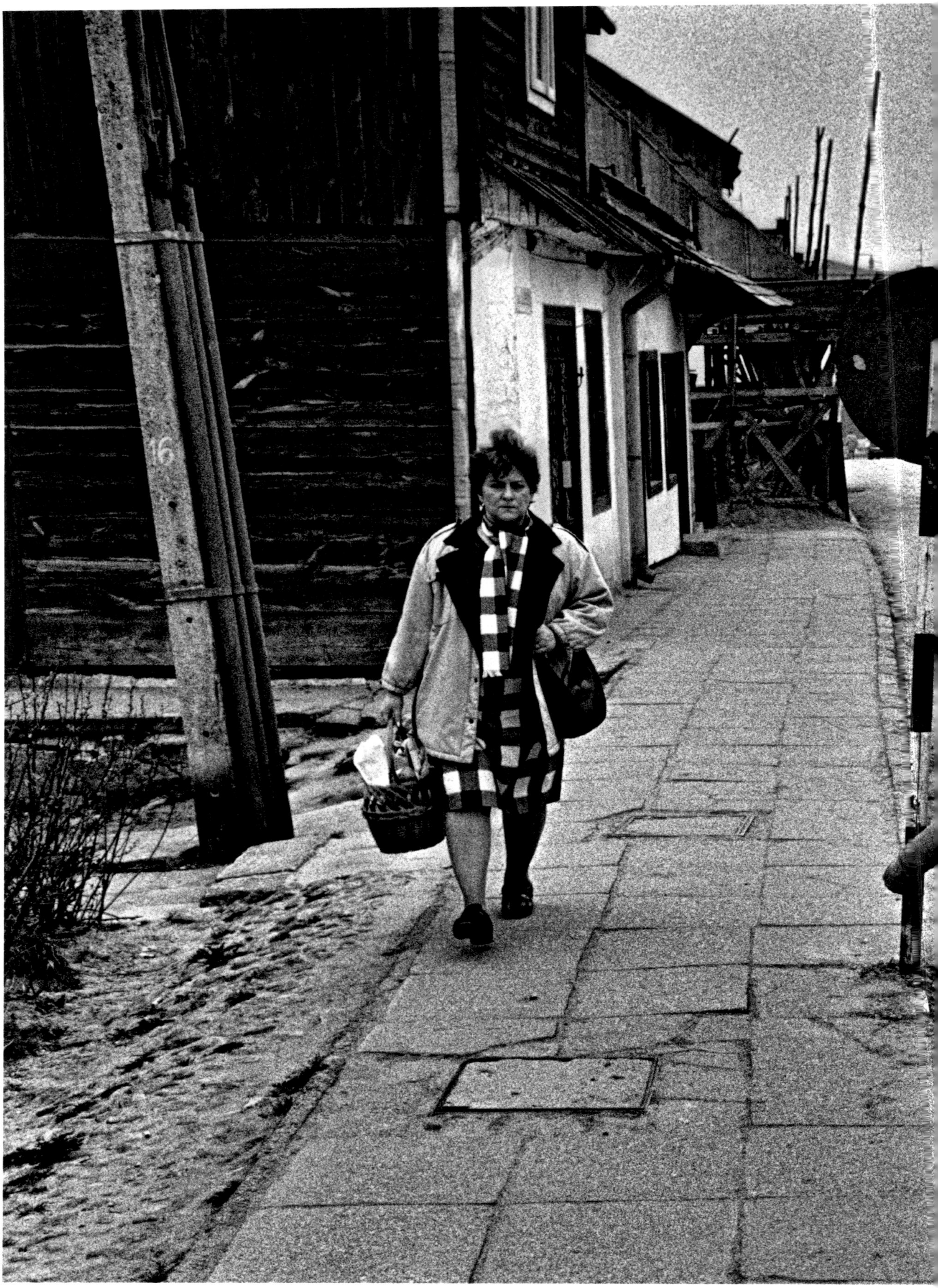

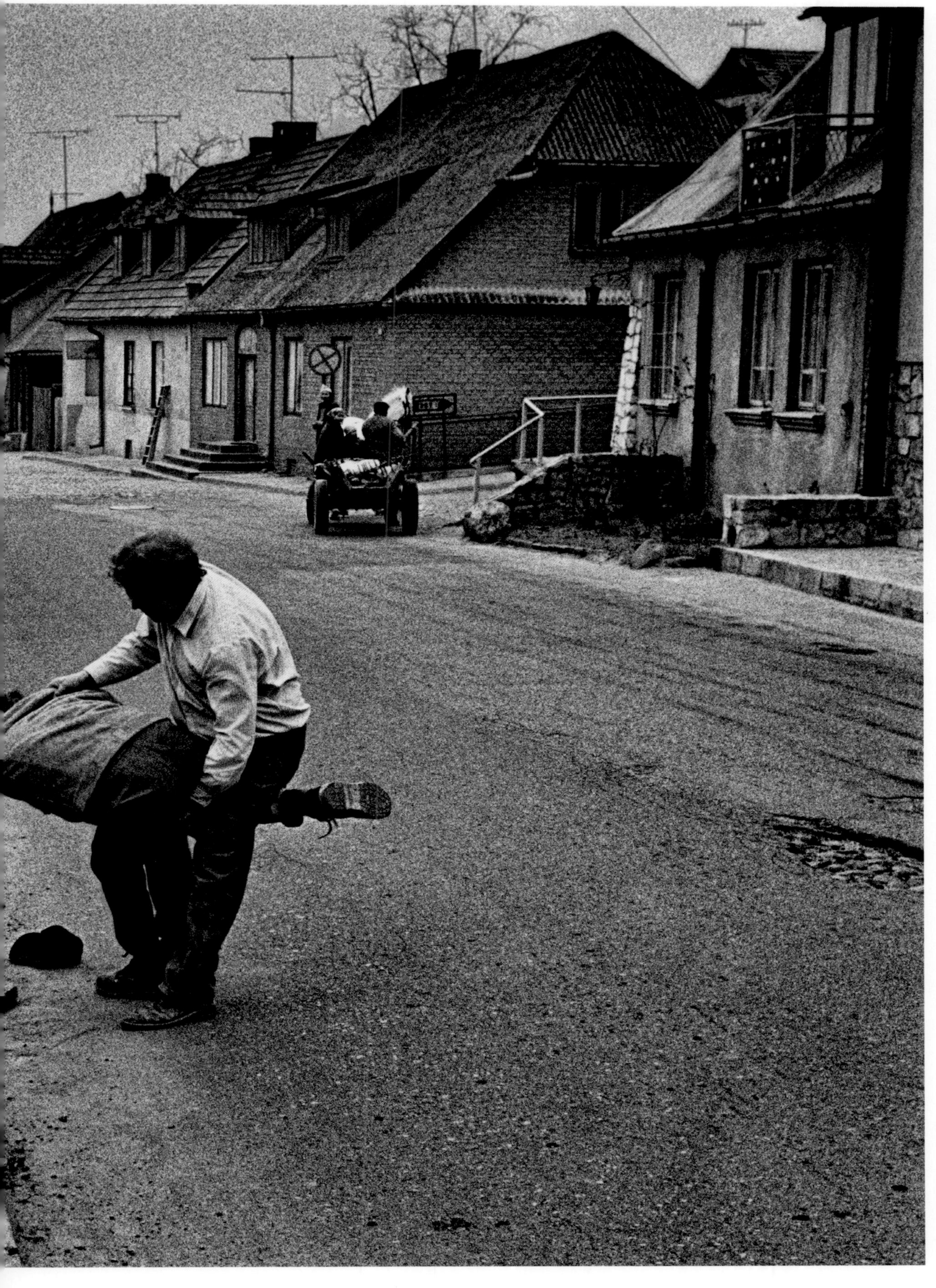

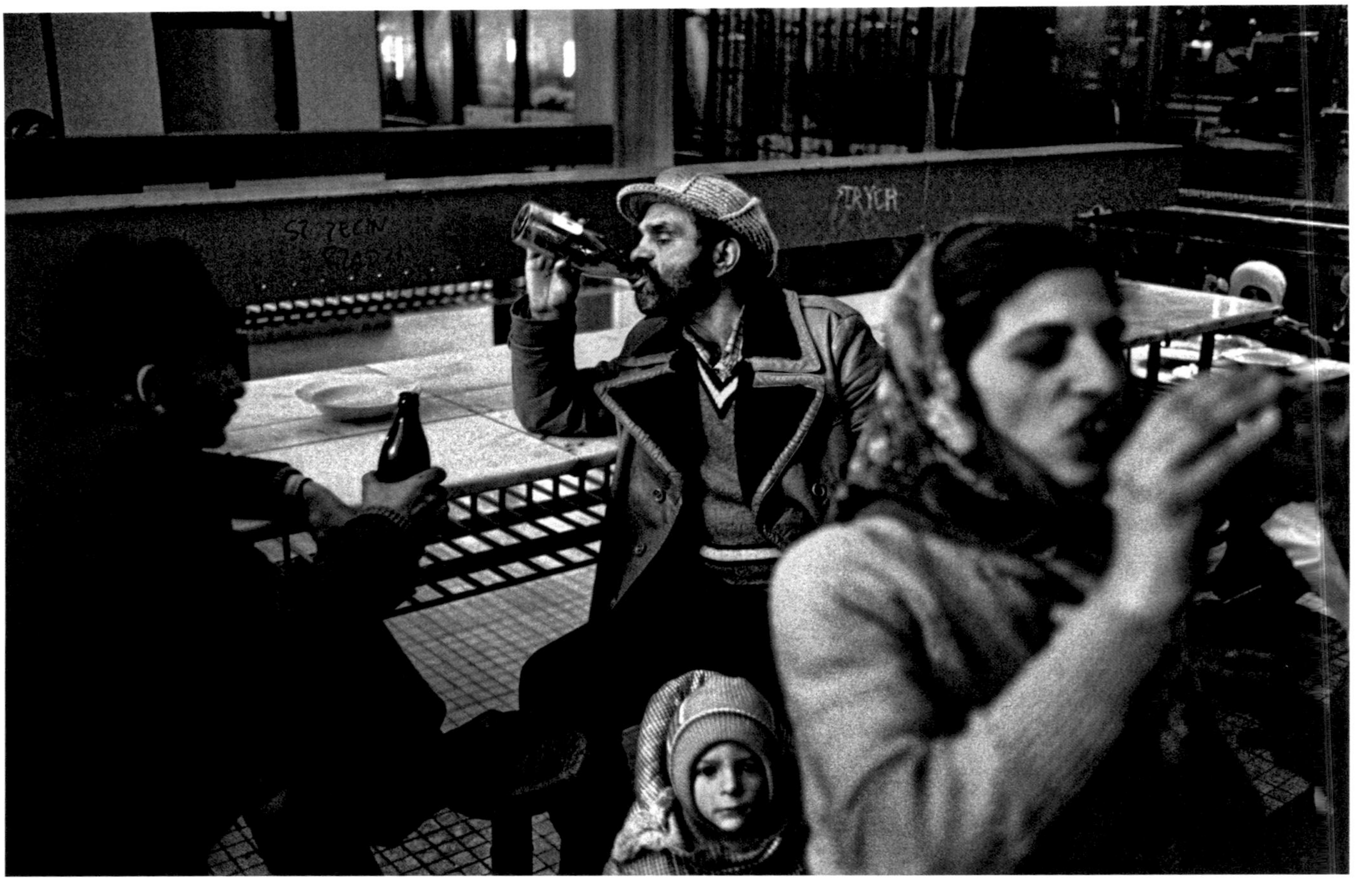

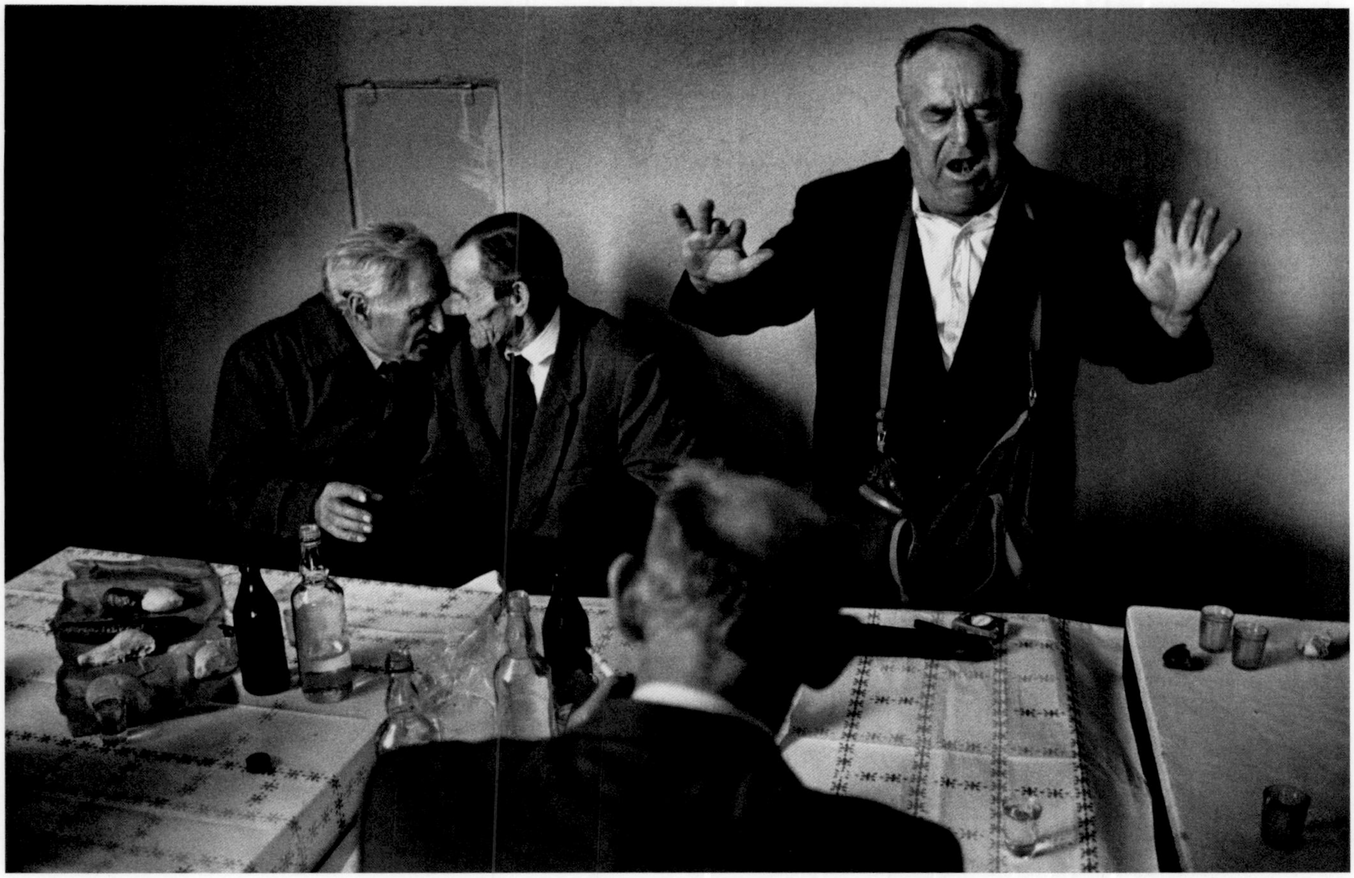

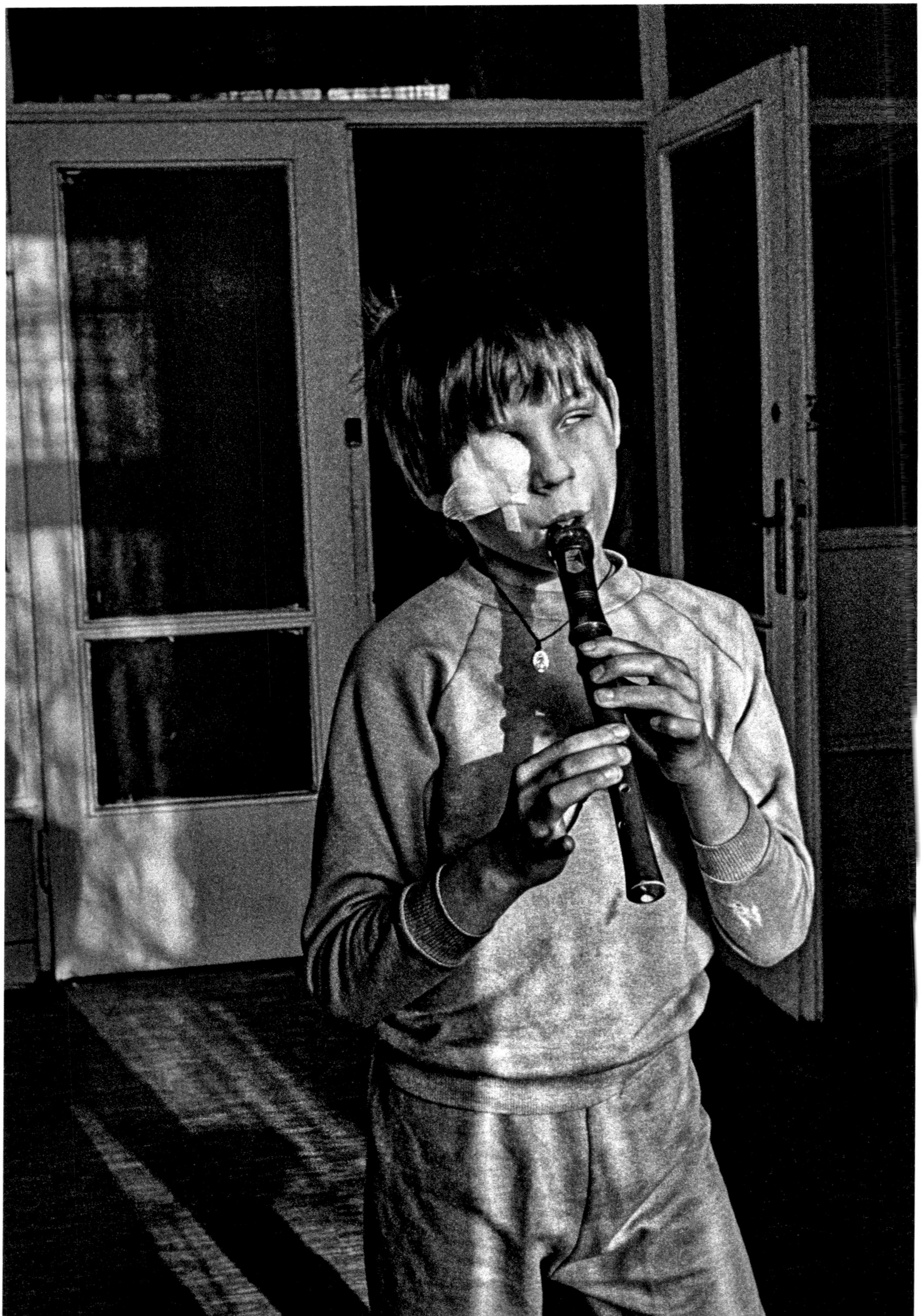

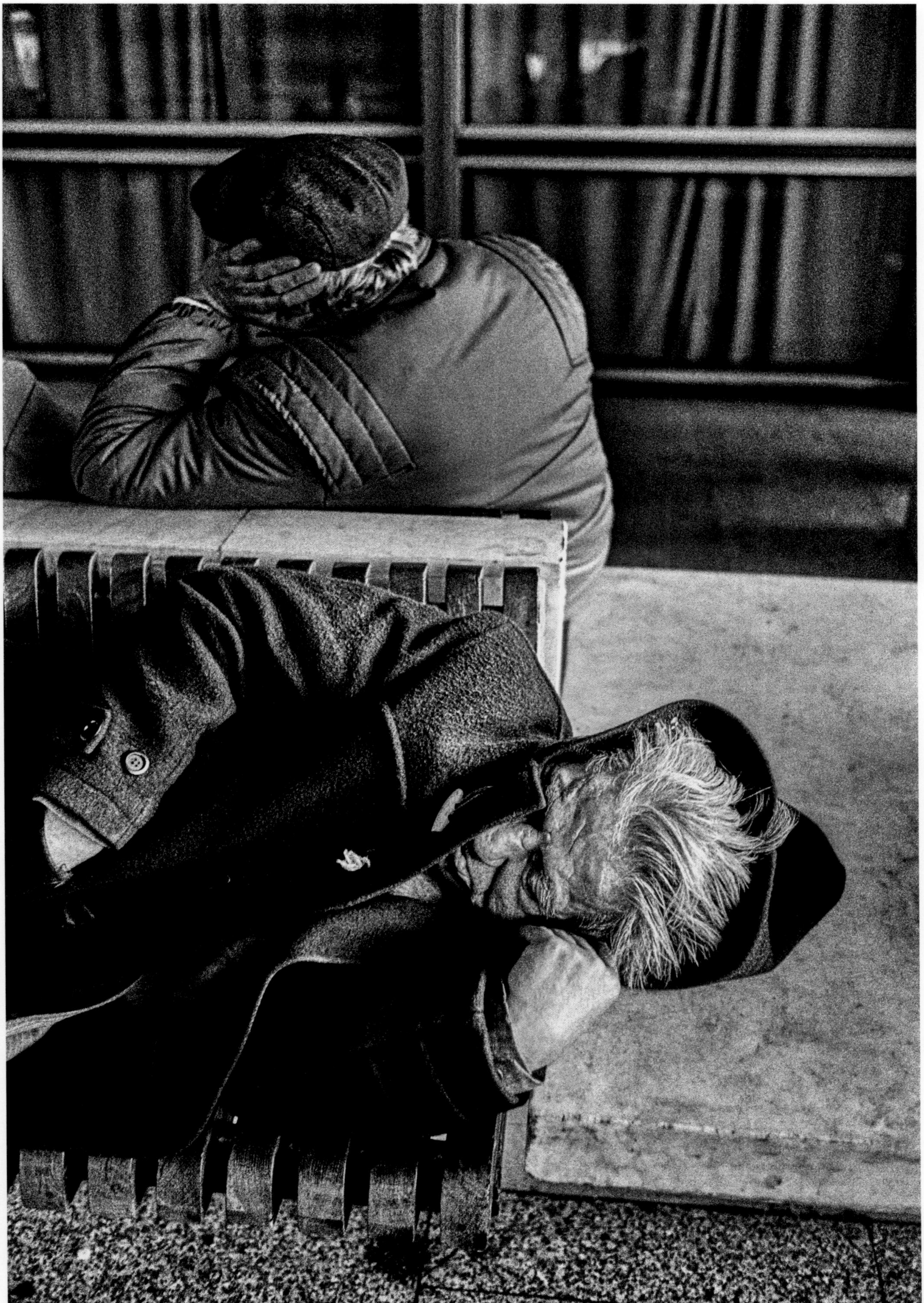

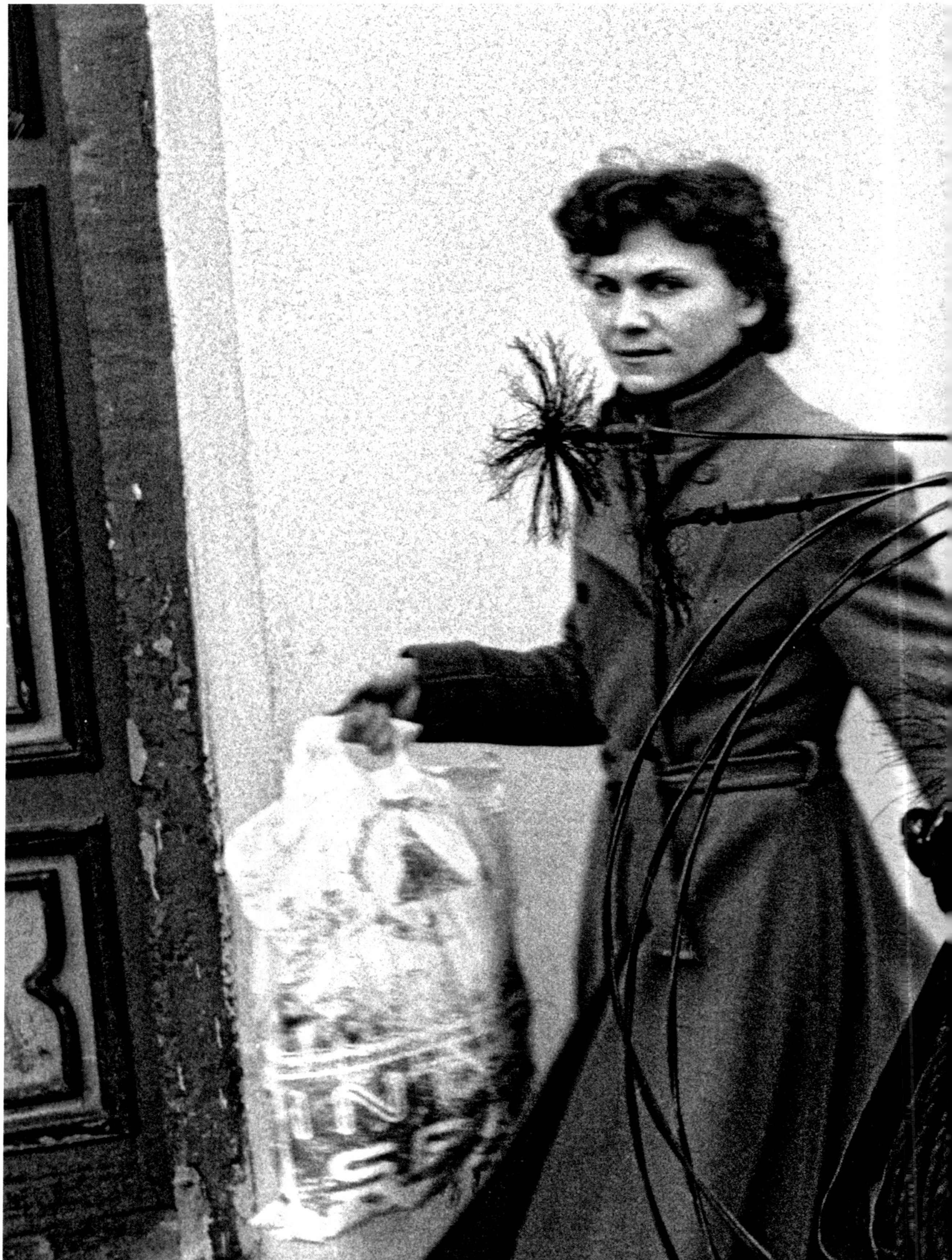

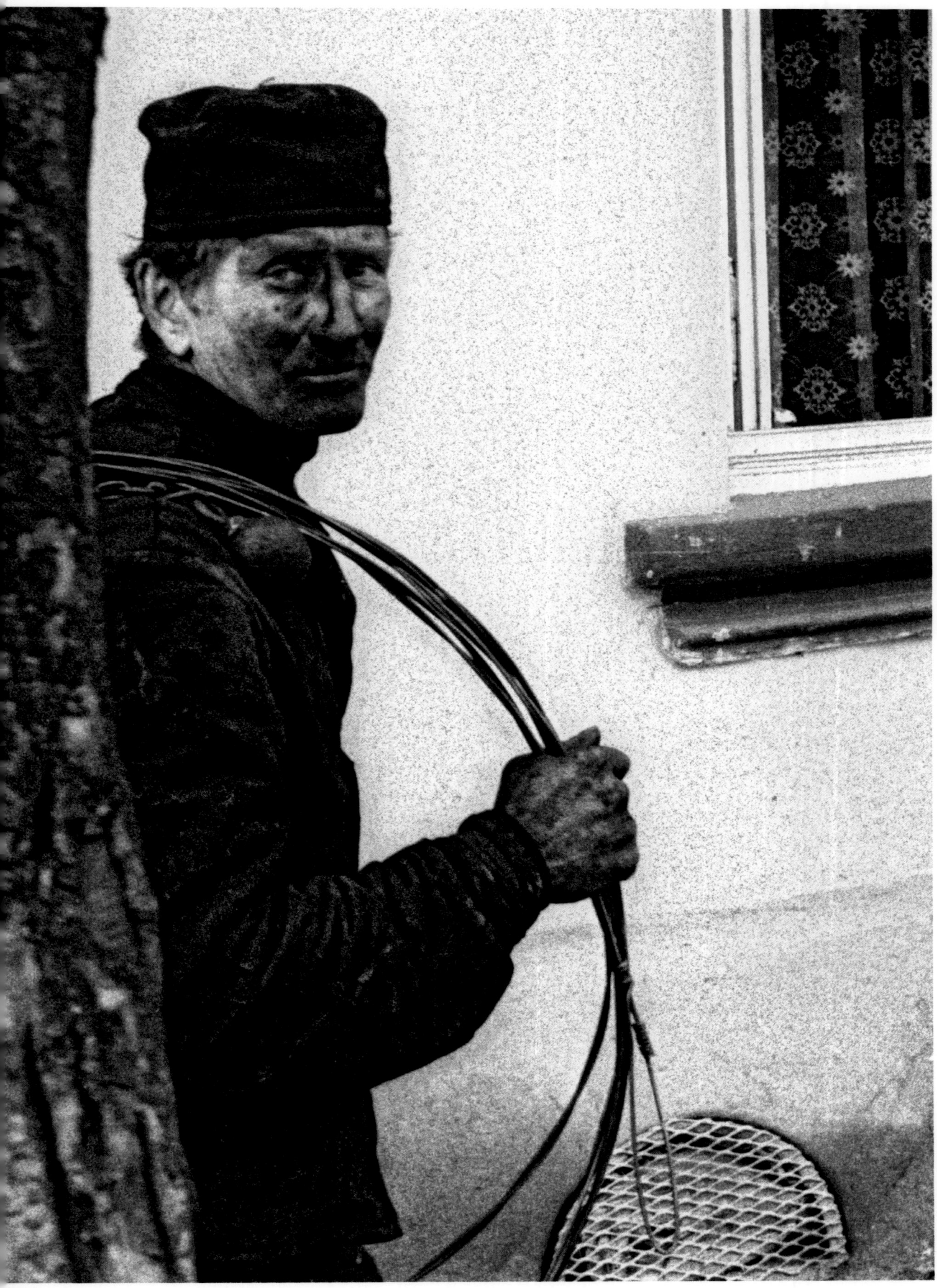

2 Poland, 1990
4–5 A wedding party walking through Fakulteta, a Roma district of Sofia, Bulgaria, 1991
6–7 The bride and bridesmaid during wedding celebrations in Fakulteta, Bulgaria, 1991
8 Henryk Strychalski, a retired miller plays an accordion during a wedding in a small village near Tomaszów Lubelski, south-eastern Poland, 1989
9 A wedding party in a garage. Fakulteta, a Roma district of Sofia, Bulgaria, 1991
10–11 A dance at the firemen's hall, Jedlińsk, Poland, 1986
12–13 Monastery near Krakow during a religious service, Kalwaria Zebrzydowska, Poland, 1987
15 Twins miss their lift home at dawn after a disco, Wierzbno, Poland, 1995
16–17 A drunk man sleeps on the street near Rynek in Kraków, Poland, 1989
18–19 Bored children, Głogówek, Poland, 1992
20–21 Renovation work, Amsterdam, the Netherlands, 2006
22–23 A man—soon to join the Russian Cossacks—at home, in Uralsk, Kazakhstan, 1993
25 Getting ready for an oath to join the Russian Cossacks organisation, Uralsk, Kazakhstan, 1993
26–27 Signing paperwork after an oath to join the Russian Cossacks organisation in Uralsk. The ceremony was organised in a flooded Soviet Scout's camp—accessible only by boat—to prevent detection from Kazakh secret police, Uralsk, Kazakhstan, 1993
28–29 A worker leaving a ship under construction in Gdańsk Shipyard where Solidarność was born, Gdańsk, 1990
31 Queuing for lunch in a cafeteria in Gdańsk Shipyard, with meal ticket at the ready, Gdańsk, Poland, 1990
32–33 Workers walk in the rain inside Gdansk Shipyard, Gdansk, Poland, 1990
34–35 Lumberjacks return to their accommodations after a day's work, Pogobie Village, Mazury Lake District, Poland, 2002

A massive storm destroyed part of the Pisz Forest and brought 3,600 lumberjacks from around the country to help with the clearing efforts.
36–37 Miners in Pailaviri Mine bring stones with tin ore to the grinder. Every bag weighs about 50 kg, Potosi, Bolivia, 2008
38–39 A blacksmith in Fakulteta neighbourhood, Sofia, Bulgaria, 1991
41 Cairo, Egypt, 1992
43 Releasing a pigeon, Fakulteta, Sofia, Bulgaria, 1991
44–45 Kids playing in Fakulteta neighbourhood, Sofia, Bulgaria, 1991
46–47 Replacing the lace curtains, Fakulteta neighbourhood, Sofia, Bulgaria, 1991
48 Grazing on a back street in the Village of Suntar, Yakutia, Russia, 2000
49 1:00 am during the Summer Solstice in Yakutia, Russia, 2000
50–51 Ciudad Bolivar, Barrio Brisas del Bolador, Bogotá, Colombia, 2007
52 The house of a landmine victim, Cúcuta, Colombia, 2007

The mines are an element of guerrilla warfare in the country.
53 Senaida Caicedo with her child and partner at home, Puente Aranda, Bogotá, Colombia, 2007
54 Senaida Caicedo, Puente Aranda, Bogotá, Colombia, 2007
55 A mine victim and his family at home, Cúcuta, Colombia, 2007
56 A girl with a parrot in Barrio Jerónimo Uribe—consisting almost entirely of displaced persons, Cúcuta, Colombia, 2007
57 Barrio Jerónimo Uribe, Cúcuta, Colombia, 2007
59 Distribution of humanitarian aid, Magdalena District, Oristunna, Colombia, 2007
60–61 Shop advertisement on a frozen canal, Żuławy District, Poland, 1997
62–63 Collecting scrap metal at a mine dump to make a living, Katowice, Poland, 1988
64–65 People living in the city dump, Katowice, Poland, 1989
66 The Circus, Żyrardów, Poland, 1983
67 Children playing around a fire of haulms, waiting for potatoes to be ready, Dęblin, Poland, 1989
68–69 A bar open all night in the Flower Market on Bakalarska St., Warsaw, Poland, 1983
70–71 Two women escape a storm, Tykocin, Poland, 1986
72–73 Selling birch brooms during the fair in Skaryszew, Poland, 1988
75 After a funeral, Katowice, Poland, 1986
76 Żuławy District, Poland, 1997
77 Going home after a horse race, Pietrowice Wielkie, Poland, 1987
78–79 Inscription on a blackboard meaning 'I love a cow.' 'Love' being the only word in English seemingly familiar to the pupils in Poland in 1984.
81 Worker in a garage, Chilsitun Rd., Kabul, Afghanistan, 1991. While men were either fighting or fleeing to Iran, children were often relied upon to work and help support the family. Kabul, Afghanistan, 1991
82–83 Evening prayer, Chilsitun Rd., Kabul, Afghanistan, 1991
84–85 Watchmaker, Kabul, Afghanistan, 1991
86–87 A child put on display to invite negotiations for a marriage offer, Kabul, Afghanistan, 1991
89 Watching a Hindu film crew working. Regular pastimes were limited during the Soviet-controlled 'puppet' regime of then-president Mohammad Najibullah, Kabul, Afghanistan, 1991
90–91 After a press conference organised by Najibullah's officials, the soliders rush the conference table fighting for the leftovers (salty sticks), Kabul, Afghanistan, 1991
92–93 A military outpost facing Pakistan, in the mountains off Jalalabad, Afghanistan, 1991
94–95 Boys play football in the famous swimming pool on Bibi Mahroo Hill. Built by the Soviets in the 1980s, it was never used for swimming. The Soviets were unable to transport water up the steep hill. During the Taliban rule in the 1990s it served as a secret execution location. Kabul, Afghanistan, 1991
96 Tel Aviv, Israel, 1992
97 The Lag BaOmer celebrations on Mount Meron, around the grave of Shimon bar Yochai, Safed, Israel, 1992
99 Praying around the grave of Shimon bar Jochai on Mount Meron, Safed, Israel, 1992
100–101 Boys studying before an exam, Potosi, Bolivia, 2008
103 Fiesta in Laykakota, a quarter in Puno, Peru, 2008
104–105 Sunrise over the sea during Easter celebrations, Trapani, Italy, 1993
107 Departure of the Greek

Orthodox procession on Easter Tuesday, Palazzo Adriano, Italy, 1993

109 Mrożek Festival, Kraków, Poland, 1990

111 A village disco in Niedzbórz, Central Poland, 1995

112–113 The participants of the Miss Poland beauty contest wait off stage for the final parade in the provincial town of Tarnobrzeg, Poland, 1992

114–115 Aleksander Kwaśniewski, presidential hopeful, distributes small calendars with his picture among the voters during his campaign trail in a commune of Turobin, Grodki, Poland, 1995

116 The Elegance Ball in a Marriott Hotel in Warsaw, Poland, 1994

117 The participants of the Miss Poland beauty contest, during the preliminary contest in Łańcut, Poland, 1992

118 A village disco, Central Poland, 1995

120–121 A police patrol picks up a drunk from the street in Rostov-on-Don, Russia, 1993

122–123 Searching for ID papers, Rostov-on-Don, Russia, 1993

124 Drunk tank in Rostov-on-Don. If aggressive, the occupants have a bucket of cold water poured over them, Rostov-on-Don, Russia, 1992

125 Intoxicated men collected from the streets in detention at a police station in Rostov-on-Don, Russia, 1993

126 The police were called regarding a domestic disturbance and found a man dripping with blood. He had been lacerated by his wife, Rostov-on-Don, Russia, 1993

127 An operation to remove a fork from a man's back, planted there during a family and friends dinner, Rostov-on-Don, Russia, 1993

128–129 Inside a prison cell in Rostov-on-Don, Russia, 1993

130 A team of volunteers, on their way to recover bodies from the rubble after the tsunami that struck Sumatra on 26 December 2004. Banda Aceh, Indonesia, 2005

131 In the city of Banda Aceh alone 167,000 people died. This team of volunteers recovered 700 bodies in two weeks. Banda Aceh, Indonesia, 2005

132–133 Waiting for a doctor in the Rosumo Camp—made up of over 150,000 refugees during the Rwandan genocide—Ngara, Tanzania, 1994

134–135 A taylor in the Rosumo Camp, working on a sewing machine transported from Rwanda on a bike, Ngara, Tanzania, 1994

136–137 A funeral in the Rosumo Camp, Ngara, Tanzania, 1994

138–139 Children queuing to fetch water at dawn, Rosumo Camp, Ngara, Tanzania, 1994

140–141 Drying dung bricks for use as fuel. Children gather the fresh dung from behind the buffalo in the streets, then the bricks are formed and thrown against walls. Once dry, they fall off. Several families make a living selling the bricks. Varanasi, India, 2000

142–143 Exercising in an akhara on the Ganges, near Varana River. The akhara must have access to soil, water and god. Varanasi, India, 1997

144–145 Varanasi, India, 1997

146–147 A brahmin praying at home, while children do homework. The bed is often the only space for family activities.

A few years after the picture was taken, this teenage girl was murdered. Varanasi, India, 2000

149 Varanasi, India, 2000

151 A street in the old town, Varanasi, India, 1997

152–153 Rikshaw on BHU Marg Street, Varanasi, India, 2000

154–155 Flying kites on the ghats, Varanasi, India, 1996

156–157 Daily bath, Oristunna village, Magdalena district, Colombia, 2007

158–159 The house of a mine victim, Cúcuta, Colombia, 2007

160–161 Mongolian massage in the Traditional Medicine Centre in Mamba Datsan monastery, Ulan Bataar, Mongolia, 2004

162–163 Voters solve a crossword on lottery coupons, after an electoral meeting with the opposition leader Lamjavyn Gündalai, in a small village near Lake Khövsgöl, Mongolia, 2004

164–165 Butcher, Ulan Bataar, Mongolia, 2004

166–167 Khatgal, Mongolia, 2004

168–169 Ulan Bataar, Mongolia, 2004

170–171 Along the line of the last steam railway, Wolsztyn, Poland, 2002

172–173 People going to a mass celebrated by John Paul II, Lublin, Poland, 1987

174–175 Rostov-on-Don, Russia, 1992

176 Waiting for a tram, Marszałkowska St., Warsaw, Poland, 1986

177 Katowice, Poland, 1988

178–179 After celebrating at the Horse Fair, Skaryszew, Poland, 1991

181 Waiting for a bus, Warsaw, Poland, 1986

183 Roma setting up home in the Warsaw East railway station, on their way to the West, Warsaw, Poland, 1990

185 A Roma family in the city centre, Warsaw, Poland, 1990

187 Warsaw, Poland, 1991

188 A short cut on the way home, Żuławy region, Poland, 1997

190–191 A fire started by a candle left in the grass, during All Saints' Day in Wólka Węglowa Cemetery, Warsaw, Poland, 1987

192–193 Żuławy district, Poland, 1997

194–195 Going to church, Drohiczyn, Poland, 1985

196–197 Kazimierz on Wisła, Poland, 1989

198 Roma setting up home in the Warsaw East railway station, on their way to the West, Warsaw, Poland, 1990

199 Celebrations during a get-together of godsons of the pre-war Polish President Ignacy Moscicki. According to tradition, many of these men are named Ignancy after him. Mierzanowo near Ciechanow, Poland, 1993

200 A young patient in the Ophthalmology unit of a hospital, Warsaw, Poland 1986

203 Homeless in the waiting room of the Warsaw Central railway station, Warsaw, Poland, 1989

204–205 Chimney sweep, Stary Sącz, Poland, 1985

Thank you to PIX.HOUSE for supporting
this project.

First published in 2020 by
GOST Books
8a West Smithfield
London
ec1a 9jr
info@gostbooks.com
gostbooks.com

Designed and produced by GOST:
Katie Clifford, Gemma Gerhard, Justine
Hucker, Allon Kaye, Eleanor Macnair,
Claudia Paladini, Ana Rocha

Printed in Italy by EBS

British Library cataloguing-in-publication
data. A catalogue record of this book is
available from the British Library.

ISBN 978-1-910401-40-8